BIRDS
of
WASHINGTON STATE

Brian H. Bell
Gregory Kennedy

with contributions from
Chris Fisher & Andy Bezener

LONE
PINE

Lone Pine Publishing International

The Distributor: Lone Pine Publishing
1808 B Street NW, Suite 140
Auburn, WA, USA 98001

Website: www.lonepinepublishing.com

Library and Archives Canada Cataloguing in Publication

Bell, Brian H., 1936–
    Birds of Washington State / Brian H. Bell & Gregory Kennedy.

Includes bibliographical references and index.
ISBN-13: 978-1-55105-430-8
ISBN-10: 1-55105-430-2

1. Birds—Washington (State)—Identification. I. Kennedy, Gregory, 1956–
II. Title.

QL684.W2B44 2006   598'.09797   C2005-905004-7

Cover Illustration: American Goldfinch by Gary Ross
Illustrations: Gary Ross, Ted Nordhagen, Eva Pluciennik
Scanning & Digital Film: Elite Lithographers Co.

PC: *13*

CONTENTS

ACKNOWLEDGMENTS

I gratefully acknowledge Sharon Colette and H. Lee Mitchell, who pestered me for years to do a book, and Hal Opperman, for introducing me to Lone Pine. I thank the many, many talented and knowledgeable people who inspired me in birding; as the old chestnut goes "they know who they are." Particular thanks go to Andy Engilis, Ed Harper, Willie Argante and Tim Manolis for the sharing of their talents and help to a then new and developing birder. The many excellent birders in the Washington Ornithological Society provide inspiration, but of note are Kevin Aanerud, Steve Mlodinow, Michael Donahue and Kraig Kemper. Dr. Dennis Paulson has been responsible for furthering my learning and curiosity about birds and has always given generously of his time, to me and to hosts of other birders. The opportunity to teach birding classes for Seattle and East Lake Washington Audubon Societies allows me to pass on my enthusiasm and knowledge to new generations of birders.

The editors at Lone Pine are great at pulling all the separate parts of the book together into a fine finished product—thank you Nicholle Carrière and Volker Bodegom.

I especially thank my wife, Penn, for her continual support and encouragement in all my birding endeavors.

—Brian H. Bell

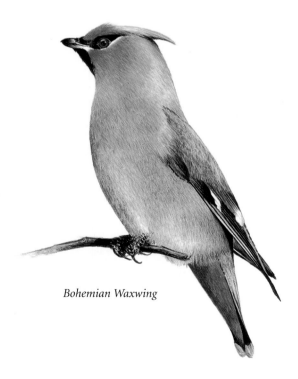

Bohemian Waxwing

Greater White-fronted Goose
size 30 in • p. 38

Snow Goose
size 30 in • p. 39

Brant
size 25 in • p. 40

Cackling Goose
size 30 in • p. 41

Canada Goose
size 40 in • p. 42

Trumpeter Swan
size 60 in • p. 43

Tundra Swan
size 54 in • p. 44

Wood Duck
size 19 in • p. 45

Gadwall
size 20 in • p. 46

Eurasian Wigeon
size 19 in • p. 47

American Wigeon
size 20 in • p. 48

Mallard
size 24 in • p. 49

Blue-winged Teal
size 15 in • p. 50

Cinnamon Teal
size 16 in • p. 51

Northern Shoveler
size 19 in • p. 52

Northern Pintail
size 23 in • p. 53

Green-winged Teal
size 14 in • p. 54

Canvasback
size 20 in • p. 55

Redhead
size 20 in • p. 56

Ring-necked Duck
size 16 in • p. 57

Greater Scaup
size 18 in • p. 58

Lesser Scaup
size 17 in • p. 59

Harlequin Duck
size 17 in • p. 60

Surf Scoter
size 19 in • p. 61

White-winged Scoter
size 21 in • p. 62

Black Scoter
size 19 in • p. 63

Long-tailed Duck
size 19 in • p. 64

Bufflehead
size 14 in • p. 65

WATERFOWL

Common Goldeneye
size 18 in • p. 66

Barrow's Goldeneye
size 19 in • p. 67

Hooded Merganser
size 18 in • p. 68

Common Merganser
size 24 in • p. 69

Red-breasted Merganser
size 23 in • p. 70

Ruddy Duck
size 15 in • p. 71

GROUSELIKE BIRDS

Chukar
size 13 in • p. 72

Gray Partridge
size 13 in • p. 73

Ring-necked Pheasant
size 28 in • p. 74

Ruffed Grouse
size 17 in • p. 75

Greater Sage-Grouse
size 26 in • p. 76

Spruce Grouse
size 15 in • p. 77

White-tailed Ptarmigan
size 13 in • p. 78

Blue Grouse
size 19 in • p. 79

Sharp-tailed Grouse
size 17 in • p. 80

Wild Turkey
size 44 in • p. 81

Mountain Quail
size 12 in • p. 82

California Quail
size 11 in • p. 83

DIVING BIRDS

Red-throated Loon
size 26 in • p. 84

Pacific Loon
size 26 in • p. 85

Common Loon
size 32 in • p. 86

Pied-billed Grebe
size 14 in • p. 87

Horned Grebe
size 14 in • p. 88

Red-necked Grebe
size 20 in • p. 89

Eared Grebe
size 13 in • p. 90

Western Grebe
size 22 in • p. 91

DIVING BIRDS

Clark's Grebe
size 22 in • p. 92

Black-footed Albatross
size 28 in • p. 93

Northern Fulmar
size 19 in • p. 94

Pink-footed Shearwater
size 20 in • p. 95

Buller's Shearwater
size 17 in • p. 96

Sooty Shearwater
size 17 in • p. 97

Short-tailed Shearwater
size 17 in • p. 98

Fork-tailed Storm-Petrel
size 9 in • p. 99

Leach's Storm-Petrel
size 9 in • p. 100

American White Pelican
size 60 in • p. 101

Brown Pelican
size 45 in • p. 102

Brandt's Cormorant
size 34 in • p. 103

HERONLIKE BIRDS

Double-crested Cormorant
size 29 in • p. 104

Pelagic Cormorant
size 27 in • p. 105

American Bittern
size 25 in • p. 106

Great Blue Heron
size 52 in • p. 107

Great Egret
size 39 in • p. 108

Green Heron
size 19 in • p. 109

Black-crowned Night-Heron
size 25 in • p. 110

Turkey Vulture
size 29 in • p. 111

BIRDS OF PREY

Osprey
size 24 in • p. 112

White-tailed Kite
size 16 in • p. 113

Bald Eagle
size 37 in • p. 114

Northern Harrier
size 20 in • p. 115

Sharp-shinned Hawk
size 12 in • p. 116

Cooper's Hawk
size 17 in • p. 117

Northern Goshawk
size 23 in • p. 118

Red-shouldered Hawk
size 19 in • p. 119

BIRDS OF PREY

Swainson's Hawk
size 20 in • p. 120

Red-tailed Hawk
size 22 in • p. 121

Ferruginous Hawk
size 25 in • p. 122

Rough-legged Hawk
size 22 in • p. 123

Golden Eagle
size 35 in • p. 124

American Kestrel
size 8 in • p. 125

Merlin
size 11 in • p. 126

Gyrfalcon
size 22 in • p. 127

Peregrine Falcon
size 17 in • p. 128

Prairie Falcon
size 16 in • p. 129

RAILS, COOTS & CRANES

Virginia Rail
size 10 in • p. 130

Sora
size 9 in • p. 131

American Coot
size 15 in • p. 132

Sandhill Crane
size 45 in • p. 133

SHOREBIRDS

Black-bellied Plover
size 12 in • p. 134

Pacific Golden-Plover
size 11 in • p. 135

Snowy Plover
size 7 in • p. 136

Semipalmated Plover
size 7 in • p. 137

Killdeer
size 10 in • p. 138

Black Oystercatcher
size 17 in • p. 139

Black-necked Stilt
size 15 in • p. 140

American Avocet
size 18 in • p. 141

Greater Yellowlegs
size 14 in • p. 142

Lesser Yellowlegs
size 11 in • p. 143

Solitary Sandpiper
size 9 in • p. 144

Willet
size 15 in • p. 145

Wandering Tattler
size 11 in • p. 146

Spotted Sandpiper
size 8 in • p. 147

Whimbrel
size 18 in • p. 148

Long-billed Curlew
size 23 in • p. 149

Marbled Godwit
size 18 in • p. 150

Ruddy Turnstone
size 10 in • p. 151

Black Turnstone
size 9 in • p. 152

Surfbird
size 10 in • p. 153

Red Knot
size 11 in • p. 154

Sanderling
size 8 in • p. 155

Semipalmated Sandpiper
size 6 in • p. 156

Western Sandpiper
size 7 in • p. 157

Least Sandpiper
size 6 in • p. 158

Baird's Sandpiper
size 7 in • p. 159

Pectoral Sandpiper
size 8 in • p. 160

Rock Sandpiper
size 9 in • p. 161

Dunlin
size 8 in • p. 162

Stilt Sandpiper
size 9 in • p. 163

Short-billed Dowitcher
size 12 in • p. 164

Long-billed Dowitcher
size 12 in • p. 165

Wilson's Snipe
size 11 in • p. 166

Wilson's Phalarope
size 9 in • p. 167

Red-necked Phalarope
size 8 in • p. 168

Red Phalarope
size 9 in • p. 169

Pomarine Jaeger
size 21 in • p. 170

Parasitic Jaeger
size 19 in • p. 171

Long-tailed Jaeger
size 21 in • p. 172

Franklin's Gull
size 15 in • p. 173

Bonaparte's Gull
size 13 in • p. 174

Heermann's Gull
size 18 in • p. 175

Mew Gull
size 16 in • p. 176

Ring-billed Gull
size 19 in • p. 177

California Gull
size 19 in • p. 178

Herring Gull
size 25 in • p. 179

Thayer's Gull
size 24 in • p. 180

Western Gull
size 25 in • p. 181

Glaucous-winged Gull
size 26 in • p. 182

Glaucous Gull
size 27 in • p. 183

Sabine's Gull
size 14 in • p. 184

Black-legged Kittiwake
size 17 in • p. 185

Caspian Tern
size 21 in • p. 186

Common Tern
size 14 in • p. 187

Arctic Tern
size 16 in • p. 188

Forster's Tern
size 15 in • p. 189

Black Tern
size 10 in • p. 190

Common Murre
size 18 in • p. 191

Pigeon Guillemot
size 14 in • p. 192

Marbled Murrelet
size 10 in • p. 193

Ancient Murrelet
size 10 in • p. 194

Cassin's Auklet
size 9 in • p. 195

Rhinoceros Auklet
size 15 in • p. 196

Tufted Puffin
size 16 in • p. 197

Rock Pigeon
size 13 in • p. 198

Band-tailed Pigeon
size 14 in • p. 199

Mourning Dove
size 12 in • p. 200

OWLS

Barn Owl
size 14 in • p. 201

Flammulated Owl
size 7 in • p. 202

Western Screech-Owl
size 10 in • p. 203

Great Horned Owl
size 22 in • p. 204

Snowy Owl
size 24 in • p. 205

Northern Pygmy-Owl
size 7 in • p. 206

Burrowing Owl
size 9 in • p. 207

Spotted Owl
size 18 in • p. 208

Barred Owl
size 21 in • p. 209

Great Gray Owl
size 29 in • p. 210

Long-eared Owl
size 15 in • p. 211

Short-eared Owl
size 15 in • p. 212

Boreal Owl
size 11 in • p. 213

Northern Saw-whet Owl
size 8 in • p. 214

NIGHTJARS, HUMMINGBIRDS & KINGFISHERS

Common Nighthawk
size 9 in • p. 215

Common Poorwill
size 8 in • p. 216

Black Swift
size 7 in • p. 217

Vaux's Swift
size 5 in • p. 218

White-throated Swift
size 7 in • p. 219

Black-chinned Hummingbird
size 4 in • p. 220

Anna's Hummingbird
size 4 in • p. 221

Calliope Hummingbird
size 3 in • p. 222

Rufous Hummingbird
size 4 in • p. 223

Belted Kingfisher
size 13 in • p. 224

WOODPECKERS

Lewis's Woodpecker
size 11 in • p. 225

Acorn Woodpecker
size 9 in • p. 226

Williamson's Sapsucker
size 9 in • p. 227

Red-naped Sapsucker
size 8 in • p. 228

Red-breasted Sapsucker
size 8 in • p. 229

Downy Woodpecker
size 7 in • p. 230

Hairy Woodpecker
size 9 in • p. 231

White-headed Woodpecker
size 9 in • p. 232

American Three-toed
Woodpecker size 9 in • p. 233

Black-backed Woodpecker
size 10 in • p. 234

Northern Flicker
size 13 in • p. 235

Pileated Woodpecker
size 18 in • p. 236

FLYCATCHERS

Olive-sided Flycatcher
size 7 in • p. 238

Western Wood-Pewee
size 6 in • p. 239

Willow Flycatcher
size 6 in • p. 240

Least Flycatcher
size 5 in • p. 241

Hammond's Flycatcher
size 5 in • p. 242

Gray Flycatcher
size 6 in • p. 243

Dusky Flycatcher
size 6 in • p. 244

Pacific-slope Flycatcher
size 5 in • p. 245

Say's Phoebe
size 7 in • p. 246

Ash-throated Flycatcher
size 9 in • p. 247

Western Kingbird
size 9 in • p. 248

Eastern Kingbird
size 8 in • p. 249

SHRIKES & VIREOS

Loggerhead Shrike
size 9 in • p. 250

Northern Shrike
size 10 in • p. 251

Cassin's Vireo
size 6 in • p. 252

Hutton's Vireo
size 5 in • p. 253

Warbling Vireo
size 6 in • p. 254

Red-eyed Vireo
size 6 in • p. 255

Gray Jay
size 11 in • p. 256

Steller's Jay
size 11 in • p. 257

Western Scrub-Jay
size 11 in • p. 258

Clark's Nutcracker
size 12 in • p. 259

Black-billed Magpie
size 20 in • p. 260

American Crow
size 19 in • p. 261

Common Raven
size 24 in • p. 262

Horned Lark
size 7 in • p. 263

Purple Martin
size 8 in • p. 264

Tree Swallow
size 6 in • p. 265

Violet-green Swallow
size 5 in • p. 266

Northern Rough-winged
Swallow size 6 in • p. 267

Bank Swallow
size 5 in • p. 268

Cliff Swallow
size 5 in • p. 269

Barn Swallow
size 7 in • p. 270

Black-capped Chickadee
size 5 in • p. 271

Mountain Chickadee
size 5 in • p. 272

Chestnut-backed Chickadee
size 5 in • p. 273

Boreal Chickadee
size 6 in • p. 274

Bushtit
size 4 in • p. 275

Red-breasted Nuthatch
size 5 in • p. 276

White-breasted Nuthatch
size 6 in • p. 277

Pygmy Nuthatch
size 4 in • p. 278

REFERENCE GUIDE

Brown Creeper
size 5 in • p. 279

Rock Wren
size 6 in • p. 280

Canyon Wren
size 6 in • p. 281

Bewick's Wren
size 5 in • p. 282

House Wren
size 5 in • p. 283

Winter Wren
size 4 in • p. 284

Marsh Wren
size 5 in • p. 285

American Dipper
size 8 in • p. 286

Golden-crowned Kinglet
size 4 in • p. 287

Ruby-crowned Kinglet
size 4 in • p. 288

Western Bluebird
size 7 in • p. 289

Mountain Bluebird
size 7 in • p. 290

Townsend's Solitaire
size 8 in • p. 291

Veery
size 7 in • p. 292

Swainson's Thrush
size 7 in • p. 293

Hermit Thrush
size 7 in • p. 294

American Robin
size 10 in • p. 295

Varied Thrush
size 9 in • p. 296

Gray Catbird
size 8 in • p. 297

Sage Thrasher
size 8 in • p. 298

European Starling
size 8 in • p. 299

American Pipit
size 7 in • p. 300

Bohemian Waxwing
size 8 in • p. 301

Cedar Waxwing
size 7 in • p. 302

Orange-crowned Warbler
size 5 in • p. 303

Nashville Warbler
size 4 in • p. 304

Yellow Warbler
size 5 in • p. 305

Yellow-rumped Warbler
size 6 in • p. 306

Black-throated Gray Warbler
size 5 in • p. 307

Townsend's Warbler
size 5 in • p. 308

Hermit Warbler
size 5 in • p. 309

Palm Warbler
size 5 in • p. 310

American Redstart
size 5 in • p. 311

Northern Waterthrush
size 6 in • p. 312

MacGillivray's Warbler
size 5 in • p. 313

Common Yellowthroat
size 5 in • p. 314

Wilson's Warbler
size 4 in • p. 315

Yellow-breasted Chat
size 7 in • p. 316

Western Tanager
size 7 in • p. 317

Green-tailed Towhee
size 7 in • p. 318

Spotted Towhee
size 8 in • p. 319

American Tree Sparrow
size 6 in • p. 320

Chipping Sparrow
size 6 in • p. 321

Brewer's Sparrow
size 6 in • p. 322

Vesper Sparrow
size 6 in • p. 323

Lark Sparrow
size 7 in • p. 324

Sage Sparrow
size 6 in • p. 325

Savannah Sparrow
size 6 in • p. 326

Grasshopper Sparrow
size 5 in • p. 327

Fox Sparrow
size 7 in • p. 328

Song Sparrow
size 6 in • p. 329

Lincoln's Sparrow
size 5 in • p. 330

Swamp Sparrow
size 6 in • p. 331

White-throated Sparrow
size 7 in • p. 332

White-crowned Sparrow
size 7 in • p. 333

SPARROWS, GROSBEAKS & BUNTINGS

Golden-crowned Sparrow
size 7 in • p. 334

Dark-eyed Junco
size 6 in • p. 335

Lapland Longspur
size 6 in • p. 336

Snow Bunting
size 7 in • p. 337

Black-headed Grosbeak
size 8 in • p. 338

Lazuli Bunting
size 6 in • p. 339

BLACKBIRDS & ALLIES

Bobolink
size 7 in • p. 340

Red-winged Blackbird
size 8 in • p. 341

Tricolored Blackbird
size 8 in • p. 342

Western Meadowlark
size 9 in • p. 343

Yellow-headed Blackbird
size 10 in • p. 344

Brewer's Blackbird
size 9 in • p. 345

Brown-headed Cowbird
size 7 in • p. 346

Bullock's Oriole
size 8 in • p. 347

FINCHLIKE BIRDS

Gray-crowned Rosy-Finch
size 6 in • p. 348

Pine Grosbeak
size 9 in • p. 349

Purple Finch
size 6 in • p. 350

Cassin's Finch
size 6 in • p. 351

House Finch
size 6 in • p. 352

Red Crossbill
size 6 in • p. 353

Pine Siskin
size 5 in • p. 354

Lesser Goldfinch
size 4 in • p. 355

American Goldfinch
size 5 in • p. 356

Evening Grosbeak
size 8 in • p. 357

House Sparrow
size 6 in • p. 358

INTRODUCTION

BIRDING IN WASHINGTON

In recent decades, birding has evolved from an eccentric pursuit practiced by a few dedicated individuals to a continent-wide activity that boasts millions of professional and amateur participants. Birding has become so popular for a variety of good reasons. Many people find it a relaxing pastime that can offer outdoor exercise and an opportunity to socialize with other bird enthusiasts. Others see it as a rewarding learning experience. Still others watch birds to reconnect with nature and enjoy the beauty of birds. A visit to any of our region's premier birding locations, such as Ocean Shores on the edge of Grays Harbor, the Samish and Skagit flats, the Okanogan or the Blue Mountains in southeastern Washington, would doubtless uncover still more reasons why people watch birds.

We are truly blessed with the geographical and biological diversity of Washington. In addition to supporting a wide range of breeding birds and year-round residents, our state hosts a large number of spring and fall migrants that move through our area on the way to their breeding and wintering grounds. In all, over 470 bird species have been seen and recorded in Washington. Of these, 370 or so make regular appearances in the state.

Birdwatching is a friendly activity with a long tradition in our state. Washington birders, the Washington Ornithological Society, Audubon chapters and bird clubs gladly help beginners and involve novices in their activities. Christmas bird counts, breeding bird surveys, nest box programs, migration monitoring and birding classes and workshops all provide a chance for novice, intermediate and expert birdwatchers to interact and share their enthusiasm for the wonder of birds.

BEGINNING TO LEARN THE BIRDS

The Challenge of Birding

Birding (or birdwatching) is sometimes challenging, but it is always rewarding. Learning to recognize all the birds in Washington with confidence takes time, and this guide will help you get started quickly. Although any standard North American field guide will help you identify local birds, such guides can be daunting because they cover the entire continent and present an overwhelming number of species. By focusing specifically on the bird life of Washington, we hope to simplify your introduction to the world of birding. Attending local birding lectures, classes and organized field trips will greatly enhance your learning experiences and enjoyment of birds.

Classification: The Order of Things

To an ornithologist (a biologist who studies birds), the species is the fundamental unit of classification. The members of a single species generally look very

Red-tailed Hawk

17

American Coot

much alike (although male, female and immature plumages can in some cases be strikingly different), behave in predictable ways and interbreed with one another. Every known species (plant or animal) has a latinized, two-part scientific name that is normally italicized. Each bird species also has a single accredited common name, so that the different popular names of a species do not cause confusion. For example, "American Coot" is an accredited common name, even though some people call this bird "Mudhen." *Fulica americana* is the American Coot's scientific name—*Fulica* is the genus name, and *americana* is the "species name" (or, more accurately, the "specific epithet").

To help make sense of the hundreds of bird species in our region, scientifically oriented birders lump species into recognizable groups. After the genus (plural is "genera"), the most commonly used groupings, in order of increasing scope, are family and order. The Red-tailed Hawk and Bald Eagle are different species in different genera (*Buteo* and *Haliaeetus,* respectively), but they are both members of the Accipitridae (the hawk family). The hawk family is in turn grouped with the falcon family in the Falconiformes, the order that contains the birds of prey. Learning some characteristics of families and orders will help speed identification when you encounter an unfamiliar species in the field.

Based on DNA and other evidence, ornithologists arrange all of the orders in a standard sequence, beginning with species most similar to the evolutionary ancestors of birds and ending with those most strongly modified by evolutionary change. For many years this sequence began with the loons (order Gaviiformes). More recently, scientists have agreed that the geese, swans and ducks (order Anseriformes) and chickenlike birds (order Galliformes) should be placed ahead of the loons. Like most other bird guides, this book is arranged according to the current standard sequence (American Ornithologists' Union, 1998, and supplements through to 2005). You will find the reference guide on the back cover of this book and on pp. 5–16 particularly helpful while you are becoming familiar with this sequence.

TECHNIQUES OF BIRDING

Being in the right place at the right time to see birds in action involves both skill and luck. The more you know about a bird—its range, preferred habitat, food preferences and hours and seasons of activity—the better your chances will be of finding it. It is much easier to locate a Northern Saw-whet Owl in the boreal forest than elsewhere, especially at night in winter and in spring, when the adults are calling for mates. Short-eared Owls, however, are most often seen on fence posts or in fields during the day in winter.

Generally, spring and fall are the busiest birding times, with a great number of birds migrating through Washington. Male songbirds are easy to identify on spring mornings as they belt out their courtship songs. Throughout much of the year, diurnal (day-active) birds are most visible in the early morning hours when they are foraging, but during winter they are often more active during the day when milder temperatures prevail.

Short-eared Owl

Binoculars

The small size, fine details and wary behavior of many birds make binoculars an essential piece of equipment for birding. Binoculars can cost anywhere from $50 to $1500. Most beginners pay less than $200 for their first pair.

Binoculars come in two basic types: Porro-prism and roof-prism. Each has advantages, which knowledgeable salespeople can explain, but in general roof-prisms are probably better choices for most birders.

The optical power of binoculars is described with a two-number code. A compact pair of binoculars might be "8 × 21," and a larger pair might be "7 × 40." The first number states the magnification, whereas the second number indicates the diameter, in millimeters, of the front lenses. Seven-power binoculars are the easiest to hold and to use for finding birds; 10-power binoculars give a more magnified but shakier view. Larger lenses gather more light, so a 35 mm or 40 mm lens will perform better at dusk than a 20 mm or 25 mm lens of the same magnification. Some binoculars have a wider field of view than others, even if the two-number code is identical. We recommend larger lenses with a wider field of view for beginners.

Look at many types of binoculars before making a purchase. Talk to other birders about their binoculars and ask to try them. See how a pair feels in your hands—can you focus them easily? Go to a store that specializes in birding; the salespeople will know from personal experience which models perform best in the field.

MacGillivray's Warbler

When birding, lift the binoculars up to your eyes without taking your eyes off the bird. This way you will not lose the bird in the magnified view. You can also note an obvious landmark near the bird (a bright flower or a dead branch, for example) and then use it as a reference point to find the bird with the binoculars.

Spotting Scopes and Cameras

The spotting scope (a small telescope with a sturdy tripod) is designed to help you view birds that are beyond the range of binoculars. Most spotting scopes magnify by a factor of 20 or more. Some will even allow you to take photographs through them.

For serious photography, you will need a 35 mm single-lens reflex (SLR) camera with a telephoto lens measuring at least 300 mm (or a high-resolution digital SLR camera with an equivalent lens). A solid tripod for the camera is essential.

Birding by Ear

Recognizing birds by their songs and calls can greatly enhance your birding experience. When experienced birders conduct breeding bird surveys in summer, they rely more on their ears than their eyes, because listening is far more efficient. Recordings are available to help you learn bird songs, and a portable player with headphones can let you quickly compare a live bird with the recording. Please avoid playing tapes or CDs through speakers during the breeding season.

A tried-and-true way to remember bird songs is to make up words for them. We have given you some of the classic renderings in the species accounts that follow, such as *"who cooks for you? who cooks for you all?"* for the Barred Owl, as well as some imitative syllables, such as *churr churr churr swee swee* for the MacGillivray's Warbler. Of course, these mnemonics are approximations; birds often add or delete syllables, and very few pronounce consonants in a recognizable fashion. Songs usually vary from region to region as well.

BIRDING BY HABITAT

Washington can be divided into 31 biophysical regions or "bioregions" based on the Vegetation Zones of the Washington Gap Analysis Project.

Westside Forests and Olympic Mountains
Sitka Spruce
Westside Western Hemlock
Olympic Douglas-fir
Silver Fir
Alpine/Parkland
Permanent Ice, Snow

Puget Trough
Puget Sound Douglas-fir
Woodland/Prairie Mosaic
Cowlitz River
Willamette Valley

Canadian Rocky Mountains
Interior Redcedar
Interior Western Hemlock
Mountain Hemlock
Alpine/Parkland

Blue Mountains
High Basalt Ridges
Open High Conifers

East Cascades and Okanogan Mountains
Ponderosa Pine
Interior Douglas-fir
Grand Fir
Oak (East Side)
Mountain Hemlock
Subalpine Fir
Lava Flows < 4000 ft
Lava Flows > 4000 ft
Alpine/Parkland (Cascade/Okaganogan Mts)
Permanent Ice, Snow

Columbia Plateau
Big Sage/Fescue
Canyon Grasslands
Wheatgrass/Fescue
Central Arid Steppe
Bitterbrush
Klickitat Meadow Steppe
Three-tip Sage
Palouse
Blue Mountain Steppe

Please refer to map on p. 25

Each bioregion is composed of a number of identifiable habitats. Simply put, a bird's habitat is the place where it normally nests, roosts or forages during a given season. Some birds prefer open water, some are found in cattail marshes, others like mature coniferous forest, and still others prefer abandoned, overgrown agricultural fields. Many species have very specific habitats that they leave only in migration or during inclement weather.

Knowing a bird's habitat increases the chances of identifying the bird correctly. If you are birding in wetlands, you will not be identifying tanagers or towhees; if you are wandering among the leafy trees of a deciduous forest, do not expect to meet Boreal Owls or Tundra Swans.

BIRD LISTING

Many birders list the species they have seen during excursions or at home. So popular is listing that the American Birding Association publishes a regular bulletin featuring the accomplishments of its members (see http://www.americanbirding.org/resources/). It is up to you to decide what kind of list—systematic or casual—you will keep, and you may choose not to make lists at all. However, lists may prove rewarding in unexpected ways. For example, after you visit a new area, your list becomes a souvenir of your experiences there. As well, keeping regular, accurate lists of birds in an area over time can yield many interesting insights about that area. Your information may also be of interest to local researchers, especially if you have recorded yearly arrival and last sighting dates of hummingbirds and other seasonal visitors, and have noted first sightings of any new visitors to your area.

Although computer programs are available for listing birds, many naturalists simply keep records in field notebooks. You can personalize your notebook with sketches and with observations of feeding, courtship and nesting behaviors. As well, the checklist in this book (p. 370) features check boxes for listing purposes.

BIRDING ACTIVITIES
Bird Conservation
Washington still boasts large areas of wilderness, including parks, wildlife refuges and public lands. Nevertheless, agriculture, forestry and housing development threaten viable bird habitat across the state. Many bird enthusiasts support groups such as Ducks Unlimited, the Nature Conservancy and the American Bird Conservancy, which help birds by providing sanctuaries and promoting conservation.

Landscaping your own property to provide native plant cover and natural foods for birds is an immediate and personal way to conserve bird habitat. The cumulative effects of such urban "nature-scaping" can be significant. If your yard is to become a bird sanctuary, try to keep neighborhood cats away—cats kill millions of birds each year. The Humane Society recommends that all pet cats be kept indoors.

Bird Feeding
Many people set up backyard bird feeders or plant native berry- or seed-producing plants in their gardens to attract birds. Staff at birding stores can suggest different foods for attracting specific birds. Hummingbird feeders are filled with a simple sugar solution made from one part sugar and three to four parts water. Red food coloring is unnecessary and is in fact harmful to the hummingbirds.

Contrary to popular opinion, birds do not become dependent on feeders, nor do they forget how to forage naturally. Birds appreciate feeders most in winter, but don't forget early spring, before flowers bloom, seeds develop and insects hatch.

There are many good books about feeding birds and landscaping your yard to provide natural foods and nest sites. A particularly good one for Washington is *Landscaping for Wildlife in the Pacific Northwest*, by Russell Link.

Western Bluebird

Rufous Hummingbird

Nest Boxes and Birdbaths

Setting out nest boxes will attract certain cavity-nesting birds, such as House Wrens, Western Bluebirds, Tree Swallows and Purple Martins. If you wish to attract small songbirds, make sure the size of the hole is specific to the bird you want (see http://www.audubon.org/educate/expert/birdbox.html). If the hole is too large, you will attract only House Sparrows and European Starlings. Other appropriately sized nest boxes can attract kestrels, owls and cavity-nesting ducks.

Birdbaths will entice birds to your yard at any time of year, and heated birdbaths are particularly appreciated in the colder months. Avoid birdbaths that have exposed metal parts, because wet birds can accidentally freeze to them in winter. Birdbaths must have the water changed frequently; see under "West Nile Virus" below.

Cleaning Feeders and Nest Boxes

Nest boxes and feeding stations must be kept clean to prevent birds from becoming ill or spreading disease. Old nesting material may harbor a number of parasites. Once the birds have left for the season, remove the old material and scrub the nest box with detergent or a 10 percent bleach solution (1 part bleach to 9 parts water). You can also scald the nest box with boiling water. Rinse it well and let it dry thoroughly before you remount it.

Unclean bird feeders can become contaminated with salmonellosis and possibly other diseases. Seed feeders should be cleaned monthly; hummingbird feeders at least weekly. Any seed, fruit or suet that is moldy or spoiled must be discarded. Clean and disinfect feeding stations with a 10 percent bleach solution, scrubbing thoroughly. Rinse the feeder well and allow it to dry completely before refilling it. Discarded seed and feces on the ground under the feeding station should also be removed.

We advise that you wear rubber gloves and a mask when cleaning nest boxes or feeders.

West Nile Virus

Since the West Nile virus surfaced in North America in 1999, it has caused fear and misunderstanding. Some people have become afraid of contracting the disease from birds, and some health departments have advised residents to eliminate feeding stations and birdbaths.

To date, the disease has reportedly killed 284 species of birds. Corvids (crows, jays and ravens) and raptors have been the most obvious victims because of their size, although the disease also affects some smaller species. The virus is transmitted among birds and to humans (and to some other mammals) by mosquitoes that have bitten infected birds. Birds do not get the disease directly from other birds, and humans cannot get it from casual contact with infected birds. As well, not all mosquito species carry the disease. According to the Centers for Disease Control and Prevention (CDC), only about 20 percent of people who are bitten and become infected will develop any symptoms at all, and fewer than 1 percent will become severely ill.

Because mosquitoes breed in standing water, birdbaths have the potential to become mosquito breeding grounds. Birdbaths should be emptied and have the water changed at least weekly. Drippers, circulating pumps, fountains or waterfalls that keep water moving will prevent mosquitoes from laying their eggs in the water. There are also bird-friendly products available to treat the water in birdbaths. Contact your local nature store or garden center for more information on these products.

TOP 50 BIRDING SITES IN WASHINGTON

There are hundreds, if not thousands, of good birding areas throughout Washington. The following 50 sites have been selected to represent a broad range of bird communities and habitats, with an emphasis on accessibility. The next section presents descriptions of some of the best of these sites, with notes on interesting species you can expect to see there.

1. Point Roberts
2. Blaine Harbor, Birch Bay & Semiahmoo
3. Samish Flats
4. Skagit Flats & Fir Island
5. Cattle Pass (San Juan Island)
6. Rosario Head
7. Crockett Lake & Fort Casey
8. Keystone–Port Townsend Ferry
9. Spencer Island (Everett)
10. Discovery Park (Seattle)
11. Union Bay Natural Area (Montlake Fill, Seattle)
12. West Seattle & Lincoln Park
13. Marymoor Park (Redmond)
14. Gog-le-hi-te Wetland (Tacoma)
15. Point No Point
16. Port Gamble & Salsbury Point
17. Fort Flagler & Oak Bay CP
18. Sequim
19. Ediz Hook (Port Angeles)
20. Hurricane Ridge (Olympic NP)
21. Ocean Shores
22. Bottle Beach & Westport
23. Long Beach
24. Nisqually NWR
25. Julia Butler Hansen NWR
26. Ridgefield NWR
27. North Cascades NP
28. Rainy Pass & Washington Pass
29. Sinlahekin Valley, Palmer Lake & Champneys Slough
30. Conconully, FR 37 & FR 39
31. Bridgeport SP & Brewster
32. Waterville Plateau
33. Grand Coulee & Sun Lakes
34. Vantage & Huntzinger Road
35. Lower Crab Creek
36. Wenas Campground
37. Mt. Rainier NP
38. Conboy Lake NWR
39. Lyle
40. Goldendale & Rock Creek
41. Potholes & Columbia NWR
42. Tri-Cities & McNary NWR
43. Walla Walla River delta
44. Republic & Curlew
45. Sanpoil River Valley
46. Mt. Spokane SP
47. Turnbull NWR
48. Steptoe Butte
49. Blue Mountains
50. Field Springs SP

BEST SITES ABBREVIATIONS

CP = County Park
FR = Forest Road
NP = National Park
NWR = National Wildlife Refuge
SP = State Park

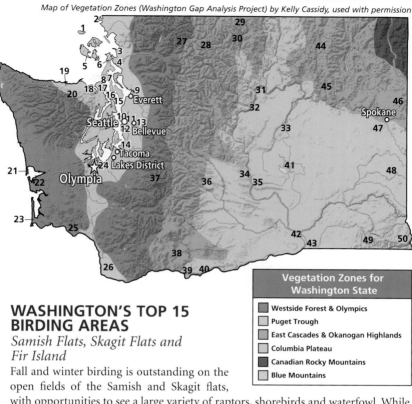

Map of Vegetation Zones (Washington Gap Analysis Project) by Kelly Cassidy, used with permission

Vegetation Zones for Washington State

- Westside Forest & Olympics
- Puget Trough
- East Cascades & Okanogan Highlands
- Columbia Plateau
- Canadian Rocky Mountains
- Blue Mountains

WASHINGTON'S TOP 15 BIRDING AREAS

Samish Flats, Skagit Flats and Fir Island

Fall and winter birding is outstanding on the open fields of the Samish and Skagit flats, with opportunities to see a large variety of raptors, shorebirds and waterfowl. While driving the roads on both flats, scan poles and fencelines for Red-tailed Hawk, Rough-legged Hawk, Northern Harrier and Bald Eagle. Pay particular attention to falcons, because it is possible to see five species here in midwinter.

On the Samish Flats, a particularly good spot is the "West 90," where Samish Island Road turns 90 degrees to the north. Scanning fields, fencelines and poles from here can turn up Peregrine Falcon, Gyrfalcon and occasionally Prairie Falcon. Northern Harrier and Short-eared Owl are common. Elsewhere on the flats, watch for Merlin, Trumpeter Swan and Tundra Swan. Often there is a pair of American Kestrels along D'Arcy Road. Working your way south along Bayview–Edison Road, a stop at the Padilla Bay Interpretive Center can yield a good variety of passerines.

Continue south to the Skagit Flats and watch the open fields for raptors. Up to 15,000 Snow Geese can be seen here in fall and winter. Turn south off Fir Island Road onto Wylie Road to reach the Skagit Wildlife Area, which features riparian woodlands along the Skagit River and the sloughs, with open fields between. Walking the dikes out to Skagit Bay brings you into an area of marsh and open water. The Skagit Wildlife Area is an excellent location for waterfowl in fall and winter and for passerines year-round. Winter can be good for kinglets, Bewick's Wren, Winter Wren, White-crowned Sparrow, Golden-crowned Sparrow and occasionally American Tree Sparrow and Northern Shrike. Spring is excellent for warblers, including Yellow-rumped, Yellow, Wilson's, Nashville, MacGillivray's and Townsend's.

Crockett Lake, Keystone Harbor and Fort Casey

This part of Whidbey Island provides many different habitats in close proximity. Sea-level Crockett Lake, with its open water and mudflats, is separated from Admiralty Inlet by a grassy and sandy spit. Adjoining both is Keystone Harbor, with its jetty, and just upslope is forested Fort Casey State Park (parking fee charged).

The entire area is an excellent shorebird spot during the southbound migration period from early July to late September. Common species include Western, Least, Spotted, Baird's and Semipalmated sandpipers, Killdeer, Black-bellied Plover, Semipalmated Plover, both yellowlegs, both dowitchers, Dunlin, Wilson's Snipe and Red-necked Phalarope. Sanderling and Whimbrel are fairly common. Uncommon to rare species include American Avocet, Stilt Sandpiper, Sharp-tailed Sandpiper, American Golden-Plover, Pacific Golden-Plover, Solitary Sandpiper, Red Knot and

Black Turnstone. The grassy margins and cattail marshes are good for sparrows and wrens, and the Virginia Rail is often heard. Northern Harrier, Red-tailed Hawk, Bald Eagle and Peregrine Falcon regularly patrol the area.

Crockett Lake may be viewed from its north and south sides. Wanamaker Road provides access from the north, and SR 20 runs along the south shore, with wide shoulders that provide good views across the lake and its mudflats (the water level is controlled by a tide gate). If you walk out toward the lake, rubber boots are advised and caution is necessary, because the mud can get very soft quickly.

Keystone Harbor can yield all three species of cormorant, alcids, loons and grebes. The jetty is good for Heermann's Gull from July to September, and the Black Oystercatcher has been seen. The woods of Fort Casey State Park are excellent for a wide variety of passerines.

Red Knot

Keystone–Port Townsend Ferry

The Washington State Ferry from Keystone Harbor to Port Townsend regularly yields all three cormorants, Common Loon, Pacific Loon, Horned, Red-necked and Western grebes, Pigeon Guillemot, Rhinoceros Auklet, Common Murre, Marbled Murrelet and Glaucous-winged, Mew and Bonaparte's gulls. The cold, nutrient-rich waters of Admiralty Inlet are forced toward the surface here, attracting many fish that in turn bring the birds in. You can park on either side and walk aboard the ferry, or you can drive aboard if you are going to continue on the other side. The best viewing is from outside on the upper deck, but dress warmly, because it can be chilly even in summer.

Discovery Park & West Point

Discovery Park in Seattle is a remarkable oasis in the midst of a large urban area. The upland forests are home to Black-capped Chickadee, Chestnut-backed Chickadee, both kinglets, Bewick's Wren, Winter Wren, Brown Creeper, Downy, Hairy and Pileated woodpeckers, Northern Flicker and Red-breasted Sapsucker. Anna's Hummingbird is regular year-round near the interpretive center, and Rufous Hummingbird is present in summer. The grasslands in the center of the park are good for Savannah Sparrow, occasional Western Meadowlark and both hummingbirds, and the brushy edges may turn up Black-headed Grosbeak, Willow Flycatcher and Orange-crowned Warbler. The dense forest on the north slope is good for Winter Wren, Swainson's Thrush, Black-throated Gray Warbler, Cassin's Vireo and Warbling Vireo. Down by Puget Sound, adjacent West Point is excellent for ducks, loons, grebes and alcids. Here you'll find all three scoters and possibly Harlequin Duck and Long-tailed Duck. During migration, Brant can be seen in the eelgrass beds offshore. This is also a good spot to carefully examine the gulls—Glaucous-winged, Bonaparte's and Mew gulls are regular, and it is possible to see Franklin's and Sabine's gulls as well. During fall migration you may see a Parasitic Jaeger harassing Common Terns.

Sequim & Dungeness Spit

The area from Sequim Bay around to Dungeness Spit is particularly rich in birdlife. One of the best locations to view Sequim Bay is from the John Wayne Marina (turn off US 101 onto West Sequim Bay Road and follow it to the marina). Usually present from fall through winter are all three cormorants, loons, grebes, all three scoters, a wide variety of ducks that includes Long-tailed Duck, and many alcids, such as Marbled Murrelet. The jetty around the marina can have Western Sandpiper, Least Sandpiper, Dunlin, Black-bellied Plover and Black Oystercatcher.

The shore from Dungeness (north of Sequim) to Dungeness Spit provides forest, grassland, marsh and mudflat habitats. Follow Sequim–Dungeness Way north out of Sequim to the Three Crabs Restaurant. From here, you are likely to see many of the same species as at the John Wayne Marina and, in addition, Eurasian Wigeon, Northern Shoveler, Northern Pintail, Gadwall, yellowlegs, Peregrine Falcon and Merlin. Just south of the restaurant is a series of ponds that can turn up many different ducks and shorebirds. In addition to the regulars, Baird's, Pectoral and Sharp-tailed sandpipers have been seen. To the west, in the open fields and forests of Dungeness National Wildlife Refuge, you may see Savannah Sparrow, Chestnut-backed Chickadee, Brown Creeper, both kinglets, Bewick's Wren and a variety of warblers, including Townsend's.

Savannah Sparrow

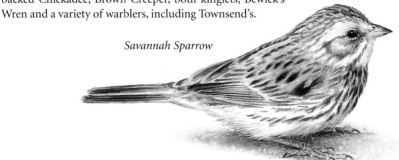

27

Ocean Shores & Grays Harbor

Ocean Shores, in Grays Harbor County, is located on a long peninsula separating Grays Harbor from the Pacific Ocean on the outer coast. Birding is outstanding in all seasons. The Point Brown jetty is an excellent spot to look for Wandering Tattler and Rock Sandpiper in winter. From the jetty, scan for loons, grebes, alcids, cormorants and sea ducks. The jetty and beach attract gulls, terns, shorebirds and often Brown Pelican. Winter storms may bring pelagic birds such as Sooty Shearwater close to shore.

Adjacent to the jetty area is the Oyhut State Wildlife Recreation Area, another good spot for shorebirds in spring and fall. You may see Sharp-tailed Sandpiper here.

On the Grays Harbor side of the peninsula is Damon Point State Park. This park is good for loons, grebes, shorebirds (particularly at low tide) and,

on the grass-covered dunes, Horned Lark and Lapland Longspur. It is also the site of a nesting area for Snowy Plover, so please observe the exclosure signs during the spring breeding season. Flocks of Black-bellied Plover should be looked over closely for American Golden-Plover and Pacific Golden-Plover.

Ocean City State Park provides freshwater ponds and forest and is very good for many passerines, including migrating warblers. To the east at Hoquiam are Grays Harbor National Wildlife Refuge and Bowerman Basin, where huge gatherings of shorebirds occur in April, including approximately 90 percent of the Western Sandpiper population.

On the south shore of Grays Harbor, just east of Westport, is Bottle Beach State Park (presently undeveloped), another excellent spot for migrating shorebirds, including Red Knot in April.

Ridgefield National Wildlife Refuge

Ridgefield NWR's River "S" Unit is a low-elevation area of ponds and marshes, and the Carty Unit offers more upland habitat. From I-5 take exit 14 to the town of Ridgefield. Take South 9th Avenue (Hillhurst Road) south to the River "S" Unit, home in fall and winter to huge populations of ducks and geese. Here you can study various subspecies of both Cackling Goose and Canada Goose. From October to April, access to this part of the refuge is limited to driving the road tour route, the entrance area and the observation blind area about midway along the road. Watch for a small population of Sandhill Crane that winters in the area. Black Tern (unusual for western Washington) has been seen in small numbers here, and nesting was recorded in 2001 and 2002. Pay particular attention to the tree copses along the way for perched raptors, including Red-shouldered Hawk (unusual for Washington).

White-breasted Nuthatch

Go back through the town of Ridgefield on North Main Avenue to reach the Carty Unit. A loop trail provides access to ponds and oak woodland where you can see a good variety of waterfowl and forest birds. This is an excellent area for woodpeckers, Western Scrub-Jay and White-breasted Nuthatch, in addition to the more usual forest songbirds such as chickadees, kinglets, wrens and Brown Creeper. Don't neglect the shrubby and grassy areas, which are good for sparrows.

Sinlahekin Valley, Palmer Lake and Champneys Slough

Spring and summer are optimal for this area on the far northeastern flank of the Okanogan Mountains, which features some of the highest breeding bird diversity in Washington. The Sinlahekin Wildlife Area, in the Sinlahekin Valley, is the oldest wildlife area in the state. A number of small lakes dot the valley and host many breeding ducks, including Cinnamon Teal, Blue-winged Teal, Barrow's Goldeneye, Lesser Scaup and Redhead. Black Tern nests here, too. Riparian areas are good for sapsuckers, flycatchers, swallows, Veery and warblers, including the Yellow-breasted Chat. The valley slopes are good for Common Nighthawk, Common Poorwill, Mountain Chickadee and Chipping Sparrow, among others. To the north, the marshy margins of Palmer Lake are good for Virginia Rail, Sora, swallows and Wilson's Snipe. Grebes can be seen on deep parts of the lake. Bobolink and sometimes Long-billed Curlew are seen in the area around Chopaka Road. Champneys Slough is good for flycatchers, warblers, woodpeckers and Gray Catbird. The cliffs above are excellent for White-throated Swift, Violet-green Swallow and Canyon Wren. Keep your eyes peeled for Lewis's Woodpecker, Bullock's Oriole and Golden Eagle.

Conconully, Forest Road 37 and Forest Road 39

As you enter Conconully, stop and look out over Conconully Lake for ducks, grebes and perhaps a rail. The surrounding ponderosa pines may have Pygmy Nuthatch. Conconully State Park may be good for warblers, chickadees and Chipping Sparrow. Take FR 37 west from Conconully for a loop with access to some of the best boreal birding in Washington. As you climb, watch for the transition from ponderosa pine into a zone with larch. This area can be good for Williamson's Sapsucker, Hairy Woodpecker and flycatchers. As you approach Baldy Pass at about 6000 feet, you enter an area with potential for Pine Grosbeak, Boreal Chickadee, American Three-toed Woodpecker and Spruce Grouse.

Farther on, FR 37 meets FR 39. Take FR 39 to the north. Stop at Roger Lake and walk around the lake. This is an excellent place to see American Three-toed Woodpecker (the Engelmann spruce here has been attacked by spruce bark beetle, providing a good woodpecker food source). Williamson's Sapsucker is also present. Roger Lake is good for Wilson's Snipe, Spotted Sandpiper, Dark-eyed Junco and Spruce Grouse. Farther north, the trail from Freezeout Pass climbs through areas yielding Spruce Grouse, Blue Grouse and Gray-crowned Rosy-Finch. Tiffany Springs Campground is a good site for Boreal Chickadee as well as American Three-toed Woodpecker and Hairy Woodpecker. Northern Goshawk is also present in the area. A number of forest fires along the ridge have left many dead trees, good habitat for Black-backed Woodpecker.

Most of FR 37 and FR 39 are at high elevation. These roads are usually open from late June until September, and they are kept in graded and graveled condition suitable for passenger vehicles.

Pygmy Nuthatch

Bridgeport & Waterville Plateau

This area is at its best in winter. Cruise the network of roads on the plateau slowly, because the agricultural fields hold large numbers of wintering Horned Lark, Snow Bunting and Lapland Longspur. Also present are predators such as Rough-legged Hawk, Northern Harrier, Gyrfalcon, American Kestrel and Red-tailed Hawk. In summer, watch for Swainson's Hawk. In the towns, watch for Common Redpoll, Bohemian Waxwing and White-crowned Sparrow. Remnants of sage–shrub steppe can yield Greater Sage-Grouse, but be careful not to disturb this sensitive endangered species. Riparian vegetation along the streams in the canyons is good for owls and sparrows, as well as for warblers in spring. More forested areas can be good for woodpeckers, Steller's Jay and, occasionally, Northern Goshawk. The Columbia River is worth scanning for loons, grebes and waterfowl.

Horned Lark

Vantage & Vicinity

Vantage lies on the Columbia River where I-90 crosses it. The area to the west of this city includes some relatively pristine sage–shrub steppe habitat. Take the Old Vantage Highway eastward from Ellensburg to reach some of the best habitat. As the road begins to drop down into Schnebly Coulee, watch for the turnoffs to the Quilomene Wildlife Area. Sage Thrashers and Sage, Brewer's and Vesper sparrows are active here from very early spring until very early summer. The rocky cliffs along the coulee and down by the Columbia are good for Rock Wren and Chukar. One mile before Vantage, turn off to the museum in Ginkgo Petrified Forest State Park for a good view over the Columbia. In spring, the trees around the museum are often filled with warblers, vireos, tanagers, orioles and other passerines. The cliff edges are frequented by Cliff Swallow and Violet-green Swallow, and White-throated Swift often zooms by. In early morning, Chukar is frequently heard, and sometimes seen, on the flats below.

Wanapum Lake, formed by the Wanapum Dam downstream from Vantage, is excellent in winter for loons, grebes and a variety of waterfowl. Unusual species can show up here, including Long-tailed Duck and Yellow-billed Loon. During spring migration, take Huntzinger Road south along the Columbia and check out Wanapum State Park. Black-throated Sparrow reaches its northern limit in this area. In winter, Cliff Swallow nests on the cliffs below Wanapum Dam often host Gray-crowned Rosy-Finches.

Mt. Rainier National Park

Whether approached from the west (SR 706) or the east (SR 410), the tremendous vertical ascent of Mt. Rainier presents us with a good selection of Washington's western and eastern vegetation zones. The western slope has a progression of wet zones, whereas the drier eastern slope zones are like those of eastern Washington. As you climb from the west side, you first experience the Douglas-fir/Western Hemlock Zone, with birds such as Ruffed Grouse and Red-breasted Sapsucker. You then enter the Silver Fir Zone, where Northern Goshawk is possible. The vegetation zones above this one resemble eastern Washington's zones. The Mountain Hemlock Zone has Blue Grouse, Olive-sided Flycatcher, Varied Thrush and Red Crossbill. In the Subalpine Zone, which is characterized by stunted whitebark pine and Engelmann spruce, Clark's Nutcracker, Gray Jay and Common Raven are present. A short hike above the highest drivable point gets you above treeline into the Alpine Zone, where American Pipit, Blue Grouse,

Gray-crowned Rosy-Finch and White-tailed Ptarmigan can be seen.

Approaching from the east, you begin in the Oak Zone, where Lewis's Woodpecker is found. As you climb through the Ponderosa Pine Zone, expect White-headed Woodpecker and Pygmy Nuthatch. Look for Mountain Chickadee and Red-Breasted Nuthatch in the Interior Douglas-fir Zone. The Grand Fir Zone, which grades into lodgepole pine, offers Williamson's Sapsucker. The Interior Western Hemlock/Interior Redcedar Zone is home to Mountain Chickadee and Townsend's Warbler. In the Subalpine Zone, with mountain hemlock and subalpine fir, watch for Gray Jay, Clark's Nutcracker and Red Crossbill.

In addition to the great variety of vegetation and birdlife, Mt. Rainier offers some of the most spectacular scenery in the lower 48 states. Enjoy the alpine views, but don't miss the old-growth forests of the Cathedral Grove on the eastern flank of the mountain near the Stevens Canyon Entrance on SR 706.

Tri-Cities and McNary National Wildlife Refuge

The Tri-Cities (Richland, Kennewick and Pasco) lie along the Columbia River and encompass a series of riverside parks and the delta of the Yakima River. The parks and delta are rich areas for birding, particularly in fall, winter and spring. Loons, grebes and waterfowl are good in fall and winter; also look for more unusual Columbia Basin species, such as Greater Scaup, Lesser Scaup, Long-tailed Duck, Surf Scoter and White-winged Scoter. Sparrows are prolific in shrubby areas. During low-water periods in fall and spring, the area around Bateman Island often yields 20 shorebird species. Gulls and jaegers may be seen as well. In spring, watch for swallows, warblers, shorebirds and terns in migration. American White Pelicans have nested on islands in the area.

Just south of the Tri-Cities along US 12, on the shore of Lake Wallula (the impoundment of the Columbia behind the McNary Dam), is McNary National Wildlife Refuge. The marshes, fields and open water are excellent in winter for terns, gulls, regular and unusual waterfowl, and sparrows, including rarities such as White-throated and Harris's.

Common Loon

Ruffed Grouse

Mt. Spokane State Park

Located about 25 miles northeast of Spokane, Mt. Spokane State Park provides good mountain birding close to a major urban area. From Spokane, take US 395/US 2 north and continue on US 2 to the junction with SR 206 and the turnoff to the state park. The Douglas-fir, lodgepole pine, western white pine and subalpine fir forest is good habitat for many species. During the breeding season you can find vireos, warblers, Ruffed Grouse, Blue Grouse, Black-backed Woodpecker, Winter Wren, Hermit Thrush, Swainson's Thrush and sparrows. In winter, look for Common Raven, Steller's Jay, Northern Pygmy-Owl, chickadees, crossbills, Cassin's Finch and Pine Grosbeak. During migration periods, higher elevations can be good for raptors, including Golden Eagle and Northern Goshawk. High, open grassy and rocky areas may turn up Mountain Bluebird, Horned Lark, Snow Bunting, Lapland Longspur and Bohemian Waxwing. The Gray-crowned Rosy-Finch is often a bonus.

Turnbull National Wildlife Refuge

Turnbull National Wildlife Refuge, south of Spokane, is an oasis in dry eastern Washington. Its open ponderosa pine forest, ponds and lakes provide a good mix of habitats and good birding year-round, although slower in the heat of summer. From Spokane, take I-90 to SR 904 and watch for signs to the refuge. Much of the refuge is off-limits to the public, but a loop road allows access to a variety of good habitats. In spring, the refuge is home to many species of breeding waterfowl, including all three teals, Redhead and Canada Goose, along with rails, grebes, Spotted Sandpiper, Black Tern and Yellow-headed Blackbird. The pine forest is good for woodpeckers, chickadees, nuthatches and Western Bluebird. Riparian vegetation regularly turns up Downy Woodpecker, Red-naped Sapsucker, flycatchers, vireos, American Redstart, Gray Catbird, House Wren and perhaps Northern Saw-whet Owl. Unusual species have turned up during migration periods (April to May and August to October). Don't limit yourself to watching for birds, because the refuge is also excellent for white-tailed deer, long-tailed weasels, red squirrels, coyotes and river otters.

BIRDING ORGANIZATIONS

Meeting other people with the same interests makes birding even more pleasurable, and there is always something to be learned when birders gather. Become involved with Christmas bird counts, birding festivals, breeding or winter bird surveys and local birding societies, and attend meetings of natural history groups. Bird hotlines provide up-to-date information on sightings of rarities and allow you to report your own sightings. The following organizations can help you get involved.

American Birding Association
P.O. Box 6599
Colorado Springs, CO 80934-6599
Phone: (800) 850-2473
Website: www.americanbirding.org/

Audubon Washington
P.O. Box 462
Olympia, WA 98507
Phone: (360) 786-8020
Website: wa.audubon.org/new/audubon/

Seattle Audubon Society
8050 35th Avenue NE
Seattle, WA 98115
Phone: (206) 523-4483
Websites: www.seattleaudubon.org/ &
www.birdweb.org/

Spokane Audubon Society
P.O. Box 9820
Spokane, WA 99209-9820
Phone: (509) 838-5828
Website: www.spokaneaudubon.org/

Washington Ornithological Society (WOS)
P.O. Box 31783
Seattle, WA 98103-1783
Website: www.wos.org/
The WOS publishes the newsletter WOSNews *and the journal* Washington Birds.

Yakima Valley Audubon Society
P.O. Box 2823
Yakima, WA 98907-2823
Phone: (509) 248-1963
Website: www.yakimaaudubon.org/

Bird Hotlines
- WOS statewide hotline (Washington BirdBox): (206) 281-9172
- Lower Columbia Basin hotline: (509) 627-2473
- Southeastern Washington/northern Idaho hotline: (208) 882-6195

Tweeters E-mail Discussion List
To learn more, and to subscribe, visit www.scn.org/earth/tweeters/

Redhead

ABOUT THE SPECIES ACCOUNTS

This book gives detailed accounts of the 320 species of birds that are listed as regular by the Washington Bird Records Committee. These species can be expected on an annual basis. Thirty-three occasional species and species of note are briefly described in an illustrated appendix (p. 359). Washington birders can expect to see small numbers of these 33 species every few years, brought here by anticipated range expansion, migration or well-documented wandering tendencies. The checklist (p. 370) lists all 477 species that have been seen in the state. The order of the birds and their common and scientific names follow the American Ornithologists' Union's *Check-list of North American Birds* (1998), and its supplements through 2005.

One of the challenges of birding is that many species look different in spring and summer than they do in fall and winter. Many birds have breeding and non-breeding plumages, and immature birds often look different from their parents. This book does not describe or illustrate all the different plumages of a species; instead, it focuses on the forms that are most likely to be seen in our area. The illustrations are of adult birds unless otherwise indicated.

As well as helping you identify the birds, the species accounts bring them to life by including points of interest about their behavior, physiology and ecology and the derivation of their names. At times our language personifies the birds, and such characterizations should not be mistaken for scientific propositions. Nonetheless, we hope that a lively, engaging text will communicate our scientific knowledge as smoothly and effectively as possible.

Mourning Dove

ID: It is difficult to describe the features of a bird without being able to visualize it, so this section is best used in combination with the illustrations. Where appropriate, the description is subdivided to highlight the differences between male and female birds, breeding and nonbreeding birds and immature and adult birds. The descriptions use as few scientific terms as possible, and they favor easily understood language. Birds may not have "jaw lines," "eyebrows" or "chins," but these and other technically inaccurate terms are easily understood by all readers. Scientific terms are used for some of the most common features of birds; see the Glossary (p. 368) and its illustration for explanations.

Size: The average length *(L)* of the bird's body from bill to tail tip, along with its wingspan *(W)* from wing tip to wing tip, give the approximate size of the bird as it is seen in nature. Separate measurements are given for male and female where the difference in size is consistent and substantial. Please note that the length measurements for birds with long tails do not necessarily reflect "body" size.

Status: A general comment, such as "common," "uncommon" or "rare," is usually sufficient to describe the relative abundance of a species. Wherever possible, we have also indicated status at different times of the year and by region. Situations are bound to vary as migratory pulses, seasonal changes and centers of activity concentrate or disperse birds.

Habitat: The habitats we list indicate where each species is most commonly found. In most cases, it is a generalized description, but, if a bird is restricted to a specific habitat, the habitat is described accordingly. Because of the freedom that flight gives them, birds can turn up in almost any type of habitat. However, they will usually be found in environments that provide the specific food, water, cover and, for breeding birds, nesting habitat they require.

Nesting: For each species that breeds in Washington, nest location and structure, clutch size, egg color, incubation period and parental duties are noted. Remember that birding ethics discourage the disturbance of active bird nests, and laws prohibit the destruction or possession of nests, eggs or young. If you disturb a nest, you may drive off the parents during a critical period or expose defenseless young to predators. Do not use tapes or recordings to attract birds during the nesting season.

Feeding: Birds spend a great deal of time foraging for food, so they are frequently encountered while foraging. If you know what a bird eats and where the food is found, you will have a good chance of finding that bird. We hope that our description of each bird's feeding styles and diets provides valuable identifying characteristics as well as interesting dietary facts.

Voice: Many birds, particularly songbirds, tend to be heard and not seen. Easily remembered imitative paraphrases of distinctive sounds will aid you in identifying a species. These phrases only loosely resemble the call, song or sound produced by the bird. Should one of our phrases not work for you, feel free to make up your own—the creative exercise will reinforce your memory of the bird's vocalizations.

Similar Species: Because bird species can differ in subtle ways, consult this section before finalizing your identification. Here you will find brief descriptions of the most relevant characteristics of easily confused species.

Concentrating on the most relevant field marks, and paying attention to habitat preferences and behavioral clues, make differences between species clearer and speed up the identification process. Don't be discouraged when you're first learning. Even experienced birders make mistakes!

Best Sites: If you are looking for a particular bird, you will have more luck in some locations than in others, even within the range shown on the range map. There are many excellent birding sites in Washington; unfortunately, we cannot list them all. In this section of the accounts we list some easily accessible places, such as nature centers, state game areas, national lakeshores and state and national parks, where you stand a good chance of seeing the species. Abbreviations are defined on p. 24.

Range Maps: The range map for each species represents the general Washington distribution of the species in an average year. Most birds confine their annual movements to this range, although each year some birds wander beyond their traditional boundaries. These small maps do not show differences in abundance within the range; areas of a range with good habitat will support a denser population than areas with poorer habitat. These maps also cannot show small pockets within the range where the species may actually be absent, or how the range may change from year to year.

Unlike many other field guides, we have attempted to show migratory pathways—areas of the region where birds may appear while en route to nesting or winter habitat. Many of these migratory routes are "best guesses," which will no doubt be refined as new discoveries are made. The representations of the pathways do not distinguish high-use migration corridors from areas that are seldom used.

Range Map Legend

limit of winter dispersal

summer

migration/ post-breeding dispersal

winter

year-round

NONPASSERINES

Waterfowl

Grouse & Allies

Diving Birds

Heronlike Birds

Birds of Prey

Rails, Coots & Cranes

Shorebirds

Gulls & Allies

Doves

Owls

Nightjars, Swifts & Hummingbirds

Woodpeckers

Nonpasserine birds represent 18 of the 19 orders of birds found in Washington and about 63 percent of the species seen here. They are grouped together and called "nonpasserines" because, with few exceptions, they are easily distinguished from the "passerines," or "perching birds," which make up the 19th order. Being from 18 different orders, however, means that nonpasserines vary considerably in their appearance and habits—they include everything from the 5-foot-tall Great Blue Heron to the 3-inch-long Calliope Hummingbird.

Generally speaking, nonpasserines do not "sing." Instead, their vocalizations are usually limited to "calls." There are also other differences in form and structure. For example, whereas the muscles and tendons in the legs of passerines are adapted to grip a perch, and the toes of passerines are never webbed, nonpasserines have feet adapted to a variety of uses.

Many nonpasserines are large, so they include some of our most notable birds. Waterfowl, raptors, gulls, shorebirds and woodpeckers are easily identified by most people. However, novice birders may mistake small nonpasserines such as doves, swifts and hummingbirds for passerines, thus complicating their identification. With a little practice, it will become easy to recognize the nonpasserines. By learning to distinguish the nonpasserines from the passerines at a glance, birders effectively reduce by about half the number of possible species for an unidentified bird.

GREATER WHITE-FRONTED GOOSE

Anser albifrons

Wild geese have come to mean many things to many people. We flatter them with the attributes of pair devotion, family tenacity and vigor. And yet, in addition to sometimes being hampered by late spring ice at their arctic breeding sites, White-fronted Geese must endure hunting and repeatedly find their traditional wetland staging and feeding areas encroached on or taken over for development. • White-fronts often travel alone or with Canada Geese (occasionally with Snow Geese in eastern Washington) and sometimes join flocks of domestic or feral geese and ducks at park and farm ponds. Some migrants visiting Washington stay over winter, but most continue down the coast to California. National wildlife refuges and local sanctuaries offer them both shelter and food crops.

ID: brownish gray overall; white patch across forehead and orangy pink bill; blackish speckling or barring across whitish lower breast and belly; white hindquarters; bright orange legs and feet. *"Tule White-front"* (from Cook Inlet, Alaska): somewhat larger; dark brown head; blackish back. *Immature:* dark around and above bill (yellow until mid-fall); mottled, brown-and-white belly.
Size: *L* 27–33 in; *W* 4½–4¾ ft.
Status: uncommon coastal winter resident, frequently with Canada Geese; usually common in migration from mid-April to mid-May, often in large flocks along the outer coast; occasional large flocks along the outer coast from late September to early October.

Habitat: *Winter:* most frequently uses open areas of grass or crop stubble in western Washington; roosts on open water, shorelines, ice and sometimes plowed fields. *In migration:* nearly anywhere.
Nesting: does not nest in Washington.
Feeding: forages on land by stripping and gleaning plant material, including grasses, sedges, seeds and crop wastes; submerges head or tips up in water for submerged and emergent vegetation.
Voice: contact and flight call in flocks is a distinctive series of far-carrying falsetto notes likened to laughing or yelping; *gig-gog* alarm call is usually given on the ground.
Similar Species: *Canada Goose* (p. 42): dark head and neck with distinctive white "chin strap"; heavier body and wings; more cackling or honking calls.
Best Sites: Grays Harbor NWR, including Hoquiam sewage treatment ponds and airport; Ocean Shores area; Willapa NWR; McNary NWR; Columbia NWR–Othello.

SNOW GOOSE
Chen caerulescens

Clannish by nature, and perhaps the noisiest of geese, Snow Geese prefer their own company but will travel with both Greater White-fronts and Canadas. Flocks are composed of family groups that assemble in highly localized groups at their wintering grounds. • Along the Pacific Flyway, Snow Geese are seen mainly in managed wetland ecosystems of national wildlife refuges and local wildlife management areas. These refuges have helped stabilize numbers on wintering grounds and in migration to the extent that fragile tundra nesting habitat is being put under pressure to support the increasing number of geese. • Most Snow Geese wintering in western Washington breed in northeastern Siberia on Wrangel Island and cross the Bering Strait twice each year in migration. Eastern Washington birds come from other areas in northeastern Siberia, Alaska and Canada. The dark-morph "Blue Goose" is very uncommonly seen.

ID: stubby, pink bill with thin, black "grinning patch" along mandible edges; pink feet. *White morph:* all white, except for black wing tips and occasional light rusty or buff orange staining on head. *Dark morph ("Blue Goose"):* white head, upper neck and sometimes belly; bluish gray to brown body. *In flight:* flocks often in large, loose "V"s.
Size: *L* 28–33 in; *W* 4¾–5 ft.
Status: common local western winter resident; small numbers in the east (from a different population) overwinter at Umatilla NWR.
Habitat: shallow freshwater lakes and wetlands, grainfields and croplands.

Nesting: does not nest in Washington.
Feeding: gleans from land, in marshes or in shallows; eats most other parts of aquatic plants, as well as berries, grains, leafy stems of crops and horsetail stems; bill is adapted to gripping and stripping vegetation.
Voice: loud, nasal, constant *houk-houk* in flight; flocks can be heard from afar.
Similar Species: *Ross's Goose* (p. 359): occasionally in eastern Washington only; smaller; more smoothly rounded head; more triangular bill; no black "grinning patch"; slightly shorter neck; sometimes hybridizes with Snow Goose, producing birds with intermediate characteristics.
Best Sites: up to 15,000 per field graze in old croplands in the Fir I. area of the Skagit R. delta (Skagit Co.) and along Boe Rd. in the Stillaguamish delta south of Stanwood (Snohomish Co.).

BRANT
Branta bernicla

Most of its larger cousins prefer the interior, but the Brant, which is coastal by nature, stays largely along the coast as it migrates between Siberia or Alaska and California or Mexico. • Brant are among the later-arriving fall migrants, appearing from November to December and overwintering in small numbers. They are conspicuous and recognizable at a great distance as they skim close to the surf line in undulating skeins. • The northward movement along the coast begins in early May. Most birds are gone by June, but a small number remain along the coast throughout summer. • Brant rely to a great extent on eelgrass, a submergent plant that has greatly suffered from human abuses of estuaries and harbors. Consequently, Brant are only locally common, staging for weeks at favored sites before migrating.

"Black"

ID: *"Black":* deep brown overall; black breast, neck and head; stubby, dark bill; barred, gray-and-white sides; belly usually dark; broken white "collar"; extensive white tail coverts; dark legs. *"Gray-bellied":* similar but with light gray belly. *Immature:* sides mostly without white barring; no "collar."
Size: *L* 25 in; *W* 3¾ ft.
Status: common migrant and local winter resident in coastal saltwater bays with extensive eelgrass beds; accidental migrant and winter visitor in east; "Gray-bellied" is local on Padilla Bay.

Habitat: tidal estuaries, river mouths and large, shallow coastal lagoons with eelgrass; occasionally found in farm fields with other grazing and gleaning waterfowl.
Nesting: does not nest in Washington.
Feeding: tips up and gleans for submergent vegetation over tidal shallows; prefers aquatic plants and algae, especially eelgrass.
Voice: deep, prolonged croak on the ground; soft clucking in flight.
Similar Species: *Cackling Goose* (p. 41): rarely seen on the coast; paler brown belly; conspicuous "chin strap."
Best Sites: Willapa NWR; Dungeness NWR; March Pt. (Skagit Co.); Birch Bay. *"Gray-bellied":* Padilla Bay.

CACKLING GOOSE
Branta hutchinsii

Three subspecies of Cackling Goose occur in Washington. The smallest, "Cackling Goose" *(B.h. minima)*, is distinguished by its cackling calls, extremely small size, stubby neck and short bill. It arrives in mid-October; most birds shortly depart again, but a few overwinter in Washington. "Aleutian Goose" *(B.h. leucopareia)*, is a rare fall migrant and uncommon local winter visitor at Willapa NWR along the coast. "Taverner's Goose" *(B.h. taverneri)* overwinters in southwestern Washington, arriving in October and leaving by mid-April. All three subspecies often travel with flocks of Canada Geese but generally split up into flocks of their own type on the wintering grounds. • All three subspecies nest in Alaska and Canada; the Aleutian also nests in the Aleutian Islands. • Ornithologists recently split the Cackling Goose off from the Canada Goose. Birders face an interesting challenge as they search through various homogeneous and mixed flocks seeking to distinguish the two species and their subspecies.

ID: generally dark brown; stubby, black bill; rounded, white "chin strap" encircles throat; relatively long, black neck ("Aleutian" shows white band at base); white rump and undertail coverts; short, black tail; black legs.
Size: *L* 25–35 in; *W* 3–4 ft.
Status: uncommon migrant and winter resident, primarily in the southwest; "Aleutian" is federal and state-listed as threatened.

Habitat: along water bodies and marshes; croplands and parks.
Nesting: does not nest in Washington.
Feeding: grazes on new sprouts, aquatic vegetation, grass, roots, berries and seeds (particularly grains); tips up for aquatic roots and tubers.
Voice: cackling call similar to Canada Goose's *ah-honk* but higher pitched.
Similar Species: *Canada Goose* (p. 42): larger; generally lighter in color. *Brant* (p. 40): no "chin strap"; more coastal.
Best Sites: *Winter:* "Cackling" and "Taverner's" at Ridgefield NWR; "Aleutian" at Willapa NWR.

CANADA GOOSE

Branta canadensis

Four of the many Canada Goose subspecies remaining after the split with the Cackling Goose occur in Washington. The largest, "Western Canada Goose" (*B.c. moffitti*), is a breeding resident. "Lesser Canada Goose" (*B.c. parvipes*), is a common migrant in Washington on its way south. "Dusky Canada Goose" (*B.c. occidentalis*) arrives in October and leaves by mid-April, overwintering in southwestern Washington. "Vancouver Canada Goose" (*B.c. fulva*) may move south into Washington in winter. Except for "Western," which breeds throughout the western states, all of these subspecies nest in Alaska or Canada. • Each subspecies shows a high degree of individuality in behaviors such as habitat selection, winter mixing and roosting. • Having adapted to western Washington's mild winters and no longer needing to migrate, "Western" is our most prevalent Canada Goose subspecies. Because it can nest earlier and has extensive areas of lawn for grazing, its population has exploded. In winter, additional "Westerns" migrate in from farther north.

ID: black bill; dark brown upperparts; light brown underparts; white rump and undertail coverts; long, black neck; rounded, white "chin strap" encircling throat; short, black tail; black legs.

Size: *L* 35–45 in; *W* 4½–5¾ ft.

Status: widespread common breeding resident; common migrant and winter resident.

Habitat: along water bodies, parks, marshes and croplands.

Nesting: on the ground on an islet, shoreline point or cliff, or in an old eagle or Osprey nest close to water; female builds a nest of grass and other vegetation lined with feather down; male guards the nest and female incubates 4–7 white eggs for 25–30 days; pair raises the young.

Feeding: grazes on new sprouts, aquatic vegetation, grass, roots, berries and seeds (particularly grains); tips up for aquatic roots and tubers.

Voice: familiar, loud *ah-honk*.

Similar Species: *Cackling Goose* (p. 41): smaller; generally darker. *Brant* (p. 40): no "chin strap"; more coastal.

Best Sites: *"Western"*: statewide. *"Lesser"*: Umatilla NWR. *"Dusky"*: Julia Butler Hansen NWR–Ridgefield NWR. *"Vancouver"*: Ridgefield NWR.

TRUMPETER SWAN

Cygnus buccinator

The majestic Trumpeter Swan is the largest of North America's native waterfowl species. It was hunted nearly to extinction for its meat and feathers during the early 1900s. Breeding populations in Alaska and Alberta, Canada, were the only ones that survived. The species began to return to western Washington in the 1970s, appearing in Skagit County fields. It is now a fairly common winter resident on the Skagit and Samish flats near Mount Vernon, in the Snohomish River valley, in other lowland river valleys and occasionally on small lakes in western Washington. • Both the common name and *buccinator* refer to the loud, bugling sounds created by the long windpipe. • These magnificent birds look especially stunning against a blue winter sky.

ID: all-white plumage; sloping head; large, all-black bill (pinkish lower mandible visible at close range); bill appears to continue straight into forehead; black skin from bill to eyes; long neck (often with a kink along back when at rest); black legs and feet. *Immature:* grayish pink bill; grayish brown plumage. *In flight:* straight neck; flies in family groups.
Size: *L* 4¾–5¼ ft; *W* 9½ ft.
Status: common winter resident on Samish and Skagit flats, in the Snohomish R. valley east of Snohomish and on the Chehalis R. floodplain, with small numbers elsewhere in coastal western Washington; rare migrant and winter visitor in eastern Washington, with small numbers near Ellensburg.

Habitat: shallow areas of large lakes and wetlands, spring-fed rivers, farm fields and flooded pastures; rarely on mudflats and salt marshes.
Nesting: does not nest in Washington.
Feeding: surface gleans and occasionally grazes submerged and emergent vegetation, grain and pasture grasses; especially young birds eat small fish, fish eggs and invertebrates.
Voice: loud, resonant, buglelike *koh-hoh*, usually by male in flight; gentle, nasal honking; immature's high-pitched calls deepen over first winter.
Similar Species: *Tundra Swan* (p. 44): smaller; more commonly in large flocks; rounder head; often shows yellow at base of bill; softer, more nasal calls. *Snow Goose* (p. 39): smaller; stubbier, pink bill; shorter neck; pink legs; black in wing tips.
Best Sites: Fir I.; Skagit Co. lowland farm areas; Samish Flats; Snohomish R. valley; Chehalis R. valley.

TUNDRA SWAN

Cygnus columbianus

W ell adapted to a life in shallow wetlands, the Tundra Swan has a long neck and powerful bill. This bird can graze and glean on land like a goose, skim the water's surface or tip up like a dabbling duck. With its exceptional underwater reach and strong bill, it can grasp and root out bottom-growing tubers and shoots—foods unavailable to geese and ducks. Such specialization allows large flocks of different waterfowl to gather together in huge numbers without overly depleting the same food resources. • Tundra Swans depend both on federally managed wetland refuges and private lowland farm fields. • Swans have long been celebrated in poetry and dance for their grace, and the first sight of swans flying in formation overhead is something that few people forget.

ID: white overall; rounded head; heavy, black, slightly concave bill; black facial skin to just in front of eye, often with yellow "teardrop"; long neck, usually carried straight up from body; big, black feet. *In flight:* holds neck horizontally; flies in family groups.

Size: L 4–4¾ ft; W 5½–6¾ ft.

Status: common winter resident in western Washington, including Skagit Valley, Samish Valley, Chehalis R. and southwestern lowlands; in spring migration, large flocks appear overhead near wetlands in western and eastern Washington.

Habitat: permanent or seasonal wetlands in undisturbed open country; large, shallow lakes, riparian marshes and shallow estuarine tidal areas with nearby grassland or cropland; prefers clear line of sight in all directions.

Nesting: does not nest in Washington.

Feeding: tips up, dabbles and surface-gleans for aquatic vegetation, mollusks and invertebrates; grazes for tubers, roots, grasses and waste grain.

Voice: muffled, hollow honking or hooting *whoo-hoo-wu-whoo* call in flight and by nervous flocks on land or water; large flocks make gooselike barking sounds.

Similar Species: *Trumpeter Swan* (p. 43): larger; heavier bill; no yellow "teardrop"; loud, buglelike calls; immature retains grayer plumage into fall; longer neck in flight. *Snow Goose* (p. 39): smaller; stubbier, pink bill; shorter neck; pink legs; black in wing tips; faster wingbeats.

Best Sites: Samish Flats; Skagit Flats; Ridgefield NWR; McNary NWR; Turnbull NWR; Calispell L.

WOOD DUCK

Aix sponsa

The image of the gaudy male Wood Duck has adorned innumerable calendars, postcards and bird-book jackets. The drake's plumage throughout much of the year suggests that he bathed in the palette left over after all the other North American birds had been painted. • Much less dramatic than the male, the female is nonetheless lovely in her own right. Clothed in a delicate mouse gray, she has large, liquid eyes that are given added expression by elongated white patches. • In the wild, Wood Ducks usually flush and fly off almost immediately after coming into view, but at park ponds they often accommodate close-range admiration. • Wood Ducks sometimes forage for seeds and plant parts well away from water, and they perch in trees and low overhanging riparian tangles more often than any other duck.

ID: *Male:* glossy, green-and-purple head with slicked-back crest has several white streaks; red eyes; orange bill with black and white markings; dark back and hindquarters; golden brown sides bordered by white and black; white-spotted, purplish chestnut breast; white "chin" and throat. *Female:* brownish gray head and upperparts; large, teardrop-shaped white eye patch; gray bill with black and white markings; mottled, brown breast streaked with white; white belly.

Size: *L* 17–21 in; *W* 28–31 in.

Status: fairly common summer resident; numbers decrease in winter.

Habitat: freshwater ponds, marshes, lakes and rivers, usually bordered by dense stands of trees.

Nesting: in a natural hollow, tree cavity or nest box, up to 30 ft above the ground and usually near water; nest is lined with down; female incubates 9–14 creamy white to tan eggs for 27–30 days.

Feeding: gleans the water's surface and tips up for aquatic vegetation; feeds in woodlands; eats fruits, nuts and waste grains.

Voice: *Male:* ascending *ter-wee-wee*. *Female:* squeaky *woo-e-e-k*.

Similar Species: *Hooded Merganser* (p. 68): slim, dark bill; white speculum with dark bar; pointed tail; male has black, crested head with white patch and black-and-white breast; female is brown overall, with shaggy crest, and has yellow lower mandible.

Best Sites: Deception Pass SP; Skagit Game Range; Lake Sammamish SP; Nisqually NWR; Washougal sewage lagoons; Yakima Sportsman SP; Columbia NWR.

GADWALL
Anas strepera

Being called an "odd duck" implies an unusual appearance and habits. The image of a plain brown duck doesn't leap to mind, yet the often-overlooked Gadwall displays nuances of habitat selection, temperament and behavior distinct from those of neighboring dabblers. • Gadwalls favor undisturbed ponds and sloughs with muddy bottoms, abundant aquatic plants and adjacent cover of marsh vegetation or overhanging willows or other trees. In such seclusion, they glean from the surface, dabble in shallows and repeatedly dive for submerged food-stuffs. Methodical feeders, they move slowly around a feeding site. • A combination of blackish bill, black-and-white speculum and black hindquarters confirms the male. A female is generally close at hand, because Gadwalls start forming pair bonds for the next breeding season as early as July, remaining together in the interim.

ID: rounded head; small, white speculum patch with black border; steeply angled forehead; yellowish orange legs. *Breeding male:* dark bill; mostly subtly barred and streaked gray; black hindquarters. *Female and eclipse male:* orangy yellow bill with dark ridge; mostly mottled brown; less white in speculum.
Size: *L* 18–22 in; *W* 29–33 in.
Status: common year-round resident in lowland wetlands and freshwater bodies, especially from Skagit Co. south to Olympia and along the Columbia Basin; common migrant.
Habitat: *Breeding:* marshes; moves with ducklings to open water with emergent vegetation. *In migration* and *winter:* ponds, lakes and coastal and brackish waters.

Nesting: often on an island; can be far from water; grassy, down-lined hollow is well concealed in tall emergent vegetation; female incubates 7–12 dull creamy white to grayish green eggs for 24–27 days.
Feeding: dabbles, tips up and dives for aquatic and estuarine plants and invertebrates; also eats waste grain, tadpoles and small fish; often steals food from American Coots.
Voice: often whistles harshly. *Male:* simple, single quack. *Female:* high *kaak kaaak kak-kak-kak* series with changing volume.
Similar Species: *Mallard* (p. 49): female has darker eye line, blue or purplish speculum with white borders and white sides to tail.
Best Sites: Union Bay Natural Area (Montlake Fill, Seattle); Everett sewage treatment ponds; Sikes L. (Carnation); Winchester Wildlife Area (west of Moses L.); Conners L. (Sinlahekin Valley).

EURASIAN WIGEON

Anas penelope

More Eurasian Wigeons overwinter in Washington than anywhere else in the other lower 48 states. Following an avian rule that echoes the saying, "when in Rome, do as the Romans do," Eurasian Wigeons consort almost exclusively with American Wigeons—any large migratory or winter flock of American Wigeons at one of our principal Pacific Flyway sites typically contains one to several Eurasians. • As with most ducks, wigeon males in their breeding plumage (mid-fall until late spring) are easily distinguished, and the females are often over-looked. Eurasian females are patterned much like their female American cousins, but with warmer buff flanks, less contrast between the neck and breast and, usually, more reddish heads. Scanning throngs of American Wigeons for Eurasian Wigeons offers observers of all abilities valuable practice in picking out the odd bird from among the host of the mundane—one of the keys to discovering rarities.

ID: black-tipped, pale bluish gray bill; white belly; dark legs and feet. *Male:* rich orangy brown head; creamy yellow forehead stripe; black-and-white hindquarters; lightly barred, gray sides and back; chestnut breast. *Female:* mottled brown head and breast, usually with rufous tints; rufous tan sides. *In flight:* green-and-black speculum; all-gray underwings.

Size: *L* 17–21 in; *W* 30–33 in.

Status: uncommon to locally common winter resident west of the Cascades; rare winter resident east of the Cascades—may be found in the Tri-Cities area.

Habitat: shallow lakes with abundant submergent vegetation; open expanses of sprouting grass close to water; intertidal eelgrass beds; sometimes in city parks.

Nesting: does not nest in Washington.

Feeding: dabbles or tips up for stems, leaves and seeds of submergent vegetation; grazes lawns and pastures; occasionally dives, especially in eelgrass beds.

Voice: *Male:* high-pitched, 2-tone *thweeeeeeer* whistle. *Female:* rougher quack than an American Wigeon's.

Similar Species: *American Wigeon* (p. 48): white "wing pits"; breeding male has clear white forehead and crown, broad, iridescent, green facial patch and rusty back and sides; female has grayish head and neck contrasting with browner breast.

Best Sites: Samish R. estuary and Samish Flats; Three Crabs Restaurant (Dungeness Bay) and Dungeness R. estuary; Ship Harbor Slough (Anacortes); Nisqually NWR; Para Ponds (Othello); Wenatchee Confluence SP.

AMERICAN WIGEON

Anas americana

Expanses of short, lush grass in open country attract flocks of American Wigeons from fall until spring. These ducks like to graze on young shoots while walking steadily along in dense, formless flocks, each individual no more than a few feet from its nearest neighbor. City parks and golf courses provide much the same opportunity for grazing. American Wigeons also occur in the managed wetlands and croplands of wildlife refuges and sanctuaries, massing by day in reed-fringed impoundments and flying off at dusk to glean waste grains and sprouting grasses from outlying agricultural lands. • Amid the wetland orchestra of buzzes, quacks and ticks, the male American Wigeon's piping, three-syllable whistle may be the most prominent sound heard.

ID: pale bluish gray bill with black tip; cinnamon breast and flanks; white belly. *Breeding male:* whitish crown and forehead; broad, iridescent, green patch behind eye; conspicuous white shoulder patch; cinnamon breast and sides. *Female:* grayish head; brown breast and sides. *Eclipse male:* like female, but with more white on upperwing and warmer brown on underparts. *In flight:* large white wing patch; green-and-black speculum; white "wing pits."
Size: *L* 18–23 in; *W* 30–33 in.
Status: common winter resident and migrant statewide; uncommon eastern breeder; rare local western breeder.
Habitat: *Breeding:* small water bodies. *In migration* and *winter:* shallow lakes and slow-moving rivers with submergent vegetation; open expanses of short grass,

protected fresh water, brackish marshes and intertidal eelgrass beds.
Nesting: always on dry ground, often far from water; well-concealed nest of grass and leaves is lined with down; female incubates 7–11 creamy white eggs for 23–25 days.
Feeding: dabbles and tips up for submergent vegetation, insects, small mollusks and crustaceans; grazes short grasses.
Voice: *Male:* frequent, repeated nasal, whistled *whee wick weew. Female:* soft, seldom-heard quack, mostly uttered when with the young.
Similar Species: *Eurasian Wigeon* (p. 47): breeding male has rich orangy brown head, creamy yellow forehead and crown, and gray back and sides; female has little contrast between rufous or grayish neck and breast.
Best Sites: Samish Flats; Three Crabs Restaurant (Dungeness Bay); Ship Harbor Slough (Anacortes); Nisqually NWR; Para Ponds (Othello); Wenatchee Confluence SP; Walla Walla R. delta.

MALLARD
Anas platyrhynchos

The Mallard is among the most abundant, distinctive and familiar of all waterfowl. In many parts of Europe, its common name translates as "wild duck," and it was likely the ancestor of many wild and domesticated species. • Mallards do well anywhere from tiny ponds to extensive wetlands. Often the last ducks to be pushed out of deteriorating habitat, they are the first to recolonize if conditions improve. • Mallard drakes will mate with females of closely related species, including domestic ducks, especially Muscovy Ducks (*Cairina moschata*). The offspring are the ducks usually accepting handouts at park ponds. • The male molts after breeding. The resulting, much plainer "eclipse" plumage provides camouflage during the flightless period. Molting into new breeding plumage usually occurs by early August.

ID: white outer tail feathers; orange feet. *Breeding male:* green head; bright yellow bill; pale gray underparts; unmarked, chestnut breast; white neck ring; iridescent, upcurled, black central tail feathers. *Female:* dark-mottled, dull orange bill; long, thin, dark eye line; finely patterned brown overall. *Eclipse male:* like female, but with dull yellow bill and richer brown breast. *In flight:* white-bordered, dark blue speculum (purple or green on hybrids).
Size: *L* 20–28 in; *W* 31–35 in.
Status: common year-round resident.
Habitat: freshwater and brackish habitats of nearly every description; favors grainfields, stubble, flooded fields and sprouting pastures but will visit city parks and even garden ponds; molting, flightless adult moves to tall emergent vegetation near open water.

Nesting: in tall vegetation or under a bush, usually near water; nest of grass and other material is lined with down; female incubates 7–10 white to olive buff eggs for 26–30 days.
Feeding: tips up, gleans and dabbles in shallows for seeds of aquatic plants; takes some mollusks and other invertebrates, larval amphibians, fish eggs and crop wastes; city ducks readily take handouts at ponds and beneath feeders.
Voice: very vocal. *Male:* quacks deeply but quietly. *Female:* quacks loudly.
Similar Species: *Northern Shoveler* (p. 52): long, wide-tipped bill; green speculum with narrow white borders; breeding male has white breast with chestnut flanks and dark back; female is paler, with fainter eye line.
Best Sites: statewide, anywhere near water.

BLUE-WINGED TEAL

Anas discors

Less common along the Pacific Coast than most other dabbling ducks and not very tolerant of cold, Blue-winged Teals arrive late at their breeding sites and leave before the cold weather sets in. They generally prefer eastern Washington over the western part of the state. Individuals, pairs and small groups frequent marshes, reed-bordered ponds, mudflats and seasonal wetlands in both spring and fall. Although a few birds linger late, they are essentially gone by mid-January. • The male defends his nesting territory and may remain with the female and brood through the early part of summer, thereby increasing nesting success. • It is difficult to consistently distinguish females and males in eclipse plumage from each other and from other teals.

ID: brown eyes; broad-based, bluish black bill; yellow legs and feet. *Breeding male:* gray head; blackish forehead and crown; white crescent in front of eye; dark brown upper-parts; black-spotted, brown breast; bluish sides. *Female:* dark eye line; whitish "chin" spot; buff-mottled, brownish gray overall. *Nonbreeding male:* like female, but with gray "chin" and faint white crescent in front of eye. *In flight:* conspicuous sky blue forewing patch; green speculum; agile flight.
Size: *L* 14–16 in; *W* 21–23 in.
Status: common breeding resident in the east and common migrant from mid-April to early May and from July to October; uncommon migrant in western Washington from mid-April to late May and from July through mid-October; fairly common breeder in the Puget Trough.

Habitat: freshwater wetlands, lakes, ponds and marshes; migrants may visit estuarine-edge habitats, such as mudflats, secluded tidal channels and salt marsh pools; rarely on coastal bays.
Nesting: in grass along a shoreline or in a wet meadow, usually near water; grass nest includes considerable amounts of down; female incubates 8–11 creamy eggs for 23–24 days.
Feeding: gleans the water's surface for sedge and grass seeds, pondweed, duck-weed and aquatic invertebrates.
Voice: *Male:* soft *keck-keck-keck* and whistles. *Female:* quacks softly.
Similar Species: *Cinnamon Teal* (p. 51): female has more uniformly colored face and broader end on longer bill.
Best Sites: Union Bay Natural Area (Montlake Fill, Seattle); Nisqually NWR seasonally; Paterson Unit, Umatilla NWR; Winchester Wildlife Area (west of Moses L.); Para Ponds (Othello); Conners L. (Sinlahekin Valley); Turnbull NWR.

CINNAMON TEAL

Anas cyanoptera

Every spring, Cinnamon Teals push northward from their wintering grounds to dot the reed-fringed ponds and marshes of Washington. • Eagerly awaited by most birders as a sign of spring, the intensely reddish brown breeding plumage of the male Cinnamon Teal, accented by his ruby red eyes, is worth an admiring gaze at any time of day. During the low, slanting light of early morning or near sunset, he can be a real showstopper. Despite his spectacular appearance, this duck is relatively shy and is often overlooked as he glides from one patch of marsh vegetation to another. • Females often have the company of their mates throughout the nesting cycle, which contributes greatly to their nesting success.

ID: broad-ended bill. *Breeding male:* intensely cinnamon red underparts, neck and head; red eyes. *Female:* plain face; brown eyes; mottled warm brown overall. *Nonbreeding male:* similar to female, but with red eyes and rufous tint. *In flight:* conspicuous, sky blue forewing patch.
Size: *L* 15–17 in; *W* 20–22 in.
Status: statewide breeder, most common in south-central and southeastern Washington; common migrant from early April to early May and from July through September; rare in winter in western Washington.
Habitat: freshwater ponds, marshes, sloughs, ditches and flooded swales with aquatic vegetation; prefers sites close to marshes.
Nesting: nest is hidden in sedges, grass or rushes, possibly in bulrushes or cattails;

female incubates 7–16 off-white to pale buff eggs for 21–25 days.
Feeding: gleans the water's surface for sedge seeds, pondweed, duckweed and aquatic invertebrates; often feeds with head partially submerged and bill held just below the surface.
Voice: usually silent. *Male:* whispered *peep;* rough *karr-karr-karr. Female:* soft, rattling *rrrrr;* somewhat weak *gack-gack-ga-ga.*
Similar Species: *Blue-winged Teal* (p. 50): narrower tip on shorter bill; nonbreeding male has white crescent in front of dark eye and more contrasting grayish brown plumage; female has sharper facial pattern and lighter blue on forewing. *Ruddy Duck* (p. 71): breeding male has white "cheek," large, blue bill and rufous-and-gray upperwing.
Best Sites: Union Bay Natural Area (Montlake Fill, Seattle); Nisqually NWR; Paterson Unit, Umatilla NWR; W.E. Johnson Park (Richland); Para Ponds (Othello); Conners L. (Sinlahekin Valley); Turnbull NWR.

NORTHERN SHOVELER

Anas clypeata

You can't fail to be impressed by the Northern Shoveler's remarkable bill. Its broad, spatulate shape and the hairlike ridges that line it allow this duck to sift small water plants and invertebrates from the surface of still waters, where it is by far the most common duck. Shovelers eat much smaller organisms than do most waterfowl, and their digestive systems are elongated to prolong the digestion of hard-bodied invertebrates. • When nesting duties are over, drake shovelers move to molting areas and, like other male dabbling ducks, acquire an eclipse plumage that resembles that of the female. This subtly attractive stage, with partially developed chestnut belly and bottle green head, lasts until late winter.

ID: large, wide-ended bill; white outer tail feathers; yellowish legs and feet.
Breeding male: green head; black bill; chestnut sides; white breast. *Female:* mottled brown overall; orange-tinged bill. *In flight:* green speculum with 1 white bar.
Size: *L* 18–20 in; *W* 27–30 in.
Status: common summer resident in the Columbia Basin, Turnbull NWR and Puget Trough; common winter resident in western Washington; uncommon in winter in the east except in protected lowland areas of the Columbia Basin.
Habitat: *Breeding:* margins of open, shallow wetlands with submergent vegetation, including ponds, marshes and sloughs. *In migration* and *winter:* sites rich in aquatic plants and invertebrates, such as sewage

and farm ponds, lagoons and mudflats with algal growth; regularly visits upper reaches of estuaries.
Nesting: usually on dry land within 150 ft of water, in a shallow scrape; female builds a nest of dry grass and down and incubates 10–12 pale blue eggs for 25 days.
Feeding: dabbles in water and gleans on land and in mud; strains most plants and animal matter, especially aquatic crustaceans and insect larvae, through the bill; sometimes gleans seeds and other plant material in croplands and stubble fields.
Voice: occasionally gives a raspy chuckle or quack, most often during spring courtship.
Similar Species: *Mallard* (p. 49): smaller bill; blue speculum with 2 white bars; breeding male has yellow bill, chestnut breast, white flanks and upcurled, black tail; female has stronger eye line and richer brown on underparts.
Best Sites: common statewide in shallow lowland waters.

NORTHERN PINTAIL
Anas acuta

Several million waterfowl, many from just a handful of migratory species, visit the marshes, lakes and grainfields of the Pacific Flyway each year. Among them are Northern Pintails, which are common winter residents, especially in western Washington lowlands. They largely depart the western part of the state in late spring and return in late summer. • Northern Pintails are particularly attracted to winter grainfields. Lands managed to provide staging and feeding habitat have relieved the pressure on croplands and proven to be of critical importance to Northern Pintails and many other ducks. • An elegant profile with a long, slender neck, a relatively slim body and an extended tail make Northern Pintails recognizable in flight.

ID: grayish blue bill; long neck; dark wings; long, pointed tail. *Breeding male:* brown head; dark nape; white neck and breast; very long, tapering central tail feathers. *Female:* mottled brown overall; slightly pointed tail. *Nonbreeding male:* similar to female, but with grayer body and whiter foreneck. *In flight:* speculum is dark green and brown (breeding male) or brown with white border; white line divides dark brown wing linings and gray flight feathers.
Size: *L* 21–25 in; *W* 30–34 in.
Status: common migrant statewide; common winter resident in western Washington; variably common to uncommon winter resident in eastern Washington; uncommon breeder in the Columbia Basin; rare breeder in western Washington.

Habitat: *Breeding:* open wetlands, especially with islands. *In migration:* shallow wetlands, large lakes and reservoirs close to foraging fields and estuarine habitats. *Winter:* wide variety of shallow freshwater and intertidal habitats.
Nesting: on the ground near water, in brushy cover; female lines a small scrape with grass and down, incubates 6–8 pale greenish or buff eggs for 22–24 days and tends young for up to 42 days.
Feeding: tips up and dabbles for seeds; also eats aquatic invertebrates, especially crustaceans and snails, and larval salamanders; grazes on waste grain during migration.
Voice: *Male:* soft whistles. *Female:* rough quack.
Similar Species: *Gadwall* (p. 46): chunkier female has grayer head, orange-and-dusky bill and shorter tail.
Best Sites: *Spring:* Conboy Lake NWR; Winchester Wildlife Area (west of Moses L.); Walla Walla R. delta. *Winter:* Carnation Farm; Oak Bay CP; Annas Bay (Hood Canal).

GREEN-WINGED TEAL

Anas crecca

The name "teal" is applied to 16 of the world's smallest waterfowl species, of which the Green-winged Teal is the best known. This widespread dabbling duck exemplifies the diminutive build, speedy flight and minimal habitat requirements of teals. It favors the frontier between the cover of marsh vegetation and open country, so it is quite likely to flush up from waterlogged ditches, over-grown irrigation canals, park ponds and any marshes offering some semi-open water with a muddy border. • Green-wings happily forage on mudflats and at salt marsh edges, sifting through semifluid mud like overgrown sandpipers. On the wing, their small size, dark plumage and habit of making tight turns in wheeling flocks further suggest shorebirds in flight.

ID: *Breeding male:* chestnut head; glossy, green swipe extends back from eye; black bill; barred, grayish back; gray sides; white belly; black-spotted, creamy or buff breast; white vertical shoulder slash. *Female:* dark eye line; dusky and yellowish bill; mottled brown overall; pale belly. *Nonbreeding male:* darker head and grayer upperparts than female. *In flight:* green to blackish speculum bordered with white or pale buff; compact, agile flocks.

Size: *L* 12–16 in; *W* 20–23 in.

Status: common migrant and winter resident; locally common summer resident in eastern Washington; locally rare in summer in the west.

Habitat: *Breeding:* marshes. *In migration:* well-vegetated, shallow, muddy inland wetlands and coastal marshes and estuaries.

Winter: wetlands, flooded farmlands, slough and backwater edges, coastal marshes and estuaries.

Nesting: on the ground; well concealed beneath a tussock or bush in tall vegetation; shallow bowl of grass and leaves is lined with down; female incubates 6–11 creamy white eggs for 20–23 days and tends young until fledging at 25–30 days.

Feeding: dabbles in shallow water; walks about probing wet mud for sedge seeds, pondweed, aquatic invertebrates and larval amphibians; forages in grainfields in winter.

Voice: *Male:* whistles crisply; distinctive gurgling and wheezing notes in a unique courtship display. *Female:* quacks softly.

Similar Species: *Blue-winged Teal* (p. 50) and *Cinnamon Teal* (p. 51): females are lighter colored, with larger bills and blue forewing patches.

Best Sites: Juanita Bay Park (Kirkland); Spencer I.; Sarge Hubbard Park (Yakima); Winchester Wildlife Area (west of Moses L.); Turnbull NWR. *Spring:* Nisqually NWR.

CANVASBACK

Aythya valisineria

The Canvasback resembles other *Aythya* ducks—a sizeable genus of diving ducks of deep marshes, larger freshwater bodies and estuaries—in being "dark at both ends and pale in the middle." With legs set far back on their bodies, these ducks are clumsy on their rare land excursions but are elegant, powerful divers and underwater swimmers. Most members of the genus, including the Canvasback, require a brief running start in order to become airborne, and they fly with rapid, flickering wingbeats. A Canvasback of either gender can be distinguished from far away by its uniquely sloping head profile, in which the long bill meets the forecrown with no apparent break in angle. • Although some Canvasbacks nest in eastern Washington marshes, most birds breed farther inland, in other western and central northern states and in Canada.

ID: hefty body; evenly sloped fore-crown; long bill. *Male:* deep chestnut red head; red eyes; whitish back and underparts; black hindquarters and breast. *Female:* pale grayish body; warm brown head, neck and breast; dark eyes.

Size: *L* 19–22 in; *W* 27–29 in.

Status: fairly common locally in the west from mid-October to mid-March; in eastern Washington, locally common from September to late April and uncommon summer breeding resident.

Habitat: *Breeding:* large ponds, lakes and reservoirs in lowland eastern Washington. *In migration* and *winter:* large lakes, reservoirs, lagoons and estuaries.

Nesting: concealed in a marsh; platform built on emergent vegetation over water has a deep inner cup lined with down; female incubates 7–9 olive gray eggs for 24–29 days and tends young until shortly before fledging at 60–70 days.

Feeding: dives to or near the bottom in water up to 30 ft deep for the roots, tubers, basal stems and seeds of aquatic and estuarine plants; prefers wild celery and eelgrass; takes some invertebrates.

Voice: generally quiet. *Male:* occasionally coos, squeaks and growls during courtship. *Female:* purring quack; growls.

Similar Species: *Redhead* (p. 56): male has more squared-off forehead profile, yellow eyes, shorter, bluish bill with black tip and darker gray back and sides.

Best Sites: *Winter:* Dugualla Bay (Whidbey I.); Everett sewage treatment ponds; Rock Creek Cove (Stevenson); Port of Wallula; Port of Clarkston. *Summer:* Molson Lakes (Okanogan Co.).

REDHEAD

Aythya americana

During the breeding season, Redhead pairs scatter across central and western North America's marshes, lake edges and wetlands. They choose clean water with plenty of skirting emergent vegetation, lush bottom growth and enough depth to accommodate foraging dives. In eastern Washington, they are common on lowland water bodies, particularly in the Potholes area and Columbia National Wildlife Refuge. Like Canvasbacks, Redheads often reappear in about the same numbers year after year to overwinter on large, shallow reservoirs and in the upper reaches of estuaries; they visit smaller lakes, reservoirs and estuaries in only token numbers. • As if eager to get her young fending for themselves, the female will lead them away from the nest within a day or so of hatching.

ID: stocky body; black-tipped, bluish gray bill. *Male:* reddish chestnut head, brightest in breeding plumage; yellow eyes; black breast; finely barred, gray back and sides. *Female:* dusky brown overall with some gray; pale facial areas; dark eyes. *In flight:* dark gray forewing and lighter hindwing.

Size: *L* 18–22 in; *W* 26–29 in.

Status: common eastern summer resident and fairly common in winter; rare in migration and winter in western Washington.

Habitat: freshwater marshes; lakes and reservoirs with bottom plants. *Winter:* estuarine shallows, tidal channels and eelgrass beds.

Nesting: well concealed at the base of emergent vegetation, suspended over water; deep basket of reeds and grass is lined with fine, white down; female incubates 9–13 creamy white eggs for 24–28 days and tends young for 21–35 days; female sometimes lays eggs in other birds' nests.

Feeding: dives for aquatic vegetation, especially pondweed and duckweed; occasionally eats aquatic invertebrates.

Voice: generally quiet. *Male:* nasal courting notes. *Female:* soft, low grunts, harsher quacks and an occasional rolling growl.

Similar Species: *Canvasback* (p. 55): elongated profile; more uniform upperwing color and whiter underparts on female; male has darker head, red eyes and whiter back. *Greater Scaup* (p. 58) and *Lesser Scaup* (p. 59): females are darker, with broader, paler bills, yellow eyes and broad, white hindwing stripes in flight.

Best Sites: *Summer:* Dodson Rd. and Potholes area (Grant Co.); Sprague–Fishtrap L.; Conners L. (Sinlahekin Valley); Turnbull NWR; Columbia NWR. *Winter:* Everett sewage treatment ponds; Paterson Unit, Umatilla NWR.

RING-NECKED DUCK
Aythya collaris

Visits to secluded ponds during the coldest months will soon reveal Ring-necked Ducks. These scauplike waterfowl typically assemble in small flocks on wooded reservoirs, along shallow, vegetated coves of lakes and in the still water of shaded river eddies. At times, however, they venture into the open in flooded fields, at sewage ponds and on exposed impoundments at waterfowl refuges, and they might be found nesting in northeastern Washington's high-elevation wooded wetlands. • The dark brown neck ring of the male, for which the species was named, is rarely visible—a more fitting name would be "Ring-billed Duck." • When alarmed, these ducks stretch their necks and raise their fluffy crowns.

ID: elevated hindcrown; black and white bands on bluish gray bill; white belly. *Breeding male:* purple-glossed head; yellow eyes; black breast and back; light gray sides. *Female:* light brown head with variable pale patches; brown eyes; white eye ring; dark back; lighter brown breast and flanks. *Nonbreeding male:* smudgy brown flanks and shoulder slash.
Size: *L* 14–18 in; *W* 23–25 in.
Status: uncommon to common summer resident in northeastern Washington; rare local breeder in the west; common winter resident and migrant statewide.
Habitat: *Breeding:* shallow, permanent freshwater wetlands, typically at higher elevations. *In migration:* small water bodies; prefers wooded or vegetated slow-moving fresh water.
Nesting: in a depression, over water on a vegetated hummock or raised shoreline with a platform of bent-over vegetation; female adds vegetation and down as eggs are laid; female incubates 8–10 olive tan eggs for 25–29 days; young can dive after 5 days, and female feeds them for several weeks.
Feeding: dives underwater for vegetation, including seeds, tubers and pondweed leaves; also eats aquatic invertebrates.
Voice: seldom heard. *Male:* hisses. *Female:* growling *churr*.
Similar Species: *Greater Scaup* (p. 58) and *Lesser Scaup* (p. 59): males have almost entirely bluish gray bills and lighter backs, with whiter flanks in breeding plumage; females have darker brown heads and necks and yellow eyes; prominent white hindwing stripe in flight.
Best Sites: *Summer:* Clear Lake Day Use Area (US 12); Teal L. (Okanogan Co.); Little Pend Oreille NWR; Sportsman Pond (Cusick). *Winter:* Everett sewage treatment ponds; Yakima Area Greenway.

GREATER SCAUP

Aythya marila

Distinguishing Greater Scaups from Lesser Scaups offers a chronic challenge. In Washington, Greater Scaups favor larger, deeper and more exposed salt-water habitats—including estuaries, coastal bays, lagoons and reservoirs in the coastal lowlands—than their cousins, and they do not nest in the state, although a few may stay over summer. In contrast, Lessers have a more widespread interior distribution, prefer fresh water and do breed here. Greaters often disperse among large, mixed-species flocks and are more inclined to mix with dabbling ducks. The observer must also rely on subtle field marks to distinguish the species, because there is significant habitat crossover. • Greater Scaups appear to be more leisurely feeders than other *Aythya* ducks and often look to be resting.

ID: heavyset; large, rounded head that usually peaks over eye; black-tipped, pale bluish bill; yellow eyes. *Breeding male:* dark head, often with green iridescence under bright light; pale gray back; dark hindquarters; white sides; dark breast. *Female:* dark to rufous brown overall; bold white area encircles base of bill. *Nonbreeding male:* brown-smudged flanks and back. *In flight:* prominent white wing stripe extends onto outer flight feathers.

Size: *L* 16–20 in; *W* 26–29 in.

Status: common migrant and winter resident in western Washington, particularly on marine waters; common migrant in eastern Washington and winter resident on the Columbia R. and Snake R. and their reservoirs.

Habitat: protected waters of estuaries, harbors, lagoons, large lakes, reservoirs and tidal rivers; often seen migrating along the outer coast and occasionally in rafts with scoters beyond the surf line.

Nesting: does not nest in Washington.

Feeding: dives for mollusks, especially mussels, other aquatic and marine inverte-brates and some vegetation.

Voice: generally quiet in migration; deep *scaup* alarm call. *Male:* possible 3-note whistle or soft *wah-hooo. Female:* some-times growls subtly.

Similar Species: *Lesser Scaup* (p. 59): slightly smaller; head peaks behind eye; smaller bill; shorter white wing stripe; male often has purplish gloss to head and shows less contrast between back and sides; female rarely shows extensive white area behind bill and on face; prefers inland habitats.

Best Sites: Everett sewage treatment ponds; Camano I.–English Boom; Drayton Harbor; Columbia R. at Vantage; Steamboat Rock SP; Port of Wallula.

LESSER SCAUP
Aythya affinis

Widespread and abundant, Lesser Scaups are more familiar to most beginner birders than the very similar Greater Scaups. Lessers tend to occur on freshwater lakes, in open marshes and along slow-flowing rivers much more commonly than Greaters, but Lessers are also common in freshwater coastal habitats, and both species mingle in unpredictable ratios. • Head iridescence on the male Lesser is not completely dependable as a field mark. In certain light, he often flashes a green gloss instead of the usual purple. • Immediately prior to submerging in a feeding dive, a Lesser can compress its plumage to squeeze out air, lowering its fluffy crown so that its head angle looks remarkably like a Greater's. Regardless, although occasionally confusing, head shape remains the most reliable identification feature.

ID: angled head with peak behind eye; yellow eyes; black-tipped, pale grayish blue bill. *Breeding male:* head often has purple gloss; black breast and hindquarters; grayish, barred back; gray-tipped, white side feathers. *Female:* dark brown (sometimes rufous) overall, with lighter sides; variable white area encircles base of bill. *Nonbreeding male:* brown-smudged flanks and back. *In flight:* white wing stripe confined to inner flight feathers.
Size: *L* 15–18 in; *W* 23–25 in.
Status: common migrant and winter resident on fresh and salt water; locally uncommon eastern resident and breeder; very rare breeder in western lowland ponds.
Habitat: *Breeding:* large, shallow freshwater lakes and seasonal or semipermanent wetlands with emergent vegetation.

In migration and *winter:* shallow, fresh and estuarine waters; prefers large wetlands and lakes.
Nesting: in tall, concealing vegetation; close to water, occasionally on an island; nest hollow of grass is lined with down; female incubates 8–10 olive buff eggs for 22–25 days.
Feeding: dives for invertebrates, especially crustaceans, but also for submergent vegetation, mainly sedges.
Voice: deep *scaup* alarm call. *Male:* courts with soft *whee-oooh. Female:* rough, purring *kwah.*
Similar Species: *Greater Scaup* (p. 58): more rounded head with less obvious, more forward peak; larger bill with more black at tip; longer wing stripe; usually prefers marine habitats.
Best Sites: Everett sewage treatment ponds; Juanita Bay Park (Kirkland); Conners L. (Sinlahekin Valley); Paterson Unit, Umatilla NWR; Snake R. at Windust Park; Swanson Lakes Wildlife Area (Lincoln Co.).

HARLEQUIN DUCK

Histrionicus histrionicus

Ocean waters surging around rocky headlands or among sea stacks and clusters of intertidal boulders attract Harlequin Ducks. These small ducks are at home in the turbulent roar-and-tumble of the roughest whitewater, diving among the crashing waves with bravado. The uniformly brown females are difficult to see among the foam and dark rocks, and even the colorful males can be surprisingly well camouflaged. • Modest numbers of Harlequins appear along the shore in fall and remain through winter. Most birds seen in the state are Washington-hatched birds from nests along the waterways of the Olympics, Cascades and Selkirks. • "Harlequin" refers to a multicolored traditional Italian court character who performed "histrionics" (tricks).

ID: rounded profile; raises and lowers tail while swimming. *Breeding male:* dark grayish blue body; white spots and stripes on head, flanks and neck; narrow chestnut stripe on lower crown; chestnut sides; longish tail. *Female:* dark brown overall; white ear spot; 2 whitish facial markings ahead of eye; pale belly. *Nonbreeding male:* similar to female, but with darker head, chestnut-tinted flanks and white-marked lower back.
Size: *L* 15–18 in; *W* 25–27 in.
Status: common local winter resident on coastal waters, with some remaining during summer; uncommon summer breeder in the Cascades, Olympics and Selkirks.
Habitat: *Breeding:* shallow, fast-flowing, low- to mid-elevation streams and rivers;

stages along banks or near gravel bars of larger rivers. *In migration* and *winter:* rocky inshore coastal waters and surf lines near kelp beds; roosts and preens on rocks.
Nesting: in a tree cavity or stump, under bushes or among rocks near a rushing watercourse; shallow nest is lined with conifer needles, moss, leaf litter, grass and down; female incubates 4–6 creamy to pale buff eggs for 27–29 days.
Feeding: dabbles; gleans from rocks; makes short, shallow dives to the bottom; eats invertebrates and small fish.
Voice: generally silent; courting pair may give high-pitched whistles.
Similar Species: *Surf Scoter* (p. 61): larger; heavier; female has different head pattern, pale eyes and larger, darker bill.
Best Sites: *Winter:* Alki Beach (west Seattle); west side of Whidbey I.; Fort Worden; Salt Creek CP (Clallam Co.). *Summer:* Tieton R. near Rimrock L.; Sullivan L. (northern Pend Oreille Co.).

SURF SCOTER

Melanitta perspicillata

Much of the year, Surf Scoters are at home within the zone of steepening swells and breaking surf along the open ocean coast. Huge rafts of these sturdy, heavily built ducks assemble at frequent intervals off beaches and headlands and around harbor entrances, and their looks and habits are easily learned. • Surf Scoters are very common here in winter, but it is the spectacle of their migration that forges the strongest impressions. Throughout most of spring and fall, immense numbers pass steadily just offshore. Flock after flock may race past a given point over the course of several hours, and a thorough scan of the ocean will reveal that the slowly wavering lines extend to the horizon and often well above it.

ID: *Male:* black overall; white patches on forehead and nape; pale yellow eyes; large bill is black, white, yellow and reddish. *Female:* deep sooty brown overall; 2 large, whitish patches on side of head; pale brown eyes; large, grayish black bill. *In flight:* flies in long lines, usually near water.
Size: *L* 17–21 in; *W* 29–31 in.
Status: common migrant and winter resident along the seashore and in rougher water, with some nonbreeding summer flocks; rare migrant in eastern Washington along the Columbia R.
Habitat: varied oceanic and estuarine situations, mostly within 1 mi of shore; sometimes visits coastal and inland freshwater bodies.
Nesting: does not nest in Washington.

Feeding: feeds singly or in large, well-coordinated flocks; dives up to 30 ft deep for mussels and clams, crustaceans and other marine invertebrates, herring eggs and some plant material; small pebbles and gravel aid digestion.
Voice: generally quiet; infrequent low, harsh croaks. *Male:* occasional whistles or gargles. *Female:* guttural *krraak krraak.*
Similar Species: *White-winged Scoter* (p. 62): white hindwing area; male's head shows white around eye only and slimmer, more ridged, less colorful bill with feathered, bulbous base; female has less pronounced forehead and crown angle. *Black Scoter* (p. 63): more smoothly rounded head; shorter bill; male has fully black head and bright yellow to orangy knob on bill; female has uniformly pale "cheeks."
Best Sites: Alki Pt. (west Seattle); Penn Cove (Whidbey I.); Drayton Harbor; Ocean Shores; Columbia R. reservoirs.

WHITE-WINGED SCOTER
Melanitta fusca

White-winged Scoters are the largest of the three North American scoter species. As mixed flocks take off, White-wings take a moment longer to become airborne, stumbling across the water on their pinkish feet and thrashing across the surface with deep wingbeats. When diving for food, their bulk, combined with a habit of projecting part of the wing's leading edge forward before submerging, causes their splash to rise 3 feet—a telltale identifying characteristic. • White-wings are typically somewhat warier than Surf Scoters, often seeming not to tolerate nearby human activity. When they aren't agitated, White-winged Scoters are elegant and efficient divers and powerful fliers. • During their extended spring and fall migrations, pairs, small lines and bunched strings of White-winged Scoters can be seen from nearly any ocean viewpoint. Although locally abundant in open harbors and over sandy bottoms offshore, White-wings are often outnumbered by Surf Scoters. • As with other scoters, the wings of White-wings whistle in flight.

ID: distinctive head profile; bulbous bill with feathered base; conspicuous white area on hindwing. *Male:* mostly black overall; pale eye within upward-curved, white crescent; orange to yellowish bill tip. *Female:* dark, brownish gray plumage; 2 large, indistinct pale patches on side of head.
Size: *L* 19–24 in; *W* 32–35 in.
Status: common migrant and winter resident in western Washington, with rare, local nonbreeding summer flocks; rare fall migrant in eastern Washington.
Habitat: varied nearshore oceanic and estuarine habitats, often just beyond the surf line; some birds may visit large inland lakes during migration.
Nesting: does not nest in Washington.
Feeding: dives up to 90 ft deep for bivalve mollusks and some crustaceans, taking larger prey than other scoters; swallows small stones to aid digestion.
Voice: courting pair produces coarse quacking; otherwise usually silent.
Similar Species: *Surf Scoter* (p. 61): all-dark wings; male has white forehead and nape and more colorful bill; female has more distinct white facial patches. *Black Scoter* (p. 63): male has completely black head and bright yellow to orangy knob on bill; female has light "cheek" and darkish crown.
Best Sites: John Wayne Marina (Sequim Bay); Ocean Shores; Penn Cove (Whidbey I.); Westport; San Juans.

BLACK SCOTER

Melanitta nigra

Black Scoters are greatly outnumbered by other scoters in Washington. Just an individual or a pair of Blacks will likely be found among scoters rafting in estuaries, and they are the least likely scoters to be found inland. Blacks are more likely to be seen in outer-coastal surge zones, often in loose associations with Harlequin Ducks, other scoters, Pelagic Cormorants, alcids and grebes. • Migrating Black Scoters are rarely seen in any numbers. Thousands of Surf Scoters and hundreds of White-winged Scoters may wing by before a pair of Blacks eventually appears. • Although adult Black males are distinctive, immature or eclipse-plumaged male Surf Scoters are routinely mistaken for them. Female Blacks are unlike the two other species but can easily be overlooked.

ID: distinctive, high-domed head. *Male:* black overall; bold, yellow to orangy knob at base of bill. *Female:* dark blackish brown overall; dark crown; pale, dingy whitish cheek, upper throat and foreneck; grayish black bill. *In flight:* rounded body and wings.
Size: *L* 19 in; *W* 27–28 in.
Status: uncommon migrant in early October along Puget Sound and the outer coast and fairly common migrant and local resident from November to mid-May; casual fall migrant in eastern Washington.
Habitat: outer coast, usually in the surf zone near rocky shores and islands, edges of kelp beds or around jetties; small flocks sometimes occupy the lee of headlands, lower reaches of estuaries or even coastal

freshwater lagoons; prefers rocky headlands and waters with gravelly bottoms.
Nesting: does not nest in Washington.
Feeding: dives for mollusks and other invertebrates, small fish and some plant material; eats herring eggs in spring; swallows gravel to assist digestion.
Voice: heard infrequently in Washington. *Male:* courts with unusual *cour-loo* and a long, drawn-out *whe-oo-hoo* or rattling *tuka-tuka-tuka-tuk*. *Female:* growls.
Similar Species: *White-winged Scoter* (p. 62): larger; longer bill; white on hindwing; female has darker face; male has white area around eye and less orangy yellow on bill; immature male has more angled head, with yellow only at bill tip. *Surf Scoter* (p. 61): larger, heavier bill; male shows white at least on nape; female has 2 whitish areas on side of head.
Best Sites: Ocean Shores; Alki Pt. (west Seattle); Discovery Park (Seattle); Ediz Hook (Port Angeles); Penn Cove (Whidbey I.).

LONG-TAILED DUCK

Clangula hyemalis

These odd-looking ducks, previously known as "Oldsquaws," summer mostly on the arctic tundra and are common winter residents in patches along the Washington coast. While in Washington, Long-tails prefer nearshore ocean shallows above shoals or in the lee of headlands or jetties. One or two, and rarely a small flock, establish winter quarters near harbor entrances, around piers and waterfronts and on lagoons, seemingly at intervals of many miles along the coast. A few turn up inland, often on sewage lagoons and ponds. Numbers vary considerably from year to year, with the great majority being either immatures or females, but nonbreeding males are more likely in summer. • The Long-tailed Duck remains distinctive throughout its complex series of plumages.

breeding

nonbreeding

ID: rounded or oval eyes; white underparts. *Nonbreeding male:* white head; grayish "cheek"; reddish eyes; black bill with broad pink ring; brownish back with white patches; blackish lower breast; white upper breast and lower neck; blackish brown neck patch; long, trailing tail feathers. *Nonbreeding female:* dark brown top of head, lower neck, breast and back; white face; brown eyes; bluish gray bill.
Size: *Male: L* 17–21 in. *Female: L* 16–17 in. *Both: W* 26–28 in.
Status: somewhat common, local winter resident in western Washington from late October to late May, usually in sheltered and northerly waters; rare in eastern Washington on Columbia R. reservoirs.
Habitat: inshore coastal waters, including bays, harbors, lagoons and estuaries; can appear some miles out to sea; rarely seen on inland freshwater lakes and ponds.
Nesting: does not nest in Washington.
Feeding: dives up to 180 ft deep (usually less than 35 ft) to catch mollusks, crustaceans and some small fish.
Voice: heard only occasionally in Washington; quiet in early winter but very vocal from February onward. *Male:* musical, throaty yodels. *Female:* soft grunts and quacks.
Similar Species: *Northern Pintail* (p. 53): male has brown head, much longer neck and bill, and mostly pale gray wings; most common on fresh water.
Best Sites: Ediz Hook (Port Angeles); Fort Flagler; Sequim Bay; west side of Whidbey I.; Birch Bay.

BUFFLEHEAD
Bucephala albeola

The energetic Bufflehead is among the first diving ducks to be positively identified by beginning birders. Simply and boldly patterned, it resembles few other species. The black-and-white male's most characteristic feature is the broad white patch on the rear of his head. The female is somber but appealing, her sooty head ornamented with a white "cheek" spot. • A small goldeneye, the Bufflehead is classified in the same genus, and it employs the same feeding techniques and nesting strategies—all three *Bucephala* species nest in tree cavities or nest boxes. • Although the female attends her brood and defends her feeding territory for 35–40 days, ducklings often switch broods.

ID: dark eyes; bluish gray or blackish bill; white belly; dark pinkish feet with brownish webs. *Breeding male:* black forecrown, lower face, neck and back; dark portion of head flashes iridescent purple and bronze; white wedge on back and sides of head. *Female:* brownish gray head and upperparts with lighter breast and flanks; elongated white patch behind and below eye. *Nonbreeding male:* similar to female, with larger white areas on head and wing.
Size: *L* 13–15 in; *W* 20–21 in.
Status: common western migrant and winter resident; fairly common eastern migrant and winter resident; rare local breeder near high northeastern mountain lakes.
Habitat: uses both fresh and salt water. *Breeding:* small ponds and lakes with wooded margins. *In migration* and *winter:*
prefers larger lakes and estuaries but also uses urban ponds.
Nesting: commonly in an aspen or poplar woodpecker cavity (also uses natural cavities and nest boxes); can be unlined or down-filled; female incubates 6–11 creamy or pale olive buff eggs for 28–33 days; egg dumping is quite common.
Feeding: mostly dives for small fish, crustaceans, insects and mollusks.
Voice: seldom heard in Washington. *Male:* growls and squeaks sharply. *Female:* quacks harshly.
Similar Species: *Hooded Merganser* (p. 68): larger; yellow eyes; slim bill; breeding male has black-bordered, white crest and buff to rufous flanks; female has brownish crest and no white on face. *Harlequin Duck* (p. 60): female has 3 small white areas on head and browner plumage; prefers turbulent water.
Best Sites: often widespread in fall and winter.

COMMON GOLDENEYE

Bucephala clangula

Whistling wings signal the return of Common Goldeneye migrants to Washington in late fall from their breeding grounds beside boreal lakes, bog pools and beaver ponds in Canada and Alaska. Among the last diving ducks to leave the mountain lakes before freeze-up, Common Goldeneyes often remain until only narrow channels or pools remain. • Single birds and small flocks usually winter at some distance from one another, but they are quite happy to join other ducks, loons, grebes, cormorants and gulls. • The boldly patterned plumage and peaked head of the male Common Goldeneye lend themselves to an elaborate series of courtship displays, beginning on the wintering grounds and continuing during the northward migration of late winter.

ID: steeply angled head; yellow eyes; white inner upperwing patches, continuing onto shoulder. *Male:* glossy, dark green head (may appear purplish); round, white "cheek" patch at base of dark bill; black back with 2 white stripes; white underparts; black tail. *Female:* dark brown head; dark bill tipped with dull yellow; grayish brown body; white belly; narrow white "collar."
Size: *L* 16–20 in; *W* 25–26 in.
Status: common winter resident beginning anywhere from early-October to mid-November; rare after mid-May in western Washington; rare breeder in mountain lakes near the Sinlahekin Valley and at Big Meadow L. in Pend Oreille Co.
Habitat: shallow coastal bays, estuaries and harbors, large inland lakes and rivers (in winter, especially those kept open by warm wastewater). *In migration:* temporary wetlands and ponds.
Nesting: in a tree cavity or nest box, often close to water; lined with wood chips and down; female incubates 6–10 bluish green eggs for 28–32 days.
Feeding: dives for aquatic or estuarine food items such as crustaceans, mollusks, amphibians, small fish and plant material; consumes several items during prolonged dives.
Voice: usually silent in migration. *Male:* nasal *peent* and a hoarse *kraaagh* in late-winter courting. *Female:* croaks harshly.
Similar Species: *Barrow's Goldeneye* (p. 67): male has longer, often purple-glossed head (forehead often appears steeper), white crescent behind bill and smaller white marks on back; female has yellower bill.
Best Sites: *In migration* and *winter:* fresh- and saltwater bodies statewide.

BARROW'S GOLDENEYE
Bucephala islandica

Often near the top of a birder's "wish list," the Barrow's Goldeneye is certainly worthy of the honor: both the male and female are neatly attired and have a subtle charm. • Barrow's Goldeneyes are loyal to favored wintering locations, with the same number of birds often returning yearly to old docks and pilings with crustaceans and mollusks. During migration, these birds are regularly seen in Washington's bays and estuaries. • Barrow's Goldeneyes breed primarily in western Canada and Alaska, but some stay on to nest on subalpine lakeshores in the Cascades. Although Barrow's Goldeneyes join Common Goldeneyes in winter and often indulge in aggressive courtship displays in a mixed flock, hybrids are extremely rare.

ID: long, angled head; bright yellow eyes; stubby bill; yellow legs and feet. *Male:* black head, often with dark purple gloss (may appear greenish); distinctive white crescent between eye and black bill; white-spotted, black back; black extension downward from shoulder. *Female:* dark brown head; yellowish orange bill; grayish brown body; white "collar."

Size: *L* 17–20 in; *W* 27–29 in.

Status: common summer resident in lakes of the Cascades, Okanogan Highlands and Selkirk Mts.; common local winter resident in sheltered waters in western Washington; uncommon winter resident in eastern Washington.

Habitat: *Breeding:* clear, still waters and fast-flowing streams and rivers with standing trees or piles of boulders. *In migration*

and *winter:* lakes, reservoirs, estuaries, lagoons and rivers.

Nesting: in an old woodpecker hole in a decaying tree or stump or in a rock pile; female revisits former or previously prospected site; down is added as eggs are laid; female incubates 8–11 whitish or bluish green eggs for 28–30 days; female sometimes dumps eggs in other nests.

Feeding: dives to 15 ft deep for invertebrates and some plant material.

Voice: generally silent. *Male:* cawing spring call. *Female:* croaks hoarsely.

Similar Species: *Common Goldeneye* (p. 66): less elongated head; male has glossy, often green head with round, white face spot and whiter shoulder marking with more lines than spots; female has dark bill with yellowish tip.

Best Sites: *Winter:* Alki Pt. (west Seattle); Penn Cove (Whidbey I.); Ruston Way (Tacoma). *Summer:* Clear L. (off US 12); Conners L. (Sinlahekin Valley).

HOODED MERGANSER

Lophodytes cucullatus

The male Hooded Merganser is always a treat to see. His colorful plumage is spectacularly obvious in the sunlight. However, it blends well with the dappled and irregular rays of sunlight cast upon the water through overarching vegetation, and, given a choice between sunny and shady shorelines or banks, Hooded Mergansers opt for the shady side. • These mergansers shun large open bodies of water, instead favoring secluded, sheltered or overgrown smaller water bodies, but they will use a variety of habitats, from coastal estuaries to mid-elevations in the Cascades. • Hooded Mergansers are most commonly seen in small flocks, but larger flocks sometimes occur, especially when migrants start reappearing in October.

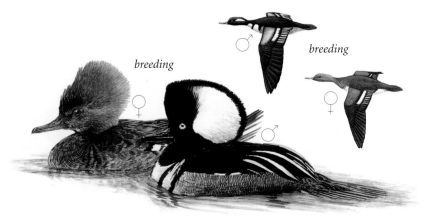

breeding

breeding

ID: crested head; yellow to brownish eyes; thin, dark bill; yellowish legs and feet. *Breeding male:* black head; bold white crest outlined in black; black back; white breast; 2 black shoulder slashes; finely barred, warm buff to deep rufous sides. *Female:* generally dusky brown; reddish brown crest; yellow lower mandible; white belly. *Nonbreeding male:* resembles female, but duller. *In flight:* white speculum with dark bar; flickering flight.
Size: *L* 16–19 in; *W* 23–24 in.
Status: fairly common year-round resident in western lowlands; uncommon year-round resident along northeastern rivers and uncommon summer resident elsewhere in the northeast.
Habitat: *Breeding:* shallow wetlands, small lakes, forested creeks and rivers. *In migration* and *winter:* forested freshwater

wetlands; tidal brackish and saltwater creeks.
Nesting: in an old woodpecker hole or natural cavity in a tree, broken stump or large limb or in a nest box, above or near water; little lining except for down; female incubates 5–13 almost spherical, white eggs for 35–40 days; female sometimes dumps eggs in other nests.
Feeding: dives for small fish, aquatic insects and larvae, snails, amphibians and crustaceans, often in murky water.
Voice: low grunts and croaks. *Male:* utters a froglike *crrrrooo* when courting. *Female:* generally quiet; gives an occasional harsh *gak* or a croaking *croo-croo-crook.*
Similar Species: *Bufflehead* (p. 65): smaller; chunkier; breeding male has white underparts and back of head; female has small white patch on side of head.
Best Sites: *Summer:* Deception Pass; County Line Ponds (Skagit Co.–Whatcom Co.). *Winter:* L. Quinault; Juanita Bay Park (Kirkland).

COMMON MERGANSER

Mergus merganser

Rafts of big, black-and-white ducks massed on fish-bearing lakes and reservoirs in winter often prove to be Common Mergansers, swimming with heads and bills extended. In spring, winter flocks break up and Common Mergansers disperse throughout much of forested Washington to nest. Pairs are soon swimming or resting every few miles along suitable waterways. • After breeding, single-sex flocks are the norm until courtship resumes in late winter. Females assume full responsibility for raising the sometimes unruly young. As family groups move downriver, they gather in larger groups at river bars, pools and smaller estuaries toward late summer. • These elongated, heavy-bodied, low-slung diving ducks require a running start for takeoff and prefer to dive to escape danger.

breeding

breeding

ID: dark eyes; long, slender, hook-tipped, red bill; red legs. *Breeding male:* mostly white body; glossy, dark green, uncrested head; black back; black stripes on shoulders and flanks. *Female:* gray body; rusty brown head; small, shaggy crest; white "chin" and throat. *Nonbreeding male:* resembles female, with larger white areas and whiter flanks.
Size: *L* 22–27 in; *W* 32–34 in.
Status: year-round resident; common at low elevations in winter and at low- to mid-elevations during breeding.
Habitat: prefers fresh or brackish water. *Breeding:* fast, deep streams and rivers; clear, tree-ringed foothill and mountain lakes with drainage channels. *In migration* and *winter:* prefers fresh water; clear rivers, lakes and estuaries.

Nesting: in a natural tree cavity or a large woodpecker hole (occasionally concealed on the ground or in a large nest box), usually near water; female incubates 8–11 creamy eggs, often nest-stained, for 30–32 days.
Feeding: singly or in a flock cooperating to drive fish, dives up to 30 ft deep for small fish, shrimp, frogs, salamanders and freshwater mussels; even takes small mammals and birds.
Voice: usually silent. *Male:* harsh *uig-a. Female:* harsh *karr karr,* usually in flight or when tending the brood.
Similar Species: *Red-breasted Merganser* (p. 70): smaller; shaggier crest; red eyes; slimmer bill; prefers salt water; breeding male has chestnut breast with dark spots, black shoulder patch with white spots and grayish sides; female has brownish "chin."
Best Sites: *Winter:* freshwater river mouths and lakes. *Summer:* fast-flowing rivers and streams.

RED-BREASTED MERGANSER

Mergus serrator

A bit of effort is required to observe the habits and habitats of Red-breasted Mergansers. Rarely seen away from open water and flat shorelines, they are relatively widespread and common waterfowl that few people know well. In Washington, in migration and winter they prefer shallows, boat channels and protected ocean waters along the outer coast. A very few birds will venture inland, generally to large, open reservoirs, during migration periods, typically in late fall and early winter. • Red-breast flocks rarely join other waterfowl or Common Mergansers, even when in the same general area, but individual birds are often seen in the company of grebes and loons, perhaps because of the presence of shared prey.

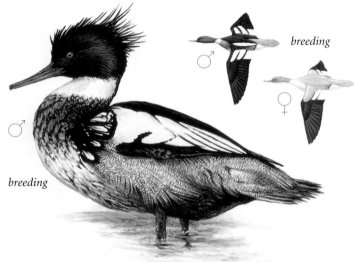

breeding

breeding

ID: shaggy, wild-looking crest; red eyes; thin, serrated, red or dull orangy yellow bill; white belly; red or pale orange legs. *Breeding male:* glossy, green head; black-spotted, light rusty breast; broad, white "collar"; black-and-white wing coverts. *Female:* reddish brown head; gray sides and lower breast. *Nonbreeding male:* similar to female.

Size: *L* 19–26 in; *W* 28–30 in.

Status: common winter resident on protected salt water; rare migrant inland and along the Columbia R.

Habitat: inshore coastal waters, including saltwater bays, harbors, lagoons and estuaries with limited tidal action; rarely freshwater lakes and large rivers.

Nesting: does not nest in Washington.

Feeding: often forages with head just underwater, sometimes in loose flocks, or makes shallow dives for small fish, aquatic insects, fish eggs, crustaceans, worms and amphibians; rarely uses its wings for underwater propulsion.

Voice: generally quiet. *Male:* catlike *yeow* when courting or feeding. *Female:* harsh *kho-kha* (mostly when tending her brood and not often heard here).

Similar Species: *Common Merganser* (p. 69): larger; more elongated look; dark eyes; breeding male has smoother crest and white breast and flanks, extending into wings; female has distinct white "chin" and lower throat.

Best Sites: Sequim Bay; Port Townsend; west side of Whidbey I.; Discovery Park (Seattle); Alki Pt. (west Seattle); Ruston Way (Tacoma).

RUDDY DUCK
Oxyura jamaicensis

Ask a kid with a box of crayons to draw a duck, and the result may well resemble a Ruddy Duck. With his big head, outsized bill, pointed tail and bold coloration, a male Ruddy Duck in his spring finery looks like a cartoon come alive. The male's intent is serious, however, as he advertises for prospective mates with a vigorous bill-pumping display accompanied by staccato grunts and a stream of surface bubbles. • The nondescript yet appealing female's main claim to fame is the extraordinarily large eggs she lays, given her size; they are 2½ inches long. • These ducks can sink slowly underwater to escape detection—easier than flying, which requires a laborious running takeoff and extremely rapid wingbeats.

breeding

breeding

ID: *Breeding male:* chestnut red overall; black crown and nape; bold white "cheek"; blue bill; pale belly. *Female:* brown overall, darker on crown and back; brown stripe across whitish "cheek." *Nonbreeding male:* grayish brown replaces chestnut; gray crown and nape; gray bill. *In flight:* head looks heavy; uniformly dark upperwings.
Size: *L* 15–16 in; *W* 18–19 in.
Status: common regular breeder in eastern lowlands, uncommon breeder in the south Puget Sound region; common regular western migrant and resident in winter, fairly common in winter in eastern Washington.
Habitat: *Breeding:* around openings in deep marshes or on marsh-skirted ponds and lakes. *In migration:* ponds, lakes, sewage ponds and reservoirs. *Winter:* large

flocks assemble on protected freshwater lakes or tidal waters.
Nesting: in emergent vegetation (occasionally on a muskrat lodge or in an abandoned waterfowl nest); basketlike, domed nest is usually suspended over water, but may be floating; female incubates 6–10 whitish eggs for 23–26 days; female often dumps eggs in other nests.
Feeding: dives to shallow bottoms for seeds, leafy plant parts and some aquatic invertebrates.
Voice: generally silent. *Male:* courts with *chuck-chuck-chuck-chur-r-r-r* display "song" punctuated with air bubbles on the water.
Similar Species: *Cinnamon Teal* (p. 51): more slender breeding male has reddish head, red eyes and smaller, dark bill.
Best Sites: *Spring* and *summer:* Dodson Rd. and Winchester Wildlife Area (west of Moses L.); Paterson Unit, Umatilla NWR. *Fall* and *winter:* Everett sewage treatment ponds; Juanita Bay Park (Kirkland); Fruit Valley sewage treatment plant (Vancouver); Turnbull NWR.

CHUKAR
Alectoris chukar

First introduced east of the Cascades in the 1940s, the Chukar was well established by 1946. Further releases have helped this Old World species become fairly common in rocky coulees in Okanogan, Douglas, Grant and Kittitas counties. Rarely seen in open grasslands or heavy forest, the Chukar does not compete for habitat with native grouse and quail species. • The Chukar has impressive reproductive capabilities—a female can lay more than 20 eggs in a single clutch, and she will sometimes provide another, usually smaller, clutch for the male to incubate separately. • In fall and winter, Chukars feed in family groups, reassembling using the distinctive call for which the bird was named. The same call may help disperse breeding pairs into separate territories in summer.

ID: grayish overall; brownish crown and back; black "mask" and "necklace" border creamy white throat and "cheek"; reddish pink eye ring and bill; black and chestnut vertical bars on pale buff sides; rufous undertail coverts; gray tail; reddish pink legs and feet. *In flight:* plain brownish wings; gray rump; red-sided, gray tail; whirring wingbeats.

Size: *L* 13 in; *W* 20 in.

Status: common year-round in eastern Washington; in the Palouse along the Snake R.

Habitat: steep, rocky hillsides, arid foothills, canyons, dry sagebrush and dry mid-elevation valleys.

Nesting: on the ground on a rocky, brush-covered slope; shallow scrape is lined with grass and feathers; female incubates 10–20 heavily spotted, pale yellow to buff eggs for 23–24 days; family stays together through winter.

Feeding: gleans the ground for weed and grass seeds; plucks grass and other green leaves; also takes berries and some insects, especially grasshoppers; uses cheatgrass in winter.

Voice: short clucking precedes a distinctive *chuc-kar chuc-kar chuc-kar;* soft, clucking *whitoo whitoo* when flushed.

Similar Species: *Gray Partridge* (p. 73): buff to rufous face with gray patch; pale bill; chestnut brown bars on gray sides; pale legs. *Northern Bobwhite:* restricted to southern Pierce Co.; much smaller; more chestnut and brown in plumage; strong facial stripes; pale legs.

Best Sites: Frenchman Coulee (Grant Co.); Huntzinger Rd. (south. of Vantage); lower Grand Coulee at Sun Lakes SP; Yakima R. canyon; Lower Granite L. (Chief Timothy SP); Wawawai River Rd. along the Snake R.

GRAY PARTRIDGE

Perdix perdix

Secretive and shy most of the year, Gray Partridges are rarely seen in the open, except when they venture onto quiet country roads, particularly in early morning. • Social outside the incubation period, Gray Partridges sometimes form coveys. If flushed, the birds burst suddenly from cover and fly off in all directions, flapping furiously and then gliding to a nearby safe haven to reunite. During cold weather, they huddle together in a circle, with each bird facing outward, always ready to burst into flight. • Like other seed-eating birds, the Gray Partridge regularly swallows small amounts of gravel to help crush hard seeds. This gravel accumulates in the bird's gizzard, a muscular pouch of the digestive system.

ID: brown eyes; pale grayish blue bill; mottled brown back; gray underparts; chestnut-barred flanks; short, gray, rufous-edged tail; pale grayish legs and feet. *Male:* orangy brown face and throat; dark brown "horseshoe" on belly. *Female:* buff face. *In flight:* low, whirring flight.

Size: *L* 12–13 in; *W* 19 in.

Status: introduced from Europe; common resident in eastern Washington; rare in the hot, arid lower Columbia Basin.

Habitat: grassy or weedy fields and croplands with hedgerows or brushy edge cover; prefers grainfields; also established in some desert areas and grasslands; moves to crop stubble and wooded cover in winter.

Nesting: in a hay field, pasture, weedy fenceline or brushy margin; scratched-out ground depression is rimmed and lined with grass; female incubates 10–20 buff, brown or olive eggs for 21–26 days; pair feeds the young; family stays together until early spring.

Feeding: at dawn and dusk in summer, throughout the day in winter; gleans the ground for waste grains, other seeds and stems; picks apart seedheads; also eats insect adults and larvae; sometimes tunnels in the snow to find waste grain.

Voice: squeaks and clucks; flushed covey utters a barrage of cackling *keep* notes. *Male: kshee-rik* dawn and dusk call sounds like a rusty hinge.

Similar Species: *Chukar* (p. 72): generally gray and brown; black-bordered, creamy "cheek" and throat; red bill; boldly dark-barred flanks; red legs and feet.

Best Sites: dry fields north of Ellensburg; Hog Ranch Buttes (Yakima Training Center; permission required); southwest of Bickleton; Waterville Plateau (Douglas Co.); Turnbull NWR.

RING-NECKED PHEASANT

Phasianus colchicus

The spectacular Asian Ring-necked Pheasant was introduced to North America in the mid-1800s and to southeastern Washington in 1883, mainly for hunting purposes. Unlike most other introductions, Ring-necks became established and thrived almost everywhere they were introduced, but ongoing releases make their true status difficult to determine. • The distinctive, loud *krahh-krawk* of male pheasants is often heard echoing near farmyards, brushy suburban parks and national wildlife refuges, but the birds themselves are less frequently observed. The drab females are even more circumspect, but they may be seen shuffling away to safety in farm fields and brushy cover. • Like other game birds, pheasants have poorly developed flight muscles and rarely fly far.

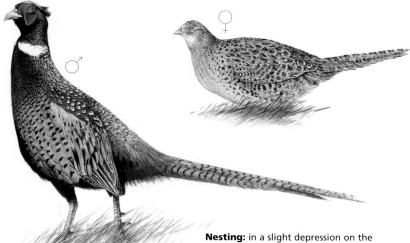

ID: unfeathered, gray legs; very long tail. *Male:* glossy, green-and-purple head; red face and wattle; yellowish pink bill; pale yellow eyes; bronze neck and underparts; white-spotted, brownish back; long, neatly barred, bronze tail. *Female:* dull buff overall; dark eyes; dark gray bill; brown-mottled back and sides. *In flight:* short, rounded wings; long tail feathers well spaced at ends.
Size: *Male: L* 30–36 in; *W* 28–33 in. *Female: L* 20–26 in; *W* 19–25 in.
Status: common resident.
Habitat: brushy and weedy fields, stubble fields and other croplands; shrubby, overgrown hillsides at lower elevations.

Nesting: in a slight depression on the ground, among grass or sparse vegetation or next to a log or other ground cover; nest is barely lined with leaves or grass; female incubates 10–12 brownish olive eggs for 23–25 days; occasionally dumps eggs in other game bird or duck nests.
Feeding: gleans the ground and lower vegetation for weed seeds and invertebrates; winter diet of buds, seeds and waste grain.
Voice: hoarse *ka-ka-ka, ka-ka* when flushed or startled. *Male:* loud, raspy *kraah-krawk,* followed by a muffled whirring of wings. *Female:* usually clucks.
Similar Species: male is unmistakable. *Greater Sage-Grouse* (p. 76): grayer brown overall; dark belly; short, feathered legs. *Ruffed Grouse* (p. 75): smaller; feathered legs; fan-shaped tail.
Best Sites: grain-growing areas on both sides of the Cascades, open fields and large open urban parks in western Washington.

RUFFED GROUSE

Bonasa umbellus

Strutting on a fallen log with his tail fanned and neck ruffled, a displaying male Ruffed Grouse beats the air with accelerating wing strokes and then falls back from the sheer force of his performance. The sounds of this "drumming" are more felt than heard. During this nonvocal display, which occurs mainly in the spring courtship season but also in fall, the male impresses females by erecting the black ruffs on the sides of his neck to appear larger. • As winter approaches, each Ruffed Grouse toe feather gains an elongated bristle, thereby providing temporary "snowshoes." • *Bonasa* is thought to compare the male's drumming sound to the bellow of a bull aurochs (an extinct species of European wild cattle known as *bonasos* in Greek and Latin); *umbellus* (Latin for "sunshade") refers to the umbrella-like black ruff. • Rufous-morph birds are most common in western Washington, and gray-morph birds dominate in the east.

gray morph

ID: grayish or rufous brown overall; small, ragged crest; black shoulder patches expand into ruff (larger on male) in display or threat; thick, dark, vertical barring on sides; brown-barred, rufous tail has broad, dark band (incomplete on female) adjoining pale tip. *In flight:* rounded wings; fan-shaped tail; stiff, shallow wingbeats; usually flies low.
Size: *L* 15–19 in; *W* 22 in.
Status: common year-round resident at low elevations and along higher-elevation riparian corridors; absent from the Columbia Basin below the ponderosa pine zone.
Habitat: forests of all types, from near sea level to over 5000 ft; prefers hardwood second-growth or mixed forests with birch or aspen; often near urban areas.

Nesting: on the ground, typically next to a tree, stump or boulder, possibly in deadfall; female lines a bowl-like depression with dry vegetation and incubates 9–14 cinnamon buff eggs for 23–24 days.
Feeding: gleans the ground, bushes and trees for buds, leaves, flowers, catkins, fruit, acorns and small invertebrates.
Voice: *Male:* quiet *queet* flushing call. *Female:* nasal squeals, soft clucks and hisses; also, squirrel-like chirps and loud *peta peta peta peta* flushing call.
Similar Species: *Spruce Grouse* (p. 77) and *Blue Grouse* (p. 79): females are darker overall, with less white and without crests or ruffs. *Northern Bobwhite:* restricted to southern Pierce Co.; smaller; white or buff "eyebrow" and throat patch; short tail.
Best Sites: low-elevation hardwood forests statewide.

GREATER SAGE-GROUSE

Centrocercus urophasianus

Groups of large, spectacular Greater Sage-Grouse assemble at their courtship "leks" at dawn in March and April to perform a traditional dance. Males enter the arena, inflate their pectoral sacs, spread their pointed tail feathers and strut their stuff to intimidate rivals and attract prospective mates. The most fit and experienced males take center stage, with the others banished to the edges. The best performer will mate with up to 75 percent of the nearby females. • Because of their threatened status, it is best not to approach too closely while the birds are gathered in leks. • Sage-grouse do not run well, preferring to hide or fly. Flocks flush with a startling burst of wingbeats.

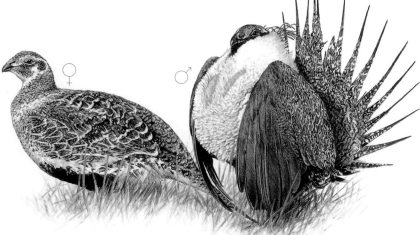

ID: yellow eye comb; stubby, dark bill; mottled, grayish brown upperparts; black belly; long, pointed, barred tail; feathered, yellowish legs and feet. *Male:* black "bib" and neck stripes; yellow pectoral sacs; white underparts; spiked tail. *Female:* smaller; paler than male; white "chin." *In flight:* heavy-looking body; brown underwings with white linings; long tail feathers widely separated at tips.

Size: *Male: L* 27–34 in; *W* 38 in. *Female: L* 18–24 in; *W* 33 in.

Status: uncommon and local; state-listed as threatened.

Habitat: sagebrush; ventures into nearby woodlands and farmlands to feed; display leks are often located in or on fields, airstrips, gravel roads or pits, ridges, grassy swales or dry beds of lakes or streams.

Nesting: on the ground, in shaded cover; shallow bowl is filled with leaves and twigs and lined with feathers; female incubates 7–9 brown-marked, pale olive or greenish eggs for 25–29 days and tends young for up to 12 weeks.

Feeding: gleans mostly sagebrush leaves and buds; pursues insects; young are fed insects for the first 20 days.

Voice: generally silent; guttural clucking and cackling notes. *Male:* courts with unique hollow *oop-la-boop* made by releasing air from quivering air sacs.

Similar Species: *Ring-necked Pheasant* (p. 74): female is smaller, with darkly marked, buff body and naked legs. *Blue Grouse* (p. 79): female is browner, with white-spotted, darkly mottled underparts and rounded tail.

Best Sites: best seen at leks in spring; central Douglas Co. in big sagebrush near Leahy Junction; Yakima Training Center (permission required).

SPRUCE GROUSE
Falcipennis canadensis

S pruce Grouse spend much of their secretive lives foraging in dark, dense sub-alpine conifer stands. They trust their camouflage even in open areas, often allowing people to approach within a few feet before flushing. • The Spruce Grouse is most conspicuous in late May and early June, when the females cackle from trees and the males strut across open areas, or from late July to August, when the females and young walk to insect-rich feeding areas. • The male's courtship call is largely beyond human hearing, but we can see him transform from a dark and somber bird to a red-browed, puff-necked, fan-tailed dandy in display. The male of the "Franklin's Grouse" *(F.c. franklinii)* race, which is found in Washington, ends his short, whirring courtship flight with two loud wing claps.

ID: grayish bill; mottled, gray-and-brown upperparts; straw-colored feet. *Male:* prominent red eye comb; heavily white-marked, dark breast and underparts; white-tipped upper tail coverts; indistinct white "collar" line; black throat and neck; dark tail. *Female:* browner upperparts than male; mottled, dark-barred, white or rufous-washed underparts. *In flight:* heavyset body; short-ish wings and tail; short flights to tree branches.
Size: *L* 14–16 in; *W* 22 in.
Status: uncommon year-round resident in subalpine areas of Okanogan Co. and northeastern Washington; rare (small population) in northwestern Yakima Co.
Habitat: young successional conifer stands but avoids single-species plantations; high-elevation stunted growth.

Nesting: on the ground in a natural or enhanced depression, often below a conifer; nest is lined with needles, leaves and some feathers; female incubates 4–5 tawny olive eggs for 22–24 days; young leave the nest when dry and can flutter to lower tree branches at 6–8 days.
Feeding: usually eats needles at mid-level of pine and spruce; also consumes shrub berries and leaves, herbs, small arthropods and snails.
Voice: guttural notes and clucks. *Male:* extremely low, barely audible hoots accompany whirring flight and 2 wing claps. *Female:* loud, wavering cackle from a tree perch at dawn and dusk.
Similar Species: *Blue Grouse* (p. 79): larger; more bluish gray overall; male has orange comb, yellow or purplish air sacs and pale-tipped tail, with less white in plumage.
Best Sites: FR 39 from Roger L. to Long Swamp (Okanogan Co.); Harts Pass (Okanogan Co.); Salmo Pass (Pend Oreille Co.).

WHITE-TAILED PTARMIGAN

Lagopus leucura

A better-adapted alpine hiker than the White-tailed Ptarmigan, the smallest of our grouse, is hard to imagine. Its plumage perfectly matches its surroundings, regardless of the season, and in winter its feathered feet, which look like fluffy bedroom slippers, allow the bird to "snowshoe" across the snowdrifts of its mountain habitat. • In severe weather, ptarmigan escape the cold by tunneling into the snow near willow bushes where, safe from the howling winds, they nibble on buds. • A brooding female White-tailed Ptarmigan will remain on her nest even if she is closely approached. However, a close approach will be very stressful to her, and sensitive hikers can make a ptarmigan's tough life somewhat easier by keeping a respectful distance.

♂

breeding

ID: black eyes and bill; fully feathered feet, white outer tail feathers. *Breeding male:* red "eyebrow" during courtship; mottled brown upperparts; white underparts, heavily dark-blotched on breast. *Female:* mottled brown overall with black barring on belly. *Nonbreeding:* all-white plumage. *In flight:* mostly white wings.
Size: *L* 12–14 in; *W* 22 in.
Status: uncommon local resident at 5000–7500 ft in the Cascades.
Habitat: mossy and lichen-covered rocky areas; willow and alder thickets at or above treeline. *Winter:* probably moves to lower elevations where vegetation is not snow covered.

Nesting: on the ground, among rocks in snow-free alpine tundra; in a depression lined with fine grass, leaves and lichen; female incubates 4–8 brown-spotted, cinnamon-washed eggs for 24–26 days; pair guards the young for up to 2 months.
Feeding: gleans and picks buds, stems, seeds, fruits and flowers from willows and other alpine plants; occasionally eats insects.
Voice: *Male:* high-pitched *ku-kriii kriii;* low *kuk-kuk-kuk. Female:* low clucks around chicks.
Similar Species: *Blue Grouse* (p. 79): much larger; all-dark tail.
Best Sites: Golden Gardens Trail to Panorama Pt., Fremont Peak, Burroughs Mt. (all at Mt. Rainier NP); Harts Pass–Slate Peak (Okanogan Co.); Chopaka Mt.

BLUE GROUSE

Dendragapus obscurus

The male Blue Grouse sometimes begins his low, owl-like hooting while patches of snow remain in the high coniferous forests. One of the earliest signs of spring, this mating call is intended to attract multiple females. So deep that the human ear can detect only a fraction of the sounds, the resonant notes produce a humming sensation in the head at close range. • Some birds fatten up on berries along timberline ridges before overwintering at more sheltered lower elevations. • *Dendragapus* is Greek for "tree-loving." This bird does roost in conifers, but it spends much of its time on the ground. • Like other forest-dwelling grouse, the Blue Grouse is often easily approached, earning it the nickname "Fool Hen."

"Pacific" subspecies

ID: dark eyes and bill; longish, broad tail; feathered legs. *Male:* bluish gray crown and nape; reddish orange eye comb; brownish upperparts; displays with inflated yellow ("Pacific" subspecies) or purplish ("Interior" subspecies) throat patches surrounded by white and blackish feathers (more white on Interior birds); black tail with light tip. *Female:* grayish brown overall, lightly white-speckled neck and back; banded brown rump and tail with paler tip.
Size: *Male: L* 18–22 in; *W* 25–27 in. *Female: L* 17–19 in; *W* 23–25 in.
Status: uncommon year-round resident.
Habitat: coniferous forests, from coastal rainforests to subalpine associations; occasionally wanders to open country, especially in summer; prefers denser forests in winter.

Nesting: female selects a site with some overhead cover; shallow scrape is sparsely lined with dead vegetation and some feathers; female incubates 6–7 buff eggs for 25–28 days; young leave the nest the morning after hatching and can flutter to cover after 9 days.
Feeding: flies into foliage and perches; eats mainly leaves, flowers and conifer needles in spring, berries and invertebrates in summer and conifer needles, buds, twigs and seeds in winter.
Voice: *Male:* series of 5–8 extremely deep hoots produced in neck sacs; other soft and harsh calls. *Female:* loud whinny and quavering cackles.
Similar Species: *Spruce Grouse* (p. 77): male has prominent red comb, black upper breast and throat, and white-spotted underparts and tail; female has more heavily barred underparts.
Best Sites: *"Pacific":* Hurricane Ridge and Deer Park (Olympic NP). *"Interior":* Okanogan Mts.

SHARP-TAILED GROUSE

Tympanuchus phasianellus

Male Sharp-tails gather at traditional dancing grounds, called "leks," to perform their mating rituals each spring. With wings drooping at their sides, tails pointing skyward and purple air sacs inflated, males furiously pummel the ground with their feet, vigorously cooing and cackling for a crowd of prospective mates. Each male has a small stage within the circular lek that he defends against rival males with kicks and warning calls. • The courtship display of the male Sharp-tailed Grouse has been emulated in the traditional dance of many native cultures on the prairies. • Although this grouse is widespread across the northern Great Plains, much of Canada and parts of Alaska, it is barely hanging on in Washington.

Nesting: on the ground; usually under cover near the lek; in a depression lined with grass and feathers; female incubates 10–13 light brown eggs, dotted with reddish brown, for about 24 days.

Feeding: eats buds, seeds, flowers, green shoots and berries; also eats insects.

Voice: *Male:* mournful *coo-oo* and cackling *cac-cac-cac-cac* during courtship.

Similar Species: *Ruffed Grouse* (p. 75): slight head crest; black patches on neck; broad, fan-shaped tail with broad, dark subterminal band. *Ring-necked Pheasant* (p. 74): female has paler markings on underparts, unfeathered legs and longer tail. *Spruce Grouse* (p. 77): black or mottled throat; black, fan-shaped tail in flight; male has red eye comb.

Best Sites: West Foster Creek along Bridgeport Hill Rd.; Colville Indian Reservation.

ID: yellow eye combs; mottled, white, brown and black neck, breast and upperparts; small, dark crescents on white belly; white throat; white undertail coverts; feathered legs; white-edged tail with long central feather. *Male:* inflates purplish pink air sacs on neck during courtship displays.

Size: *L* 17 in; *W* 25–26 in.

Status: nearly extirpated in Washington; rare and very local in the Okanogan Valley and northern Douglas Co., mostly on private lands; state-listed as threatened.

Habitat: grasslands and shrub savannah in sage and arid steppe zones.

WILD TURKEY
Meleagris gallopavo

The wary Wild Turkey has acute senses and a highly developed social system. Feeding largely in the open and highly visible to predators, it forms flocks of up to 60 birds, with some individuals always on alert. Turkeys sometimes cooperatively flush grasshoppers. • Like other game birds, turkeys consume grit to assist in grinding down hard-shelled foods in the gizzard. Objects requiring more than 400 pounds of pressure per square inch to crush have been found flattened within a day when fed to a turkey. • The turkey is the only widely domesticated animal native to North America. Perhaps with that fact in mind, Benjamin Franklin offered the Wild Turkey as his first choice for America's national emblem, but it lost to the Bald Eagle by one congressional vote.

ID: naked, bluish head; dark, glossy, iridescent plumage of green, copper and brown; barred copper tail tipped with white; long, unfeathered pinkish legs. *Male:* red wattles; conspicuous central breast tuft. *Female:* smaller; less iridescent body.
Size: *Male: L* 4–4¼ ft; *W* 5¼ ft. *Female: L* 3 ft; *W* 4¼ ft.
Status: locally common to uncommon in eastern Washington.
Habitat: chiefly openings and forest edges in the oak–conifer zone of valley edges, rolling foothills and lower mountain slopes; prefers oak, hackberry and cotton-wood; needs adequate surface water and is often near streams.
Nesting: in open woods or a forest glade; female scratches a slight depression at the base of a tree, close to shrubs or under a brush pile and lines it with grass and leaves; female incubates 5–17 pale buff eggs with reddish spots for 27–31 days.
Feeding: omnivorous diet includes sedge and grass seeds, fruits, bulbs, leaves, nuts, berries, roots, invertebrates and even small amphibians and reptiles.
Voice: wide array of sounds; birds cackle when leaving the roosting area. *Male:* gobbles loudly. *Female:* clucks and whines.
Similar Species: none.
Best Sites: Turnbull NWR; Sinlahekin Valley; Little Pend Oreille NWR; North Fork, Coppei Creek (Walla Walla Co.); Rowland L. (SR 14, Klickitat Co.).

MOUNTAIN QUAIL

Oreortyx pictus

With spring's arrival, foothill and mountain slopes in widely separated locales of Washington come alive with the resonant, querulous calls of the male Mountain Quail. In other seasons, the secretive Mountain Quail is less readily detected. Family groups vanish from roadsides, quickly concealing themselves among dense brush and sheltering thickets. Flushed coveys scatter and then reunite. • The Mountain Quail is known for its ability to exploit a wide variety of plant food and to travel long distances to take advantage of seasonally abundant food. Newly hatched quails quickly follow their parents as they travel many miles per day by foot, often moving to lower elevations where there is more cover. • The largest of the North American quails, the Mountain Quail also displays the least sexual dimorphism.

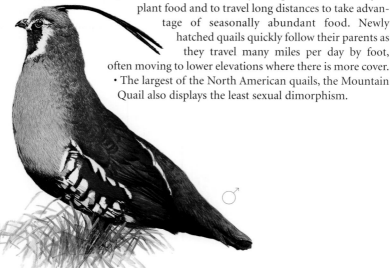

ID: bluish gray head, neck and breast; white-bordered, brown "cheek" and throat; 2 straight, black head plumes (may intertwine); brownish gray back, wings, rump and tail; rufous underparts, strongly white-barred on sides and paler on under-tail coverts; short tail. *In flight:* grayish underwings.

Size: *L* 11–12 in; *W* 16 in.

Status: rare local resident; small populations in the southeast; scattered populations on the Kitsap Peninsula and into Mason Co. and Thurston Co.

Habitat: shrubby growth after a fire or clear-cutting; woodlands; streamside habitats; birds may move downslope to the coast in winter.

Nesting: on the ground, usually in dense cover; shallow nest scrape in loose, dry soil is lined with dry pine needles and grass; pair incubates 6–14 cream or buff eggs for 24–25 days.

Feeding: digs and scratches among leaf litter; sometimes gleans in trees or shrubs; eats seeds, berries, bulbs, green leaves, flowers, acorns, fungi and grit; female eats bone fragments and forages for ants and other insects when with young.

Voice: calls include a whistling *wit-wit-wit* and *tu-tu-tu-tu* assembly call. *Male:* distinctive loud, clear, 2-noted, whistling *quee-yark* courtship call; similar, less raucous alarm call.

Similar Species: *California Quail* (p. 83): grayer plumage; horizontally streaked flanks; "scaly" belly and neck; male has darker face and teardrop-shaped plume; female has plainer face and short, upright plume.

Best Sites: Capitol State Forest, particularly C-4000 and C-Line roads (Thurston Co.); west of Belfair (Mason Co.); Chief Joseph Wildlife Area (Asotin Co.).

CALIFORNIA QUAIL
Callipepla californica

Although the male's spring courtship call sounds remarkably like the name of mid-America's famous windy city, Chicago, the California Quail rarely strays from its western homeland. Apparently first introduced to Washington around 1857, the California Quail has, since the 1880s, been successfully introduced to various parts of the state, but it is largely absent from the northern coast, heavily forested areas and higher elevations. • Spending most of their time scuttling about in tight, cohesive coveys of up to 200 birds, these quails run the risk of attracting feral cats and other predators. Even though they stay largely within the protective confines of their brushland habitat, noisy scratching for food and soft vocalizations to keep the covey together usually give them away. A flushed covey will erupt from cover, scatter and later reassemble.

ID: gray breast, back and tail; horizontal, white streaking on brown sides; very "scaly" belly and neck. *Male:* prominent white "eyebrow"; forward-drooping black plume; dark crown; white-bordered, black "cheek" and throat. *Female:* grayish brown face and throat; small, upright black plume. *In flight:* gray underwings.
Size: *L* 10–11 in; *W* 14 in.
Status: common resident at low elevations in eastern Washington; fairly common but local in western Washington.
Habitat: chaparral; brush, even in suburban parks; oak and riparian woodlands.
Nesting: usually on the ground, well concealed under cover of a shrub, log, brush pile or debris; sometimes in an abandoned nest of another species; shallow depression lined with leaves and grass can be quite substantial; mostly the female incubates up to 21 brown-blotched, off-white eggs for 22–23 days.
Feeding: gleans and scratches on the ground; eats seeds, fresh leaves, plant shoots, berries, acorns, bulbs, flowers and catkins, plus occasional plant galls, insects and waste grain; sometimes takes birdseed.
Voice: soft calls, usually 2 notes; spitting alarm call (mostly by the male). *Male:* loud, low-pitched *chi-ca-go* call in courtship (April to May) and at other times of year.
Similar Species: *Mountain Quail* (p. 82): 1–2 long, straight head plumes; strongly white-barred, rufous sides; unbarred, rufous belly.
Best Sites: open shrubby habitats, parks, urban areas and farmlands.

RED-THROATED LOON

Gavia stellata

O ur smallest and lightest loon, the Red-throated Loon is the only member of its family that can take off from small ponds or, in an emergency, from land. • Red-throated Loons prefer the coast and are only occasionally seen inland in Washington. Most birds migrate through our region to winter southward, but others remain in estuaries and more sheltered inshore ocean waters until the first northbound migrants reappear. • Reliable as meteorologists, Red-throats often become very noisy before the onset of foul weather, possibly sensing changes in barometric pressure. • The word *stellata* refers to the white, starlike speckles on this bird's back in its nonbreeding plumage.

nonbreeding

breeding

ID: small, slim bill points upward. *Breeding:* gray head; plain dark back; deep reddish throat. *Nonbreeding:* eye surrounded narrowly by white; dark gray upperparts; small white spots on upper back; light underparts.
Size: *L* 24–27 in; *W* 3½–3¾ ft.
Status: common migrant and winter resident in protected marine waters; rare fall migrant on lowland freshwater lakes west of the Cascades; casual in fall and winter on reservoirs east of the Cascades; fall migration begins in late July and peaks in mid-September before declining; migrants reappear in late March, with only a few birds lingering until June or possibly beyond.

Habitat: primarily inshore coastal waters, including river mouths, bays and estuaries; large bodies of water inland.
Nesting: does not nest in Washington.
Feeding: dives for small fish and aquatic invertebrates in shallower water than other loons.
Voice: Mallard-like *kwuk-kwuk-kwuk-kwuk* in flight; loud *gayorwork* distraction call; mournful, gull-like wail during courtship; spring pair duets seldom heard here.
Similar Species: *Common Loon* (p. 86): larger; much darker; much heavier, straighter bill; all-dark back in nonbreeding plumage; immature can be finely barred. *Pacific Loon* (p. 85): eye indistinct on all-dark face; bill held level; nonbreeding plumage uniform dark gray above, often with dark "chin strap."
Best Sites: Deception Pass area; Sequim Bay; Dungeness NWR; Birch Bay; Ocean Shores; Tokeland.

PACIFIC LOON
Gavia pacifica

Sporting twin white racing stripes across the shoulders, a blackish throat and a lustrous, gray head and nape, this loon is easily recognized in breeding plumage, but more somberly attired fall migrants are much less easily detected. • Pacific Loons migrate in huge numbers within sight of land in both spring and fall. These movements can involve large, open flocks that sometimes stretch over a distance of one mile or more. Small numbers migrate before and after the peak periods. • Pacific Loons generally avoid upper-estuarine waters used by Red-throated Loons and inshore waters favored by Common Loons, preferring to raft on the open ocean beyond the surf line, often in the immediate shelter of a headland or jetty.

nonbreeding

ID: slender body; high, smoothly rounded crown; thin, straight bill is held level. *Breeding:* gleaming, silver gray crown and nape; dark back with large, bold white spots; finely white-streaked, blackish throat. *Nonbreeding:* dark face; dark gray upperparts; white underparts; thin, black trim at sides of neck; often has very thin, dark "chin strap."
Size: *L* 23–29 in; *W* 3½–4 ft.
Status: common migrant on outer coast in spring and fall; common winter resident in deep inland marine waters; uncommon migrant and rare winter resident in eastern Washington; migration occurs from mid-May to early June and from mid-September to October.
Habitat: coastal ocean waters, including harbors and bays; occasionally large inland water bodies.

Nesting: does not nest in Washington.
Feeding: dives deeply for small fish; summer diet includes aquatic invertebrates and some plant material.
Voice: largely silent away from breeding sites; sharp *kwao* flight call.
Similar Species: *Common Loon* (p. 86): larger; heavier bill; regular rows of white spots on sides and more extensive white spotting on black upperparts in breeding plumage; pale ring around eye and white notch along line between dark and light on neck in nonbreeding plumage. *Red-throated Loon* (p. 84): smaller head; slimmer, upward-tilted bill; plain upperparts and reddish throat in breeding plumage; fine, white spotting on back and more distinct white around eye in nonbreeding plumage; faster, deeper wingbeats in flight.
Best Sites: Deception Pass; Cattle Pass (San Juan Is.); Admiralty Inlet; Point No Point. *In migration:* Ocean Shores jetty.

85

COMMON LOON
Gavia immer

Common Loons are a regular sight on our coastal waters from late summer to spring, but they breed mostly in Canada and Alaska. A few nest inland in Washington, and the few birds that summer on the Washington coast are usually in nonbreeding plumage. • Loons are well adapted to their diving lifestyle: solid bones make them less buoyant (most birds have hollow bones), and their feet are placed well back on their bodies for effective propulsion. • The word "loon" is derived from the Scandinavian *lom*, meaning "clumsy," perhaps referring to this bird's awkwardness on land. However, many people would also say that "loony" is a good description of the weird wails and behavior at loon breeding sites.

breeding

ID: heavy, daggerlike bill; full or partial white "collar." *Breeding:* green-glossed, black head; red eyes; black bill; white-spotted, dark upperparts; white underparts mottled and striped with black on sides and flanks; black-and-white-striped "necklace." *Nonbreeding:* much duller plumage; dark eyes; pale eye-arcs; dark-topped, gray bill; dark, unmarked gray above; white below.
Size: *L* 28–35 in; *W* 4–4¾ ft.
Status: common coastal migrant and resident from late August to June, with small numbers of birds summering; fairly common migrant and winter resident on inland lakes and reservoirs east of the Cascades; uncommon but regular breeder at large, secluded northeastern lakes; nests regularly at Chester Morse L. in the Cedar River Watershed (closed to visitors).

Habitat: mainly open ocean close to shore, estuaries and freshwater lakes.
Nesting: on a muskrat lodge, small island or projecting shoreline; always very near water; pair builds nest mound of aquatic vegetation; pair incubates 1–3 olive eggs with dark spots for 24–31 days; pair rears the young.
Feeding: pursues fish to depths of 180 ft; occasionally eats aquatic invertebrates and amphibians.
Voice: quavering tremolo alarm call, often called "loon laughter"; long but simple wailing contact call. *Male:* summer territorial call is an undulating, complex yodel.
Similar Species: *Pacific Loon* (p. 85): smaller; more rounded crown; slimmer bill; no white "collar"; distinctive, silver gray head and nape in breeding plumage; grayer sides to neck and dark "chin strap" are usual in nonbreeding plumage.
Best Sites: *Late summer* to *spring:* coastal and inland marine waters; eastern inland reservoirs.

PIED-BILLED GREBE

Podilymbus podiceps

The Pied-billed Grebe is the most widespread grebe species in North America, yet it is not always easy to find. Shy and retiring by nature, this grebe most often hides behind shady, protective cover in its marshland habitat. Its exuberant call is sometimes the only clue to its presence. • In breeding season, the male is bold, aggressively chasing off any intruders, even those that are much larger than he is. At other times of the year, when frightened by an intruder, this grebe will slide noiselessly under the water's surface, with only its bill and eyes exposed. • Pied-billed Grebes breed throughout Washington and are year-round residents in western Washington, with numbers increasing toward winter. They prefer fresh water but sometimes use brackish upper estuaries.

breeding

ID: rich brown plumage; oversized head; whitish "cheek"; dark eyes; stubby, laterally compressed bill; short tail; individually lobed toes. *Breeding:* black forehead and throat; narrow, white eye ring; black ring neatly divides white bill. *Nonbreeding:* white "chin"; yellowish bill. *Immature:* dark stripes on side of head.

Size: *L* 12–15 in; *W* 22–25 in.

Status: common to fairly common year-round resident statewide; statewide migrant.

Habitat: *Breeding:* marshy ponds and sloughs; freshwater lakes and reservoirs with dense aquatic vegetation. *Nonbreeding:* various open and semi-open fresh and estuarine waters; rarely visits salt water or eelgrass beds.

Nesting: in the densely vegetated margin of a lake or marsh; platform with a shallow saucer of wet and decaying plants is anchored to emergent vegetation; pair incubates 3–10 bluish or greenish white eggs for 23–27 days and raises young together until late summer.

Feeding: opportunistic feeder; dives in pursuit of fish, amphibians, invertebrates and water plants; gleans seeds and insects from the water's surface.

Voice: loud, whooping *kuk-kuk-kuk cow cow cow cowp cowp cowp* call begins quickly, then slows down; other calls are short and rail-like.

Similar Species: *Other small grebes* (pp. 88–90): slimmer bills; nonbreeding birds have more white or pale coloration on lower part of face, belly and wings.

Best Sites: freshwater habitats such as marshes, wetlands, shallow lakes, rivers or open bays that have emergent vegetation.

HORNED GREBE

Podiceps auritus

Horned Grebes are unmistakable in their breeding finery, with bright rufous underparts and golden "ear" tufts. As soon as this striking plumage fades, however, they become nondescript until they attain their contrasting black-and-white winter plumage. • Outside the breeding season, Horned Grebes commonly patrol harbors, industrial waterfronts and shipping channels for underwater food, which places them at risk from oil spills and surface pollution. • Like loons, grebes appear hunchbacked in flight, with hastily beating wings, head held low and feet trailing behind the stubby tail. • Grebes migrate mainly at night to avoid detection by predators. • *Auritus* refers to the golden feather tufts, or "horns," acquired in breeding plumage.

nonbreeding

ID: flat crown; red eyes; small, dark, whitish-tipped bill; white underparts; stubby tail. *Breeding:* black "cheek" and forehead; golden "ear" tufts; rufous neck and flanks; white shoulder patch. *Nonbreeding:* dark crown and upperparts; well-defined dark nape; white "cheek"; pale spot ahead of eye.
Size: *L* 12–15 in; *W* 23–25 in.
Status: common western resident in winter; fairly common locally in winter in the east, particularly on Columbia R. reservoirs; uncommon summer resident in the east; rare breeder in the northeast and Okanogan Co.
Habitat: *Breeding:* shallow, well-vegetated wetlands and marshes with some open water. *Nonbreeding:* inshore ocean waters, brackish estuaries and open fresh water.

Nesting: singly or in small, loose colonies; in thick vegetation at the water's edge; platform of wet plant material is usually attached to emergent vegetation; pair incubates 4–7 brown-stained, white eggs for 23–24 days; pair raises the young.
Feeding: makes shallow dives and gleans the water's surface for aquatic invertebrates, small fish and amphibians.
Voice: usually quiet outside the breeding season; during courtship, a loud series of croaks and shrieking notes and also a sharp *keark keark;* shrill *kowee* alarm call.
Similar Species: *Eared Grebe* (p. 90): smaller, more peaked, asymmetric head; finer, all-dark bill; black neck in breeding plumage; black "cheek" and whitish ear patch in nonbreeding plumage.
Best Sites: west side of Whidbey I.; West Pt. (Discovery Park, Seattle); Union Bay (Seattle); Grays Harbor north of Damon Pt.; Potholes SP (Grant Co.); Banks L.

RED-NECKED GREBE

Podiceps grisegena

Sparsely scattered among more sharply patterned diving birds at harbor entrances and estuaries, unobtrusive Red-necked Grebes in nonbreeding plumage might easily go unrecognized. In this plumage of mostly grays and whites, they are often mistaken for loons, but a little study usually reveals the differences. Red-necked Grebes do, however, develop their showy breeding plumage with a black "cap," a white "cheek" and a rusty red neck before leaving for their breeding grounds. • Although Red-necks are fairly common breeders in northeastern Washington, very few birds stray inland in migration or in winter, preferring salt water up to a quarter of a mile from shore. • The *grisegena* ("gray cheek") part of the scientific name reflects a distinctive field mark of this bird's nonbreeding plumage.

nonbreeding

ID: dark eyes; thick bill; brownish gray upperparts; white underparts; long neck. *Breeding:* black crown; white "cheek"; bright yellow-and-black bill; red neck. *Nonbreeding:* dingy brown "cheek" and neck; dusky yellow bill. *In flight:* 2 white upperwing patches; feet extend beyond tail.
Size: *L* 17–22 in; *W* 30–33 in.
Status: common fall and winter resident west of the Cascades, particularly in protected marine waters; occasionally on large lakes; common breeder on Okanogan lakes and in the northeast.
Habitat: *Breeding:* emergent vegetation zone of large lakes and ponds. *Nonbreeding:* protected bays, estuaries and harbors.
Nesting: singly, or in small, loose colonies; floating platform of aquatic vegetation is anchored to submerged plants; pair incubates 4–5 light blue to chalky white, usually stained eggs for 25–35 days.
Feeding: dives and gleans the water's surface for small fish and crustaceans and other invertebrates.
Voice: usually silent away from breeding sites; often-repeated, laughlike, excited *ah-ooo ah-ooo ah-ooo ah-ah-ah-ah-ah;* calls include ducklike quacks and grunts.
Similar Species: *Western Grebe* (p. 91) and *Clark's Grebe* (p. 92): larger; black-and-white plumage; slender, bright yellow or yellowish orange bill. *Horned Grebe* (p. 88): smaller; shorter, darker bill with white tip; golden "ear" tufts and rufous flanks in breeding plumage; white lower face and foreneck in nonbreeding plumage.
Best Sites: *Winter:* Port Townsend bay; Deception Pass SP; L. Washington; Westport. *Summer:* Sinlahekin Valley; Molson Lakes (Okanogan Co.).

EARED GREBE

Podiceps nigricollis

Wearing their black-and-rufous breeding plumage and adorned with bright golden "ears," Eared Grebes arrive at ponds and marshes east of the Cascades, where they are common summer residents. Much more distinctive than their dingy nonbreeding plumage, this color pattern makes the colonial breeding pairs easy to pick out among the cattails. • The molting process leaves some nonbreeding birds flightless for much of the year, and even breeding adults are grounded for three to four months. • Like all grebes, Eared Grebes consume feathers to aid in digestion and to protect the stomach lining and intestines from sharp fish bones. • The black neck of the breeding plumage is responsible for the *nigricollis* part of the scientific name.

breeding

ID: small, peaked head; red eyes; thin bill; black back; white underparts, including fluffy undertail. *Breeding:* black face and forehead; golden-plumed "ear" tufts; dark bill; rufous flanks; thin, black neck. *Nonbreeding:* white behind ear and "chin" and on foreneck; gray bill; gray-mottled, white flanks; generally dusky neck. *In flight:* white hindwing patch; feet extend beyond tail.
Size: *L* 12–14 in; *W* 22–23 in.
Status: reasonably common summer resident in eastern Washington; large migratory flocks on eastern lakes; uncommon winter resident in western Washington.
Habitat: *Breeding:* freshwater or slightly alkaline shallow lakes and wetlands with floating or emergent vegetation. *Nonbreeding:* coastal and interior water bodies.

Nesting: strongly colonial; in thick vegetation of a lake edge, pond or marsh; pair builds a shallow, flimsy platform of floating wet and decaying plants; pair incubates 4–7 bluish white, often brownish-stained eggs for 20–23 days.
Feeding: makes shallow dives and gleans the water's surface for aquatic invertebrates, small fish and amphibians.
Voice: usually silent away from breeding sites; loud, chirping *kowee* threat call; mellow *poo-eee-chk* during courtship.
Similar Species: *Horned Grebe* (p. 88): more rounded head; straighter, chunkier bill with white tip; rufous neck and denser golden "ear" tufts in breeding plumage; solidly white "cheek" and often foreneck in nonbreeding plumage. *Pied-billed Grebe* (p. 87): browner plumage; dark eyes; thicker bill.
Best Sites: *Summer:* Soap L.; Molson Lakes (Okanogan Co.); Okanogan Highlands; Turnbull NWR. *Fall:* Mystery Bay SP. *Winter:* Kennedys Lagoon (Whidbey I.).

WESTERN GREBE

Aechmophorus occidentalis

A medium-sized, long-necked, black-and-white diving bird with a long, daggerlike, yellow bill seen on open water could be either a Western Grebe or its recently split-off sibling species, the Clark's Grebe. Both grebes exhibit a spectacular courtship display in which participants posture with bits of water plants in their bills, then arise from the surface to patter frantically on parallel courses, heads held high, ultimately dropping back into the water or diving below the surface. • Western Grebes are more likely than Clark's to be seen on estuaries and lagoons much of the year, but most Westerns move to freshwater lakes and marshes to breed. • *Aechmophorus* is derived from Greek words that mean "spear bearer."

ID: dark crown extends below red eye; long, daggerlike, yellowish to yellowish green bill; black upperparts; white underparts; long, slender neck with broad, dark stripe on nape. *In flight:* long, pointed body and wings; inconspicuous white upperwing stripe.

Size: *L* 20–24 in; *W* 30–40 in.

Status: common summer resident in large eastern lakes; common winter resident in marine waters and local coastal freshwater lakes; uncommon winter resident along the Columbia R.; candidate for state threatened list.

Habitat: *Breeding:* large freshwater lakes with dense areas of emergent vegetation or thick mats of floating aquatic plants. *Nonbreeding:* large, open water bodies, fresh or salt.

Nesting: colonial; pair builds floating nest of wet or decaying vegetation anchored to submerged plants; pair incubates 2–4 pale bluish white, brown-stained eggs for about 24 days.

Feeding: dives for small fish, invertebrates and other small aquatic or marine prey; sometimes eats small birds and salamanders.

Voice: often heard at both breeding and wintering sites; shrill, brief, 2-note *kreee-krreeet* or *krrrik krrrikk;* female's calls are reminiscent of Killdeer's.

Similar Species: *Clark's Grebe* (p. 92): brighter, yellowish orange bill; white around eye and to base of bill; narrower nape stripe; different calls. *Red-necked Grebe* (p. 89): duller yellow bill; shorter neck; red neck and white "cheek" in breeding plumage; grayish white "cheek" and grayer, dingier neck in nonbreeding plumage.

Best Sites: *Summer:* Moses L.; Potholes Reservoir; Banks L. *Winter:* Quartermaster Harbor (Maury I.); Birch Bay–Drayton Harbor; virtually any open, protected marine body of water.

CLARK'S GREBE
Aechmophorus clarkii

Ornithologists once believed that Western Grebes came in two varieties: those with duller yellow bills and red eyes on a black background, and those with bright yellowish orange bills and red eyes clearly visible below the black crown on a white face. What they eventually realized—something the grebes had known all along—was that there are two separate species. We now know the less widespread, paler-faced birds with paler downy young as Clark's Grebes, but, particularly in winter, identification remains an intriguing challenge. The two species are often found together, but for the most part they do not interbreed, even when both share a breeding site. • Clark's Grebe was named in honor of John Henry Clark, a mathematician, surveyor and successful bird collector who procured the first scientific specimen in 1858.

ID: white on face extends to surround red eyes; long, dagger-like, yellowish orange bill; black upperparts; white underparts; long, slender neck with slender black stripe on nape. *Male:* longer bill. *In flight:* long, pointed body and wings; conspicuous white wing stripe.

Size: *L* 20–23 in; *W* 31–38 in.

Status: uncommon summer resident on large eastern lakes; rare migrant and winter resident on marine waters.

Habitat: *Breeding:* large lakes with dense areas of emergent vegetation or thick mats of floating aquatic plants. *Nonbreeding:* sizeable water bodies, including sluggish rivers and lagoons, and open coast up to 1 mi offshore.

Nesting: colonial; floating nest of wet or decaying vegetation anchored to submerged plants; pair incubates 2–4 bluish white eggs for about 24 days.

Feeding: dives for small fish, invertebrates and other small aquatic or marine prey.

Voice: brief 2-note *kreee-krreeet;* similar to the Western Grebe's, but generally higher pitched and uttered as single notes.

Similar Species: *Western Grebe* (p. 91): black on face extends beyond eye; duller yellow to yellowish green bill; broader black nape stripe; lower-pitched calls. *Other grebes* (pp. 87–90): smaller; shorter, less daggerlike bills.

Best Sites: *Summer:* Potholes Reservoir; Moses L.; Banks L. *Winter:* find occasional birds amid large flocks of Western Grebes.

BLACK-FOOTED ALBATROSS
Phoebastria nigripes

Albatrosses are the ultimate ocean wanderers, logging thousands of miles and enduring the toughest storms the oceans have to offer even before they reach breeding age. Black-footed Albatrosses visit offshore Washington waters year-round in varying numbers. From April until October, when most adults return to Pacific islands to nest, Black-foots in our area are most common from 10 miles offshore to the edge of the continental shelf. Small numbers, probably nonbreeding immature birds, remain through winter. • Like other albatrosses, Black-foots have a well-developed sense of smell and are often attracted to fishing vessels. • With extremely long, slender wings designed to take advantage of strong ocean wind currents, these large birds can fly for long periods of time without flapping, needing only an occasional deep dip of the wings to stay aloft. • In calm conditions, or when loafing, albatrosses will gather together on the water in flocks of up to two dozen birds.

ID: ashy brown overall, becoming paler with age; white on face at base of bill and under eye; heavy, dark bill, darkest at tip; undertail coverts may be white; white crescent at base of tail in all but immature plumage. *In flight:* long, narrow wings; black feet extend beyond tail.
Size: *L* 27–29 in; *W* 6¼–7 ft.
Status: common offshore from April to October; uncommon in winter.
Habitat: open ocean, except during breeding; prefers continental shelf waters.
Nesting: does not nest in Washington.
Feeding: snatches fish, flying-fish eggs, squid, crustaceans, natural marine oils and carrion from the water's surface; plunges to just below the surface; follows fishing vessels, consuming remains of discarded fish and other marine creatures caught in fishing nets.
Voice: generally silent; sometimes groans, shrieks or squawks, especially in feeding flocks.
Similar Species: *Laysan Albatross* (p. 360): white head, neck and underparts; pale yellow bill. *Short-tailed Albatross:* rare; larger; black-and-white plumage; creamy head; heavier, pale pink bill; immature is brown overall.
Best Sites: open ocean, usually 10 mi or more from shore; most often seen on pelagic trips leaving from Westport; near commercial fishing vessels.

93

NORTHERN FULMAR

Fulmarus glacialis

Northern Fulmars are the only mid-sized tubenoses that breed in the North Pacific and spend all their lives north of the equator. Regularly found well out to sea, Northern Fulmars follow fishing vessels and sometimes enter bays and harbors in search of food scraps and refuse, so they might be seen from land, most often in winter. • Relatively slim-winged but thick-necked and bull-headed, the Northern Fulmar shares many physical attributes—except for its stubby, pale greenish yellow bill—with the closely related shearwaters. • Northern Fulmar color morphs range from all-dark to all-pale, with darker morphs predominating in Washington waters. • Fulmars are among the longest-lived birds, and some have been known to breed for 40 or more years. • "Fulmar" is derived from the Old Norse words meaning "foul gull," a derivation obvious to anyone who has approached one of these birds too closely and received a shot of foul-smelling fish oil.

dark morph

light morph

ID: dark eyes; short, pale greenish yellow to slightly orangy, tubed bill; thick neck; stubby, rounded tail. *Light morph:* white overall; patchy, pale bluish gray mantle. *Dark morph:* blue-tinged, deep brownish gray overall; paler flight feathers. *In flight:* long, pointed wings.
Size: *L* 17–20 in; *W* 3½ ft.
Status: common well offshore from late July to late April; uncommon from mid-May to mid-July; occasional winter records in inland marine waters; rare close to shore and in bays.
Habitat: open ocean waters over upwellings and along the outer continental shelf.

Nesting: does not nest in Washington.
Feeding: seizes almost any edible item when swimming, including fish, squid, invertebrates and carrion; makes shallow plunges beneath water's surface; cannot feed in flight.
Voice: generally silent; possible low quacking call when competing for food.
Similar Species: *Shearwaters* (pp. 95–98, 360): slimmer heads and necks; more slender bills. *Albatrosses* (pp. 93, 360): much larger; longer, heavier bills; more leisurely flight. *Gulls* (pp. 173–84, 363): slimmer body and neck; bill not tubed.
Best Sites: open ocean waters far offshore, usually seen from pelagic boat trips leaving from Westport; occasionally seen from shore during fall and winter storms.

PINK-FOOTED SHEARWATER

Puffinus creatopus

Beginning in April, when their nesting duties are complete, until November, Pink-footed Shearwaters migrate north along the continental shelf into our area to search out large schools of fish and squid. Like other members of the shearwater family, Pink-foots assemble astonishingly quickly at any food source. They will closely approach any boat if food of any description is tossed overboard. In the Pacific Northwest, Pink-footed Shearwaters are nonbreeding birds of the open ocean, and small numbers of Pink-foots may be present among the swarms of other shearwaters encountered at sea. Infrequently seen from land, Pink-foots are best spotted from strategic coastal points with the aid of a telescope. • Like other shearwaters, Pink-foots are long-winged seabirds that fly with shallow, rapid wingbeats and stiff-winged glides.

ID: slender, pinkish bill with hooked, black tip; dark brown upperparts; white underparts with dark mottling on sides, wing linings and tips of undertail coverts; pink legs.

Size: *L* 19–20 in; *W* 43 in.

Status: rare offshore visitor, most common in fall, usually near trawlers.

Habitat: open ocean, usually well out over the continental shelf; rarely within several miles of shore.

Nesting: does not nest in Washington.

Feeding: plunges into water or dives shallowly from water's surface; swims underwater over short distances; gleans from the surface; fish, squid and crustaceans probably form bulk of diet.

Voice: generally silent; birds competing for food may make quarrelsome noises.

Similar Species: *Northern Fulmar* (p. 94): stouter body; light morph has unmarked, white head and underparts, and stout, greenish yellow to orangy bill. *Buller's Shearwater* (p. 96): all-black bill; gray-and-black upperwing pattern in flight, with more gleaming, thoroughly white underparts, especially the narrow-bordered underwing. *Flesh-footed Shearwater* (p. 360) and *Sooty Shearwater* (p. 97): entirely dark bodies.

Best Sites: open ocean well offshore; occasionally seen on pelagic boat trips leaving from Westport.

BULLER'S SHEARWATER

Puffinus bulleri

With a clear "W" pattern on its back, the Buller's Shearwater declares its home turf: the water. A common visitor to Washington's offshore waters in early fall, this large bird glides effortlessly over the ocean between the U.S. Pacific Coast and New Zealand, where it nests. It is eagerly watched for on pelagic boat trips that depart from Westport, and sightings are always cause for celebration. • This bird's population on the Poor Knights Islands off the coast of New Zealand, one of their main breeding areas, has recovered from near extinction following the eradication of feral pigs there. • Shearwaters were named *Puffinus* in the 15th century, when the word was freely used to describe various pelagic seabirds such as shearwaters, puffins and razorbills. • Formerly known as "New Zealand Shearwater," Buller's Shearwater was renamed for Sir Walter Lowry Buller, one of New Zealand's foremost ornithologists.

ID: black "cap"; black bill; white underparts. *In flight:* gray back with black "W"; white underwings outlined with black; dark wing and tail tips.
Size: *L* 16–18 in; *W* 3–3½ ft.
Status: common offshore visitor from August through October.
Habitat: open ocean.

Nesting: does not nest in Washington.
Feeding: techniques include hovering to dip bill in water and submerging head; eats small fish and squid.
Voice: silent at sea.
Similar Species: *Pink-footed Shearwater* (p. 95): black-tipped, pink bill; all-brown above, with no distinct back pattern; white underparts with dark smudges; pink legs; underwings show thicker dark outline.
Best Sites: open ocean far offshore; usually seen on pelagic boat trips leaving from Westport; very occasionally from land at Westport or Ocean Shores.

SOOTY SHEARWATER
Puffinus griseus

Each summer, in numbers beyond estimation, shearwaters of several species arrive from breeding islands in the southern hemisphere. One of the world's commonest birds, the Sooty Shearwater dominates the tens of thousands of birds spread out on the open ocean. Any boat trip between May and September will reveal scattered individuals or huge flocks. Because these shearwaters are the most numerous birds in most mixed-seabird foraging flocks on the continental shelf, it is often easiest to identify other shearwater species by their differences from the Sooty. • The Sooty is one of the few shearwater species that prefers water close to land. Large concentrations of fish often draw it there and into competition with other seabirds, including pelicans, cormorants and gulls. Using a telescope, you may well find some Sooties without even venturing out to sea.

ID: sooty brown overall, with slightly paler underparts; grayer "chin" and throat; long, slender, black bill; blackish, rounded tail; black to gray legs and feet. *In flight:* possible silvery flash in underwings; feet extend just beyond tail; strong, direct flight with several deep flaps followed by long glide.
Size: *L* 16–18 in; *W* 3–3½ ft.
Status: common offshore visitor from late April to mid-October, occasionally with large numbers close to shore or in Grays Harbor or Willapa Bay; rare in winter.
Habitat: open ocean, especially at upwellings and within a few miles of shore; some birds enter larger estuaries.

Nesting: does not nest in Washington.
Feeding: gleans the water's surface or snatches underwater prey in a shallow dive or plunge; eats mostly fish, squid and crustaceans; gathers in large concentrations around fishing vessels but ignores other ships.
Voice: usually silent; occasionally utters quarrelsome calls when competing for food.
Similar Species: *Short-tailed Shearwater* (p. 98): slightly smaller; sometimes has pale "chin" and throat; smaller bill; more uniformly colored underwings. *Flesh-footed Shearwater* (p. 360): black-tipped, pinkish bill; pale pinkish legs and feet; uniformly dark underwings; slower wingbeats.
Best Sites: pelagic boat trips leaving from Westport; Pt. Brown jetty, Ocean Shores; Westport jetty; North Head Lighthouse and North Jetty (Columbia R. mouth); Cape Flattery.

97

SHORT-TAILED SHEARWATER

Puffinus tenuirostris

Cruising the pelagic zone with quick wingbeats and short, efficient glides, flocks of Short-tailed Shearwaters are best seen off the coast of Washington from fall through early spring. These birds are found mostly off the shores of Alaska and the Bering Strait during summer, but they move as far south as California in winter. Often seen in the large shearwater flocks gathered around deep-sea trawlers to partake of the discarded bycatch, Short-tails prefer cold, deep waters and are commonly found far out to sea. The young birds tarry along our coastline awhile, but the adults head to Australia to breed, beginning the traverse over the South Pacific's tropical waters in fall. • The name "shearwater" was given to this low-flying group of birds because, as a bird banks left or right, its lower wing tip appears to slit or "shear" the surface of the water.

ID: usually dark overall; may have dark "cap" or pale throat; steep forehead with bulbous crown; short bill. *In flight:* possibly pale wing linings.
Size: *L* 17 in; *W* 3¼ ft.
Status: uncommon offshore from October through April; rare from May to early June and mid-August to late September.
Habitat: open ocean; over continental shelf; over cool waters or upwellings.

Nesting: does not nest in Washington.
Feeding: food varies with region; dives or drops feetfirst into water; may dive to depths of 60 ft; commonly eats fish, crustaceans, squid or octopus; sometimes takes jellyfish, aquatic worms or insects; occasionally forages with whale pods or dolphins.
Voice: generally silent at sea.
Similar Species: *Sooty Shearwater* (p. 97): crown not as rounded; longer bill; more prominent pale wing linings.
Best Sites: open ocean far offshore; rarely seen from pelagic boat trips leaving from Westport.

FORK-TAILED STORM-PETREL

Oceanodroma furcata

The Fork-tailed Storm-Petrel's secretive nesting strategy typifies the breeding habits of the small tubenoses. To minimize predation, a pair will place its single egg at the end of an underground burrow. The adults maintain a strictly nocturnal schedule of incubation shift changes and make nightly visits with food for the growing nestling. Foraging miles from the nest during the day, members of the colony disperse over the open ocean to feed in colder water over banks on the continental shelf. • Although they sometimes fly alongside ships, Fork-tails are usually attracted only by fishing vessels discarding fish oil and small waste items. • These storm-petrels can appear inshore (but very rarely inland), closely approaching beaches, jetties and piers, in April and May. They may also be seen inshore when ocean temperatures rise in late summer or if driven there by westerly gales in late fall.

ID: dark eye patch; pale bluish gray upperparts, darker at wing tips; pale gray underparts. *In flight:* deeply forked tail; flutters low across the ocean's surface with rapid, shallow wingbeats interspersed with brief glides.
Size: *L* 8–9 in; *W* 18 in.
Status: common offshore from mid-April through October and uncommon to rare the rest of the year; annual but uncommon on inland waters, usually after storms.
Habitat: cold, open ocean waters from near shore to beyond the continental shelf; occasionally visits bays and estuaries; often found in large Leach's Storm-Petrel colonies.

Nesting: colonial; on a vegetated offshore islet; in a self-excavated burrow, rock crevice or old burrow excavated by other species, sometimes having many side channels with additional nest chambers; pair incubates 1 white egg with dark terminal dots for 37 or more days; pair takes turns at night feeding the nestling.
Feeding: skims or snatches small fish, crustaceans and floating natural oils from the surface while hovering; will drop briefly onto the water or glean and pick while swimming.
Voice: usually silent away from breeding sites; low-pitched trilling calls at the nest.
Similar Species: *Leach's Storm-Petrel* (p. 100): much darker; white rump; dark wing linings; erratic, bouncy flight.
Best Sites: offshore; usually seen from pelagic boat trips leaving from Westport; very occasionally seen from Ocean Shores or Westport.

LEACH'S STORM-PETREL

Oceanodroma leucorhoa

Familiar to many coastal residents, the Leach's Storm-Petrel is one of the more widespread small storm-petrels. Appearing longer-winged than most, it has a buoyant and graceful, weaving flight that incorporates deep, ternlike wing-beats and very short, shearwater-like glides on bowed wings for an overall nighthawk-like effect. • The presence of storm-petrels was once believed to foretell an approaching storm. The word "petrel" may derive from "Peter," comparing the apostle's water-walking attempt to the habit some storm-petrels have of dangling their feet to patter on the water's surface. Because of their tiny size and erratic flight, storm-petrels are sometimes called "Sea Swallows." • Storm-petrel colonies can be extremely large, but the highly nocturnal parents are rarely seen nearby.

ID: dark brown head and underparts; slender, black bill; whitish rump with gray center line; black legs. *In flight:* conspicuous lighter diagonal band separates brown and blackish parts of upperwings; often shows deep fork in tail; buoyant, graceful, weaving flight with deep wingbeats and short glides; occasionally hangs motionless with wings raised slightly and feet pattering on the water's surface.

Size: *L* 8–9 in; *W* 18–19 in.

Status: common to uncommon far offshore from March to September, rare from October through February; locally common breeder on the outer Olympic coast from May to August; storms occasionally force birds inland.

Habitat: warmer waters at least 75 mi from shore.

Nesting: strongly colonial; on an offshore island or islet; uses a rock crevice or an old burrow excavated by another species, or the male excavates a burrow; pair incubates 1 white egg, purplish-dotted at the large end, for 37–50 days.

Feeding: skims or snatches small fish, squid, crustaceans, jellyfish and floating natural oils from the water's surface while hovering; rarely picks and gleans while swimming.

Voice: usually silent; commonly gives purring, chattering and trilling nocturnal notes at the nest site.

Similar Species: *Fork-tailed Storm-Petrel* (p. 99): paler bluish gray and gray; pale flight feathers and dark wing linings; more direct flight. *Sooty* (p. 97), *Short-tailed* (p. 98) and *Flesh-footed* (p. 360) *shearwaters:* much larger; all-dark rumps; strong, direct flight; short flaps and longer glides.

Best Sites: open ocean far offshore; occasional on Westport pelagic trips from late July to early August and rarely from late April to early May.

AMERICAN WHITE PELICAN
Pelecanus erythrorhynchos

When foraging, American White Pelicans swim through schools of small fish, plunging their bills beneath the surface. As they lift their bills from the water, they keep one or more fish trapped within their flexible pouches as they drain the water out before swallowing. These huge birds sometimes forage alone, but typically they work together in flocks to herd schools of fish into shallows. • Unlike Brown Pelicans, American White Pelicans breed in colonies on undisturbed, barren, rocky islands in large lakes and freshwater marshes—they are rarely seen with their cousins on saltwater estuaries. • The true grace of the White Pelican is appreciated when a flock is seen gliding and soaring effortlessly using thermals.

nonbreeding

ID: white overall; orange throat patch; naked, orange skin patch around eyes; massive, yellowish orange bill; short, white tail. *Breeding:* pale yellow crest on back of head; small, keeled, upright plate on upper mandible. *In flight:* black flight feathers; S-shaped neck.
Size: *L* 4–6 ft; *W* 9–12 ft.
Status: fairly common from February through mid-October along the Columbia R. in eastern Washington and otherwise less common; rare visitor to the west; summer breeder on Crescent I. and Badger I. in the Columbia R. and at Sprague L.; state-listed as endangered.
Habitat: *Breeding:* large interior lakes with barren islands. *In migration* and *winter:* lakes, rivers and large ponds.
Nesting: colonial; on a bare, low-lying, rocky island; nest scrape is rimmed with

gravel soil and nearby material and may be lined with pebbles; pair incubates 2 chalky white eggs for 30–33 days; first-hatched nestling is always fed first with regurgitated food.
Feeding: dips along the surface for small fish, amphibians and sluggish bottom-feeders; small groups often herd fish cooperatively; sometimes steals fish from other birds.
Voice: generally silent; brief, low grunts at colony site; loud squawks and "begging" calls by young.
Similar Species: *Brown Pelican* (p. 102): smaller; much darker; duskier bill; coastal. *Snow Goose* (p. 39): much smaller; smaller bill; neck extended in flight. *Tundra Swan* (p. 44) and *Trumpeter Swan* (p. 43): smaller, dark bills; longer, thinner necks held straight in flight; all-white wings.
Best Sites: below Wanapum Dam (Kittitas Co.); Paterson Unit, Umatilla NWR; Columbia R. in Tri-Cities area; Hanford Reach (Columbia R.); Wilson Creek near town of Wilson Creek.

BROWN PELICAN
Pelecanus occidentalis

Often seen perched on rocks or pilings, lined up on the water or flying past in single file, Brown Pelicans tolerate close inspection. Their easy grace in flight and tumbling dives elicit admiration from even the most blasé observer. • Numbers have recovered following a DDT-related decline in California's nesting population in the 1950s and 1960s, increasing the post-breeding dispersal into Washington, but these birds are still considered endangered. • Some of Washington's Brown Pelicans arrive from Mexico as early as late April, spending summer and fall in estuaries, at river mouths and along the open seacoast, although no nesting has been reported yet. The majority of migrants arrive in July and August. More and more birds are lingering beyond October, but most are gone by the end of November.

breeding

ID: very large, dusky bill; grayish brown upperparts; dark brown underparts; relatively short tail. *Nonbreeding:* yellow wash on head; pale yellowish pouch; white neck. *Breeding:* yellow head; red pouch; dark rufous brown nape and lower neck patch; white foreneck.
Size: *L* 3½–4 ft; *W* 6½–7 ft.
Status: fairly common in relatively small flocks along the outer coast from early July to late October, uncommon from mid-May to early July and rare to accidental the rest of the year; federally and state-listed as endangered.

Habitat: coastal and estuarine waters within 1 mi of shore; visits offshore islands; roosts on islets, sea stacks, sandbars, piers and jetties.
Nesting: does not nest in Washington
Feeding: forages almost exclusively for fish, caught by diving headfirst into water from heights of up to 60 ft; holds fish in its flexible pouch until the water has drained out.
Voice: usually silent; possible heronlike alarm call when startled.
Similar Species: *American White Pelican* (p. 101): all-white body; yellowish orange bill and legs; black flight feathers.
Best Sites: Damon Pt., Pt. Brown jetty and Grays Harbor (all Ocean Shores); Westport; North Head Lighthouse and North Jetty (Columbia R. mouth).

BRANDT'S CORMORANT

Phalacrocorax penicillatus

The largest of the three species of cormorants found along Washington's coast year-round is the Brandt's Cormorant. It and the Pelagic Cormorant often nest and forage in close proximity. The Brandt's Cormorant nests in more expansive colonies than the Pelagic, which prefers near-inaccessible small ledges and nooks. • Brandt's colonies are often isolated from each other, with breeding adults scattering widely to feed anywhere from within the surf zone to several miles offshore. • The species is named for J.F. Brandt, who distinguished the first specimen in Russia's St. Petersburg Academy of Sciences collection.

breeding

ID: dark bluish green eyes; heavy, hooked, blackish brown bill; buff brown throat patch. *Breeding:* green-glossed, blackish plumage; bright blue throat patch; white plumes on neck and upper back. *Nonbreeding:* duller, grayer plumage; less glossy head and rump. *In flight:* straight neck.

Size: *L* 32–35 in; *W* 3¾–4 ft.

Status: fairly common year-round coastal resident; migrants increase fall numbers; breeds on the northern part of Olympic Peninsula and at Cape Disappointment; nonbreeders are common in summer in the San Juans, northern Puget Sound and the Olympic Peninsula; candidate for state threatened list.

Habitat: restricted to marine waters. *Foraging:* sandy and rocky underwater substrates, offshore during migration but close to shore in winter. *Roosting:* offshore reefs, rocks and breakwaters.

Nesting: colonial; on a barren area on an offshore island, islet or sea stack or protected headland; pair cements nest of sticks and seaweed with guano and lines it

with eelgrass or seaweed; pair incubates 3–4 pale blue to whitish, nest-stained eggs on their webbed feet for 29–31 days.

Feeding: forages 150 ft deep or more for fish; also takes some crabs, shrimp and other invertebrates.

Voice: deep, low grunts and croaks at the nesting colony.

Similar Species: *Double-crested Cormorant* (p. 104): yellowish to orangy throat region; longer wings and tail; flies with neck bent; more vocal. *Pelagic Cormorant* (p. 105): slender bill; small red throat patch and white flank patches in breeding plumage.

Best Sites: *Summer:* small groups at Cape Disappointment (Columbia R. mouth) and the outer Olympic Peninsula coast. *Winter:* Point No Point; San Juans; Pt. Wilson (Port Townsend) and Keystone (Whidbey I.); Ocean Shores.

DOUBLE-CRESTED CORMORANT

Phalacrocorax auritus

Double-crested Cormorants are a familiar sight at most large bodies of water and are easy to recognize, whether flying past in loose formation, swimming, diving or loafing and drying their wings atop pilings or in trees. Unlike Washington's other two cormorant species, this one is equally at home on the coast or inland, and coastal birds will go far up rivers and onto freshwater lakes to forage. • Cormorants often partially spread their wings to dry the flight feathers. Waterlogged feathers (which decrease buoyancy), rudderlike tails, sealed nostrils and excellent underwater vision all enhance their aquatic abilities. • The common name and *auritis* both refer to the crest of short, whitish "eyebrow" plumes of the breeding plumage.

juvenille

breeding

ID: blackish overall, sometimes with greenish gloss; green eyes; thin, hook-tipped, gray bill; yellowish throat pouch; black-scaled, coppery brown back; long neck; long tail. *Breeding:* intensified throat-pouch color; fine, whitish "eyebrow" plumes (darkening in late summer). *In flight:* long wings; short tail; bent neck.
Size: *L* 26–32 in; *W* 4–4½ ft.
Status: common year-round along the coast and in western inland waters; common breeder at large eastern reservoirs from May through September.
Habitat: *Breeding:* interior wetlands, lakes, reservoirs and rivers; offshore islands, sea stacks and various coastal habitats. *In migration* and *winter:* lowland and near-coastal waters.
Nesting: colonial, often with other species; on a low-lying island, in an extensive marsh, high in a tree, or on a sea stack; mass of sticks, vegetation and debris is cemented into the platform with guano; pair incubates 3–4 pale blue, nest-stained eggs for 25–28 days.
Feeding: makes long dives up to 30 ft deep to catch fish and, less often, amphibians and invertebrates.
Voice: generally quiet; possible piglike grunts or croaks, especially near nest colonies.
Similar Species: *Brandt's Cormorant* (p. 103): buff brown throat patch; bluish green eyes; all-black bill; shorter tail; bluish throat patch in breeding plumage; flies with neck straight. *Pelagic Cormorant* (p. 105): slender, all-black bill; small red throat patch and white flank patches in breeding plumage.
Best Sites: *West:* Puget Trough; San Juans; Olympic Peninsula; outer coast (Ocean Shores, Westport and Tokeland). *East:* Moses L. and Potholes Reservoir in summer.

PELAGIC CORMORANT

Phalacrocorax pelagicus

Despite its name, the Pelagic Cormorant prefers the nearshore zone, leaving offshore waters to the Brandt's Cormorant. • The Pelagic Cormorant is an almost reptilian-looking bird, sleek and black with a subtle iridescent green and purplish blue gloss at close range. Its long, slender neck and slender bill can be twisted and turned at will. This bird appears particularly elegant in its breeding plumage. It is the smallest of Washington's three cormorant species. • Cormorants have powerful, fully webbed feet that aid swimming and diving, plus a naked, extensible throat patch. The throat patch is used in a panting behavior known as "gular fluttering," perhaps to cool the body by bringing air across the blood vessels of the throat. • Pelagic Cormorants are less colonial than other cormorants and less sociable, almost never forming feeding flocks or flying in formation.

ID: dark, greenish-glossed plumage; small head; slender, all-black bill; slender neck. *Breeding:* 2 scruffy head crests; small, red throat patch (visible at close range); white flank patches.

Size: *L* 25–28 in; *W* 3–3¼ ft.

Status: common year-round in marine waters.

Habitat: restricted to marine waters. *Breeding:* along the coast and on offshore islands and sea stacks. *Foraging:* open ocean within 1 mi of shore and lower reaches of estuaries and harbors.

Nesting: loosely colonial; on a narrow cliff ledge or flat area; pair builds (and reuses) a nest of grass, seaweed, moss and sticks; pair incubates 3–5 greenish white eggs for 25–33 days.

breeding

Feeding: forages by swimming up to 120 ft deep to catch mainly fish but also shrimp, crabs, crustaceans, marine worms and some algae.

Voice: generally silent; sometimes utters low groans at the nest site.

Similar Species: *Brandt's Cormorant* (p. 103): larger; heavier bill. *Double-crested Cormorant* (p. 104): larger; larger head; heavier bill; conspicuous pale yellow or yellowish orange throat patch.

Best Sites: Keystone and Libbey Beach (Whidbey I.); Port Townsend; Cape Flattery; San Juans; Ocean Shores; Cape Disappointment (Columbia R. mouth).

AMERICAN BITTERN

Botaurus lentiginosus

The deep, booming call of the American Bittern is as characteristic of a spring marsh as the sounds of croaking frogs. • When approached by an intruder, this bird's first reaction is to stay put, point its bill skyward and keep its streaked breast toward danger, swaying in time with surrounding plant stems. An American Bittern will instinctively adopt this tactic even if completely in the open, apparently unaware that a lack of cover betrays its presence! Its camouflage also helps it forage more stealthily in its marshy freshwater hunting grounds. • At first glance, an adult American Bittern might be mistaken for a young night-heron or Green Heron, both of which have streaked necks.

ID: large; stocky; noticeable black "whisker"; straight, straw-colored bill; buff-mottled, brown upperparts; pale buff underparts with brown streaking from "chin" down through breast and flanks; conspicuous white patch visible on shoulders when bird calls; yellowish green legs and feet. *In flight:* dark flight feathers and outer half of upperwing; faster wingbeats than other herons; neck held tucked in.

Size: *L* 23–27 in; *W* 3½ ft.

Status: uncommon and local in marshes, from mid-April through mid-November in the west and from mid-April to late September in the east; rare in winter.

Habitat: freshwater and brackish marshes with tall, dense emergent vegetation; migrants can visit almost any body of water, including ditches, wet fields and urban ponds.

Nesting: above the waterline in a dense cattail or bulrush marsh; nest platform is made of grass, sedges and dead reeds; nest often has separate entrance and exit paths; female incubates 4–5 plain buff eggs for 24–28 days and feeds the young by regurgitation.

Feeding: stand-and-wait predator; forages at any time, especially dawn and dusk; stabs for small fish, amphibians, aquatic insects and crustaceans; occasionally takes small mammals and snakes.

Voice: deep, slow, resonant, repetitive *pomp-er-lunk* or *onk-a-blonk;* most often heard in the evening or at night.

Similar Species: *Green Heron* (p. 109): immature is smaller, more heavily marked and has different facial markings. *Black-crowned Night-Heron* (p. 110): immature is grayer overall, has white-spotted upperparts and different facial markings and is more active at night.

Best Sites: Nisqually NWR; Ocean City SP; Skagit Game Range; Union Bay Natural Area (Montlake Fill, Seattle); Ridgefield NWR; Toppenish NWR.

GREAT BLUE HERON

Ardea herodias

Even the smallest and most isolated patches of suitable habitat can attract Great Blue Herons. Because they frequent rivers, lakeshores, beaches, sand flats and piers—and even some urban parks—visited by people, they are seen more often at close range than any other heron. The north-central states know these birds only as summer residents, but we can see them year-round in Washington. • Although these herons appear clumsy when taking off, once airborne, their slow, steady progress enables them to travel long distances with ease. • Slow-motion movements and an absence of fluffy, bunched feathers hanging over the tail distinguish these herons from cranes. Also, Great Blues fly with their necks held in a shallow "S," whereas cranes keep their necks straight. • The Great Blue Heron has been the official bird of the City of Seattle since 2003.

breeding

ID: bluish gray overall; long, straight, daggerlike bill; long, dark-striped, gray neck; long, dark legs with chestnut thighs. *Breeding:* intensified colors; thin, pointed plumes extend from crown and throat. *In flight:* head and upper neck held in "S"; legs and feet extend well beyond tail; chestnut stripe on leading edge of underwing.
Size: *L* 4¼–4½ ft; *W* 6 ft.
Status: common year-round resident statewide.
Habitat: almost any freshwater habitat or calm-water intertidal habitat, including farmlands and occasionally urban areas.

Nesting: colonial; in a tree, snag, tall bush or marsh vegetation; stick-and-twig platform nest up to 4 ft in diameter is lined with pine needles, moss, reeds and dry grass; may be refurbished for reuse; pair incubates 3–5 pale blue eggs for 27–29 days; pair feeds the young by regurgitation.
Feeding: stand-and-wait predator or slowly stalks prey in shallow water or grass; impales fish, amphibians, reptiles, invertebrates, small mammals and birds with its bill; occasionally scavenges carrion, including discarded fish remains and domestic animal carcasses in winter.
Voice: usually quiet away from the nest; occasionally gives a deep, harsh *fwaark* call at takeoff.
Similar Species: none in this region.
Best Sites: wetlands; riparian corridors; marshes.

GREAT EGRET

Ardea alba

Foraging individually over a wide area by day, Great Egrets gather at sunset before returning to communal nighttime roosting sites in undisturbed stands of trees or, in summer, to their nests. • During the breeding season, egrets develop their characteristic ornamental plumes, and the color of face and leg skin intensifies. • Great Egrets are the largest of a nearly worldwide group of generally white, small to medium-large herons. In the 1800s, Great Egrets and many other showy, colony-nesting waterbirds were nearly extirpated in North America because their plumes were used to decorate women's hats. Outrage over the destruction of adults and the starvation of orphaned nestlings helped change public opinion and start the National Audubon Society (with the Great Egret as its symbol). Great Egrets are increasing in Washington and nest in several locations.

nonbreeding

breeding

Habitat: almost any open or semi-open wetland habitat; favors expansive shallows, marshes and rushy lakeshores; regularly found on inner estuarine tidal flats.

Nesting: colonial; in a tree, shrub or thicket; pair builds a stick platform and incubates 3–4 pale bluish green eggs for 23–26 days; both adults feed the young by regurgitation.

ID: white plumage; yellow bill; short tail; long, all-black legs and feet. *Breeding:* orangy yellow bill; white plumes trail from throat and rump. *In flight:* black feet extend well beyond tail.

Size: *L* 3–3½ ft; *W* 4¼ ft.

Status: fairly common breeder from late April to early October in the Potholes area and the Columbia Basin; uncommon visitor to the southwest from mid-July to late October; uncommon breeder at Ridgefield NWR; rare winter visitor along the southwestern coast.

Feeding: stand-and-wait predator or actively forages in shallow water; eats mostly fish but also takes aquatic and inter-tidal invertebrates, amphibians, reptiles, rodents and small birds.

Voice: rapid, low-pitched, loud *kuk-kuk-kuk,* usually only when flushed or alarmed.

Similar Species: *Cattle Egret* (p. 361): smaller; stockier; yellow or purplish patch above shorter, yellow or reddish orange bill; dusky red legs and feet; buff plumes in breeding plumage. *Snowy Egret* (p. 360): smaller; stockier; mostly black bill; black-and-yellow legs; yellow feet; white plumes in breeding plumage.

Best Sites: *Summer:* Potholes Reservoir (breeding); Hanford Reach (Columbia R.); Ridgefield NWR.

GREEN HERON

Butorides virescens

Green Herons favor shrubby stream meanders, the backwaters of sluggish rivers, undisturbed pond margins and protected estuarine shallows, where they can feed without being discovered. While foraging, these small, colorful herons move furtively within easy flight distance of sheltering vegetation. However, they will risk exposed stream outflows, rushy tidal channels, breakwaters, disused piers and sheltered mudflats, often using the cover of logs and branches, to get closer to their prey. Green Herons will also drop feathers, leaves and other small objects onto the water's surface to lure small fish within striking distance. • Green Herons arrive in Washington earlier in spring than most other herons and leave later in fall. • The Latin word *virescens* means "becoming green," referring to the transition from a streaky brown juvenile to a greenish adult.

ID: greenish black crown; chestnut face; bluish gray back and wings with iridescent, green sheen; white-streaked, brownish purple underparts and throat; chestnut neck; short, yellowish orange legs. *Breeding male:* bright orange legs. *Immature:* dusky bill; dull brown upperparts; heavier streaking on underparts; greenish legs. *In flight:* contrasting feet extend past tail.

Size: *L* 15–22 in; *W* 26 in.

Status: uncommon in the west from April to late October and rare visitor for the rest of the year; very rare in the east from mid-September to mid-October.

Habitat: freshwater and tidal shores, ponds, streamside willows, mudflat edges and similar sheltered or semi-wooded situations.

Nesting: singly or in small, loose groups; male constructs a stick platform in a tree or shrub, very close to water; pair incubates 3–5 pale green to bluish, brown-stained eggs for 19–21 days; young are fed by regurgitation.

Feeding: stabs prey with bill after slowly stalking or while standing and waiting; adult occasionally plunges into deeper water; eats mostly small fish, frogs, tadpoles, crustaceans and aquatic insects.

Voice: generally silent except when startled; loud *kowp, kyow* or *skow* alarm and flight calls; harsh *raah* in aggression.

Similar Species: *American Bittern* (p. 106): larger; noticeable black "whisker"; buff neck and breast with heavy, brown streaks; dark flight feathers.

Best Sites: Ocean City SP; Skagit Game Range; Union Bay Natural Area (Montlake Fill, Seattle); Marymoor Park (Redmond); Three Forks Natural Area (North Bend); Black River NWR.

BLACK-CROWNED NIGHT-HERON

Nycticorax nycticorax

Herons offer a clear example of successful diversification. All have relatively large, pointed bills with which they spear prey, but these birds can be large or tiny, brilliantly colored or drab, reclusive or highly social, and diurnal or nocturnal. • Average in most regards, Black-crowned Night-Herons have large, light-sensitive eyes, allowing them to feed in much lower light situations than other herons and egrets. Hunting mostly by night, thereby avoiding competition, Black-crowns disperse widely into almost any habitat offering aquatic or estuarine prey. • The adults are boldly patterned, yet their countershading and relative lack of movement render them inconspicuous in the dappled shadows of their daytime hangouts. The streaked plumage of immatures also provides excellent camouflage among tree branches and in marsh vegetation.

breeding

immature

ID: black "cap"; large, red eyes; stout, black bill; black back; pale gray wings; dull yellow legs. *Breeding:* 2 long, white plumes trail from crown. *Immature:* streaked, brown-and-white head and underparts; dark-topped, pale bill; white-spotted, brownish gray upperwings; gray underwings. *In flight:* "lazy" wingstrokes; stubby neck; little foot extension.
Size: *L* 23–26 in; *W* 3½ ft.
Status: common breeder from mid-April to late August in the Columbia Basin and uncommon for the rest of the year; rare in the west.
Habitat: *Foraging:* marshes, mudflats, cropland, ponds and slow-moving streams.

Breeding: dense stands of trees and brush, often in seclusion.
Nesting: colonial; female uses material gathered by the male to make a loose stick nest lined with roots and grass; pair incubates 3–5 greenish eggs for 23–26 days.
Feeding: chiefly at night, but also by day; stalks or waits quietly for fish, amphibians, reptiles, invertebrates, such as mollusks, and small birds and mammals.
Voice: deep, guttural *quark* or *wok*, often on takeoff.
Similar Species: *American Bittern* (p. 106): buff-mottled, brown back; dark flight feathers and upperwing tip; rarely sits hunched in waterside shrubbery. *Great Blue Heron* (p. 107): much larger; longer, more heavily marked neck; longer legs.
Best Sites: Potholes Reservoir; Desert Wildlife Area; Marsh Unit 1, Columbia NWR; Dry Falls Dam–Banks L.; Madame Dorian Park (Walla Walla Co.); Whitman Mission Historic Park.

TURKEY VULTURE

Cathartes aura

Turkey Vultures are among North America's greatest wanderers, literally "following their noses." Their advanced sense of smell, coupled with a large wing area relative to their weight, have enabled Turkey Vultures to patrol broad stretches of countryside for dead animals. They move from one bubble of warm, rising air to another, soaring with long wings and tail spread to the fullest extent, teasing the greatest performance possible for minimal energy expenditure. • Turkey Vultures are dependent on carrion, and their bills and feet are not designed to kill or crush living animals. Often maligned by the general public, they perform a valuable service by disposing of smelly carcasses. The naked head, like that of some carrion-eating storks, is an adaptation to deter bacteria and parasites.

ID: very large; mostly dark brown; small, featherless, red head; dark "collar." *Immature:* gray head. *In flight:* head seems hunched between shoulders; silvery gray flight feathers; black wing linings; wings held in shallow "V"; tilts when soaring.
Size: *L* 26–32 in; *W* 5¾–6 ft.
Status: fairly common breeder from April to October on the east slopes of the Cascades; fairly common breeder from April to September in the west; common western migrant from mid-September to early October; absent from the Columbia Basin.
Habitat: cruises over almost all terrestrial and shoreline habitats but favors valley edges and foothills for regular thermals; roosts, sometimes colonially, in large trees, especially cottonwoods.
Nesting: on bare ground, among boulders, in a hollow tree or on the forest floor; no nest material is used; pair incubates 2–3 dull or creamy white eggs for 30–40 days; feeds nestlings by regurgitation.
Feeding: scavenger; eats carrion of nearly any type, including mammals, reptiles and beached fish.
Voice: generally silent; occasionally hisses or grunts if threatened.
Similar Species: *Golden Eagle* (p. 124): generally brown plumage, lighter on head; darker flight feathers; brown wing linings; wings appear flat or slightly uptilted in profile; does not rock in flight. *Hawks* (pp. 116–23): generally smaller; shorter, broader wings usually flat when soaring; many have distinctive tail color or pattern.
Best Sites: Teanaway River Valley (Kittitas Co.); Audubon Rd. (Wenas); Oak Creek Wildlife Area (Yakima Co.); Klickitat River Gorge; Meadow Rd. (Cusick). *Fall:* Salt Creek CP (Clallam Co.).

OSPREY
Pandion haliaetus

The highly successful Osprey is thriving on all continents except Antarctica. The only species in its genus, the Osprey is so superbly adapted for catching fish that it has been able to succeed in many different situations. Its primarily white undersides disappear against the sky as it flies high above lakes, rivers and bays in search of fish just below the surface, and its dark "mask" reduces the blinding glare of sunshine skipping off the water. Two other important features also aid in catching fish. Two toes facing forward and two toes facing backward, and a heavily scaled sole, help the Osprey clamp tightly onto slippery fish. Also, frequent preening makes Osprey feathers more water resistant than those of other raptors.

ID: light crown; dark eye line; yellow eyes; dark brown upperparts; long wings extend beyond tail at rest; white underparts; white throat; fine "necklace," darkest on female; bluish gray legs and feet. *In flight:* long, narrow, distinctively kinked wings; dark "wrist" patch; narrowly banded tail.
Size: *L* 22–25 in; *W* 4½–6 ft.
Status: fairly common breeder in the west from April to early September; fairly common breeder in the east from late March to late August; casual to rare in winter.
Habitat: lakes, reservoirs and rivers; open seacoast. *In migration:* urban lakes and ponds.
Nesting: on an exposed treetop, pole or tower; builds a nest of sticks and twigs,

possibly on a platform or base of sticks; male helps female incubate 2–3 pale, usually pinkish eggs with brown or olive markings for 32–43 days.
Feeding: hovers, then dives feetfirst from up to 100 ft in the air for small fish, usually under 2 lb in weight, sometimes plunging below the surface; also eats rodents, birds, other small vertebrates and crustaceans.
Voice: pair is very vocal around the nest site; piercing, whistled *chewk-chewk-chewk* and far-carrying *kip-kip-kip*.
Similar Species: *Red-tailed Hawk* (p. 121): smaller; dark head; pale rufous to dark brown underparts; shorter, broader wings, held flat when soaring; darker wing linings; reddish tail.
Best Sites: Port Gardner (mouth of Snohomish R.); Pend Oreille R.; riparian areas statewide.

WHITE-TAILED KITE

Elanus leucurus

Formerly known as "Black-shouldered Kite," the White-tailed Kite is the North American representative of a widespread family. Flying with grace and buoyancy uncommon among raptors, it has the look and general color pattern of a tern. • The White-tailed Kite hunts from dawn until deep evening twilight. When it spots a vole scurrying through the grass, it parachutes down on the rodent with wings held high. • Perhaps as protection against arboreal predators, the White-tailed Kite places its bulky nest near the top of a tree, away from the main trunk and larger limbs. • After being persecuted almost to extinction in the early 1900s, the White-tailed Kite was first sighted in Washington in the late 1980s and is now regular but local. Population fluctuations, apparently in tune with prey populations, are normal.

ID: dark eye patch; red eyes; yellow cere; small bill; light gray back (female is darkest); dark shoulders; white underparts; long, gray-centered, white tail; yellow feet. *In flight:* pointed wings; small, black "wrist" patch; buoyant flapping; hovers with body at steep angle; flies with wings in shallow "V."
Size: *L* 15–17 in; *W* 3¼ ft.
Status: uncommon and local, largely in the southwest, from mid-September to mid-May (particularly in winter); uncommon to rare summer breeder in the southwest.
Habitat: tree-dotted lowland or hillside fields; ungrazed or fallow grasslands; croplands; marshes; loose groups sometimes form in open fields.

Nesting: high in a tree, often an oak; pair builds a bulky stick platform lined with grass and other soft vegetation; female incubates 4 brown-blotched, creamy white eggs for 26–32 days.
Feeding: hovers over open country and dives after prey feetfirst; eats rodents, especially voles, but also small birds, snakes, frogs, lizards and large insects.
Voice: largely silent; short, repeated *keep keep keep* call; also utters a raspy *keerak* and a more guttural *grrrkkk*.
Similar Species: *Northern Harrier* (p. 115): male in flight is gray above and white beneath, with dark wing tips and trailing edges and banded tail, and he hovers infrequently. *Hawks* (pp. 116–23): shorter, broader, rounded wings. *Falcons* (pp. 125–29): more pointed wings; longer, narrower tails.
Best Sites: Raymond Airport; Chinook Valley Rd.; west of Littlerock; Julia Butler Hansen NWR; west of Centralia.

113

BALD EAGLE
Haliaeetus leucocephalus

Symbolic in both aboriginal myth and modern American culture, the threatened Bald Eagle has been helped in Washington by habitat protection, restoration of salmon stocks and less harassment at nesting and feeding sites. However, its resurgence may be adversely affecting Great Blue Heron and Common Murre nesting colonies. • Benjamin Franklin, a respected naturalist of his day, opposed selecting the Bald Eagle as our national bird because of its "dishonorable" habits of scavenging carrion and stealing fish from the smaller Osprey. Although most of an adult's food does consist of spawned-out salmon and other carrion, a Bald Eagle can catch its own prey. • A female returning to her nest site puts her mate through a series of aerial maneuvers to confirm his suitability, and not all males pass the test.

immature

the east; uncommon breeder in the Okanogan region and the northeast; federally and state-listed as threatened.

Habitat: *Breeding:* lakeshores, river corridors, estuaries and seacoasts. *In migration* and *winter:* coastal and inland waterways; occasionally farmlands.

Nesting: in a tree bordering a lake or wide river, occasionally on a cliff ledge or nest platform; huge stick nest; pair incubates 2 (rarely 3) white eggs for 34–36 days.

Feeding: opportunistic; swoops to the water's surface for fish or pirates fish from Osprey; some birds eat waterfowl; scavenges fish and carcasses.

ID: generally dark brown; white head; large, yellow cere and bill; white tail. *1st year:* brown overall; white patches; dark eyes. *2nd year:* dark head; whiter back and underparts; light belly; dark-tipped, white tail. *3rd year:* some white on head; dark eye stripe; paler eyes; yellow cere. *4th year:* largely white head and tail; some white on back and underwings; mainly dark underparts.

Size: *L* 30–43 in; *W* 5½–8 ft.

Status: common western year-round resident and increasing breeder; fairly common from December through early April in

Voice: weak squeaks and chirps; sometimes *kek-kek-kek-kek;* argumentative squawks and shrieks in group foraging; immature's calls are somewhat shriller.

Similar Species: adult is unmistakable. *Golden Eagle* (p. 124): resembles immature Bald Eagle, but with fully feathered legs and broad, dark terminal tail band; golden "hackles" on upper back and head.

Best Sites: *Summer:* San Juans; Olympic Peninsula; Seattle and suburbs. *Winter:* Skagit R.; Skagit Flats; Samish Flats; Banks L.

NORTHERN HARRIER
Circus cyaneus

The Northern Harrier, the only North American representative of its world-wide genus, may be the easiest raptor to identify on the wing, because no other hawk routinely flies so low. As it cruises across fields, meadows and marshes in search of prey, it uses both its excellent vision and its hearing, which is enhanced by its owl-like parabolic facial disc. • Males are less numerous than females. In areas with a plentiful food supply, a male can have as many as five mates and supply all five ground nests with food. • The genus name *Circus* is a reference to this bird's somewhat erratic flight pattern. The high maneuverability of this species inspired the British Royal Air Force's name for its Harrier aircraft.

ID: facial disc; small bill and talons; banded tail. *Male:* gray upperparts; white underparts; black wing tips and trailing edge; white underwings. *Female:* brown overall; brown-streaked, buff underparts; dark-barred underwings. *In flight:* long, somewhat pointed wings; white rump patch; long, narrow tail; unmistakable when coursing with wings held in a clear "V."

Size: *L* 16–24 in; *W* 3¾–4 ft.

Status: fairly common year-round in eastern Washington; fairly common from mid-August to May in the west, becoming uncommon and local from May to mid-August.

Habitat: open country, including fields, marshes and alpine meadows.

Nesting: on the ground, often on a mound started by the male and completed by the female; usually in shrubs, cattails or tall vegetation; nest of grass, sticks and cattails; female incubates 4–6 pale bluish eggs for 30–32 days; male provides food.

Feeding: glides low to the ground; eats mostly small prey, especially mice and voles, reptiles, amphibians and grasshoppers.

Voice: vocal during courtship, near the nest site and when repelling other harriers; rather peevish, high-pitched, repeated *kek* or *ke* alarm notes. *Female:* piercing, attention-getting, descending *eeyah eeyah* scream.

Similar Species: *Red-tailed Hawk* (p. 121) and *Swainson's Hawk* (p. 120): chunkier; brownish rumps; shorter, wider tails. *Rough-legged Hawk* (p. 123) and *Ferruginous Hawk* (p. 122): larger; broader wings; distinctively patterned, fanlike tails; different underwing patterns.

Best Sites: Samish Flats; Skagit Flats; Crockett L.; Spencer I.; open country and wetlands in the east. *Winter:* Ocean Shores and other grassy open areas.

SHARP-SHINNED HAWK

Accipiter striatus

When delivering food to his nestlings, a male Sharp-shinned Hawk is understandably cautious around his mate; the female is typically one-third larger. The small prey he supplies is suitable for small nestlings, but the female does much of the hunting when they get larger. Preying on different-sized mammals and birds helps increase the total food available. • Accipiters have short, rounded wings, long, rudder-like tails and a flap-and-glide flight, allowing these woodland hawks to negotiate a maze of tree trunks and foliage at high speed. They prefer using concealment and sneak attacks, however. • Sharp-shins can be secretive in summer, until the nest is approached. They are more visible in migration and at urban sites in winter. Small and medium-sized songbirds at rural bird feeders attract Sharp-shins, especially immatures, that might otherwise not overwinter here.

ID: bluish gray crown, upperwings and back; red eyes; fine rufous bars on white underparts; yellow legs. *Immature:* yellow eyes; brown upperparts; thick, brown markings on white underparts. *In flight:* small head; short, rounded wings; buff rufous wing linings; pale flight feathers spotted and barred with dark brown; long, heavily barred, squared-off tail.
Size: *Male: L* 10–12 in; *W* 20–24 in. *Female: L* 12–14 in; *W* 24–28 in.
Status: fairly common in migration from early April to May and from late August to mid-October and otherwise uncommon.

Habitat: dense to semi-open forests; riparian edges; small woodlots. *In migration:* alpine areas; foothills. *Winter:* feeders.
Nesting: in a tree, often in an abandoned crow nest; stick or twig nest is normally about 2 ft across; female incubates 4–5 pale bluish white eggs for up to 35 days; male brings food for the incubating female and hatchlings.
Feeding: mainly from a perch, pursues small birds in rapid, high-speed chases, taking more birds than other accipiters; occasionally takes small mammals, amphibians and insects.
Voice: generally silent; intense, repeated *kik-kik-kik-kik* warns intruders during the breeding season; migrating fall immature utters a clear *tewp*.
Similar Species: *Cooper's Hawk* (p. 117): usually larger; heavy-headed; rounded tail with more noticeable white terminal band.
Best Sites: appropriate habitats statewide. *In migration:* Cooper Ridge (Okanogan Co.–Chelan Co.), Entiat Ridge and Red Top Mt. (Kittitas Co.).

COOPER'S HAWK
Accipiter cooperii

With blinding speed, the Cooper's Hawk bursts from an overhead perch to ambush and pursue songbirds, grabbing them in midair with its sharp talons. • Even where it is common, the Cooper's Hawk is generally secretive and inconspicuous in breeding season. • Since DDT was banned in the U.S. and Canada, these forest hawks have slowly recolonized many of their former breeding sites, but many of them still suffer from the use of insecticides on their South and Central American wintering ranges. • Misinformed farmers and poultry producers sometimes shoot Cooper's Hawks, calling them "Chicken-Hawks." Although they do take some domestic poultry and wild grouse, they usually target smaller birds and small mammals.

immature

ID: bluish gray crown, upperwings and back; red eyes; yellow cere; fine, horizontal reddish barring on white underparts; yellow feet. *Immature:* yellow eyes; brown upperparts; thin, vertical blackish streaks on underparts. *In flight:* longish wings; long, round-ended, banded, white-tipped tail; white undertail coverts.
Size: *Male: L* 15–17 in; *W* 27–32 in. *Female: L* 17–19 in; *W* 32–37 in.
Status: fairly common from August to mid-October and otherwise uncommon.
Habitat: *Breeding:* broken woodlands, including woodlots, and brushland, especially in riparian areas, canyons and floodplains. *In migration* and *winter:* soars on thermals in open areas and along ridgelines; often visits urban areas and winters near feeders.
Nesting: in a tree fork, often in a Douglas-fir's outer branches, sometimes in a remodeled crow's nest; stick-and-twig nest is lined with bark flakes; female incubates 4–5 bluish eggs for 34–36 days and broods the young for 14 days; male brings food until

the female resumes hunting; pair feeds nestlings until fledging at around 50 days.
Feeding: often from a perch, pursues prey in rapid flight through the forest or at its edges; takes prey to a "plucking-post" or eats on the ground; male hunts birds up to robin-sized and mammals up to chipmunk-sized; female pursues grouse and occasional small ducks, squirrels and hares.
Voice: largely silent, except around nest; fast, barking, woodpecker-like *cac-cac-cac-cac* in alarm.
Similar Species: *Sharp-shinned Hawk* (p. 116): usually smaller; smaller head; darker nape; square-ended tail; thicker, redder streaks on immature's underparts.
Best Sites: present in most suitable habitats. *In migration:* Cooper Ridge (Okanogan Co.–Chelan Co.), Entiat Ridge and Red Top Mt. (Kittitas Co.).

117

NORTHERN GOSHAWK
Accipiter gentilis

The Northern Goshawk, the largest of the accipiters, has a legendary disposition. This hawk will attack a perceived threat of any size, including people too near its nest. It chases and catches prey in a high-speed aerial sprint and will even crash through brush to chase its quarry on foot. The Northern Goshawk kills by repeatedly stabbing its victim's internal organs with its long talons. • Attila the Hun, impressed by this hawk's strength and tenacity, had one adorning his helmet. • The *gentilis* part of the species name derives from this hawk's use as the preferred "falcon" of the gentry, with the similar-sized Gyrfalcon and smaller Peregrine Falcon reserved for kings and emperors.

immature

ID: dark "cap" and "cheek" patch; white "eyebrow"; yellow cere; bluish gray nape, back and upperwings; finely barred, gray underparts; white undertail; long, faintly banded tail; well-feathered legs; yellow feet. *Immature:* yellow eyes; brown-streaked, white underparts; dark-banded tail. *In flight:* robust and uniformly colored; short, broad wings; dark flight feathers on gray upperwing; purposeful flight; immature has brown-and-white-barred wings.
Size: *Male: L* 21–23 in; *W* 3¼–3½ ft. *Female: L* 23–25 in; *W* 3½–4 ft.
Status: uncommon migrant from mid-September to early November; rare to uncommon in lowlands in winter; rare

summer mountain resident; candidate for state threatened list.
Habitat: *Breeding:* mature montane coniferous forests (nonbreeders summer in riparian and open woodlands, canyons and forest edges); adversely affected by clear-cutting. *In migration* and *winter:* above mountain ridges and open country; any forest.
Nesting: in deep woods; in a fork, usually high in a hardwood; repeatedly used, bulky nest is made of sticks and twigs; female incubates 2–4 dirty white eggs for 28–32 days.
Feeding: perches briefly or flies low across open areas; flies through cover to snatch ground-dwelling birds, especially grouse, and rabbits and ground squirrels.
Voice: silent, except around nest site; loud, aggressive *kyk-kyk-kyk* and other loud, accipiter-type calls.
Similar Species: *Cooper's Hawk* (p. 117): smaller; fine, reddish breast bars; narrower tail; immature is whiter below, with narrower underpart streaking.
Best Sites: *Summer:* Hoh Rain Forest; North Fork, Teanaway R. (Kittitas Co.); Bumping River Rd. (off SR 410, Yakima Co.); FR 39 (Okanogan Co.); Silver Creek Rd. (Ferry Co.); Salmo Pass (Pend Oreille Co.). *Winter:* Steamboat Rock SP.

RED-SHOULDERED HAWK

Buteo lineatus

Preferring wetter habitats than the closely related Red-tailed Hawk, the Red-shouldered Hawk nests in mature trees, usually around river bottoms and in lowland tracts of woods alongside creeks. As spring approaches and pair bonds are formed, this normally quiet hawk utters loud, shrieking *key-ah* calls. Be forewarned, though, that Blue Jays offer impressive imitations of this vocalization. • During summer, the dense cover of this hawk's forested breeding habitat allows few viewing opportunities. However, during spring and fall migration, this hawk can be found hunting from exposed perches such as utility poles and fence posts. Some individuals may even hunt as far as one-half mile from the nearest stand of trees. • Left undisturbed, Red-shouldered Hawks remain faithful to productive nesting sites, returning yearly. After the parents die, one of the young will carry on the family nesting tradition.

ID: dark brown upper-parts; chestnut red shoulders; densely rust-barred white underparts; narrow white bars on dark tail. *Immature:* large, brown "teardrop" streaks on white underparts; whitish undertail coverts. *In flight:* white crescent or "window" near upperwing tip; rust-barred wing linings; light and dark barring on underside of flight feathers and tail.

Size: *L* 19 in; *W* 3½ ft.

Status: rare visitor to southwestern riparian forests from October through March, regularly at Ridgefield NWR; state range may be expanding.

Habitat: mature hardwood and mixed forests, wooded riparian areas, swampy woodlands and large, mature woodlots.

Nesting: usually 15–80 ft above the ground in the crotch of a hardwood (prefers a mature maple, ash or beech); pair assembles (or reuses) a bulky nest of sticks and twigs; female incubates 2–4 darkly blotched, bluish white eggs for about 33 days; pair raises the young.

Feeding: prey is usually detected from a fence post, tree or utility pole and caught in a swooping attack; may catch prey flushed by low flight; eats small mammals, birds, reptiles and amphibians.

Voice: repeated series of high *key-ah* notes.

Similar Species: *Broad-winged Hawk:* very rare fall migrant; brown shoulder; wider white tail bands; broader wing is more whitish and dark-edged underneath. *Red-tailed Hawk* (p. 121): rufous tail; no "window" near upperwing tip.

Best Sites: Ridgefield NWR; Julia Butler Hansen NWR; Steigerwald NWR (no public access—view from perimeter).

SWAINSON'S HAWK

Buteo swainsoni

The Red-tailed Hawk dominates much of Washington's skies, but the Swainson's Hawk takes center stage in the state's eastern open country, especially where ground squirrels are abundant. • Traveling in large flocks, North America's Swainson's Hawks migrate to South American wintering areas as far as Patagonia—a feat exceeded among raptors only by the arctic-breeding *tundrius* Peregrine Falcon race. However, Swainson's numbers have diminished with the loss of native grasslands and with pesticide use in South America. • This bird's name honors William Swainson, who illustrated a bird collected on the 1825–27 Franklin expedition by John Richardson. Incorrectly identified as "European Common Buzzard," 10 years later it was correctly named by Charles-Lucien Bonaparte.

dark morph

light morph

Habitat: open grasslands and pastures, low-crop fields and small woodlands; sometimes with other hawks over mountain ridges.

Nesting: in a well-spaced tree in an open area or riparian edge, sometimes in a bush, abandoned building or haystack; male chooses the site; female adds sticks and debris plus a lining of leaves, grass, stalks and bark; female incubates 1–4 plain whitish eggs for 34–35 days.

Feeding: swoops to the ground for voles, mice and ground squirrels; also eats snakes, small birds and large insects.

Voice: not very vocal; shrill, somewhat plaintive, screaming *kreeee* and repeated *pi-tik*.

ID: white or pale face; dark eyes; yellow cere; gray bill; dark brown upperparts; white or reddish to dark brown underparts; pale undertail coverts; reddish or dark "bib"; yellow feet. *Immature:* mottled dark and white. *In flight:* dark-barred flight feathers; dark wing tips; white to reddish brown wing linings; broad, finely barred, white-tipped tail with dark subterminal band.

Size: *Male: L* 19–20 in; *W* 4¼ ft. *Female: L* 20–22 in; *W* 4¼ ft.

Status: fairly common from mid-April to September, uncommon for a month on either side in the east; casual from late March to mid-May in the west.

Similar Species: *Red-tailed Hawk* (p. 121): bulkier; larger bill; reddish tail; silvery underwing flight feathers; reddish to dark wing linings; broader tail on immature.

Best Sites: Yakima Training Center (permission required); Moxee area; Othello; Sprague–Fishtrap L.; Havillah; Walla Walla valley; Rose Creek Preserve area (Pullman).

RED-TAILED HAWK

Buteo jamaicensis

One of North America's best-known, most widely distributed hawks, the Red-tailed Hawk is often seen perched on a branch or pole overlooking open fields, or even soaring over downtown Seattle. • Size, coloration and tail markings distinguish up to 16 subspecies of Redtail. Most races exhibit dark, intermediate and light morphs. Western Red-tails usually have deep cinnamon to brick red tails, except for the less colorful immatures and the rare "Harlan's Hawk." • Most Red-tails are year-round residents, but others migrate through from late August to late October. • This hawk's distinctive, shrill "scream" is often used in movies to lend wildness to outdoor scenes, but it is sometimes wrongly attributed to another species, such as the Bald Eagle.

dark morph

ID: brown eyes; yellow cere; dark upperparts with indistinct pale markings; yellow feet. *Light morph:* dark head; pale rufous breast; streaky belly band. *"Harlan's":* dark overall; black-and-white-streaked breast; pale grayish, possibly banded tail. *Immature:* yellow eyes; whitish outer wing; clearly banded tail. *In flight:* variable dark wing lining with diagnostic darker leading edge and whitish underwing flight feathers; dark wing tips and trailing edges; fan-shaped, rufous tail.
Size: *Male: L* 18–23 in; *W* 3¾–4¾ ft. *Female: L* 20–25 in; *W* 4–4¾ ft.
Status: common summer resident, migrant and winter resident; fairly common in spring.
Habitat: almost open areas with high perches.
Nesting: in the crown of a woodlot tree, usually hardwood, or on a cliff; commonly next to open fields or shrublands; bulky platform nest is augmented yearly with sticks and twigs and lined with other plant materials; pair incubates 2–3 brown-blotched, whitish eggs for 28–35 days.
Feeding: hunts from an elevated perch; also dives after prey while soaring or pursues prey on the ground; eats small mammals,

midsized birds, amphibians and reptiles, with occasional insects and fresh carrion.
Voice: distinctive, exuberant, down-slurred, single *keee-(eee)-rrrr;* shrill *chwirk* and low, nasal *gannk.*
Similar Species: *Other medium and large hawks:* tail not rufous; immature and dark-morph adults are often distinguishable only at close range. *Swainson's Hawk* (p. 120): white face, dark "bib" and light underwing linings on pale and intermediate morphs.
Best Sites: statewide in open to semi-open habitat with thermals; migrates over mountain ridges.

FERRUGINOUS HAWK
Buteo regalis

The largest of the buteos, the majestic Ferruginous Hawk is often seen coursing the contours of rolling, grassy hills, circling high above, or sitting alertly in a barren field, but it spends much of its time perched low in a tree or on a fence post watching for prey. When hunting from the air, this grassland hawk swoops from great heights, striking with great force. • Formerly shot and poisoned as perceived pests, Ferruginous Hawks eat mostly rabbits, ground squirrels and gophers, so they actually aid farmers and ranchers. Rodent control campaigns and the conversion of grasslands to agriculture have further reduced and localized these hawks. Approximately 40 to 50 pairs now live in Washington. • In parts of this hawk's range, wandering bison formerly provided bones and wool as nest material.

dark morph

light morph

ID: heavy head; pale brown eyes; yellow cere; feathered legs; yellow feet. *Light morph:* pale head; brown-mottled, rusty upperparts; white underparts; rusty flanks and "leggings"; pale tail washed with cinnamon above. *Dark morph:* gray-mottled, dark reddish brown upperparts, underparts and wing linings. *Immature:* dark brown instead of rusty; yellow eyes. *In flight:* long wings; dark-lined, white underwings; pale upperwing patch.
Size: *L* 22–27 in; *W* 4½–4¾ ft.
Status: uncommon local summer resident from late February to mid-July; rare to casual the rest of the year; state-listed as threatened.
Habitat: arid grasslands. *In migration:* foothills and mountain ridges.

Nesting: typically on a cliff in the Columbia Basin or on the ground; wide, massive platform of sticks, twigs, sagebrush stems and debris is lined with finer, drier material; male helps female incubate 2–4 creamy white, heavily spotted and blotched eggs for 32–33 days.
Feeding: hunts from a soaring flight, low perch or the ground; preys on ground squirrels, rabbits, mice, pocket gophers, snakes and small birds.
Voice: generally silent; loud, squealing alarm call, usually a down-slurred *kaaarr*.
Similar Species: *Red-tailed Hawk* (p. 121): smaller; darker underparts; tail is cinnamon to red, immature's tail is darker and more banded. *Swainson's Hawk* (p. 120): smaller; all-dark underwing or pale wing lining with dark flight feathers; banded tail.
Best Sites: east of Wilson Creek (Grant Co.); Washtucna Coulee (Walla Walla Co.–Adams Co.); Eureka Flat; Esquatzel Coulee and Juniper Dunes Wilderness area; south of Benson City.

ROUGH-LEGGED HAWK

Buteo lagopus

Each fall, subarctic-nesting Rough-legged Hawks drift south in search of warmer open areas. Their abundance in Washington varies with the weather to the north and the success of the breeding season. When small mammals are common in the north, a pair of Rough-legs can fledge up to seven young, but in lean years one chick is the norm. Most birds return north by early April, but some linger until late May. • Easily identified from afar when foraging, the Rough-legged Hawk is one of the few large hawks that routinely hovers over prey. • Oddly, light-morph females generally appear much darker than light-morph males and the reverse is true in dark-morph birds. • The word *lagopus*, meaning "hare's foot," refers to this bird's distinctive feathered feet, an adaptation to its subarctic lifestyle.

dark morph

♀

light morph

ID: brown eyes; yellow cere; legs feathered down to yellow toes. *Light morph:* white-streaked, dark brown head and breast; dark upperparts mottled with buff and white; wide, dark belly band. *Dark morph:* generally dark; white-and-dark underwings and undertail. *Immature:* paler eyes. *In flight:* indistinctly barred, white underwing flight feathers; dark patch at "wrist"; white tail with broad, dark subterminal band tipped with white; shallow, effortless wingbeats; soars and glides with wings held in a slight "V"; regularly hovers when hunting.

Size: *L* 19–24 in; *W* 4–4¾ ft.

Status: fairly common from late October to mid-March; uncommon for about 1 month on either side of this period.

Habitat: open grasslands, sagebrush flats, coastal plains, fields and meadows.

Nesting: does not nest in Washington.

Feeding: hunts from a perch, from a hovering flight or on the ground; eats mostly small rodents, especially mice and voles; occasionally captures small birds, amphibians, reptiles and large insects.

Voice: rarely vocal; catlike *kee-eer* alarm call.

Similar Species: *Other* Buteos (pp. 119–22): rarely hover; much smaller "wrist" patches; 1-color or multi-banded tails. *Northern Harrier* (p. 115): smaller; slimmer; facial disc; white rump; long, narrow tail; slow, low-level cruising. *Golden Eagle* (p. 124): much larger; broader wings; dark, unpatterned underwings; immature's broader white tail has dark band at tip.

Best Sites: Samish Flats; Skagit Flats; Kittitas Valley; Moses Coulee (Douglas Co.); Waterville Plateau (Douglas Co.); Bickleton; Moses L.

123

GOLDEN EAGLE

Aquila chrysaetos

Throughout the world, the Golden Eagle with wings spread is a symbol of corporate and national strength and power. Few people forget their first encounter with a Golden Eagle—an adult's wingspan exceeds 7 feet. • Washington's high mountains and uplands east of the Cascades provide a spectrum of varied habitats for these impressive hunters. With their remarkable eyesight, these birds have taken prey from a launch point more than 1 mile away or when the bird was so high that it was invisible to the naked human eye. In summer, observers might chance upon a breeding pair of Golden Eagles hunting together or displaying breathtaking aerial acrobatics. In spring and fall, migrating eagles that breed farther north can be seen soaring over mountain ridges, often appearing as no more than specks in the sky.

immature

ID: brown overall; gold-tinted head and neck; yellow cere; gray bill; pale-edged wing feathers; buff undertail; banded tail with broad, dark terminal band; yellow feet. *Immature:* white on wings and tail. *In flight:* relatively long tail; measured, effortless wingbeats; soars with wings held in a slight "V."

Size: *L* 30–40 in; *W* 6½–7½ ft.

Status: fairly common eastern migrant from September to early November and otherwise uncommon; casual breeder in the Olympics; rare in the San Juans; candidate for the state threatened list.

Habitat: open or broken woodlands and open country, from lower foothills to high alpine in summer, dropping to lower elevations afterward.

Nesting: on a cliff ledge or in a tall tree; nest platform to 10 ft across is built of sticks, branches and roots; pair incubates 2–3 creamy buff, brown-marked eggs for 43–45 days.

Feeding: swoops on prey from a fast, soaring flight; opportunistically feeds on small mammals and birds; also lizards, snakes and some larger mammals (usually stillbirths or carrion).

Voice: generally quiet; utters yelps, lower *chiup* calls and short barks.

Similar Species: *Bald Eagle* (p. 114): immature has larger head, heavier bill, bare legs and more diffuse white patches on wings and holds wings flat in flight. *Turkey Vulture* (p. 111): naked head looks small in flight; dark wing linings; silvery flight feathers; rocks and teeters in flight with wings in a sharp "V."

Best Sites: eastern slopes of the Cascades; Okanogan Highlands; Snake River Canyon; Blue Mts.; Selkirks.

AMERICAN KESTREL

Falco sparverius

The American Kestrel is North America's smallest falcon. It is more buoyant in flight than its relatives, and it is not inclined toward the all-out, full-speed aerial attacks that have made other falcons such admired predators. The kestrel often "wind-hovers" to scan the ground, flapping rapidly to maintain a stationary position while facing upwind. It also perches on telephone wires above roadsides and along open fields, peering intently downward into the grass below for any sign of small rodents or birds, but large insects form most of its summer diet. • Even though sparrows are only an occasional prey item, old field guides referred to this bird as "Sparrow Hawk," and *sparverius*, Latin for "pertaining to sparrows," was applied to it.

ID: gray forehead and crown; white "chin"; 2 distinctive dark facial stripes and nape patch; yellow cere; small bill; rufous back; long tail; yellow feet. *Male:* rufous upper crown patch; dark spotting on bluish gray wings and pale buff underparts; rufous tail with broad, blackish band adjoining white tip. *Female:* less contrasting head pattern and browner back; dark-barred, rufous wings; heavily rufous-streaked, pale underparts; dark-banded, rufous tail. *In flight:* long, thin, pointed wings; much lighter flight than other falcons.
Size: *L* 7½–8 in; *W* 20–24 in.
Status: common summer resident in the east; uncommon in summer and common in winter in southwest; uncommon elsewhere in the west.

Habitat: open fields, oak woodlands, forest edges, grasslands, sagebrush flats, roadsides and farmland with hunting perches; post-breeding birds may move into mountain alpine areas.
Nesting: in a natural cavity or an abandoned woodpecker hole, old magpie or crow nest, or in a nest box; pair incubates 4–6 brown-spotted, white to buff eggs for 28–31 days; pair feeds the young until fledging at 30–31 days and sometimes beyond.
Feeding: swoops from a perch or hovers; eats mostly insects (including grasshoppers, crickets, dragonflies and beetles), small rodents, birds, reptiles and amphibians.
Voice: loud, often repeated, shrill piping notes.
Similar Species: *Merlin* (p. 126): slightly larger; stockier; plainer face; gray or brown back and wings; dark or dark-banded tail.
Best Sites: Samish Flats; west of Centralia; open habitats and farmlands in the east.

125

MERLIN

Falco columbarius

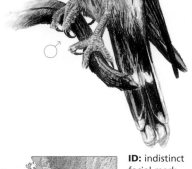

Only slightly larger than an American Kestrel, the Merlin considers itself the equal of any falcon, emulating the Peregrine Falcon in high-speed flight and in snatching other birds in midair. The elements of speed and surprise work best in open country close to forest edges, where the Merlin is most at home. • Both *columbarius*, Latin for "dove" or "pigeon," and the former name "Pigeon Hawk" refer to the bird's appearance in flight, not its preferred prey. • The "Black Merlin" (*F.c. suckleyi*) is most often seen along the coast and inland in western regions. The less dark "Taiga Merlin" (*F.c. columbarius*) is seen mostly east of the Cascades. The paler "Prairie Merlin" (*F.c. richardsonii*) may occur rarely in eastern Washington.

ID: indistinct facial markings; yellow eye ring; dark eyes; heavily brown-streaked, white or buff underparts; long, narrow, dark or heavily banded tail; yellow feet. *Male:* plain bluish gray crown and back. *Female:* plain brown crown and back. *In flight:* rapid, shallow, swiftlike wingbeats; pointed wing with straight trailing edge; light-speckled, generally dark underwings.
Size: *L* 10–12 in; *W* 23–26 in.
Status: uncommon resident and breeder in the Olympics and western Cascades; rare breeder high in the Cascades and in the northeast; common migrant and winter resident around coastal and nearby inland waters; uncommon to rare winter

resident near towns in Puget Sound and central and eastern Washington; candidate for state threatened list.
Habitat: semi-open to open country, including estuaries, seacoast, open woodlands, windbreaks, forest glades and hedgerows; often winters in towns and cities.
Nesting: in a tree; usually reuses an abandoned raptor, crow, jay or squirrel nest; mostly the female incubates 4–5 chestnut-marked, whitish eggs for 28–32 days; male feeds the female; pair raises the young.
Feeding: stoops or pursues smaller birds, particularly flocking songbirds and shorebirds, and large flying insects, especially dragonflies; also eats other insects, small mammals and reptiles, usually pouncing from a perch.
Voice: rapid, high-pitched *ki-ki-ki-kee*, sometimes imitated by jays.
Similar Species: *American Kestrel* (p. 125): more colorful; 2 bold facial stripes; rufous tail; often hovers; perches on wires. *Prairie Falcon* (p. 129): much larger; sandy brown upperparts; whiter underparts; dark "wing pits."
Best Sites: Samish Flats; Skagit Flats; Dungeness NWR; Nisqually NWR; Ocean Shores; Leadbetter Pt.

GYRFALCON

Falco rusticolus

The speedy Gyrfalcon is a rare winter visitor to Washington, which makes its presence all the more satisfying to birders who catch a glimpse of it rocketing by in hot pursuit of an unfortunate duck or shorebird. Most birds reaching Washington are dark morphs, but gray morphs can also be found if conditions farther north drive them southward. • The Gyrfalcon is one of the world's most powerful avian hunters. Unlike the Peregrine Falcon, the Gyrfalcon rarely swoops from above with its wings closed—it prefers to outfly its prey, often attacking from below. For a duck unlucky enough to be its target, the only possible escape might be to plunge into the water headfirst.

gray morph

gray morph

Habitat: open and semi-open areas, including marshes, fields and open wetlands, where prey is abundant.

Nesting: does not nest in Washington.

ID: possible thin, dark "mustache"; yellowish cere; dark brown or gray upperparts; white underparts with brown or gray streaks or blotches; yellow feet; wings appear distinctly shorter than tail when perched. *Immature:* darker and more heavily patterned than adult; gray cere; gray feet. *In flight:* white-flecked, brown wing linings with whitish flight feathers below or barred, gray-and-white underwing.

Feeding: strikes prey in mid-air and carries or follows it to the ground; locates prey from an elevated perch, by coursing low over the ground or by soaring; eats mainly birds, especially upland gamebirds, shorebirds, waterfowl and Rock Pigeon.

Voice: loud, harsh *kak-kak-kak*.

Similar Species: *Other falcons:* smaller. *Prairie Falcon* (p. 129): dark "wing pits"; shorter tail. *Peregrine Falcon* (p. 128): dark "mustache" joins "cap" to form distinctive "helmet"; shorter tail. *Northern Goshawk* (p. 118): deceptively similar at times; dark "cap"; light "eyebrow"; rounded wings in flight.

Size: *Male: L* 20–22 in; *W* 4–4¼ ft. *Female: L* 22–25 in; *W* 4¼–4½ ft.

Status: rare and local from late October to late March.

Best Sites: Samish Flats; Skagit Flats; Dungeness Spit, Ocean Shores (coastal beaches); Waterville Plateau (Douglas Co.); Davenport–Reardan area; north of Moses L.

PEREGRINE FALCON

Falco peregrinus

Although migrants and wintering birds commonly hunt waterfowl and shore-birds (hence the former name "Duck Hawk"), summering Peregrines typically concentrate on birds of the forest canopy or, in cities, species such as the Rock Pigeon. • The Peregrine's legendary speed was no defense against the insidious effects of pesticides. Over just 30 years during the mid-1900s, the Peregrine almost disappeared across the U.S., prompting a public outcry that resulted in a 1972 ban on DDT. Intensive conservation and reintroduction efforts have brought about a heartening recovery across much of the Peregrine's North American range. A pair has successfully nested in Seattle for several years, and, more recently, one has done so in Tacoma.

ID: broad, dark "mus-tache" joins "cap" to form distinctive "helmet"; bluish gray back, wings and tail; light underparts with fine, dark gray barring and spotting. *Immature:* dark areas are brown, not gray. *In flight:* broad-based, pointed wings; dark-banded tail; strong, steady wingbeats.
Size: *Male: L* 15–17 in; *W* 3–3½ ft. *Female: L* 17–19 in; *W* 3½–3¾ ft.
Status: fairly common fall migrant; uncommon summer resident on the San Juans and the outer Olympic Peninsula but local in the Cascades; uncommon winter resident in open country and along coastlines.
Habitat: lakeshores, seacoast, estuaries and coastal marshlands; mountainous areas

with cliffs and open country; recently urban areas.
Nesting: wild birds use cliff ledges or rocky ridges; many introduced birds use artificial platforms and flat, protected sites on ledges and bridges; reuses nest sites without adding material; male helps the female incubate 3–4 cinnamon-spotted, yellowish white eggs for 32–36 days; pair feeds the nestlings for 49–56 days until fledging.
Feeding: stoops at high speed from a soaring flight, striking birds in midair with clenched feet; also chases down birds on the wing.
Voice: generally silent; loud, harsh, persistent *kak-kak-kak-kak* near the nest.
Similar Species: *Prairie Falcon* (p. 129): smaller "mustache" separate from crown patch; sandy brown above; brown-spotted underparts; dark "wing pit" on whiter underwing.
Best Sites: *Summer:* San Juans. *In migration* and *winter:* Samish Flats; Skagit Flats; Ocean Shores; Columbia R.; Seattle.

PRAIRIE FALCON

Falco mexicanus

Rocketing overhead like a supercharged fighter jet, the Prairie Falcon often seems to appear out of nowhere. It can outfly the closely related Peregrine in level flight and can rival it in downward stoops. • In spring and summer, Prairie Falcons often concentrate their hunting over ground squirrel colonies, swooping over windswept grass to pick off naïve youngsters. As summer fades to fall, large flocks of migrating songbirds capture their attention. • Inexperienced and over-eager Prairie Falcons risk serious injury or death when pushing their limits in early hunting forays. Young falcons stooping at close to 200 miles per hour can easily misjudge their flight speed or their ability to pull out of a dive. • Prairie Falcons commonly soar for long periods on updrafts or along ridgelines.

ID: pale face; narrow, dark brown "mustache"; yellow eye ring; brown eyes; yellow cere; sandy brown upperparts; white underparts with brown spots heaviest on flanks; barred tail; yellow feet. *In flight:* diagnostic broad, blackish "wing pit" line.
Size: *Male: L* 14–15 in; *W* 3–3¼ ft. *Female: L* 17–18 in; *W* 3½ ft.
Status: uncommon year-round resident in the east; uncommon mountain migrant in fall; rare from late summer through early spring in the west.
Habitat: arid grasslands. *Breeding:* deserts; cliffs and rocky promontories. *In migration* and *winter:* croplands and pastures; hardly ever along the coast.
Nesting: on a cliff ledge, in a crevice or on a rocky promontory, rarely in an abandoned crow or hawk nest or on an artificial structure; nest is usually unlined; mainly the female incubates 3–5 pale, darkly speckled eggs for 29–33 days.
Feeding: high-speed strike-and-kill follows stoop, low flight or chase on the wing, sometimes from a perch; eats ground squirrels, pocket gophers, small birds and other small vertebrates, supplemented by large insects.
Voice: generally silent; yelping *kik-kik-kik-kik* alarm call.
Similar Species: *Peregrine Falcon* (p. 128): distinctive dark "helmet"; broader, pointier wings; uniform underwing coloration. *Merlin* (p. 126): much smaller; female usually has darker back, upperwings and underwings and narrower, dark or heavily banded tail.
Best Sites: Yakima R. canyon; Moses Coulee (Douglas Co.); Grand Coulee; Bethel Ridge Rd. (off US 12); Rattlesnake Mt.; Lower Crab Creek; Columbia NWR.

129

VIRGINIA RAIL
Rallus limicola

A time-honored way to meet a Virginia Rail is to visit a marsh, clap your hands three or four times and wait. With luck, this slim bird may reveal itself for an instant, but more often a metallic return call is all that betrays a Virginia Rail's presence. • With its short, stubby wings, the Virginia Rail prefers to escape the attention of an intruder or predator by scurrying off into dense vegetation, particularly in late summer, when molted wing and tail feathers leave it temporarily flightless. Escape is made easier by the laterally compressed body, modified feather tips resistant to wear and tear, and flexible vertebrae. • The ability of rails to disappear so quickly and their habit of feeding by twilight ensure that their numbers are almost always underestimated.

ID: gray face; red eyes; long, down-curved, orange bill; brown-mottled, rusty back; rusty orange breast and throat; white undertail coverts; black-and-white, vertically barred flanks; short tail; pinkish orange legs and feet; long toes. *In flight:* broad-tipped, forward-swept wings; rusty shoulders on brownish upperwings; gray underwings, white at leading edge only; dangling feet.

Size: *L* 9–11 in; *W* 13 in.

Status: fairly common statewide in summer; uncommon in winter, particularly east of the Cascades.

Habitat: *Breeding:* freshwater wetlands, especially cattail, bulrush and tule marshes; flooded riparian woodlands; sometimes coastal saltwater marshes. *In migration* and *winter:* wetland areas with suitable overhead cover, particularly coastal freshwater marshes in winter.

Nesting: usually suspended just over the water in emergent marsh vegetation; concealed loose basket nest of coarse grass, cattail stems or sedges; pair incubates 7–12 brown-dotted, pale buff eggs for 18–20 days; pair feeds and tends the young.

Feeding: probes soft substrates for soft-bellied invertebrates; often snatches prey from vegetation; sometimes eats seeds or small fish.

Voice: easily imitated, repeated, metallic *kid-dik* given day or night; also gives an accelerating series of wheezy grunts that eventually trail off. *Female:* ends a series of sharp notes with a rough trill.

Similar Species: *Sora* (p. 131): black "mask"; short, yellow bill; greenish yellow legs; straight wings.

Best Sites: widespread in marshes, but secretive. *Winter:* good quality marshes in the west; open, unfrozen marshes in the east.

SORA

Porzana carolina

ounding halfway between a crazed laugh and a horse's whinny, the call of a male Sora hidden deep within a marsh puzzles the uninitiated. Easier to imitate is the plaintive, two-note whistle that the Sora gives day and night, but most often in the clear, still twilight hours. This call is often the only definite sign of a Sora's presence, because this bird is elusive even where it is common. • Even without webbing between its toes, the Sora swims well as it moves from one patch of wet vegetation to another, and its wings are strong enough to enable many North American birds to migrate to South America. • The Sora habitually flicks its short, stubby tail, perhaps to confuse prey. • *Porzana*, meaning "crake," indicates this bird's resemblance to Europe's Corn Crake *(Crex crex)*.

breeding

ID: gray face, neck and breast; brown crown and nape; black "mask" in front of eye; reddish brown eyes; yellow bill; white-streaked, black-mottled brown back and tail; flanks vertically streaked in black, brown and white; whitish undertail coverts; greenish yellow legs and feet. *Breeding:* black "chin" and throat.
Size: *L* 8–10 in; *W* 14 in.
Status: uncommon in summer in the west and rare in winter; fairly common in summer in the east.
Habitat: *Breeding:* freshwater marshes with standing water and abundant emergent vegetation; grassy or marshy borders of streams, lakes and ponds; up to 4000 ft. *In migration* and *winter:* freshwater

wetlands; saltwater and brackish coastal marshes.
Nesting: under concealing vegetation, usually over water, but possibly in a wet meadow; well-built basket nest of grass and aquatic vegetation; pair incubates 10–12 brown-spotted, buff eggs for 16–19 days; pair feeds and tends the young until just beyond fledging at 20–25 days.
Feeding: gleans and probes vegetation for seeds, plants, aquatic insects and mollusks; also picks food from the ground or the water's surface.
Voice: distinctive, loud, uneven whinny; also a high, clear, 2-note, whistling *koo-ee* and a sharp alarm call.
Similar Species: *Virginia Rail* (p. 130): long, orange, downcurved bill; rusty underparts; pinkish legs; less likely to be found at high elevations.
Best Sites: freshwater marshes and wetlands.

AMERICAN COOT

Fulica americana

The expression "crazy as a coot" may at first seem inappropriate for such well-adapted, successful waterbirds, but watch American Coots through the seasons and the expression will make sense. During the breeding season, coots are among the most spirited and aggressive waterbirds in the world, quick to take offense and always finding something to squabble about. They can often be seen running across the surface of the water on their lobed feet or swimming head down with white frontal "shields" flashing to intimidate rivals and other, larger waterfowl. Yet, in winter American Coots are highly sociable and often form large rafts, swimming and diving together as if they didn't have a care in the world.

ID: dark gray overall; black head; white forehead "shield" with reddish spot; red eyes; sturdy, white bill with broken dark ring; white undertail coverts; sturdy, greenish yellow legs; long, individually lobed toes. *Immature:* dark brown upperparts; pale grayish brown underparts. *In flight:* trailing legs; white trailing edge on inner half of wing.

Size: *L* 13–16 in; *W* 24 in.

Status: common in winter in large numbers on open lakes and reservoirs; fairly common summer lake resident.

Habitat: freshwater marshes, ponds and wetlands with open water and emergent vegetation; city parks and golf courses.

Winter: coastal saltwater marshes, lagoons and estuaries.

Nesting: in emergent marsh vegetation; pair builds a bulky, floating nest of cattails and grass; pair incubates 8–12 brown-spotted, pale buff eggs for 21–25 days.

Feeding: gleans the water's surface for algae, aquatic vegetation and invertebrates; grazes short grasses; dives for submerged water plants, tadpoles and fish.

Voice: usually very vocal; single notes often accelerated into a long, loud *priki priki priki* series with emphasis on *ki.*

Similar Species: *Scoters* (pp. 61–63): larger, males have colorful bills and smaller, webbed, pinkish feet; found on open salt water in winter.

Best Sites: *Winter:* marshes, lakes and ponds statewide. *Summer:* marshes and lakes east of the Cascades; L. Washington; other marshes and lakes with cover.

SANDHILL CRANE

Grus canadensis

Deep, resonant, rattling yet melodious croaks betray the approach of migrating Sandhill Cranes. At some locations, flock after flock may sail effortlessly overhead. The expansive, V-shaped lines suggest geese, but the long necks, trailing legs and distinctive bugles quickly establish the birds as cranes. • As the "Lesser Sandhill Crane" (*G.c. canadensis*) migrates through Washington between wintering areas in California and breeding grounds in Alaska, it is most evident in the Othello area. Except for a small population at Conboy Lake National Wildlife Refuge, the larger "Greater Sandhill Crane" (*G.c. tabida*) has been virtually extirpated here. • Cranes mate for life, reinforcing their pair bonds each spring with elaborate, exuberant courtship dances in which partners leap high into the air with their wings half spread and then bow like courtiers.

ID: pale gray plumage, often rust-stained; red "cap" above pale "cheek" patch; bright yellow eyes; long, straight bill; scapular feathers form large "bustle"; long neck; long, dark legs. *In flight:* straight neck; trailing legs; black-tipped, silvery flight feathers; slow, steady wingbeats; flocks form line or "V" formation.
Size: *"Greater Sandhill":* L 3¾–4¼ ft; W 6¼–7 ft. *"Lesser Sandhill":* L 3¼–3¾ ft; W 5¾–6¼ ft.
Status: *"Greater Sandhill":* rare local breeder at Conboy Lake NWR; state-listed as endangered. *"Lesser Sandhill":* common fall and spring migrant around Othello; common local winter resident in the southwest.
Habitat: *Breeding:* isolated, open, wet grassy meadows and shallow marshlands; grasslands, mudflats and freshwater lakeshores. *In migration* and *winter:* agricultural fields.

Nesting: on a large mound of aquatic vegetation over water or along a shoreline; platform of vegetation is lined with finer material selected by the female; pair incubates 1–3 pale, olive-splotched eggs for 29–32 days.
Feeding: probes and gleans the ground and shallow water for insects, soft-bodied invertebrates (especially worms), berries, waste grain, shoots and tubers.
Voice: unmistakable, loud, resonant, rattling, croaking *gu-rrroo gu-rrroo gurrroo,* sometimes extended into a long, exuberant chorus, especially with several birds calling.
Similar Species: *Great Blue Heron* (p. 107): black crown stripe; mainly yellow bill; chestnut thighs; black head plumes and pale neck plumes in breeding plumage; flies with neck folded back; all-gray underwings.
Best Sites: *"Greater Sandhill":* Conboy Lake NWR. *"Lesser Sandhill":* Othello in migration; Ridgefield NWR, Woodland and Vancouver lowlands in winter and in migration.

133

BLACK-BELLIED PLOVER

Pluvialis squatarola

Most often seen in its nonbreeding plumage, the Black-bellied Plover breeds across the High Arctic. Some of the most northerly breeding birds winter in the tropics, whereas others winter as far north as coastal British Columbia, Canada. • Black-bellies benefit from their sociable nature and ability to adopt a variety of feeding strategies. Dense flocks roost together in migration and at wintering grounds but spread out to forage on mudflats as the tide recedes. At high tide, they forsake the shore for freshwater and field habitats. Their large eyes allow them to feed easily at night. • Wary and quick to give alarm and take flight, the Black-bellied Plover serves as a sentinel for mixed flocks of shorebirds.

nonbreeding

breeding

ID: black bill; relatively long, blackish legs. *Breeding:* black face, breast and belly (less bold on female); light gray crown; white shoulders; white-spangled, black back; white undertail coverts. *Nonbreeding:* grayish brown upperparts; brown-smudged, pale underparts; traces of black on belly until September. *In flight:* diagnostic black "wing pits."

Size: *L* 11–13 in; *W* 29 in.

Status: common fall migrant and winter resident on coastal mudflats and plowed fields; uncommon fall migrant and rare spring migrant in the east.

Habitat: coastal and inland sand- and mudflats; fields flooded by heavy rain; roosts on salt marshes, dunes and pastures and above beaches.

Nesting: does not nest in Washington.

Feeding: run-and-snatch technique to pick prey from the surface; sometimes probes in mud or moist soil; winter diet of mollusks, crustaceans and marine worms, also insects and some plant material.

Voice: rich, plaintive 3-syllable *pee-oo-ee* whistle; flocks may utter mellow 2-note whistles.

Similar Species: *Pacific Golden-Plover* (p. 135) and *American Golden-Plover* (p. 361): gold-flecked upperparts; more black on crown and rump in breeding plumage; buffier head and breast in non-breeding plumage; grayish underwings.

Best Sites: Sequim; Samish Flats; Skagit Flats; Crockett L.; Ocean Shores; Bowerman Basin (Hoquiam); Bottle Beach (Ocosta); Tokeland.

PACIFIC GOLDEN-PLOVER
Pluvialis fulva

Until 1993, the Pacific Golden-Plover and the American Golden-Plover were known collectively as "Lesser Golden-Plover." Because there is no evidence of hybridization in the few locations where both breed together in Alaska, they were determined to be separate species. • Although both species pass through Washington each fall, and in smaller numbers in spring, only the Pacific Golden-Plover has been positively identified in winter. The Pacific is the commoner species along the coast but is rarely seen in inland locations. • It has been suggested that the oceanic migratory cycle of the Pacific Golden-Plover led seafaring Polynesians to Hawaii. This theory led to the bird being portrayed on the 1984 U.S. postage stamp commemorating the 25th anniversary of Hawaii's statehood.

nonbreeding

ID: dark "cap"; straight, blackish bill; gold, white and brown flecking on upperparts; dark barring on rump and tail; long, bluish black legs. *Breeding:* black face and underparts; white "S" stripe extends from forehead to shoulder; black-and-white splotching on flanks and undertail coverts; female has more white on "cheeks," flanks and undertail coverts. *Nonbreeding:* conspicuous dark ear spot; brown-spotted, pale buff gray underparts; finely brown-streaked, buff neck and breast. *In flight:* fairly long, pointed wings; indistinct pale upperwing stripe.
Size: *L* 10–11 in; *W* 24 in.
Status: uncommon fall and rare spring migrant on the outer coast; casual in winter.

Habitat: estuaries; drier tidal mudflats; upper intertidal zone of sandy beaches; coastal salt marshes; inland on fields and large areas of short grass.
Nesting: does not nest in Washington.
Feeding: pecks and probes for insects, spiders, small mollusks and crustaceans; also eats some berries.
Voice: loud, whistled *chu-wee* call; also a short *peee* or a longer *deed-leek* alarm call.
Similar Species: *American Golden-Plover* (p. 361): shorter bill and legs; black flanks and undertail coverts on breeding male; folded wings extend well beyond tail. *Black-bellied Plover* (p. 134): upperparts are black, white and gray in breeding plumage; plainer, gray-and-white upperparts in nonbreeding plumage; white undertail coverts; black "wing pits"; stronger upperwing stripe; dark barring on white tail.
Best Sites: Damon Pt. (Ocean Shores); Midway Beach (Grayland); Leadbetter Pt.; Dungeness NWR.

SNOWY PLOVER
Charadrius alexandrinus

A pale and often ghostlike, year-round occupant of a few relatively undisturbed coastal beaches, the Snowy Plover has become an endangered species in Washington. • Human activity and development threaten this unassuming little plover, which blends almost unseen into isolated coastal dunes, open sandy beaches and blazing white alkali pans. • Attempts by birders to find Snowy Plovers and their well-camouflaged nests and young usually result in disruption of the parents' activities and can lead to the crushing of eggs or death of the young. During the breeding season, most nesting locations are marked as off-limits, and these signs should be respected. Snowies are best sought out in the nonbreeding season, when human disturbances are less harmful.

breeding

breeding

ID: white forehead, eye ring and "collar"; dark eyes; thin, black bill; light brown upperparts; white underparts; wings shorter than tail at rest; gray legs. *Breeding:* black patches (dark gray on female) on forehead, ear and shoulder. *Nonbreeding:* brown ear and shoulder patches. *In flight:* broad white upperwing stripe; whitish underwings; gray-tipped, white-edged upper tail.
Size: *L* 6–7 in; *W* 16–17 in.
Status: uncommon and local year-round resident on a few outer coastal beaches; federally listed as threatened and state-listed as endangered.

Habitat: sandy beaches, dunes, sandspits, drier areas of tidal estuaries and sand flats, and shorelines of alkaline lakes.
Nesting: on bare ground, often near cover of grass or driftwood; shallow scrape is lined with pebbles, shells, grass and other debris; pair incubates 3 darkly spotted, pale buff eggs for 26–32 days.
Feeding: run-and-stop foraging is supplemented by probing in sand; eats mainly tiny invertebrates; scavenges some items from beached marine mammal carcasses.
Voice: both genders make soft *purrt* calls and utter low, tinkling *ti* alarm notes; male's flight call is a soft, whistled *tur-wheet*.
Similar Species: *Semipalmated Plover* (p. 137): slightly larger; much darker on head and upperparts; heavier, dark-tipped, orange bill; full dark breast band; yellowish orange legs; longer wings.
Best Sites: Damon Pt. (Ocean Shores); Midway Beach (Grayland); Leadbetter Pt.

SEMIPALMATED PLOVER

Charadrius semipalmatus

During their seasonal long-distance flights, flocks of Semipalmated Plovers routinely touch down on Washington's shorelines for a brief stopover—or sometimes an extended winter stay. Darting here and there in short runs interspersed with deliberate pauses or stabbing probes, their attention-grabbing feeding methods and small, plump, rounded profile distinguish them amidst flocks of sandpipers. • The Semipalmated Plover's varied food choices and habitats have enabled it to expand its range while other plovers have declined in numbers. • This bird is primarily an arctic and subarctic breeder. One pair has successfully raised young at Damon Point, but not on a regular basis. • The designation *semipalmatus* reflects the partial webbing between the toes.

nonbreeding

ID: dark crown and facial patch; white forehead spot; yellow eye ring; dark eyes; stubby, black-tipped, orange bill; sandy brown upperparts; white underparts; full dark breast band (narrowing at neck and throat and less dark on female); yellowish orange legs; folded wings extend just beyond tail. *Breeding:* black forecrown extends to black "mask." *In flight:* longish, pointed wings; broad, white upperwing stripe; mainly dark tail.

Size: *L* 7 in; *W* 18–19 in.

Status: common migrant on the coast from mid-April to mid-May and from July to September; uncommon winter coastal resident; uncommon inland migrant; rare, irregular nester on the coast.

Habitat: drier areas of coastal mudflats and estuaries and upper intertidal beach areas; shorelines of interior lakes, rivers and marshes; sometimes uses city ponds and sewage lagoons.

Nesting: nests on sand or gravel, usually near extensive salt or brackish marshes; in a depression sparsely lined with vegetation; pair incubates 4 darkly marked, creamy buff eggs for 23–25 days.

Feeding: run-and-snatch technique; occasional probing; eats bottom-dwelling invertebrates in both salt and fresh water, including crustaceans, worms and mollusks.

Voice: crisp, high-pitched, rising *tu-wee* whistle.

Similar Species: *Snowy Plover* (p. 136): less distinct facial markings; shorter, black bill; much paler upperparts; narrow, incomplete breast band; gray legs. *Killdeer* (p. 138): much larger and heavier; red eye ring; longer, heavier, dark bill; 2 black breast bands; rusty rump; long tail; pale pink-tinged legs; more relaxed flight.

Best Sites: Dungeness NWR; Ocean Shores; Bottle Beach (Ocosta); Midway Beach (Grayland); Tokeland; Leadbetter Pt.

KILLDEER

Charadrius vociferus

The Killdeer is among North America's most widely distributed shorebirds, and it is certainly the best known. No other shorebird has its combination of double black breast bands and rusty tail, and its boisterous call accurately reflects its name. • Unlike most of its family, the Killdeer often uses habitats many miles from water, including urban ones. Active at any hour, it might be heard calling overhead at night, lured by lights in parking lots and ball fields. • Like many other plovers and some other shorebirds and ducks, the Killdeer has a method of luring intruders away from its nest or young. Feigning injury, one of the pair will drag a wing along the ground and fan its conspicuous tail while its mate utters loud cries—hence *vociferus*, which means "very loud voiced."

ID: brown head; white forehead and "eyebrow"; red eye ring; dark eyes; black bill; brown back and wings; white breast with 2 black bands; rusty rump and tail with dark tip; tail projects beyond tips of folded wings; pale legs. *In flight:* white underwing with dark trailing edge; black outer upperwing with white stripe; unhurried, bouncy, somewhat erratic flight.

Size: *L* 9–11 in; *W* 23–24 in.

Status: common year-round resident in the west; common summer resident in the east; uncommon to rare in winter in the east.

Habitat: any wet or dry open environment, from gravel to grass, including urban waste-land, anywhere from sea level to mountains; most numerous at low elevations.

Nesting: on any open ground, such as a shoreline, beach, field or the edge of a gravel road; in a shallow depression, usually unlined but sometimes lined with pebbles, grass or debris; pair incubates 4 dark-blotched, pale eggs for 24–28 days; may have 2 broods.

Feeding: typical plover technique of run-stop-snatch, mainly for insects, but also eats some seeds.

Voice: loud, distinctive *kill-dee kill-dee kill-deer* and variations, including *deer-deer;* high, rapid trilling when nervous or before flight.

Similar Species: *Semipalmated Plover* (p. 137): smaller; shorter, black-tipped, orange bill; single breast band; color of uppertail and rump match that of back; yellowish orange legs.

Best Sites: open country, marshes, beaches, fields and parks.

BLACK OYSTERCATCHER

Haematopus bachmani

Above the background roar of surf and the cries of gulls, piercing flight calls announce the most conspicuous member of the rocky intertidal community. Whereas other birds desert the shoreline to roost, feed or nest, the Black Oystercatcher rarely leaves its chosen gravel or rocky shorelines—they provide both feeding and nesting territory for breeding pairs, which tend to return to the same site each year. • The distinctive long, narrow bill of the Black Oystercatcher is well adapted for prying open the tightly sealed shells of mollusks and other shellfish. • The genus name *Haematopus*, Greek for "blood red eye," refers to a related Old World species. The *bachmani* part of the scientific name honors Reverend John Bachman, a close friend of John James Audubon, who first described the bird in the 19th century.

ID: brownish black overall, with black head, neck and breast; orangy red eye ring; bright yellow eyes; long, straight, blood red bill; sturdy, pale pink legs. *Female:* longer bill. *In flight:* short tail; broad wings; underwing feathers are slightly paler on immature.

Size: *L* 16–18 in; *W* 31–32 in.

Status: uncommon year-round coastal resident on rocky shorelines.

Habitat: rocky shorelines and islands; sea stacks; breakwaters, jetties and reefs; bathes at freshwater outfalls.

Nesting: on bare ground or rocks well above the high-water mark; nest is sometimes lined with pebbles and shells; pair incubates 1–3 dark-marked, buff eggs for 26–28 days; pair tends the young until fledging at 38–40 days and then moves them to remote feeding sites for winter.

Feeding: forages at low tide on mussel beds, prying open shells; pries limpets, barnacles and other shellfish from rocks and cavities; also eats sea urchins, marine worms, crabs and other invertebrates; rarely eats oysters.

Voice: loud, piercing *wheep* or *wik* repetitions are usually given in flight; longer series of notes, accelerating into a frantic, uneven trill, is given in spring or in territorial disputes.

Similar Species: none.

Best Sites: San Juans; Neah Bay; Cape Flattery; Libbey Beach and Hastie Lake Rd. boat launch (Whidbey I.); Washington Park (Anacortes).

BLACK-NECKED STILT

Himantopus mexicanus

A bird of contrasts, the Black-necked Stilt is black above and white below. It wades with dignity on its long, pink legs along the margin of a smelly sewage lagoon or a stark, white, alkaline lakeshore—but all semblance of dignity disappears as the agitated adults scream at any intruder who approaches their nest. • The male and female Black-necked Stilt each take their turn sheltering their eggs from the warmth of the hot sun. Some individuals may even be observed wetting their belly feathers to cool off their offspring during their next stint of incubation duty. • Border disputes commonly erupt between neighboring pairs. Unlike American Avocets, their colony-nesting colleagues, Black-necked Stilts are fiercely territorial. • This loud-voiced bird serves as a sentinel for other shorebirds.

ID: black crown extends around eyes on otherwise white face; short, white "eyebrow"; red eyes; long, needlelike black bill; black back and nape; white flanks and underparts; very long, orangy pink legs. *Male:* black parts are glossy. *Female:* dark parts are brownish. *In flight:* white triangle from back onto tail; extremely pointed, dark wings with white "wing pits"; legs extend far beyond tail.
Size: *L* 14–15 in; *W* 29 in.
Status: locally fairly common migrant and resident in the Columbia Basin from May to September; rare summer resident in western Washington.
Habitat: *Breeding:* edges of salt ponds, sewage lagoons and shallow, inland wetlands. *In migration:* may visit shallow lagoons with muddy shores.

Nesting: on the ground near water, on a dike, island or mound with sparse vegetation; shallow depression is lined with items such as shells and pebbles; pair incubates 3–4 heavily dark-marked, drab brown or gray eggs for 24–29 days.
Feeding: picks prey, mostly aquatic invertebrates, from the water's surface or from the bottom.
Voice: loud, shrill *yip yap yip yap* at the nest site; also utters *kik-a-rik* or *kek kek kek kek* flight calls.
Similar Species: *American Avocet* (p. 141): bulkier; peach-colored (breeding) or light gray (nonbreeding) head and neck; upturned black bill; shorter, bluish legs; broad wings with striking black-and-white upperwing pattern.
Best Sites: Potholes Wildlife Area (Grant Co.); Dodson Rd. at Desert Wildlife Area; Toppenish NWR; Columbia NWR; occasionally summers at Ridgefield NWR.

AMERICAN AVOCET
Recurvirostra americana

Unlike avocets elsewhere in the world, the American Avocet develops a characteristic peach glow on its head, neck and upper breast in early spring, making it one of North America's most elegant birds. • In any season, avocets can be identified, even at a distance, by their habit of whisking their long, upward-curved bills back and forth through shallow water when feeding. The tip of the bill is so sensitive that it will recoil at the slightest touch. Female avocets are slightly smaller than the males and have shorter, more curved bills, enabling them to locate different aquatic prey than their mates. • The sometimes-noisy avocet parents are noted for their complicated array of both deceptive and aggressive antipredator behaviors.

breeding

breeding

ID: dark eyes; long, slim, upturned, black bill; black wings with broad white patches; white underparts; long, light bluish gray legs. *Breeding:* peach-colored upper breast, neck and head. *Nonbreeding:* light gray replaces peach. *In flight:* white back with black-and-white-patterned upperwings; white underwing has large dark triangle at tip; long legs extend beyond tail.
Size: *L* 17–18 in; *W* 30–31 in.
Status: fairly common local migrant and resident in the Columbia Basin from March to mid-September; rare migrant and summer resident in western Washington.
Habitat: shallow alkaline ponds and depressions; mudflats; marshes with short vegetation; sewage lagoons.

Nesting: semi-colonial; along a dried mudflat or exposed shoreline, in an open area or on a mound or island; in a shallow depression, usually with sparse vegetation; pair incubates 3–4 darkly marked, dusky eggs for 22–29 days.
Feeding: scythes bill through shallow water (male goes deeper) to pick up small fish and crustaceans, aquatic insects and sometimes seeds; sometimes wades or swims into deeper water and pecks, plunges, lunges or tips up.
Voice: noisy aerial pursuits near the nest; melodic *kleet* repetitions are usually loud and shrill.
Similar Species: *Black-necked Stilt* (p. 140): black pattern on head; slimmer; straight bill; mostly white body; largely black back, wings and nape; orangy pink legs.
Best Sites: Potholes Wildlife Area (Grant Co.); Dodson Rd. at Desert Wildlife Area; Toppenish NWR; Columbia NWR; Lower Crab Creek; Crockett L.

141

GREATER YELLOWLEGS
Tringa melanoleuca

The Greater Yellowlegs is the most widespread North American shorebird of a group once collectively termed "tattlers" or "tell-tales." Around the world, these species serve as sentinels among mixed flocks of shorebirds. At the first sign of danger, a Greater Yellowlegs begins calling, bobbing its head and moving slowly away from any perceived threat, eventually retreating into deeper water or taking flight, still uttering its three- or four-note warning call. This loud, whistled alarm helps distinguish the Greater Yellowlegs from the smaller Lesser Yellowlegs, one of the first identification challenges to face a novice birdwatcher in Washington. • The heavy black streaking and barring of the breeding plumage, seen here on northward-migrating birds in spring, explains the choice of *melanoleuca*, Greek for "black-and-white," to describe this species.

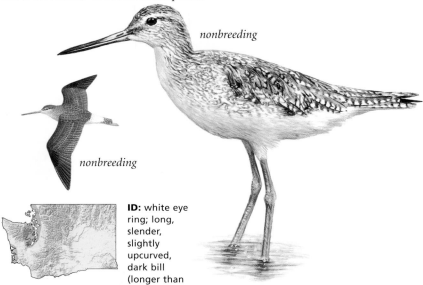

nonbreeding

nonbreeding

ID: white eye ring; long, slender, slightly upcurved, dark bill (longer than head); long, yellow legs. *Breeding:* fine, dark streaking on white head, neck and upper breast; white-spangled, brownish black back and wings; dark-barred, white flanks and lower breast. *Nonbreeding:* white-speckled, brownish gray upperparts and lighter-streaked neck; white belly and flanks. *In flight:* dark grayish upperwings; paler underwings; dark streaking on white tail.

Size: *L* 13–15 in; *W* 27–28 in.

Status: common statewide migrant from late March to mid-May and from late June to mid-October; uncommon winter resident in the west and rare in the east.

Habitat: almost any wetland habitat, including river shorelines and flooded fields.

Nesting: does not nest in Washington.

Feeding: wades in water and snatches prey from the surface or just below, or probes into soft mud; eats mostly aquatic invertebrates but also takes small fish and frogs plus some seeds and berries.

Voice: quick, whistled *tew-tew-tew* series (sometimes 4 notes); soft, single notes when feeding.

Similar Species: *Lesser Yellowlegs* (p. 143): smaller; shorter bill; legs extend farther beyond tail in flight; softer, typically 1–2 note calls. *Willet* (p. 145): stockier; stouter bill; grayish legs; flashy black-and-white wing markings in flight; different calls.

Best Sites: Skagit Game Range; Crockett L.; Nisqually NWR; Bowerman Basin (Hoquiam); Potholes Wildlife Area (Grant Co.); Columbia Basin NWR–Othello.

LESSER YELLOWLEGS

Tringa flavipes

A daintier version of its larger cousin, the Lesser Yellowlegs nevertheless appears considerably larger than the small sandpipers with which it readily mixes. It is a shorter-billed, longer-legged, less stocky bird than any accompanying dowitchers. • All but a few of the Lesser Yellowlegs seen in Washington are merely passing through on their way between nest sites in boreal woodlands and tundra in northern Canada and Alaska and their wintering grounds along Gulf and South American shorelines. Compared to the Greater Yellowlegs, it migrates northward a little earlier and is less likely to be seen in winter. • In the late 1800s, when the Lesser Yellowlegs was a popular game bird, the tendency of flockmates to hover over a wounded bird made them easy targets.

nonbreeding

nonbreeding

November) and uncommon from mid-April to mid-May; immatures rarely overwinter in the west.

ID: white "eyebrow" and eye ring; slender, straight, dark bill about as long as head; folded wings extend well beyond tail; long, yellow legs. *Breeding:* fine, dense, dark streaking on white head, neck and upper breast; white-spangled, brownish black back and wing coverts; limited dark barring on white lower breast and flanks. *Nonbreeding:* fine, pale brownish gray streaking on white head, neck and breast; white-speckled, brownish gray upperparts; white belly and flanks. *In flight:* grayish upperwings and paler underwings; dark-streaked, white tail.

Size: *L* 10–11 in; *W* 23–24 in.

Status: common statewide migrant from early July to October (stragglers to late

Habitat: equally likely in freshwater and saltwater habitats; lake, pond and marsh edges, flooded fields, wet meadows, mudflats and coastal estuaries.

Nesting: does not nest in Washington.

Feeding: makes quick probes into shallow water and mud and scythes bill back and forth for aquatic invertebrates, small fish and tadpoles; snatches airborne insects and picks prey off vegetation.

Voice: typically gives a high-pitched pair of *tew* or *tip* notes; rising, trilled *kleet* alarm call.

Similar Species: *Greater Yellowlegs* (p. 142): larger; much longer, slightly upturned bill; more dark barring on flanks in breeding plumage; legs extend less beyond tail in flight; more ringing alarm call with more notes.

Best Sites: Skagit Game Range; Crockett L.; Nisqually NWR; Bowerman Basin (Hoquiam); Potholes Wildlife Area (Grant Co.); Columbia Basin NWR–Othello.

143

SOLITARY SANDPIPER

Tringa solitaria

The nesting strategy of the Solitary Sandpiper remained a mystery until someone discovered shorebird eggs in an abandoned songbird nest in a tree. Even though the closely related yellowlegs species regularly perch in trees, the Solitary Sandpiper is the only North American shorebird to take the next logical step. • Shorebirds lay relatively large eggs that are incubated long enough for the young to grow body feathers before they hatch. Such highly developed hatchlings, known as precocial young, must learn quickly to fend for themselves. Even though they hatch in a different style of nest, once hatchling Solitary Sandpipers are lured down to the ground by the waiting parents, they behave like typical shorebird young. • Somewhat reclusive, the Solitary Sandpiper is rarely seen in flocks, but single birds may forage close together.

nonbreeding

nonbreeding

ID: white eye ring; dusky bill; white-spotted, dark back and wings; white underparts; greenish yellow legs. *Breeding:* fine dark streaking on head and neck extends onto upper breast; darker upperparts. *Nonbreeding* and *immature:* brown-streaked head and neck; grayish brown upperparts. *In flight:* center of tail and rump are dark; dark-barred outer tail; unique, butterfly-like flight close to the water's surface.
Size: *L* 8–9 in; *W* 21–22 in.
Status: uncommon migrant from mid-April to late May and rare to uncommon from July to October.
Habitat: small, wet or muddy areas.

Nesting: does not nest in Washington.
Feeding: gleans at the water's surface, probes in water and soft mud and stirs up food with its feet; eats aquatic and terrestrial invertebrates.
Voice: high, thin *peet-wheet* and clipped *plik*.
Similar Species: *Spotted Sandpiper* (p. 147): dark eye line and white "eyebrow"; dark-tipped, orange bill, dark spotting on underparts and upperparts (most conspicuous on breast) and orange legs in breeding plumage; unmarked, brown upperparts, white underparts (with extension of white at bend of wing), throat and breast (brown-smudged at edges) and yellowish legs in nonbreeding plumage.
Best Sites: Crockett L.; Union Bay Natural Area (Montlake Fill, Seattle); Nisqually NWR; Ocean Shores; Potholes Wildlife Area (Grant Co.); Reardan Ponds.

WILLET

Catoptrophorus semipalmatus

Just as "you can't judge a book by its cover," you certainly can't judge a bird solely by its initial appearance. If you spot a Willet walking slowly along a wetland shore, there is little to indicate its spirited nature. This stocky shorebird cuts a rather staid, dull, gray figure on the ground, but the instant it begins to take off, it becomes a whirling dervish of flashing black-and-white wings and loud, rhythmic *will-will-willet!* calls. The bold wing flashes may serve as a warning signal to other shorebirds or may intimidate predators during a parent's dive-bombing defense of its young. • The common name imitates the Willet's calls, and *Catoptrophorus*, Latin for "mirror-bearing," is an obvious reference to the flashy white wing patches of this genus.

nonbreeding

ID: dark-tipped, bluish gray bill; light belly; white tail with dark terminal barring; bluish gray legs. *Breeding:* dark blotches and bars on gray back and wings; buff neck and breast with dark streaks; wavy-barred flanks. *Nonbreeding:* lightly mottled, dull gray upperparts; gray breast; white throat, belly and undertail. *In flight:* distinctive black-and-white wing pattern.
Size: *L* 14–16 in; *W* 25–26 in.
Status: uncommon from July through early April; most often seen as a local coastal winter resident.

Habitat: *In migration:* wet fields; shores of marshes, ponds, lakes, estuaries and lagoons; tidal flats, beaches, rocky coastal reefs and breakwaters.
Nesting: does not nest in Washington.
Feeding: walks in shallow water, probes muddy areas and gleans the ground for insects, worms, crustaceans, mollusks and fish; occasionally eats shoots and seeds.
Voice: loud, rolling *will-will willet, will-will-willet;* monotonous repeated *wik* alarm call.
Similar Species: *Hudsonian Godwit* (p. 361): nonbreeder is grayer overall, with darker crown, longer and slightly upcurved, orangy bill with dark tip, longer, black legs, black tail and narrower white stripe on more pointed wing with unique black coverts.
Best Sites: Tokeland.

145

WANDERING TATTLER

Heteroscelus incanus

Named for its migratory prowess, the Wandering Tattler remains little known to most Washington residents. Its breeding sites were unknown until the first nest was discovered on a gravel bar alongside a Yukon, Canada, stream in 1912; others were later found in northeastern Siberia, Alaska and northwestern British Columbia, Canada. • Many birds head out to sea and overwinter on distant shores, but a small number hug the Pacific coastline and linger at rocky headlands, jetties and tide pools before continuing on as far south as Peru and as far west as eastern New Guinea and Australia. • The Wandering Tattler tends to stand and walk in a horizontal posture, bobbing its tail and occasionally its head.

nonbreeding

nonbreeding

ID: dark eye line; stout, dark bill; unmarked, gray upperparts; shortish, stout yellowish legs. *Breeding:* dense, blackish barring on head and underparts. *Nonbreeding* and *immature:* gray underparts with white belly and undertail coverts. *In flight:* 2-tone gray wings; gray tail; low, flicking flight.

Size: *L* 10–11 in; *W* 25–26 in.

Status: fairly common outer coast migrant in May and from mid-July to mid-September and rare in winter.

Habitat: rocky coastlines, gravel beaches, jetties and breakwaters; rarely on lower portions of sandy beaches among freshly washed-up seaweed or on tidal mudflats.

Nesting: does not nest in Washington.

Feeding: creeps deliberately among intertidal rocks and seaweed, picking off crustaceans, mollusks, marine worms and other invertebrates.

Voice: generally silent; short 1-pitch series of rapid-fire whistles, *lidididi,* or a crisp *klee-ik* in alarm.

Similar Species: *Willet* (p. 145): larger; paler and browner; longer, bluish gray legs; black and white patches on wings in flight; rarely seen among rocks. *Surfbird* (p. 153): chunkier; browner; stubby, dark-tipped, yellow bill; white wings and tail in flight. *Black Turnstone* (p. 152): black head, breast and upperparts; short, dark bill; complex white pattern on back, wings and tail in flight. *Rock Sandpiper* (p. 161): nonbreeding bird has slightly downcurved bill, dark breast, dark-flecked belly and sides, and white upperwing stripe in flight.

Best Sites: Ediz Hook (Port Angeles); La Push; Kalaloch; Pt. Brown jetty (Ocean Shores); Westport jetty; North Jetty (Columbia R. mouth).

SPOTTED SANDPIPER

Actitis macularius

Apart from the ubiquitous Killdeer, the Spotted Sandpiper is perhaps North America's best-known and most easily identified shorebird. Its characteristic "teeter-totter" behavior, stiff-winged flight and conspicuous breast spots all make it instantly recognizable in summer. • The Spotted Sandpiper is among a tiny minority of birds with atypical gender roles. As with phalaropes, the females arrive on the breeding grounds first and stake out territories. A large female may mate with up to four males, each of which incubates her eggs and cares for the young (but some females are loyal to one mate and help raise their chicks). The male's relatively high level of prolactin—a hormone known to promote parental care—helps ensure his involvement.

breeding

nonbreeding

ID: white "eyebrow"; dark eye line; tail bobs distinctively and extends well beyond folded wings. *Breeding:* dark-tipped, orange bill; white underparts are heavily dark-spotted, especially in female; white undertail coverts; yellowish orange legs. *Nonbreeding:* dingier bill; brown back; white throat, neck, belly and breast (brown-smudged at edges), with upward extension of white at bend of wing; yellower legs. *In flight:* short white streak on dark trailing edge of upperwing; gray-patterned, white underwing with dark trailing edge; distinctive, flickering flight with wings bowed below horizontal and short glides close to water.
Size: *L* 7–8 in; *W* 14–15 in.
Status: fairly common statewide breeder from May to September; uncommon to rare in winter in western coastal and lowland areas.

Habitat: beaches and gravel bars along freshwater streams, lakes, ponds and estuaries; wet meadow margins.
Nesting: among logs or under bushes, usually well above the water's edge; shallow depression is lined with grass; mostly the male incubates 4 brown-blotched, buff eggs for 20–24 days and tends the young.
Feeding: picks and gleans along shorelines for invertebrates; occasionally snatches flying insects from the air.
Voice: sharp, crisp *eat-wheat, eat-wheat, wheat-wheat-wheat-wheat.*
Similar Species: *Solitary Sandpiper* (p. 144): complete eye ring; white-speckled back and wings; streaked upper breast and white underparts year-round; greenish yellow legs; dark-barred, white outer tail. *Lesser Yellowlegs* (p. 143): larger; slimmer; all-dark bill; white-speckled back, streaked breast and white belly year-round; longer, bright yellow legs; white uppertail; deeper wingbeats.
Best Sites: wetland habitats, particularly along streams and rivers. *Winter:* western lowlands and coastal estuaries.

WHIMBREL
Numenius phaeopus

Whimbrels nest across the northern latitudes of North America, Europe and Asia. They spend their winters on the shores of six continents, with some migrants undertaking nonstop ocean flights of up to 2500 miles. • Unlike its smaller relative, the probably extinct Eskimo Curlew *(N. borealis)*, the Whimbrel withstood the ravages of 19th-century market hunters largely because of its more wary nature. • Heard long before they come into sight, Whimbrels fly in V-formations and keep in touch with almost continuous whistles—one of the wild sounds of fall and spring. Flocks spread out to feed and often forage on the drier parts of mudflats, which most other shorebirds avoid. • The genus name for curlews comes from the Greek words *neos* and *mene*, meaning "new moon"—a clear reference to the crescent-shaped bills.

ID: dark-striped head with lighter central strip; brown-streaked lower face, neck and breast; partial white eye ring; dark eyes; long, downcurved, dark bill (lower mandible may have pinkish base); pale-dappled, grayish brown back and upperwings; pale, buff-washed underparts; brown-barred flanks and tail; stocky, bluish legs. *In flight:* brown-barred, buff wing linings; gray flight feathers.
Size: *L* 17–18 in; *W* 31–32 in.
Status: fairly common migrant in the west from mid-April to mid-May and from July through August; local western winter resident.
Habitat: various coastal habitats, including beaches, mudflats, estuaries, rocky shores, saltwater marshes, reefs and breakwaters; also uses pastures, flooded fields, freshwater marshes and coastal lake and river margins.
Nesting: does not nest in Washington.
Feeding: picks from the ground or probes just under the surface in mud or vegetation; eats mainly marine invertebrates, especially small crabs, marine worms and mollusks.
Voice: incoming flocks utter a distinctive, rippling *bibibibibibibi.*
Similar Species: *Long-billed Curlew* (p. 149): larger; unstriped crown; much longer bill; distinctly buff underparts; warm cinnamon wing linings and upper flight feathers. *Willet* (p. 145): smaller; much grayer; gray crown; shorter, straight bill; distinctive black-and-white wing pattern in flight.
Best Sites: Ediz Hook (Port Angeles); Crockett L.; Butler Flat (Burlington); Drayton Harbor; West Pt. (Discovery Park, Seattle); Ocean Shores Game Range.

LONG-BILLED CURLEW
Numenius americanus

North America's largest sandpiper, the Long-billed Curlew, comes equipped with a downcurved bill that may be more than 7 inches long on some females. The bill is used as a dexterous tool to pick grasshoppers and beetles from dense prairie grasslands or extract deeply buried aquatic invertebrates from soft mud. • Male curlews engage in spectacular displays over their nesting territory, uttering loud, ringing calls while fluttering high and then gliding down in an undulating flight. • The Long-billed Curlew breeds on grasslands, often in areas with scattered lakes and marshes. Its future is largely tied to the adoption of conservative range and grassland management strategies designed to provide enough grassland habitat for nesting.

ID: streaked crown, neck and breast; partial dark eye stripe; pale eye ring; very long, downcurved bill with pink base; mottled brown upperparts; buff-brown underparts; long, bluish legs. *In flight:* barred, rufous brown upperwing flight feathers; cinnamon wing linings; toes extend just beyond tail.
Size: *L* 20–26 in; *W* 34–35 in.
Status: uncommon breeding resident east of the Cascades from mid-March to late July and uncommon migrant; uncommon coastal migrant and winter resident from late July to late March.

Habitat: *Breeding:* grasslands often interspersed with freshwater lakes and marshes. *In migration:* tidal mudflats, estuaries and saltwater marshes; grasslands and pastures.
Nesting: on the ground in the open, often near a rock, bush or other small landmark; slight depression is sparsely lined with grass and other debris; pair incubates 4 brown-spotted, olive or buff eggs for 27–30 days.
Feeding: probes tall grass for insects, especially grasshoppers and beetles; probes shorelines and coastal mudflats for invertebrates; may take eggs, nestlings and berries.
Voice: most common call is a loud, whistling *cur-lee cur-lee cur-lee;* also gives shorter whistles; male's display song is a low whistle series with a slurred crescendo.
Similar Species: *Whimbrel* (p. 148): smaller; dark and pale crown stripes; shorter bill; unmarked, pale belly; plain, brown wings in flight. *Marbled Godwit* (p. 150): smaller; shorter bill slightly upturned toward tip; dark legs; plain orange upperwing flight feathers.
Best Sites: occasional at Bill's Spit (Ocean Shores). *Winter:* Tokeland.

149

MARBLED GODWIT

Limosa fedoa

Its large size, warm brown color and long, pink-based, slightly upturned bill make the Marbled Godwit easy to recognize. Unlike other North American godwits, it has a summer plumage not much different from what it wears the rest of the year. • The Marbled Godwit is generally a scarce migrant in Washington, although it is common on Willapa Bay, and it is found in coastal California as well. Some Washington migrants go up the coast in flocks to Alaska to nest, whereas others migrate across the state to breed in Montana or the Canadian prairie provinces. • In recognition of the foraging habitats preferred by many godwits, the genus name, *Limosa,* comes from a Latin word that means "mud."

nonbreeding

breeding

ID: buff brown overall; fairly noticeable dark crown and eye stripes; dark eyes; long, slightly upturned, dark-tipped, pinkish bill; dark-and-light-patterned back; pale tan underparts; long neck; long, dark legs. *Breeding:* fine dark barring on underparts; brown streaks on neck. *In flight:* unbarred, cinnamon underwing; unmarked, orangy buff inner flight feathers; darker leading edge on upperwing.
Size: *L* 16–20 in; *W* 29–30 in.
Status: common Tokeland resident from August through April; uncommon migrant at other coastal locations from early to late May and mid-July to August and resident from August to early May.
Habitat: coastal estuaries, salt marshes, lagoons, sandy beaches, wet fields and lake margins.

Nesting: does not nest in Washington.
Feeding: walks slowly and probes deeply in soft substrates for worms, small bivalves and crabs.
Voice: unique resonant, anxious, gull-like *ka-rek* cries.
Similar Species: *Long-billed Curlew* (p. 149): larger; longer, downcurved bill; bluish gray legs; barred, rufous brown upperwing flight feathers. *Hudsonian Godwit* (p. 361) and *Bar-tailed Godwit* (p. 362): less common; breeding females are similar to nonbreeding and immature Marbled Godwits but with mostly gray or black underwings; immature Hudsonian has plain brown back; immature Bar-tailed has pale "eyebrow" and eye line. *Long-billed Dowitcher* (p. 165) and *Short-billed Dowitcher* (p. 164): much smaller; stockier; long, straight, dark bills; white back patch; greenish legs; grayish underwing with light trailing edge.
Best Sites: Tokeland; occasional at Bill's Spit and Damon Pt. (Ocean Shores).

RUDDY TURNSTONE
Arenaria interpres

Painted faces and eye-catching black-and-red backs set Ruddy Turnstones apart from the multitudes of little brown-and-white sandpipers. Stocky and with heavier bills than most of their companions, Ruddies walk with a comical, rolling gait and sometimes tilt sideways to counteract the influence of strong winds. • The Ruddy Turnstone's summer and winter ranges are among the most widely separated of any bird species. It breeds in the arctic tundra of North America and Eurasia and overwinters in tropical and temperate habitats well into the southern hemisphere. • As their name suggests, turnstones find food by flipping over pebbles, shells, driftwood and other objects to find invertebrates, exploiting a foraging niche unused by other shorebirds.

breeding ♂

nonbreeding

ID: short, tapered, black bill; white belly. *Breeding:* dark-streaked crown; black-and-white face; ruddy upperparts; black bands on upper and lower back; U-shaped black "bib" curves up to shoulders; orangy red legs. *Nonbreeding:* brown upperparts mottled with black, buff and white; weaker "bib"; dusky brown breast and head markings; yellowish orange legs. *In flight:* red (or brown), black and white bands on upperwings, back and tail; white underwings with dark trailing edges.
Size: *L* 9–10 in; *W* 21 in.
Status: fairly common coastal migrant from early to mid-May and from mid-July through August and rare winter resident.
Habitat: sand or cobble beaches with pebbles, shells and abundant wrack and wave-tossed debris; estuarine mudflats, tide pools and breakwaters.
Nesting: does not nest in Washington.
Feeding: forages by gleaning from the ground or probing in mud and sand or under dislodged objects; takes mostly invertebrates but will eat carrion, moss, fish eggs and discarded human food.
Voice: clear, rattling, staccato *cut-a-cut* alarm call and lower, repeated contact notes.
Similar Species: *Black Turnstone* (p. 152): black upperparts; whitish edges accent back and wing feathers; more hectic, higher-pitched calls; similar upperwing pattern is all black and white. *Surfbird* (p. 153): bulkier; stout, dark-tipped, yellowish orange bill; yellow legs; streaky, grayish head, black-spotted flanks and paler pinkish brown back in breeding plumage; nonbreeder is mostly plain gray.
Best Sites: Tokeland; Long Beach Peninsula; Leadbetter Pt.; Kennedys Lagoon (Whidbey I.).

BLACK TURNSTONE

Arenaria melanocephala

Living up to its name, the Black Turnstone does much of its foraging by flipping over small, loose objects to expose concealed food items. This visual feeder also moves slowly over rocks, dislodging barnacles and hammering or prying them open to extract the soft parts. • Black Turnstones prefer rocky habitats, which they share with Black Oystercatchers, Surfbirds and Rock Sandpipers, but they also occur in small numbers on sand beaches and mudflats, often with Ruddy Turnstones. Unlike Ruddies, Black Turnstones have a fairly constant plumage year-round. • Flocks are usually small, and individuals always show a certain amount of aggression toward each other and to other species. • The Greek-derived species name *melanocephala* means "black head."

nonbreeding

ID: black head and breast; short, tapered, black bill; black upperparts with whitish feather edges; white belly; brownish or blackish orange legs. *Breeding:* white "eyebrow" and "teardrop" in front of eye. *In flight:* distinctive black-and-white pattern on upperwings, back and tail.
Size: *L* 9 in; *W* 21 in.
Status: common coastal migrant and winter resident from mid-August to late April; uncommon coastal migrant from mid-July to mid-August and from early to mid-May.
Habitat: rocky shorelines, breakwaters, jetties and reefs; may also visit beaches with seaweed wracks as well as mudflats, gravel bars and temporary ponds.
Nesting: does not nest in Washington.

Feeding: flips over pebbles and other items or forages on rocks; pries open shells or hammers them apart; eats mostly crustaceans and mollusks such as barnacles and limpets.
Voice: shrill, high-pitched *skirrr* call turns into chatter as flock erupts into flight.
Similar Species: *Ruddy Turnstone* (p. 151): reddish to yellowish orange legs; distinctive black markings on head and breast, and ruddy back and wing bars in breeding plumage; lightly mottled, brownish head and upperparts in nonbreeding plumage; lower-pitched calls. *Surfbird* (p. 153): larger; dark-tipped, yellow bill; mostly gray upperparts; back and wing coverts all gray or with pinkish brown; black- or gray-spotted flanks; yellowish legs. *Wandering Tattler* (p. 146): slimmer; longer bill; all-gray upperparts, wings and tail; white belly; dark-barred underparts in breeding plumage; teeters and bobs as it feeds.
Best Sites: Ediz Hook (Port Angeles); Pt. Brown jetty (Ocean Shores); Westport jetty; Tokeland; Long Beach Peninsula; North Jetty (Columbia R. mouth).

SURFBIRD
Aphriza virgata

Wreathed in mist from yet another breaking Pacific roller, a Surfbird treks slowly but surely through a mix of tide pools and seaweed-covered rocks until a larger wave forces it to take off. At this point, the three or four birds in view suddenly transform into a flock of two dozen or more birds that had been hidden in the backdrop of dark, glistening seaweed and mussel-encrusted boulders. In its tight foraging flocks, the Surfbird occasionally appears by the hundreds at favored feeding sites. • The Surfbird has the longest wintering range of any North American shorebird breeder. It migrates more than 10,000 miles from Kodiak Island, Alaska, to Chile's southernmost peninsula, never straying far above the tide line during its journey. When not feeding, it frequents rocky shores or jetties, staying close to the waterline.

nonbreeding

ID: mainly dull gray overall; dark eyes; sturdy, yellow-based bill with dark tip; white belly; yellow legs. *Breeding:* more fine, white streaking on head; black-marked, pinkish brown wing coverts; blackish spots and chevrons on flanks and lower breast. *Nonbreeding* and *immature:* gray-spotted flanks. *In flight:* white stripe on gray upper-wing; black-tipped, white tail; white underwings with gray edges.
Size: *L* 9–10 in; *W* 26 in.
Status: fairly common migrant and local resident along the coast from winter to early spring.
Habitat: wave-washed rocky shorelines, including ledges, reefs and pinnacles; rarely on sand beaches or intertidal mudflats.

Nesting: does not nest in Washington.
Feeding: pries young mussels, barnacles and limpets from rocks to eat whole, later regurgitating shells; picks invertebrates, such as snails, from intertidal rocks.
Voice: generally silent; soft, single, high-pitched notes and a *yif-yif-yif* flight call; feeding flocks may utter turnstonelike nasal chatter.
Similar Species: *Black Turnstone* (p. 152) and *Ruddy Turnstone* (p. 151): slightly smaller; more striking plumage; pointier, darker bills; orange or dark orange legs; white-striped back in flight; much noisier. *Rock Sandpiper* (p. 161): nonbreeding bird has longer, thinner, darker, slightly down-curved bill, dusky greenish legs and white tail with gray center on top.
Best Sites: Westport jetty; Pt. Brown jetty (Ocean Shores); Neah Bay; Ediz Hook (Port Angeles).

RED KNOT
Calidris canutus

Surely the Cinderella of shorebirds, the Red Knot, although lost in a mass of brown and gray sandpipers in rare fall appearances, is an absolute knockout during its brief spring appearance. Among its usual tidal-flat neighbors, only the dowitchers undergo a similar transformation. Whereas the Red Knot's dull non-breeding plumage blends into the uniform grays and browns of mudflats and sandy beaches, its bright summer wardrobe matches rusty-tinged arctic grasses, sedges, shrubs and wildflowers. • Red Knots feeding in tightly packed groups at a few favored spots along Washington's coast in spring may have started their trek as far south as the shores of South America. • The *canutus* part of the scientific name refers to King Canute, who commanded the tide to halt, something a flock of Red Knots may seem to be doing on its shoreline food patrol.

breeding

nonbreeding

ID: dark eyes; straight, head-length, dark bill; light gray tail; blackish yellow legs.
Breeding: largely rufous orange head, neck and underparts; grayish upperparts flecked with dark brown and chestnut; dark barring on white undertail coverts.
Nonbreeding: dark eye line; pale brownish gray upperparts; white underparts with buff wash; faint brown streaks on breast; some brownish gray barring on flanks.
Size: *L* 10–11 in; *W* 23 in.
Status: very localized, fairly common to common migrant from mid-April to mid-May; rare fall migrant from mid-July to October.
Habitat: almost entirely coastal; prefers tidal and estuary margins; also in saltwater marshes with tidal channels and sandy beaches.
Nesting: does not nest in Washington.
Feeding: probes in sand and mud; occa-sionally pecks at washed-up seaweed; eats invertebrates and various plant materials; may join Ruddy Turnstones to pick at beach carcasses.
Voice: usually silent; utters occasionally repeated low *knut* (with a softly voiced "k") reminiscent of its name.
Similar Species: *Surfbird* (p. 153): stubby, dark-tipped, yellow bill; yellow legs; dark-tipped, white tail; more contrast on under-wings; nonbreeder has gray-spotted flanks. *Wandering Tattler* (p. 146): yellow legs; nonbreeder has more uniformly gray upperparts, head, breast, wings and tail.
Best Sites: Bottle Beach (Ocosta); Ocean Shores Game Range; Bowerman Basin (Hoquiam).

SANDERLING

Calidris alba

Anyone who has spent time on a sandy beach between late summer and late spring knows Sanderlings. They scamper about like wheeled mechanical toys as flocks zigzag up and down the beach following every wave. Resembling fledgling surfers having fun, they are pursuing tiny crustaceans. If a wave catches a flock unprepared, the birds will rise in unison. Sanderlings also peck and probe with other sandpipers on sand flats and mudflats. After feeding, the birds slowly reassemble in densely packed roosting flocks, seemingly asleep but ready to escape at any disturbance. • Sanderlings breed across the Arctic and overwinter on beaches in more hospitable climes on every continent except Antarctica. • Adult Sanderlings have unique plumages, but immatures resemble several small sandpipers, though with less conspicuous wing stripes.

nonbreeding

nonbreeding

ID: black bill; white underparts; black legs. *Breeding:* rusty orange head and breast with dark spots and streaks (much grayer female has hints of rufous); rufous-marked, grayish brown upperparts; dark centered, pale-edged feathers on and near back. *Nonbreeding:* pale gray upperparts; small black patch on shoulder. *Immature:* checkered, black-and-white back. *In flight:* gray upperwing with darker edges and conspicuous white stripe; gray-edged, white underwing.
Size: *L* 7–8 in; *W* 16–17 in.
Status: common migrant and resident from August to late May along coastal beaches; uncommon migrant from late August to late September east of the Cascades.
Habitat: sand beaches; also estuaries, rocky shores, wet grassy fields and shorelines of large reservoirs.

Nesting: does not nest in Washington.
Feeding: runs and pecks along the line of advancing and retreating waves; eats various coastal invertebrates, especially sand crabs, marine worms, crustaceans, insects and small mollusks.
Voice: easily distinguished sharp *kip* flight call.
Similar Species: *Western Sandpiper* (p. 157): smaller; breeding bird has black-tipped scapular feathers and dark-spotted breast and flanks, with rufous restricted to crown, ear patch and sides of back; non-breeder has lightly streaked upper breast area. *Semipalmated Sandpiper* (p. 156): smaller; darker "cap" and mark in front of eye; lightly brown-marked breast; "scaly" upperparts; little rufous in breeding plumage.
Best Sites: Crockett L.; West Pt. (Discovery Park, Seattle); Dungeness NWR; Ediz Hook (Port Angeles); Ocean Shores beaches; Long Beach Peninsula.

SEMIPALMATED SANDPIPER
Calidris pusilla

Semipalmated Sandpipers migrate almost the entire length of the Americas, and their migratory pit stops have to provide ample food resources. In the eastern U.S., "Semis" fly in tight flocks; they peck and probe in mechanized fury, replenishing their body fat for the remainder of their long migrations. It is vital that these birds acquire just the right amount of fat—too much slows them down, making them easy targets for fast-flying falcons, but with too little they will run out of energy before they reach the next feeding ground. Only scattered remnants of these large eastern U.S. flocks migrate through Washington. Small numbers of Semipalmated Sandpipers visit our mudflats annually, with numbers decreasing from inland areas toward the coast. • "Semipalmated" refers to the slight webbing between this bird's front toes, and *pusilla* means "small."

nonbreeding

nonbreeding

ID: short, straight, dark bill; dark legs. *Breeding:* rufous ear patch; mottled upperparts; faint streaks on upper breast and flanks. *Nonbreeding:* faint, white "eyebrow"; pale grayish brown upperparts; white underparts. *In flight:* narrow, white wing stripe; white rump is split by black line.
Size: *L* 6¼ in; *W* 14 in.
Status: uncommon southbound migrant from early July to mid-August in the west and from the middle to the end of August in the east.

Habitat: mudflats and the shores of ponds and lakes.
Nesting: does not nest in Washington.
Feeding: probes soft substrates and gleans for aquatic insects and crustaceans.
Voice: flight call is a harsh *cherk*.
Similar Species: *Least Sandpiper* (p. 158): browner overall color; pale legs. *Dunlin* (p. 162): longer, downcurved bill. *Western Sandpiper* (p. 157): longer, slightly downcurved bill.
Best Sites: Crockett L.; Wenas L. (Yakima Co.).; Columbia R. near the Tri-Cities; County Line Ponds (SR 26, Adams Co.–Grant Co.); Swanson Lakes Wildlife Area (Lincoln Co.); Walla Walla R. delta.

WESTERN SANDPIPER

Calidris mauri

The Western Sandpiper and the Semipalmated Sandpiper both belong to a group of small *Calidris* sandpipers known as "peeps" in North America and "stints" elsewhere in the English-speaking world. Similarities in plumages and other characteristics can make the members of this group notoriously difficult to identify. If subtleties of size, plumage and calls are not of particular interest, then enjoy these sprites for their sheer exuberance and grace of movement. Just about everyone appreciates the aerial maneuvers of a Western Sandpiper flock wheeling over estuarine tidal flats in April. • Western Sandpipers breed only in Alaska and extreme northeastern Siberia, but they fan out across the continent in migration, wintering as far south as the coasts of South America.

breeding

nonbreeding

ID: long, slightly down-curved, black bill (longer in female); white belly and undertail coverts; black legs and feet. *Breeding:* rusty crown, ear and scapular patches; heavily dark-spotted and chevroned upper breast and flanks (less so on upper belly). *Nonbreeding:* pale gray head; indistinct white "eyebrow" and lower face; grayish brown upperparts; faint streaks on sides of breast. *In flight:* gray upperwing with white stripe; dark-edged, white underwing; dark-centered tail; large, tightly packed flocks.
Size: *L* 6–7 in; *W* 14 in.
Status: very abundant migrant in the west from mid-April to mid-May and common migrant from July to September; fairly common migrant in the east from July to mid-September.

Habitat: tidal estuaries, saltwater marshes and sandy beaches; freshwater shorelines, flooded fields and pools.
Nesting: does not nest in Washington.
Feeding: gleans and probes in soft mud, moist sand, washed-up seaweed and shallow water (occasionally submerges its head); eats mainly small aquatic invertebrates.
Voice: squeaky, high-pitched *cheep* or *chir-eep* flight call, more liquid than that of other peeps; twittering chatter from flocks.
Similar Species: *Semipalmated Sandpiper* (p. 156): breeding bird is plainer brown, with a few rufous tints and less spotting on flanks; nonbreeder has slightly darker mottling. *Dunlin* (p. 162): larger; longer bill; breeding bird has black area on lower belly and more rufous on back; nonbreeding bird is darker and browner.
Best Sites: Crockett L.; Union Bay Natural Area (Montlake Fill, Seattle); Ocean Shores–Bowerman Basin; Willapa Bay; Long Beach Peninsula; Lind Coulee.

157

LEAST SANDPIPER

Calidris minutilla

Just as its common name and *minutilla* suggest, the Least Sandpaper is the smallest of our sandpipers, yet it still manages impressive migratory feats. As with most peeps and other small sandpipers, some females migrate from the Arctic to South America and back again each year. • Least Sandpipers breed during the brief arctic summer, and in fall the parents start their journey south earlier than their brood. The juveniles are left to fatten up, learn to fly and prepare for the long journey south all on their own. Many birds stop off at well-vegetated areas of coastal salt marshes and tidal estuaries to replenish their food supplies and to get some protection from aerial predators.

nonbreeding

breeding

ID: sharp, black bill; clearly defined white belly; white flanks and undertail coverts; distinctive yellowish or greenish legs. *Breeding:* mottled, warm brown head, breast and upperparts; dark-centered back and wing feathers. *Nonbreeding:* darkly marked, dull grayish brown head, breast and upperparts. *Immature:* brighter than adult; extensive dark-centered, rufous feathering on back and wings. *In flight:* short, dark wings, often bent, with white lining and thin upperwing stripe.
Size: *L* 6 in; *W* 13 in.
Status: common to fairly common western migrant from July to mid-November and in early May; fairly common eastern migrant from July to mid-September; uncommon western resident in winter and early spring.
Habitat: tidal estuaries, saltwater marshes, lagoons and kelp-wracked sandy beaches along the coast; flooded fields and freshwater shorelines inland.

Nesting: does not nest in Washington.
Feeding: picks and probes in mud, sand and low marsh vegetation for insects, crustaceans, snails, marine worms, other aquatic invertebrates and occasional seeds; does not wade much.
Voice: usual call is a high-pitched *kreee*. *Male:* often utters a high, fast trill during spring courtship flight, with each phrase rising to a crescendo during descent.
Similar Species: *Other small sandpipers:* dark legs. *Semipalmated Sandpiper* (p. 156): little rufous on plain grayish brown breeding bird; dull, uniformly gray upperparts on nonbreeder; no rufous and less distinctly streaked breast on immature. *Western Sandpiper* (p. 157): longer bill; rufous accents on breeding bird; less defined breast streaking on grayish brown nonbreeder.
Best Sites: Crockett L.; Union Bay Natural Area (Montlake Fill, Seattle); Dungeness NWR; Ocean Shores; Long Beach Peninsula; Lind Coulee.

BAIRD'S SANDPIPER

Calidris bairdii

Baird's Sandpipers are the largest of the small sandpipers commonly referred to as "peeps." • As with other arctic-nesting shorebirds, when the chicks can fend for themselves, the parents abandon them and then embark on the long, arduous return trip to wintering areas in western and southern South America. A few weeks later, the juveniles are ready to make their first migration flights, with some following the adults' interior routes and others spreading out across Canada to reach both the Atlantic and Pacific coasts. The juveniles join up with other species of sandpipers from early August to late September; they can be picked out in roosting flocks by their taller stature. • This modestly plumaged but elegant shorebird was named for Spencer Fullerton Baird, an early Smithsonian Institute official who organized several natural history expeditions across North America in the mid- to late 1800s.

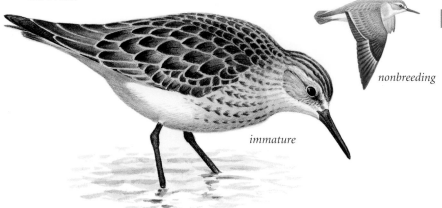

nonbreeding

immature

ID: straight, black bill; white under-parts; upper breast has brownish wash with fine darker streaks; black legs; long wings project well beyond tail when folded. *Breeding:* silvery scapulars with large dark spots. *Nonbreeding:* indistinctly "scaly," grayish brown back. *Immature:* "scaly" back; light brown upper breast.
Size: *L* 7 in; *W* 17 in.
Status: uncommon migrant in the west from mid-August to October; uncommon to fairly common migrant in the east from August to late September; rare to casual statewide in spring.
Habitat: upper tide lines on ocean beaches, dry estuarine flats, damp freshwater alkaline flats and margins of sewage ponds; grassy fields and dunes; even above timberline during fall migration.
Nesting: does not nest in Washington.
Feeding: alone, with other small sand-pipers or with plovers; walks slowly and picks insects and other invertebrates from the water's surface; rarely probes; not inclined to wade, it feeds mostly on higher, drier ground.
Voice: usually silent; soft, reedy *creeeep, creeep* is often extended into a trill in flight.
Similar Species: *Pectoral Sandpiper* (p. 160): dull, yellow legs; streaky breast band is darker and more clearly defined; male is noticeably larger; undertail coverts are more obvious in flight.
Best Sites: Crockett L.; Damon Pt. (Ocean Shores); Union Bay Natural Area (Montlake Fill, Seattle); Potholes Wildlife Area (Grant Co.); County Line Ponds (SR 26, Adams Co.–Grant Co.); Walla Walla R. delta.

159

PECTORAL SANDPIPER

Calidris melanotos

Widespread world travelers, Pectoral Sandpipers have been observed throughout North America during their epic migrations from Alaska and the Siberian and Canadian Arctic to the pampas of South America—and even to Australia and New Zealand in small numbers. Siberian individuals may undertake a return trip of 20,000 miles—comparable to that of the Arctic Tern. In spring, most migrants take an inland route to the Arctic. Once there, the males court by filling their pectoral sacs with air and producing a remarkable rapid, foghornlike hooting, but in migration they hide in long grass and give no indication of their unique abilities. • Adults first appear in Washington in mid-July and then leave by early September, but immatures are most abundant from late August to the end of October, with a few birds lingering until late November.

immature

ID: dark-tipped, dusky yellowish bill; dark breast streaking with distinct boundary contrasts with white underparts; yellow-tinged legs; dark-centered tail with white sides;. *Breeding:* pale buff edges to upper feathers; darker breast streaking and back markings. *Immature:* brighter, more rufous upperparts; 2 distinctive white back and scapular stripes.
Size: *Male:* L 8–9 in; W 17–18 in. *Female:* L 6–7 in; W 16–17 in.
Status: common to fairly common western migrant from early September through October; common to fairly common eastern migrant from early September through October.
Habitat: coastal salt marshes; also grassy margins of saltwater and brackish pools and lagoons, wet or grassy fields, ponds and drained lake beds.
Nesting: does not nest in Washington.
Feeding: pecks and probes the ground and grass for small invertebrates; also takes some seeds and algae.
Voice: gives a sharp, short, low and distinctive *krrick krrick* when flushed. *Male:* occasionally utters a low, throaty note series or louder, more persistent threat call when feeding.
Similar Species: *Sharp-tailed Sandpiper* (p. 362): less and coarser breast streaking; nonbreeder usually has some rufous on crown; immature has brighter reddish "cap" and upperparts, strong white "eyebrow" and buffier, mostly unstreaked breast. *Buff-breasted Sandpiper* (p. 362): small, rounded head; unmarked "cheeks" and throat; warm buff underparts.
Best Sites: Leadbetter Pt.; Ocean Shores Game Range; Crockett L.; Union Bay Natural Area (Montlake Fill, Seattle); Potholes Wildlife Area; Soap L.

ROCK SANDPIPER

Calidris ptilocnemis

This well-camouflaged bird is the smallest and rarest of the several "rock-pipers" seen along the Washington coast. With the shape and size of a Dunlin and the overall plumage of a Surfbird, the Rock Sandpiper might easily be overlooked as it feeds with larger, showier Black Turnstones and Surfbirds on wave-washed jetties, rock ledges and rocky shorelines. In Washington it is almost always seen in the cryptic gray nonbreeding plumage rather than the more colorful breeding or immature plumages. • Rock Sandpipers are almost always seen in small numbers. A few adults return to our coast as soon as early October, and a few lingerers stay until mid-May. Point Brown jetty at Ocean Shores is the most reliable site.

nonbreeding

ID: blackish bill with dull olive base; bold, gray spots on sides and undertail coverts; short, dusky olive legs; folded wings shorter than tail. *Nonbreeding:* uniformly gray head and neck; pale mark between base of bill and eye; mottled, gray back, wings and breast. *Immature:* back feathers narrowly edged in rufous; indistinct, pale mantle stripe.
Size: *L* 9 in; *W* 17 in.
Status: uncommon local migrant and resident from October to April.
Habitat: rocky shorelines, jetties, breakwaters, sea stacks and tide pools; very rarely on estuarine sites.

Nesting: does not nest in Washington.
Feeding: picks small marine invertebrates off rocks and seaweed; may also eat plant material.
Voice: generally silent; scratchy, low *keesh* flight call may change to a rougher *cherk;* flocks utter a sharper *kwititit-kwit.*
Similar Species: *Dunlin* (p. 162): slightly longer, more downcurved bill; brownish gray upperparts and plainer underparts in nonbreeding plumage; immature has more, darker streaking on breast and black-marked belly. *Surfbird* (p. 153): much heavier; stubbier bill; black-tipped, white tail; yellow legs; paler gray upperparts in nonbreeding plumage.
Best Sites: Pt. Brown jetty (Ocean Shores); Westport jetty; Ediz Hook (Port Angeles); North Jetty (Columbia R. mouth).

161

DUNLIN

Calidris alpina

Named for its brownish color and small size, the Dunlin (originally "Dunling") fully lives up to its name only in winter, when grayish brown flocks of this small sandpiper are scattered along chilly shorelines. The Dunlin prefers to fly with its own kind and can often be seen in very large, more discrete flocks at tide-line roosts. As spring approaches, the dingy nonbreeding bird gradually takes on a dazzling russet back and bold black belly. Dynamic, swirling clouds of up to 10,000 birds fly wing tip to wing tip, all changing course simultaneously, often to elude falcons. But, all too soon, the flocks leave for more northerly destinations. • The Dunlin is our most common winter shorebird and is among the swiftest of shorebird migrants. Its speed helps it escape from raptors such as the Merlin and the Peregrine Falcon.

breeding

nonbreeding

ID: long, slightly down-curved, black bill; black legs. *Breeding:* gray, lightly streaked head and neck; russet crown, scapulars and back; black belly; white undertail coverts. *Nonbreeding:* brownish gray upperparts; pale underparts. *In flight:* prominent white stripe on dark upperwing; long wings; dark-centered tail.

Size: *L* 7–9 in; *W* 17 in.

Status: common migrant and winter resident in the west from late October to early May; uncommon in early October and early April in the east.

Habitat: tidal and saltwater marshes, estuaries and lagoon shorelines; open, sandy ocean beaches; flooded fields and muddy edges of freshwater wetlands; occasionally seen beside city ponds and sewage lagoons.

Nesting: does not nest in Washington.

Feeding: jabs, picks and probes, often with the bill open and usually at the tide line; varied diet of mostly bivalves, crustaceans and other invertebrates, small fish and some plant material.

Voice: grating *cheezp* or *treezp* flight call. *Male:* display song is a descending, creaky, high-pitched trill.

Similar Species: *Rock Sandpiper* (p. 161): slightly shorter bill; gray upperparts and heavily gray-marked underparts in nonbreeding plumage; immature has whitish belly; prefers rocky areas. *Curlew Sandpiper:* accidental to casual; slightly longer bill and legs; all-white rump; breeding adult is deep rufous over most of body; nonbreeding adult has white "eyebrow" and lighter gray upperparts.

Best Sites: Samish Flats–Skagit Flats; Ocean Shores; Westport; Bottle Beach (Ocosta); Willapa Bay.

STILT SANDPIPER

Calidris himantopus

With the silhouette of a yellowlegs and the foraging behaviour of a dowitcher—two birds with which it often associates—the Stilt Sandpiper is often overlooked by birdwatchers. • Stilt Sandpipers love water, and they often wade breast deep or plunge their heads underwater in search of food. They are the most vegetarian of shorebirds, and one-third of their diet consists of plant matter. A foraging Stilt Sandpiper occasionally sweeps its bill side-to-side through the water, like an avocet. Stilt Sandpipers have also been seen holding their bills submerged for prolonged periods in sand or water, waiting for prey to touch the bill and trigger a strike. • Several shorebirds have longer legs, but the Stilt Sandpiper is deserving of its title in comparison with other members of the genus *Calidris.*

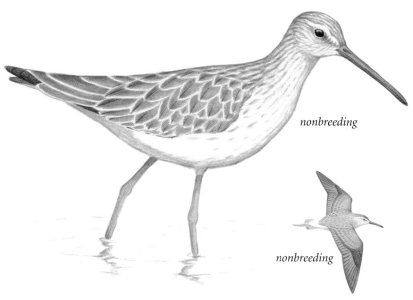

nonbreeding

nonbreeding

ID: long bill, drooping at tip; long legs. *Breeding:* striped crown; chestnut red ear patch; white "eyebrow"; barred underparts; blackish yellow legs. *Nonbreeding:* dark gray upperparts; dirty white underparts; yellow legs. *In flight:* pale wings and tail; legs trail behind tail.
Size: *L* 8–9 in; *W* 18 in.
Status: uncommon fall migrant from mid-August to mid-October in eastern Washington; rare migrant from August to mid-September in western Washington.

Habitat: shores of lakes, reservoirs and marshes.
Nesting: does not nest in Washington.
Feeding: forages in shallow water, probing deeply; occasionally picks insects from the water's surface or the ground; feeds mostly on invertebrates; also eats seeds, roots and leaves.
Voice: simple, sharp *querp* in flight.
Similar Species: *Greater Yellowlegs* (p. 142) and *Lesser Yellowlegs* (p. 143): no red ear patch; yellow legs; pick for food rather than probe.
Best Sites: Crockett L.; Jensen Access, Skagit Wildlife Area; Paterson Unit, Umatilla NWR; Potholes Wildlife Area; Walla Walla R. delta.

SHORT-BILLED DOWITCHER

Limnodromus griseus

Having short legs, dowitchers feed in mud or in shallow pools, where their extra-long, flexible-tipped bills can reach hidden invertebrates unavailable to longer-legged shorebirds with shorter bills. While foraging along shorelines, these birds "stitch" up and down into the mud with a rhythm like a sewing machine's. • Bill length is unreliable for identification—the bills of female Short-bills are often as long as, if not longer than, the bills of male Long-bills. Feeding habits more reliably distinguish the two species: Short-billed Dowitchers are saltwater mudflat specialists, whereas Long-billed Dowitchers prefer freshwater pools and marshes, but there is enough of an overlap to cause confusion. Calls (if the birds oblige) are very distinctive. Another reliable identification feature, in good light and at least for immatures, is a combination of wing and tail feather patterns.

breeding

nonbreeding

ID: conspicuous white "eyebrow"; dark line from bill to eye; long, sturdy bill; white belly; greenish yellow legs; spotted, rarely barred, undertail coverts. *Breeding:* mostly orange head and spotted neck; lighter orange on barred and spotted breast and heavily barred sides; dark centers and pale buff edges to scapulars. *Nonbreeding:* pale grayish overall; gray-speckled breast; heavily dark-barred flanks. *Immature:* blackish innermost flight feathers with reddish margins and markings; indistinctly streaked, orangy buff breast. *In flight:* equal dark-and-white tail barring; white triangle on lower back.
Size: *L* 11–12 in; *W* 19 in.
Status: common coastal migrant and rare in the east from mid-July to mid-September and mid-April to mid-May.

Habitat: estuaries and salt marshes along the coast; lakeshores, shallow marshes, sewage lagoons, ponds and flooded fields inland.
Nesting: does not nest in Washington.
Feeding: wades in shallow water or soft mud, picking off surface and swimming invertebrates; probes for buried prey with the whole bill; occasionally eats seeds, aquatic plants and grasses.
Voice: generally silent; flight call is a mellow, repeated *tututu, toodulu* or *toodu*.
Similar Species: *Long-billed Dowitcher* (p. 165): sides of breast usually barred or chevroned; heavier dark barring on uppertail; redder orange continues onto flanks and belly of breeding bird; more uniform brownish gray head and upperparts in nonbreeding plumage.
Best Sites: Crockett L.; Bowerman Basin (Hoquiam); Damon Pt. (Ocean Shores); Bottle Beach (Ocosta); Willapa Bay; Long Beach Peninsula.

LONG-BILLED DOWITCHER
Limnodromus scolopaceus

Long-billed Dowitchers favor freshwater habitats, even along the coast, prefer-ring lakeshores, flooded pastures, grass-dotted marshes and the mouths of brackish tidal channels, where their slightly longer legs give them an advan-tage over Short-billed Dowitchers. • Nesting only along the edge of the Beaufort Sea in extreme northern Alaska and northwestern Canada, Long-bills spread out over the continent and make a more leisurely fall migration than their cousins, with immatures appearing as late as November at coastal and southern wintering sites. Long-bills are also later to leave their wintering areas, not getting on the move until mid-April to early May. Their beautiful breeding plumage makes them one of Washington's most anticipated returning shorebirds.

breeding

nonbreeding

ID: conspicu-ous pale "eye-brow"; long, sturdy bill; greenish yellow legs; dark-barred undertail coverts. *Breeding:* rufous head and underparts; dark-streaked neck; some white streaking on dark-barred breast and sides. *Nonbreeding:* drab brownish gray overall; heavily barred pale flanks. *Immature:* buff gray breast. *In flight:* thickly dark-barred; white tail; white triangle on lower back; dark-barred wing linings.
Size: *L* 11–12 in; *W* 19 in.
Status: fairly common statewide migrant on fresh water from early to mid-May (numbers may be very large) and from the end of July to mid- or late October; uncommon winter and spring resident in the west; rare to casual winter and spring resident in the east.
Habitat: along lakeshores, shallow marshes and fresh water; even along the coast.
Nesting: does not nest in Washington.
Feeding: probes in shallow water and moist mud with a rapid up-and-down bill motion, often with the head underwater; eats mostly larval flies, worms and other soft-bodied invertebrates but will take mollusks, crustaceans and seeds of aquatic plants.
Voice: usual call is a single *peek,* some-times quickening into *kik-kik-kik-kik;* feed-ing flocks chatter steadily.
Similar Species: *Short-billed Dowitcher* (p. 164): breeding plumage is less rufous, with white belly; nonbreeding bird has browner upperparts, usually spotted sides of breast (not barred) and more obvious streaking and barring on underparts.
Best Sites: Crockett L.; Bos L. (Whidbey I.); Spencer I.; Kennedy Creek (Hood Canal); Lind Coulee.

165

WILSON'S SNIPE
Gallinago delicata

The eerie, hollow, ascending winnowing of the male Wilson's Snipe (formerly included in Common Snipe, *G. gallinago*) is one of spring's most memorable wetland sounds. Specialized outspread outer tail feathers vibrate like saxophone reeds as the courting bird performs aerial maneuvers. • Both genders are well camouflaged and normally secretive. With large eyes set far back on the head, Wilson's Snipes can detect predators approaching from almost any direction. They explode from cover of grass or sedges and escape in a characteristic zigzag flight, usually uttering a rasping call. • "Snipe" comes from *snite*, an old version of "snout," in reference to the long bill and the bird's habit of probing for prey in soft ground.

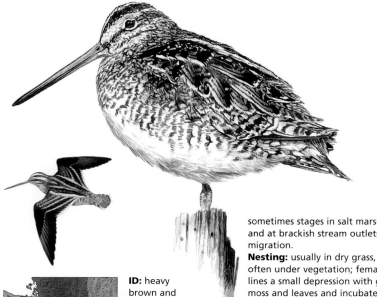

ID: heavy brown and white stripes on head and back; large, dark eyes; long, straight, grayish bill; dark-barred breast and sides; white belly; rusty tail; relatively short, pale yellowish or bluish legs. *In flight:* short wings; dark underwings with barred linings; rapid wingbeats; often rises high in the air and then drops rapidly back into cover.
Size: *L* 10–12 in; *W* 18 in.
Status: common to fairly common year-round in the west; fairly common migrant statewide; fairly common spring and summer resident in the east.
Habitat: grassy edges of freshwater marshes, ponds, lakes, rivers and streams, beaver meadows and flooded grasslands;

sometimes stages in salt marshes and at brackish stream outlets in migration.
Nesting: usually in dry grass, often under vegetation; female lines a small depression with grass, moss and leaves and incubates 4 brown-marked, olive buff to brown eggs for 18–20 days; pair splits the brood, feeding them for about 20 days, sometimes up to 60 days.
Feeding: probes deliberately into soft substrates for soft-bodied invertebrates, mostly larvae and earthworms; also eats small amphibians and some seeds.
Voice: nasal *scaip* alarm call; often sings *wheat wheatawheat* from an elevated perch. *Male:* uses tail feathers to produce an accelerating *woo-woo-woo-woo-woo-woo* courtship song in flight.
Similar Species: *Dowitchers* (pp. 164–65): triangular, white back area; more orangy breeding plumage and otherwise grayer; usually seen in flocks in the open; rapid up-and-down feeding method.
Best Sites: almost any grassy wetland.

WILSON'S PHALAROPE

Phalaropus tricolor

Phalaropes are among the most colorful and graceful of North American shorebirds, and they have unusual breeding habits. The flashy females pursue the less colorful males, sometimes mating with several, laying eggs in each of their nests and then leaving the males with all the duties of a single parent. For the most part, however, female Wilson's Phalaropes are monogamous and defend the nesting territory. • Soon after the young hatch, the females head for several lakes in Washington and Oregon, as well as California's Mono Lake, to fatten up and partially molt. The males and immatures join them later. As many as 100,000 phalaropes may gather at one such location before they all leave for Bolivia or Argentina.

nonbreeding

♂

breeding

♀

ID: white "eyebrow" and "cheek"; dark eyes; long, dark, needlelike bill; white belly, sides and undertail coverts; lobed toes. *Breeding female:* gray "cap"; black eye stripe; gray back with 2 chestnut stripes; brownish upperwings; cinnamon foreneck and upper breast; black-sided neck; black legs. *Breeding male:* grayish brown upperparts and "cap"; chestnut and light brown neck; white throat; black legs. *Nonbreeding:* light gray upperparts; yellow legs.
Size: *L* 8–9 in; *W* 17 in.
Status: fairly common late spring and early fall migrant and summer breeding resident in the east and rare in the west.
Habitat: *Breeding:* boggy ponds, marshes, wet meadows and marshy mountain lakes. *In migration:* alkaline lakes, sewage treatment ponds, freshwater shorelines and flooded fields.

Nesting: near water; usually well concealed; depression is lined with vegetation; male incubates 3–4 brown-blotched, buff eggs for 22–25 days and tends the young.
Feeding: whirls in tight circles in water to stir up aquatic invertebrates and picks prey from the surface or just below; short jabs for land invertebrates.
Voice: deep, grunting *work work* or *wu wu wu*, usually in flight on the breeding grounds.
Similar Species: *Red-necked Phalarope* (p. 168): shorter bill; dark "cap"; white upperwing stripe; red (female) or buff (male) neck sides and gray breast in breeding plumage. *Red Phalarope* (p. 169): stouter bill; dark "cap," yellow bill, white eye patch and rufous (female) or cinnamon (male) neck, breast and underparts in breeding plumage; extremely pelagic.
Best Sites: Nisqually NWR; Desert Wildlife Area; Paterson Unit, Umatilla NWR; almost any pond or sewage lagoon east of the Columbia R. and Okanogan R. *Fall:* Spencer I.

167

RED-NECKED PHALAROPE

Phalaropus lobatus

This tiny mite of a shorebird is among the world's smallest seabirds. Seeming all but lost among the troughs, the dainty Red-necked Phalarope rides out all the open ocean has to offer. • Other sea-feeding birds search far and wide for concentrations of food and then plunge, dive or swim to reach their food. Phalaropes use their individually lobed toes to swim and dab in tight circles, stirring up tiny invertebrates that live in the upper layer of seawater. As prey items funnel toward the water's surface, phalaropes pick and choose with their needlelike bills. • Most of these arctic breeders migrate along the coast or well out to sea, but small flocks of Red-necks may suddenly appear along freshwater shores.

breeding

nonbreeding

ID: long, thin, dark bill; white "chin" and belly; dark legs; lobed toes. *Breeding female:* dark gray head; tiny, white "eyebrow"; buff-striped, gray back; gray breast; chestnut on upper breast and neck. *Breeding male:* black "cap" and eye line; whitish "eyebrow"; dark gray upperparts with buff stripe; cinnamon neck stripe. *Nonbreeding:* white face and underparts; black eye patch; gray-streaked upperparts. *Immature:* dark "cap"; black eye patch; buff stripes on dark back; smudgy breast. **Size:** *L* 7–8 in; *W* 15 in.
Status: common western migrant in May and from mid-August to October (particularly pelagic); fairly common eastern migrant from mid-August to mid-September and uncommon in mid- to late May.
Habitat: open ocean, from just beyond the surf line to well offshore; harbors, estuaries,

lagoons and saltwater marshes with tidal channels; alkaline lakes; sewage ponds; open freshwater marshes.
Nesting: does not nest in Washington.
Feeding: whirls in tight circles in shallow or deep water, picking small invertebrates from the surface or just below; totters jerkily on land, lunging for invertebrates with short jabs.
Voice: often noisy with a soft *krit krit krit* in migration.
Similar Species: *Red Phalarope* (p. 169): chunkier; heavier bill; rufous or cinnamon underparts in breeding plumage; paler, plainer upperparts in nonbreeding plumage. *Wilson's Phalarope* (p. 167): longer, thinner bill; breeding female has black on neck and cinnamon foreneck; male and nonbreeding female have mostly white face and pale gray upperparts; plainer wings.
Best Sites: pelagic trips from Westport; Ocean Shores Game Range; Hoquiam sewage treatment ponds; Crockett L.; Paterson Unit, Umatilla NWR; Lind Coulee.

RED PHALAROPE

Phalaropus fulicarius

Getting a good view of a Red Phalarope, the most pelagic of shorebirds, usually requires a boat trip well offshore—or going out in a storm on land. The effort is worth it, especially in spring, when the birds are in their striking breeding plumage. Heavy weather in November and December may drive hundreds of exhausted Red Phalaropes onto beaches, coastal ponds, wet meadows and even parking lots. • Red Phalaropes have been seen snatching parasites off the backs of surfacing whales, acting much like the tickbirds of the African plains. • John James Audubon, fooled by female phalaropes assuming typical male roles on their arctic breeding grounds, mislabeled the genders on his phalarope illustrations.

nonbreeding

ID: grayish legs; lobed toes. *Breeding female:* black crown, forehead and "chin"; white eye patch; black-tipped, bright yellow bill; buff-striped, brown back; striking reddish orange underparts and neck. *Breeding male:* like female, but paler. *Nonbreeding:* white head, neck and underparts; black nape and eye patch; black bill has pale base; plain, light gray upperparts.
Size: *L* 8–9 in; *W* 17 in.
Status: fairly common offshore migrant from mid-September to mid-November; uncommon offshore migrant from May to early June and from mid-August to mid-September; rare offshore resident in winter and spring.
Habitat: open ocean far from shore, preferring upwellings and current edges; occasionally seen close to shore off headlands

and jetties, and inshore in bays, lagoons and estuaries; hardly ever found inland, except when blown in by storms.
Nesting: does not nest in Washington.
Feeding: gleans the ocean's surface, largely for tiny crustaceans, usually while swimming in tight circles; eats small invertebrates on land.
Voice: calls include a shrill, high-pitched *wit* or *creep* and a low *clink clink*.
Similar Species: *Red-necked Phalarope* (p. 168): daintier; slimmer bill; white underparts year-round; breeding bird has different facial pattern and gray upper breast; nonbreeding bird has darker, streakier upperparts. *Wilson's Phalarope* (p. 167): longer, thinner, dark bill; white underparts year-round; breeding female has black eye line and black-and-cinnamon neck; breeding male has grayer upperparts and light brown neck; nonbreeding bird has gray eye line and yellow legs; plainer wings.
Best Sites: pelagic trips from Westport.

POMARINE JAEGER

Stercorarius pomarinus

Powerful, swift pirates of the open ocean, jaegers chase down hapless terns and small gulls to steal their hard-earned food. On their arctic nesting grounds, jaegers defend their eggs and young by attacking any intruders with stooping dives or hectic pursuits. • Most jaegers occur singly or in loose groups far from land, where ocean currents and upwellings bring food to the surface. Some can be seen from land, and a few may even make it to a harbor entrance or inland lake. • The "Pom" appears heavier than other jaegers. Its wings have broader bases, and its flight is more labored, with slower wingbeats. • With their heavy build and prominent white patch, immatures can be mistaken for South Polar Skuas (*Stercorarius maccormicki*).

dark morph immature

light morph nonbreeding

ID: dark-tipped, pale yellowish bill; twisted, spoon-shaped tail feathers; dark legs.
Light morph: dark "cap" and front of face; dark brown upperparts; white underparts, often with dark brown or barred flanks and undertail; possible brownish black breast band; creamy yellow upper neck. *Dark morph:* all-dark plumage. *Immature:* brown head and underparts; light-tipped, dark upperpart feathers; dark-barred white rump. *In flight:* prominent white primary underwing flash with corresponding white shafts visible on upperwing.
Size: *L* 18–23 in; *W* 4¼ ft.
Status: fairly common offshore migrant from mid-August to mid-September;

uncommon offshore migrant from mid- to late May and from early August to late October; rare from late October to early May; rarely seen from shore.
Habitat: usually open ocean, often far from land; regularly seen around fishing vessels.
Nesting: does not nest in Washington.
Feeding: snatches food from the ocean's surface; harasses other birds, including larger shearwaters and gulls, into dropping or ejecting their food; chases and eats small birds.
Voice: generally silent; may give a sharp *which-yew*, a squealing *weak-weak* or a squeaky, whistled note during migration.
Similar Species: *Parasitic Jaeger* (p. 171): more slender; smaller head; all-dark bill; long, pointed tail feathers.
Best Sites: pelagic trips from Westport; Pt. Roberts.

PARASITIC JAEGER

Stercorarius parasiticus

Concentrations of feeding seabirds attract these vigilant "falcons of the sea." Parasitic Jaegers chase down and intimidate their victims into dropping or coughing up their latest meal. They will also follow people and bird-hunting mammals in hopes of getting any eggs and young left behind by fleeing nesters of other bird species. • Parasitic Jaegers occur in three color morphs. About one in five immatures is either a light or dark morph, with the rest being intermediate, but dark-morph adults are more common. • Of the three jaeger species found along the Washington coast, the Parasitic is the most widely and regularly seen from shore. It is also a rare visitor to inland lakes. • In the Arctic, pairs of nesting jaegers will cooperate to drive off predators.

light morph immature

light morph breeding

ID: dark "cap," eye patch, bill, upperparts and legs; pointed central tail feathers. *Light morph:* white face and neck tinged with pale yellow; white underparts; dull brown bars or streaks on flanks and undertail coverts. *Dark morph:* all-dark plumage. *Immature:* dark-streaked, lighter brown head and underparts; dark upperpart feathers with lighter tips. *In flight:* long, pointed, dark wings; white underwing flash with white shafts on upperwing.

Size: *L* 16–21 in; *W* 3¾ ft.

Status: fairly common to uncommon offshore migrant from mid-August to late October, often shadowing Common Tern migration; rare in the east from late August to late September.

Habitat: mainly on the open ocean from the outer surf zone to the continental shelf edge; some birds, especially immatures, enter estuaries, harbors or Puget Sound, or visit inland lakes.

Nesting: does not nest in Washington.

Feeding: eats small schooling fish (usually stolen from gulls, kittiwakes or terns); scavenges food from the ocean's surface.

Voice: generally silent; may make shrill calls in migrating groups of the same or other jaegers.

Similar Species: *Pomarine Jaeger* (p. 170): bulkier; larger dark "cap"; dark-tipped, pale bill; blunt, twisted, elongated central tail feathers. *Long-tailed Jaeger* (p. 172): slimmer; whitish lower head and neck; pale underparts; crisp black "cap" and particularly long, pointed central tail feathers on breeding bird; all-brown underwings.

Best Sites: pelagic trips from Westport; Pt. Brown jetty (Ocean Shores); North Jetty (Columbia R. mouth); Pt. Roberts. *Fall:* with Common Terns at Sequim Bay and Point No Point; along Columbia R.

LONG-TAILED JAEGER

Stercorarius longicaudus

Aerial pirates easily identified on land or water, Long-tailed Jaegers smugly rest with their neat black "caps" held high and their long tails angled gracefully upward. • Jaegers are masters of the air, whether lazily bouncing aloft or engaging in a falconlike power dive. While on its arctic nesting grounds, the Long-tailed Jaeger, like its cousin the Pomarine Jaeger, preys heavily on lemmings, which it catches in powerful, swooping aerial attacks. During migration, it hunts for fish over ocean waters and large lakes. It is less inclined than its jaeger relatives to pirate food from other seabirds, but it will certainly do so if a good opportunity arises. • Jaegers are members of the skua family.

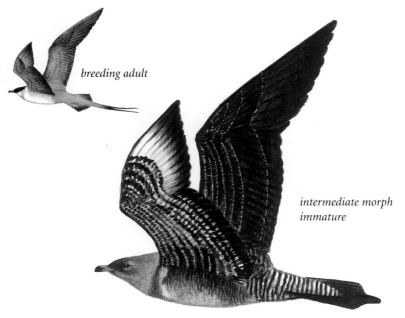

breeding adult

intermediate morph immature

ID: dark "cap"; gray upperparts; white throat and belly; yellow "collar"; long, twinned tail feathers. *Immature:* no dark cap; whitish feather edging on upperparts, darkish barring on flanks and undertail coverts. *In flight:* dark flight feathers.
Size: *L* 20–22 in; *W* 32 in.
Status: uncommon offshore migrant from mid-August to early September (peaking in August); rare offshore spring migrant from late April to the end of May; very rare in spring in the east along the Columbia R.

Habitat: mainly on the open ocean from well offshore to the edge of the continental shelf; some birds, especially immatures, enter estuaries, harbors or Puget Sound, or visit inland lakes.
Nesting: does not nest in Washington.
Feeding: hunts rodents and birds; pirates from gulls; scavenges at landfills.
Voice: generally not vocal in Washington.
Similar Species: *Parasitic Jaeger* (p. 171) and *Pomarine Jaeger* (p. 170): stockier; possible dark breast band; no long tail streamers. *Gulls* (pp. 173–84, 363): no elongated central tail feathers.
Best Sites: pelagic trips from Westport.

FRANKLIN'S GULL

Larus pipixcan

The Franklin's Gull, more than any other gull, is no "seagull." Affectionately known on the Great Plains as "Prairie Dove" because of its dovelike profile, it follows tractors to find stirred-up food in much the same way its cousins follow fishing boats. This bird nests in large colonies in marshes, and the locations of the colonies and nests may change from year to year depending on the condition of the marsh. • The Franklin's Gull winters largely south of the equator, migrating in large flocks through the central U.S., with isolated birds toward the coasts. It is seen annually in both eastern and western Washington, and each year this small gull with its long wings and buoyant flight is awaited.

nonbreeding

nonbreeding

ID: gray mantle; prominent white spots on small black area at wing tip; dark, red-tinged legs. *Breeding:* black "hood"; partial broad white eye crescents; red bill; possible pinkish tinge on breast. *Nonbreeding:* partial "hood"; dark bill; white forehead and "chin." *Immature:* light brown upperparts and nape. *In flight:* gray upperwing with white trailing edge; white underwing; white tail.
Size: *L* 14–15 in; *W* 3 ft.
Status: rare migrant in the west from early August to the end of October; rare migrant in the east from mid-May to late June and from late September to mid-October.

Habitat: marshlands, meadows, farm fields, lakes and river mouths.
Nesting: does not nest in Washington.
Feeding: opportunistic; follows agricultural machinery to seize flushed insects and worms; catches flying insects in midair.
Voice: gives shrill, "mewing" *weeeh-ah* and hollow *kowee-ee* calls; longer calls are more varied than those of other inland gulls.
Similar Species: *Bonaparte's Gull* (p. 174): slimmer; thinner, black bill; paler back; pink or red legs; conspicuous white wedge and narrow, black strip on trailing edge above and below on wing tip; dark ear spot in nonbreeding plumage.
Best Sites: Everett sewage treatment ponds; Point No Point; Kennedy Creek (Hood Canal); Tri-Cities; Grand Coulee lakes; Walla Walla R. delta.

173

BONAPARTE'S GULL

Larus philadelphia

Bonaparte's Gulls migrate in large numbers through western Washington, and significant numbers remain for winter. These birds flock up in spring and are joined by northbound migrants on a coastal migration route to boreal and subarctic breeding areas. A similar influx is seen from early August to mid-November, when these gulls are common on estuaries and in Puget Sound. The birds that stay here in winter rest and feed at estuaries, sewage ponds and flooded fields and on water close to shore. • This elegant gull was named after the French emperor's nephew, zoologist Charles Lucien Bonaparte. The first specimen was collected in Philadelphia.

nonbreeding

breeding

ID: thin, black bill; pale gray upperparts; white underparts; short tail. *Breeding:* black "hood"; white eye-arcs; orangy red legs. *Nonbreeding:* white head; neat, round, dark ear patch; pink legs. *1st winter:* elongated ear patch; paler legs; dark upperwing trim. *In flight:* conspicuous white wedge and narrow, black trailing edge above and below on wing tip; white tail; 1st-winter bird has dark terminal tail band and thin, dark "M" on upperwings.
Size: *L* 12–14 in; *W* 32–33 in.
Status: common migrant in the west from mid-March to mid-May and from early August to late November; fairly common in the west from mid-July to August and as a winter resident; casual in the east in spring and fall.

Habitat: protected coastal waters; beaches; sewage ponds; rivers; large lakes; reservoirs; open ocean.
Nesting: does not nest in Washington.
Feeding: dabbles and tips up for small fish and freshwater and marine invertebrates (especially shrimp and other crustaceans) and tadpoles; gleans the ground for land invertebrates; catches flying insects in midair.
Voice: utters a scratchy, soft *ear ear;* large flocks can be very noisy when feeding.
Similar Species: *Franklin's Gull* (p. 173): larger; darker back; prominent white spots on black wing tips; dark, red-tinged legs; slightly heavier bill is red in breeding plumage; half "hood" in nonbreeding plumage.
Best Sites: San Juans; Whidbey I.; Discovery Park (Seattle); Point No Point; Salsbury Pt. (Kitsap Co.); Pt. Wilson (Port Townsend).

HEERMANN'S GULL

Larus heermanni

Coastal birders struggling to identify gulls can be grateful to the Heermann's Gull for providing a sequence of completely distinctive plumages. Something else sets this dusky gull apart: whereas most gulls migrate north to breed and return south for winter, the Heermann's Gull travels south to small, sun-baked Isla Raza in the Sea of Cortez to raise its chicks and then heads north for the balance of summer and much of fall. • The Heermann's Gull often steals food from waterbirds it can bully into giving up their catch. Jaegers, which also pirate food, have feathers that are not very water resistant, but the Heermann's Gull is quite capable of taking fish directly from the water, so it has no such excuse for its kleptoparasitism.

nonbreeding

breeding

ID: dark eye has red orbital ring; black-tipped, red bill; dark back and wings; light ashy gray underparts and neck; black legs; white-tipped, black tail. *Breeding:* white head. *Nonbreeding:* brownish gray mottling or streaking on head. *1st winter:* dark brown overall, darkest on head, wing tips and tail; pale bill with dark tip. *In flight:* wings and tail usually all dark except for white trailing edges (narrower on 2nd-winter bird).
Size: *L* 16–19 in; *W* 4¼ ft.
Status: common post-breeding dispersal summer resident in the west from early July to mid-October and rare to casual after November.
Habitat: coastal ocean waters, usually close to shore, including bays, beaches, offshore islands, lagoons and coastal creek outfalls.

Nesting: does not nest in Washington.
Feeding: dips to the water's surface to snatch items while in flight; often pirates food from other birds, especially immature Brown Pelicans; eats mainly small fish but also invertebrates, eggs, carrion and human waste.
Voice: common call is a nasal *kawak;* also gives a series of whining *ye* notes and low-pitched honking; noisy and argumentative when feeding.
Similar Species: *Pomarine Jaeger* (p. 170) and *Parasitic Jaeger* (p. 171): dark morphs resemble immature Heermann's but have white primary flashes and narrower tails, often with projecting central feathers; Parasitic has much smaller bill.
Best Sites: Crockett L.–Keystone; Pt. Wilson (Port Townsend); Ediz Hook (Port Angeles); La Push; Ocean Shores; Westport; Point No Point.

175

MEW GULL

Larus canus

Characterized by distinctive light, buoyant flight and rapid walking, the Mew Gull stages a major invasion of our coastal shoreline habitats from early September to early December. It is a common nester from British Columbia northward only, so few purely white-headed adults are seen in Washington. • Winter storms bring Mew Gulls from their usual open-coast estuary habitats into flooded fields and pastures, where they forage for earthworms and other invertebrates driven to the surface. Some birds, starting to adopt the fast-food approach favored by Ring-billed Gulls, scavenge food scraps instead. • The word *canus* is Latin for "dog," but the "mewing" calls made by this small, dainty gull are more catlike.

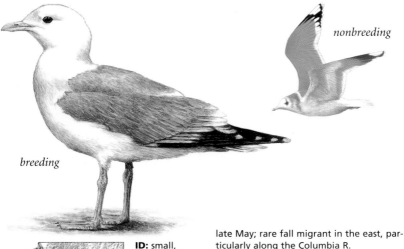

nonbreeding

breeding

ID: small, rounded head; dark eyes; small, thin, yellow bill; medium gray mantle; folded wings extend well beyond tail. *Breeding:* all-white head and neck; red-tinted eyes. *Nonbreeding:* variable dusky streaking or smudging on head, neck and upper breast; bill has indistinct dark spot; greenish yellow legs. *1st winter:* dark-tipped, dull pink bill; smudgy brown underparts; barred tail coverts. *In flight:* mostly pale underwing and gray upperwing have wide white trailing edge and white-spotted, black tip (visible at rest); broad, white tail; mostly grayish brown 1st-winter bird has dusky wedge and trailing edge on upperwing.
Size: *L* 16 in; *W* 3½ ft.
Status: fairly common to common coastal migrant and resident from early August to

late May; rare fall migrant in the east, particularly along the Columbia R.
Habitat: tidal waters, ranging from upper estuaries out to the open coast; concentrates in and around agricultural fields, harbors, river mouths and ocean beaches.
Nesting: does not nest in Washington.
Feeding: opportunistic; captures fish and invertebrates by plunging to the water's surface or plucking from wave-washed seaweed or the ground; does not normally visit garbage dumps or accept handouts.
Voice: relatively quiet; high, squeaky, nasal notes; "mewing" call; high-pitched, coughing *queeoh*.
Similar Species: *Ring-billed Gull* (p. 177): paler eyes; heavier, black-ringed, yellow bill or black-tipped, pink (immature) bill; paler gray above; nonbreeder has less brown on head; more black and less white at wing tips.
Best Sites: coastal areas of San Juans; Admiralty Inlet; Puget Sound; outer Olympic Peninsula; Ocean Shores; Willapa Bay; Columbia R. in eastern Washington; lower Columbia R.

RING-BILLED GULL

Larus delawarensis

Having developed a taste for the urban lifestyle, Ring-billed Gulls are at home amid buildings and paved roads and have become a routine sight at many shopping mall parking lots, ball fields and garbage dumps. Some Ring-bills have learned the fine art of pursuing lunch handouts at city parks, followed by dinner outside a choice fast-food outlet. To be fair, Ring-bills also help out farmers by following agricultural machinery to feast on many crop pests, and they are unobtrusive in most places. • Long-established and temporary nesting colonies are found along the Columbia River and its tributaries in central and southcentral Washington, and in Willapa Bay and Grays Harbor in the west.

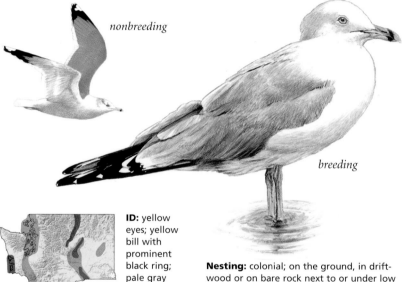

nonbreeding

breeding

ID: yellow eyes; yellow bill with prominent black ring; pale gray upperparts; white neck and underparts; yellow legs. *Breeding:* all-white head. *Nonbreeding:* faintly brown-streaked lower crown and nape. *1st winter:* black-tipped, pink bill; gray-and-brown mantle; dark-barred neck and flanks; pink legs. *In flight:* mostly pale underwing; white trailing wing edge; white spot on black wing tip (visible at rest); white tail (1st-winter bird has blackish band).
Size: *L* 18–20 in; *W* 4 ft.
Status: common migrant and winter resident in the west and locally common in summer; common in the east from late winter to the end of summer breeding and otherwise locally fairly common.
Habitat: *Breeding:* sandbars; beaches in freshwater wetlands. *In migration* and *winter:* various open environments close to water, including urban ones.

Nesting: colonial; on the ground, in driftwood or on bare rock next to or under low plants; nest of twigs, sticks, grass and leaves is lined with lichens and mosses; pair incubates 2–4 brown-splotched, grayish eggs for 25–28 days.
Feeding: opportunistic; gleans and stabs for fish, earthworms, termites and rodents; and flycatches for insects, scavenges for carrion, human leftovers and waste grain.
Voice: high-pitched *kakakaka-akakaka*; low, laughlike *yook-yook-yook.*
Similar Species: *Mew Gull* (p. 176): smaller; dark eyes; smaller, faintly ringed or unringed bill; darker mantle; larger white spots on wing tips; breeding bird has streakier head and neck; less contrasting immature plumages.
Best Sites: *Summer:* lakes and rivers of Columbia R. system; Grays Harbor; Willapa Bay. *Winter:* Skagit R. delta; Walla Walla R. delta; Tri-Cities.

CALIFORNIA GULL

Larus californicus

Seeing a "seagull" so far from the ocean may puzzle summer observers in eastern Washington, but the California Gull makes use of fluctuating inland water bodies, even in arid environments, by breeding only when the water level is right. Wherever there are islands for nesting, this opportunistic gull can find food on the water—or, more often, in surrounding terrain. • In winter, California Gulls are more common in eastern Washington than in the west. In late summer and fall, large numbers can be found along the coast and well out to sea. • Despite the California Gull's name and coastal abundance, this interior prairie-and-basin nester first became well known to the general public when it was celebrated for consuming hordes of crop-threatening grasshoppers in Utah in 1848 and 1855.

nonbreeding

breeding

ID: dark eyes; heavy, yellow bill with variable black mark and red spot on lower mandible (diagnostic combination); medium gray mantle; pale greenish yellow legs. *Breeding:* white head. *Nonbreeding:* brown-streaked hindcrown and nape. *1st winter:* black-tipped, pink bill; blotched brown back; dark-streaked breast, neck and head; pinkish gray legs; barred tail coverts; dark brown tail. *In flight:* mostly gray upperwing; white spot on dark wing tip; white underwing and tail.
Size: *L* 18–20 in; *W* 4–4½ ft.
Status: locally common to fairly common migrant statewide; locally common to fairly common year-round in the east; common along the coast and offshore in summer and fall; uncommon in the west in winter and spring.
Habitat: lakes; marshes; estuaries; croplands; cities; garbage dumps; open ocean, especially in fall.
Nesting: colonial; usually on an island, often next to shrubs; in a depression lined with bones, feathers and other materials; pair incubates 2–3 buff, olive or greenish eggs with dark markings for 24–27 days.
Feeding: takes a large variety of insects, brine shrimp, worms, fish, birds and small mammals, as well as garbage.
Voice: usual calls are loud, ringing *kyow-kyow* barks and mellower, laughlike notes, mostly at nesting colonies.
Similar Species: *Ring-billed Gull* (p. 177): yellow eyes; shorter bill without red spot; much lighter mantle; yellower legs. *Herring Gull* (p. 179): larger; yellowish eyes; pinkish legs.
Best Sites: *Summer:* Potholes Reservoir; Banks L.; Columbia R. north of Tri-Cities; Ocean Shores; Long Beach Peninsula. *Winter:* Tri-Cities; Walla Walla R. delta. *In migration:* Cape Flattery; La Push.

HERRING GULL
Larus argentatus

Although it is aggressive and opportunistic, the Herring Gull still finds itself outcompeted by Western Gulls and Glaucous-winged Gulls at many coastal feeding sites. It is, therefore, generally more common well up in large coastal estuaries and at landfills beyond the normal foraging range of its larger competitors. • The proliferation of gull species and subspecies designations and continuing hybridization make it difficult to confidently identify a Herring Gull. These gulls hybridize freely with other large, white-headed gulls, including the Glaucous-winged Gull. Because these species readily crossbreed, some ornithologists consider them a "superspecies"—an intermediate grouping of several species within a genus. • The word *argentatus* ("silver") is a description of this gull's mantle.

nonbreeding

nonbreeding

ID: flat forehead; pale yellow eyes; heavy, yellow bill with red spot; light gray back and wings; pinkish legs. *Breeding:* all-white head and neck. *Nonbreeding:* heavy brown streaking on head, neck and upper breast. *1st winter* and *2nd winter:* pale brown plumage, usually mottled; blackish bill, often with pink base; barred undertail coverts; dark tail. *3rd winter:* residual brownish areas; dark-tipped, yellow bill. *In flight:* white tail and underwing; mostly gray upperwing; white spot on dark wing tip; 1st- and 2nd-winter birds are mostly brown, with lighter primary upperwing patch.
Size: *L* 23–26 in; *W* 4¾ ft.
Status: locally common during March smelt runs on the Columbia R.; fairly common in winter and early spring on Columbia R. and Snake R.; uncommon in western Washington (mainly coastal).

Habitat: generally any habitat near water; concentrates at landfills, river mouths and on agricultural land; migrates along beaches and the surf line.
Nesting: does not nest in Washington.
Feeding: scavenges dead fish, carrion and human food waste; catches crabs, snails, insects and other invertebrates on or under the water's surface; major predator of colonial seabird eggs and young.
Voice: utters a loud, bugling *kleew-kleew*; alarm call is a loud *kak-kak-kak*.
Similar Species: *California Gull* (p. 178): smaller; dark eyes; black band and red spot on bill; darker mantle; greenish yellow legs (pinkish gray on immature). *Thayer's Gull* (p. 180): eyes mostly dark; shorter, slimmer bill; pale underwing tips; "bubble gum pink" legs.
Best Sites: *Fall* and *winter:* Columbia R., Snake R., Grand Coulee lakes; outer coast. *March:* Columbia R. between Washington and Oregon.

THAYER'S GULL

Larus thayeri

Just when you thought you had your gulls sorted out, along comes a Thayer's Gull and everything goes out the window. Long considered to be a subspecies of the Herring Gull, the Thayer's Gull was elevated to full species status by the American Ornithologists' Union in 1973. A majority of gull researchers now argue that its closest ally is the Iceland Gull (*L. glaucoides*), which shares the same nest sites in the eastern Canadian Arctic but winters along the Atlantic Coast. • Thayer's Gulls are found most often on the northern part of the Olympic Peninsula and in the southern reaches of Puget Sound. • Harvard ornithologist W.S. Brooks named this gull for John Eliot Thayer, the sponsor of the 1913 Alaska expedition on which he collected scientific specimens.

nonbreeding

nonbreeding

ID: dark eyes; yellow bill with red spot; light gray mantle; black wing tips with prominent white spots; pinkish (often bright pinkish) legs. *Breeding:* white head; brighter bill. *Nonbreeding:* heavy brown streaking on upper head, neck and breast. *1st winter* and *2nd winter:* pale brown plumage; blackish bill with pink base; blackish brown tail; barred undertail coverts. *3rd winter:* dark-ringed, yellow bill; all-black wing tips. *In flight:* gray upperwings with white trailing edges; black markings at wing tips; white underwings.
Size: *L* 22–25 in; *W* 4½ ft.
Status: locally common to uncommon resident on inland coastal waters from mid-October to late March; rare on outer coastal waters and in eastern Washington.

Habitat: disperses widely from night roosts and concentrates in harbors, river mouths, plowed fields and pastures.
Nesting: does not nest in Washington.
Feeding: omnivorous and opportunistic but not predatory; gleans and picks food items from the ground and the water's surface.
Voice: generally silent in winter; typically short, flat notes.
Similar Species: *Herring Gull* (p. 179): pale yellow eyes; longer, heavier bill; more black on wing tips; more heavily streaked and patterned immature. *Glaucous-winged Gull* (p. 182): heavier head and bill; dark eyes; gray-and-white wing tips; paler immature. *Glaucous-winged* x *Western Gull hybrid:* confusing plumages, generally with wing tips not black; heavier head and bill.
Best Sites: Ediz Hook (Port Angeles); Elwha R. mouth; Gog-le-hi-te Wetland (Tacoma); City of Tukwila shops (adjacent to south end of Foster Golf Links).

WESTERN GULL

Larus occidentalis

Big, bold and married to salt water, the dark-backed Western Gull is the casual observer's Pacific Coast "seagull." This heavyset gull is conspicuous whether sitting atop a piling, splashing in a stream outfall or sailing on a stiff breeze above coastal bluffs. • Many large, pink-footed gulls inhabit Washington's coast, but the Western Gull is the only one that stays and nests on the outer coast, rather than in estuaries. • The Western Gull has a smaller population than most other North American gulls, with fewer than 200 breeding colonies in total. It is also of possible conservation concern because of the effects of pesticides on reproduction, threats from oil spills and extensive hybridization with other species.

nonbreeding

breeding

ID: large, white head; yellow to dark eyes; stout, yellow bill with red spot; dark gray mantle; white underparts; pink legs. *1st winter:* mainly dark bill; patterned medium brown overall; barred tail coverts. *2nd winter:* completely brownish wings; streaked head; dark-tipped, pinkish bill. *3rd winter:* black-ringed, yellow bill; black wing tips. *In flight:* long, gray triangle on white underwing; dark wing tips; white tail; 1st- and 2nd-winter birds have pale brownish underwings and dark tail.
Size: *L* 24–26 in; *W* 4¾ ft.
Status: common year-round outer-coast resident; much less common on inland marine waters; rare winter visitor to eastern rivers and reservoirs.
Habitat: offshore rocks. *In migration* and *winter:* intertidal and shallow inshore zones; open ocean upwellings; coastal fields; coastal towns.

Nesting: colonial; on or near rock with vegetation cover; scrape nest is filled with vegetation; pair incubates 2–3 heavily marked, pale eggs for 30–32 days.
Feeding: eats various invertebrates and fish; follows feeding marine mammals to scavenge fish; major predator (eggs to adults) at seabird colonies; also eats human refuse.
Voice: commonest call is a *keow* note.
Similar Species: *Herring Gull* (p. 179): paler eyes; paler upperparts; whiter underwings; nonbreeder has brown-streaked head and neck; immature is often indistinguishable. *Thayer's Gull* (p. 180): eyes normally dark; paler upperparts; whiter underwings; much paler immature. *Glaucous-winged* x *Western Gull hybrid:* variable, with smaller head and bill, lighter mantle and wing tips not black.
Best Sites: La Push; Taholah; Pt. Brown jetty (Ocean Shores); Westport; Long Beach Peninsula; North Jetty (Columbia R. mouth).

GLAUCOUS-WINGED GULL

Larus glaucescens

Look for large, heavyset Glaucous-winged Gulls among winter gatherings of Western Gulls along the open coast, on inland marine waters and in estuaries. The paler-mantled Glaucous-winged adults have indistinct white "mirrors" at their wing tips. Scattered immature birds remain through spring and early summer, their drab, brownish first-winter plumage wearing and fading visibly before most of them leave for summer. • Over the last few decades, the Glaucous-winged Gull has begun to move up estuaries and river systems well beyond the influence of the tides. • In Washington and northern Oregon, the Glaucous-winged Gull routinely hybridizes with the Western Gull, resulting in a confusing range of intergrades.

nonbreeding

breeding

ID: usually darkish eyes; heavy, yellow bill with red spot; pale gray upperparts, including wings out to tips; pinkish legs. *Breeding:* white head, neck and upper breast. *Nonbreeding:* dingy head, neck and upper breast. *1st winter:* buff white or pale brown overall; dark bill; paler flight feathers. *2nd winter:* grayish brown overall; mainly dark bill; gray mantle; white throat and tail coverts. *3rd winter:* dark-tipped, pinkish bill. *In flight:* gray spots on white trailing edge near wing tip.
Size: *L* 24–27 in; *W* 4¾ ft.
Status: common year-round on the coast and inland marine waters; uncommon in winter and early spring in the east along reservoirs on the Columbia R. and Snake R.
Habitat: saltwater and brackish bays, estuaries, harbors and the open ocean; also city

dumps and parks, wet fields and offshore islands.
Nesting: colonial but territorial; on bare rock or in low ground cover on island ledges; nest consists of loosely stacked plant materials, string and bones; pair incubates 2–4 heavily marked, greenish eggs for 27–28 days.
Feeding: forages while walking, wading, swimming or plunging; omnivorous diet includes fish, mollusks, crustaceans, nestling birds, plant material, garbage and carrion.
Voice: usual calls are a squealing *kjau,* a high-pitched, repeated *kea* and a "mewing" *ma-ah;* flight call is a single, throaty *kwoh;* attack call is *eeja-ah.*
Similar Species: *Herring Gull* (p. 179): pale yellow eyes; black-and-white wing tips; darker, more patterned immature. *Western Gull* (p. 181): darker upperparts; eyes usually yellow; whiter head and neck on nonbreeder; darker, more patterned immature.
Best Sites: virtually anywhere along the outer coast and inland marine waters. *Winter:* Columbia R.; Snake R.

GLAUCOUS GULL
Larus hyperboreus

Glaucous Gulls are at heart arctic birds, wintering southward only slightly into temperate latitudes and in small numbers. They can make a living through scavenging but are also powerful predators, taking small mammals and birds during the northern summer. • Adults often linger farther north in winter than do immatures, so that most of the modest number of Glaucous Gulls seen each year in Washington are in subadult plumages. Despite their inexperience with the competitive rigors of a gull's world, first-winter Glaucous Gulls found in Washington are notable among gulls of their age class for their ability to defend food sources. • Teetering atop a mound of freshly bulldozed garbage, a gull secures a chosen food item through an intimidating "mantling" (covering) with widespread wings and by the well-aimed, no-nonsense jabs of a snapping bill.

nonbreeding

1st winter

ID: large and stout; white wing tips. *Nonbreeding* (rarely seen in Washington): variable head and neck streaking; pale eyes; yellow bill with red spot near tip of lower mandible; very pale gray mantle; pure white wing tips. *1st-winter:* pale, often whitish overall; subtle broken, white eye-arcs on darker individuals; long, heavy pinkish bill tipped with black; dusky-barred undertail coverts.
Size: *L* 27 in; *W* 5 ft.
Status: rare winter to early spring resident statewide; immatures are more common near the coast, with adults more plentiful inland.
Habitat: chiefly marine and estuarine habitats including the ocean, river mouths, beaches, industrial waterfronts and garbage dumps.
Nesting: does not nest in Washington.
Feeding: omnivorous; like other large gulls, snatches almost any edible item, living or dead.
Voice: similar to that of other large gulls but seldom heard in Washington.
Similar Species: *Glaucous-winged Gull* (p. 182): 1st-winter bird usually has somewhat smaller head and all-dark bill, is usually dark-eyed and has nearly uniformly dingy grayish brown flight feathers and pale gray wing tips with small white spots ("mirrors"). *Other large gulls* (pp. 177–81, 363): usually smaller and with at least some black or blackish on wing tips.
Best Sites: Ediz Hook (Port Angeles); mouth of Elwha R.; Gog-le-hi-te Wetland (Tacoma); most frequently on the Columbia R. near the Tri-Cities and the Walla Walla R. delta.

SABINE'S GULL

Xema sabini

The easy, buoyant flight and highly contrasting plumage of the Sabine's Gull make it instantly recognizable and unforgettable. Commercial fishers and residents of the Arctic have the best regular opportunities to appreciate this dainty and stunning bird, which wanders far out to sea, often beyond the limits of the continental shelf. Avid birders occasionally see single Sabine's Gulls or small flocks from shoreline viewpoints in Washington, mostly in May and September and usually with the aid of a spotting scope, but most birds pass by far from view. The best bet, as for other open-ocean species, is a boat trip. • Considering the pelagic nature of the species, the arrival of a few immature Sabine's Gulls inland each fall is somewhat surprising but highly anticipated. Beware, though, of misidentifying immature Black-legged Kittiwakes.

nonbreeding

breeding

ID: red-ringed, dark eyes; yellow-tipped, black bill; medium gray upper-parts; dark legs. *Breeding:* dark gray "hood." *Nonbreeding:* partial "hood." *Immature:* brownish partial "hood," neck and back; barred back and wings; pale legs. *In flight:* upperwing has gray triangle, white triangle and extensive black strip; mostly pale underwing; notched white tail (black-tipped on immature).

Size: *L* 13–14 in; *W* 3 ft.

Status: uncommon to fairly common spring and fall pelagic migrant; rare inland.

Habitat: highly pelagic; most birds remain well out of sight of land throughout their stay in Washington waters.

Nesting: does not nest in Washington.

Feeding: dips or swoops to the water's surface; gleans small fish and crustaceans while swimming; if forced to shore by storms, picks marine worms, crustaceans and insects from the water's surface or scavenges dead or dying fish.

Voice: generally silent; high-pitched calls at sea resemble those of the Arctic Tern.

Similar Species: *Black-legged Kittiwake* (p. 185): immature has black-marked, gray mantle, black "collar" and dark "M" on upperwings in flight. *Bonaparte's Gull* (p. 174): paler mantle; pink or orangy (breeding) legs; head of nonbreeding bird is white except crown and ear spot; rounded tail and different white areas on underwing in flight. *Franklin's Gull* (p. 173): partial white eye ring; red bill; darker mantle; mostly gray upperwing; reddish legs.

Best Sites: pelagic trips from Westport; Pt. Brown and Westport jetties (occasionally after storms); Columbia R.

BLACK-LEGGED KITTIWAKE

Rissa tridactyla

Apart from the usually open-ocean Sabine's Gull, the Black-legged Kittiwake is the only true "seagull" (pelagic gull) regularly found in Washington. This small, highly marine gull breeds on coastal cliffs at higher latitudes and spends the balance of the year on the open ocean, although some immature birds may spend the entire summer at sea farther south. Most sightings in Washington are from pelagic boat trips or coastal headlands in fall, winter and spring. • Late fall and winter storms that persist for several days may tire these small gulls and push them into nearshore waters and even onto beaches, sheltered harbors and estuaries. At such times, the unique combination of short, black legs, wing tips "dipped in ink" and yellow bill readily identify the Black-legged Kittiwake as a "bird of a different feather."

breeding

1st winter

nonbreeding

ID: white head; dark eyes; yellow bill; medium gray upperparts; white underparts; black legs. *Nonbreeding:* smudgy, grayish ear patch. *1st winter:* black ear patch and "collar"; black bill; gray mantle; dark wing markings. *In flight:* small, crisply defined black wing tips; white underwings; notched tail; immature has heavy, black "M" on upperwings and black-tipped tail.
Size: *L* 16–18 in; *W* 3 ft.
Status: fairly common offshore resident from fall until spring; uncommon otherwise and absent in early summer.
Habitat: mainly the open ocean, preferring areas along the edge of the continental

shelf and upwellings; young birds occasionally associate with other gulls in coastal locations.
Nesting: does not nest in Washington.
Feeding: plunges, dips and surface-feeds for marine invertebrates, fish and offal; can dive to 20 ft below the surface.
Voice: generally silent in Washington.
Similar Species: *Sabine's Gull* (p. 184): much smaller; yellow-tipped, black bill; more black on upper wing tip and less below; gray wing coverts, wider tail; nonbreeding bird has partial dark "hood." *Bonaparte's Gull* (p. 174): much smaller; small, black bill; black-tipped, white wing tips; rounded tail.
Best Sites: pelagic trips from Westport; Pt. Brown and Westport jetties; North Jetty (Columbia R. mouth); occasionally Cape Flattery.

CASPIAN TERN

Sterna caspia

A giant among terns, the Caspian Tern makes its presence known even to the casual observer by its robustness, size, eye-catching whiteness and commanding voice. Its heavy bill, deliberate flight and broad wings seem to span the conceptual gap between gulls and terns, but, unlike even the smaller gulls, this tern is almost strictly a fish-eater. • The breeding colony on Sand Island at the mouth of the Columbia River, with over 9000 pairs, is the world's largest for this species, and birds from this Oregon colony are regularly seen in adjoining areas of Washington. Other breeding colonies once existed in Washington, but the birds left after the habitat was degraded or the sites were disturbed.

breeding

ID: dagger-like, blood red bill; light gray mantle; white or pale gray underparts; black legs; folded wings extend beyond short tail. *Breeding:* peaked black "cap." *Nonbreeding:* white-streaked, dark "cap." *Immature:* white-streaked, dark "cap"; dull orange bill; "scaly" back. *In flight:* wings mostly pale gray above and white below, darker areas near tips; short, notched tail.
Size: *L* 19–23 in; *W* 4¼–4½ ft.
Status: common spring and summer resident on the outer coast; fairly common nonbreeding summer resident on inland marine waters; fairly common spring and summer resident in eastern Washington; absent in winter.
Habitat: *Breeding:* freshwater sandy islands and spits; reservoirs and large rivers; less often in mixed colonies on flat, rocky islands. *In migration:* large bodies of water; estuaries; coastal beaches.
Nesting: colonial, often with other species; in sand or gravel; scrape nest is lined with mollusk and crayfish shells, rocks, twigs or vegetation; pair incubates 1–3 lightly spotted, buff eggs for 25–28 days; family remains together until spring.
Feeding: hovers over water and plunges headfirst after small fish; also eats tadpoles and aquatic invertebrates.
Voice: low, harsh *ca-arr;* immatures answer loud *kraa-uh* of parents with a high-pitched whistle.
Similar Species: *Forster's* (p. 189), *Arctic* (p. 188) and *Common* (p. 187) *terns:* much smaller; long, forked tails; red to orangy bills (thinner, with dark tip, except on Arctic) and legs on breeding birds; black bill on nonbreeding birds.
Best Sites: Sand I. (Columbia R. mouth); Long Beach Peninsula; Westport–Ocean Shores; Crockett L.; Potholes Reservoir; Walla Walla R. delta; Paterson Unit, Umatilla NWR.

COMMON TERN
Sterna hirundo

Terns are effortless fliers, and most people concede the title of "world's best long-distance traveler" to the Arctic Tern. Recently, however, a Common Tern banded in Great Britain was recovered in Australia—a record distance for any bird. • Preferring to hug the coastline in migration, the Common Tern regularly visits beaches and estuaries. It is especially common in large estuaries in fall migration. • Difficulty in identifying the three smaller *Sterna* terns seen in Washington makes many out-of-habitat and out-of-season sighting claims questionable. In general, any terns seen in eastern Washington are most likely Forster's Terns, those in coastal habitats are probably Common Terns, and any flocks seen well out at sea are very likely Arctic Terns.

nonbreeding

breeding

ID: light gray upperparts; white underparts; white rump and undertail coverts; tail streamers (longest on breeding bird) normally do not reach tips of folded wings. *Breeding:* black "cap"; thin, orangy red bill, usually with black tip; grayish belly and breast; short, orangy red legs. *Nonbreeding:* partial black "cap"; white forehead; black bill; dark shoulder bar; black legs. *Immature:* brownish or gray upperparts with white barring. *In flight:* gray upperwings; strongly forked, white tail with gray outer edges; nonbreeding bird has dark flight feathers near tip of upperwing; immature has shorter outer tail streamers.
Size: *L* 12–15 in; *W* 29–30 in.
Status: fairly common to common end-of-summer migrant on the coast and fairly common late-spring migrant; less common migrant on inland marine waters; uncommon fall migrant in the east.

Habitat: open ocean offshore, coast, bays, harbors and lagoons; rarely (especially in fall migration) on interior freshwater lakes, reservoirs and rivers.
Nesting: does not nest in Washington.
Feeding: hovers over water and plunges headfirst, mostly for small fish, but also crustaceans and insects.
Voice: high-pitched, drawn-out *keee-are*, mostly at the colony but also during foraging.
Similar Species: *Forster's Tern* (p. 189): slightly bulkier; pale mantle; thicker bill (orange on breeding bird); underparts always white; longer legs; black eye-to-ear patch is diagnostic on nonbreeding bird and immature; broader wings; more white on upperwings; longer outer tail feathers are white on outer edges.
Best Sites: Ocean Shores; Westport; Long Beach Peninsula; Admiralty Inlet; Point No Point; Salsbury Pt. (Kitsap Co.).

187

ARCTIC TERN

Sterna paradisaea

This elegant tern rates among the most accomplished avian migrants, with some arctic-nesting birds flying to and from the Antarctic each year. Most Arctic Terns take the oceanic route, and any small "white" terns seen far out to sea are likely to be Arctic Terns. • These terns take short rests at sea, using any piece of driftwood or other floating platform that comes along. They are often harassed by Parasitic Jaegers, which follow them southward from the Arctic. • Except for the few that nest in our state, Arctic Terns are rarely seen from land in Washington, but sometimes hundreds of migrants are blown inshore by spring or fall storms, often in association with Red Phalaropes.

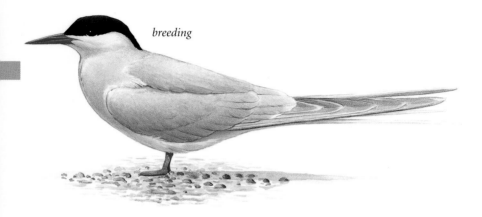

breeding

ID: white "cheek"; light gray upperparts; white rump and undertail coverts; long tail streamers reach beyond wing tips at rest. *Breeding:* black "cap"; small, red bill; gray underparts; very short, red legs. *Nonbreeding:* partial black "cap"; black bill; indistinct dark shoulder bar; clearly defined white forehead; black legs. *Immature:* white bars on upperparts; dusky legs; short, notched tail. *In flight:* little darkening at wing tips; long, forked, darker-edged, white tail.
Size: *L* 14–17 in; *W* 31 in.
Status: uncommon pelagic migrant in August and September and in late April; 1–2 pairs nest at Jetty I.
Habitat: open ocean in migration; occasionally visits estuaries, beaches and jetties if driven inshore by storms.

Nesting: colonial; on sand, gravel or rock; in a shallow, generally unlined scrape; pair incubates 2–3 darkly blotched, pale olive to buff eggs for 20–24 days.
Feeding: hovers over water and swoops or plunges for small fish and crustaceans.
Voice: harsh, high-pitched, down-slurred *kee kahr;* dry, nasal *raaaaz* attack call; also utters single short *kip* notes.
Similar Species: *Common Tern* (p. 187): larger bill, usually black-tipped on breeding bird; longer legs; shorter tail streamers compared to folded wings; nonbreeding bird has darker feathers at wing tip and more pronounced shoulder bar; immature has bolder shoulder bar and often some brown on upperparts. *Forster's Tern* (p. 189): thicker bill, orange and black-tipped on breeding bird; longer legs; black eye-to-ear patch is diagnostic on nonbreeding bird and immature.
Best Sites: *Late summer:* pelagic trips from Westport; *Summer:* Jetty I. (Everett). *Fall:* rare at North Jetty (Columbia R. mouth).

FORSTER'S TERN

Sterna forsteri

Washington's only strictly North American tern, the Forster's Tern was once considered the same species as the very similar Common Tern. German naturalist Johann Reinhold Forster was the first person to recommend, based on specimens sent to him from the Hudson Bay region of Canada, that the Forster's Tern deserved full species status. • Widespread in interior Washington, this tern is fairly common as a colony-nester on the large, shallow lakes and marshes adjoining the Potholes Reservoir. Where it breeds near the Black Tern, the Forster's prefers higher, drier locations. • Noted for its long-winged, buoyant flight and long, forked tail, the Forster's (like some of its cousins) often hovers before diving down to catch its prey.

breeding

nonbreeding

ID: light gray upperparts; white underparts, rump and undertail coverts; tail normally longer than folded wings. *Breeding:* black "cap"; black-tipped, orange bill; short, orangy red legs. *Nonbreeding:* white crown; black eye-to-ear patch; dull orange legs. *Immature:* initially tan-barred upperparts. *In flight:* long, forked, mostly white tail (shorter, darker streamers on immature); generally darkish outer flight feathers turn white above on breeding bird.
Size: *L* 13–16 in; *W* 30–31 in.
Status: fairly common and local summer Great Basin resident, particularly from the Potholes area and along the Columbia R. to the Tri-Cities; casual in the west in fall.
Habitat: *Breeding:* large freshwater lakes and marshes; large rivers with islands; alkaline lakes. *In migration:* wetlands; coastal estuaries; open beaches.

Nesting: mainly colonial, often with other species; on the ground, in mud or sand, or on a muskrat house, old grebe nest or floating vegetation platform; nest is lined with shells and grass; pair incubates 2–5 brown-marked, buff eggs for 23–24 days.
Feeding: hovers above the water and plunges headfirst after small fish, frogs and aquatic invertebrates; also catches airborne insects and eats carrion.
Voice: short, nasal *keer keer* flight call; grating *tzaap* repels intruders.
Similar Species: *Common Tern* (p. 187): slimmer; redder bill and gray underparts in breeding plumage; dark shoulder bar, partial "cap" and black legs in nonbreeding plumage; grayer upperwings; gray outer (not inner) tail feathers; more coastal.
Best Sites: Potholes Reservoir; Desert Wildlife Area; Wanapum Dam (Kittitas Co.); Hanford Reach (Columbia R.); Tri-Cities; Paterson Unit, Umatilla NWR.

BLACK TERN

Chlidonias niger

Even without brilliant colors, Black Terns are strikingly beautiful birds, unmistakable in their breeding plumage. Depending on what they are doing, their flight can be reminiscent of nighthawks, flycatchers, swallows or butterflies. Their zest and grace is unparalleled as they fly erratically but buoyantly across their nesting marsh. • These highly social birds often breed in colonies and forage in flocks. • Black Tern populations have dropped in the past few decades, partly as a result of wetland breeding habitat loss and degradation, but they often benefit from the restoration of upland habitat surrounding managed wetlands and the reduction of contamination by agricultural runoff. • The Black Tern overwinters along tropical coastlines.

nonbreeding

breeding

ID: slender, black bill; gray back, wings and tail; white undertail coverts. *Breeding:* black head, breast and belly; reddish black legs. *Nonbreeding:* white forehead, neck and underparts; black hindcrown, nape, eye spot and ear spot; partial dark gray "collar." *Immature:* browner plumage than nonbreeding bird, and with pale barring on back and wings; orange legs. *In flight:* plain, dark gray wings; white undertail; shallow-notched tail; irregular, wandering flight.
Size: *L* 9–10 in; *W* 24 in.
Status: fairly common and local breeding resident in eastern Washington from mid-May to late August; rare migrant in western Washington; uncommon at Ridgefield NWR (with nest records from 2001–02).

Habitat: shallow freshwater marshes, ponds and lakes. *In migration:* flooded fields; rarely on coastal estuaries.
Nesting: loosely colonial, sometimes with Forster's Terns; in still water with emergent vegetation; on a muskrat house, abandoned grebe nest or platform of loose, dead vegetation; nest is usually flimsy and unlined; pair incubates 2–4 dark-blotched, buff to olive eggs for 19–21 days.
Feeding: flies across water and vegetation, hovering, dipping and landing for brief moments; snatches insects from the air or tall grass; takes fish and aquatic insects from the water's surface; also eats small amphibians, earthworms, spiders, small crustaceans and leeches.
Voice: shrill, metallic *kik-kik-kik-kik-kik* greeting call; *kreea* alarm call.
Similar Species: *Forster's Tern* (p. 189) and *Common Tern* (p. 187): larger; much lighter coloration; different head patterns; much longer tail streamers.
Best Sites: Conboy Lake NWR; Desert Wildlife Area; Sprague L.; Conners L. (Sinlahekin Valley); Beth L. and Beaver L. (Okanogan Co.); Turnbull NWR.

COMMON MURRE

Uria aalge

The alcids (auk family) occupy the niche in the Northern Hemisphere that penguins do in the south, and the word "penguin" comes from *Pinguinus pinguinus,* the now-extinct large, flightless Great Auk of the northern Atlantic. • The slender, upright-standing Common Murre has typical alcid attributes: small wings, webbed feet and sleek, waterproof plumage for pursuing fish underwater, and it nests in huge, tightly packed colonies on offshore islands. • Washington's nesting murres arrive at their colonies beginning in late March, possibly following a winter visit. From August to October, additional postbreeding birds disperse northward into Washington. • Although shaped to roll in circles and stay on the nesting ledge, many murre eggs are dislodged in panic departures caused by predators or boat approaches. Food availability and water temperature also affect nesting success.

breeding

ID: long, straight, pointed, black bill; gray-streaked flanks; white underparts; dark legs and feet. *Breeding:* dark brown head and upperparts, with sharp demarcation on upper breast. *Nonbreeding:* white lower face, "chin" and neck; thin, dark line curving down from eye; blackish brown upperparts. *In flight:* stocky body tilted upward; rapid, whirring wingbeats.

Size: *L* 17–18 in; *W* 26 in.

Status: common year-round resident of the outer coast and off-shore islands; fairly common in winter on inland marine waters; candidate for state threatened list.

Habitat: *Breeding:* offshore islands and sea stacks; rarely at headland cliff ledges. *Foraging:* open ocean from just beyond the surf line; father and chick pairs regularly visit the lower reaches of estuaries from July to August.

Nesting: highly colonial; on bare, flat rock on a cliff ledge or island close to water; pair incubates 1 heavily marked, pale egg for 30–35 days; young bird leaves the nest at 21 days and joins the father in the water below.

Feeding: dives for fish, squid, crustaceans, mollusks and marine worms.

Voice: utters a low, harsh *murrr;* dependent immature gives a high-pitched, quavering, repeated *feed-me-now* whistle.

Similar Species: *Marbled Murrelet* (p. 193) and *Ancient Murrelet* (p. 194): much smaller; stocky bodies; stubby bills; very fast wingbeats; more erratic flight. *Rhinoceros Auklet* (p. 196): slightly smaller; stockier; generally grayish brown; stubbier, yellowish bill; white belly and undertail.

Best Sites: Cape Flattery–Tatoosh I.; Kalaloch–Destruction I.; Pt. Grenville (Grays Harbor); Pt. Brown and Westport jetties; Pt. Wilson (Port Townsend).

PIGEON GUILLEMOT

Cepphus columba

Pigeon Guillemots are among the most widespread and commonly seen alcids along the Pacific Coast, and they are also the most likely to remain inshore. During summer, these black-and-white seabirds forage close to their small colony sites. • The distinctively patterned black breeding plumage, with its large white wing patches, vermilion gape and startling red feet, is designed for breeding displays and for visual stimulation of the chicks at the often dark nest site. The Pigeon Guillemot's much different gray-and-white winter look, which is reminiscent of the Rock Pigeon, as well as its similarity in size and body form, inspired its common and scientific names. It is still called "Sea Pigeon" in Alaska.

nonbreeding

breeding

ID: *Breeding:* black overall, except for white wing patch; dark eyes and bill; bright red legs and feet. *Nonbreeding:* whitish head, neck and underparts; dark eye patch; mottled, gray-and-white crown and back. *In flight:* stubby wings; white wing patch split by brownish black line; gray underwings; conspicuous trailing red feet.

Size: *L* 13–14 in; *W* 23 in.

Status: fairly common year-round resident of coastal and inland marine waters.

Habitat: shallow water with offshore islands; rocky or cliff-edged seashores with deep water. *Breeding:* estuaries with shoreline structures.

Nesting: loosely colonial or solitary; on the ground or a rock, inside a rock crevice or boulder rubble or on an artificial structure; nest scrape is lined with loose stones and shells; pair incubates 1–2 pale cream eggs with gray-and-brown blotches for 29–32

days; fledged young leave the nest at 33–37 days.

Feeding: prefers 30–95 ft deep inshore water; dives to seabed for small fish and probes underwater rocky recesses and vegetation for invertebrates; also eats herring eggs.

Voice: distinctive series of wheezy, stuttering, whistled trills and screams, especially near the nest site.

Similar Species: *Common Murre* (p. 191): larger; longer bill; dark legs and feet; breeding plumage has dark brown upperparts, white underparts and all-dark upperwing; highly colonial on ledges and stack tops. *Marbled Murrelet* (p. 193) and *Ancient Murrelet* (p. 194): smaller; small bills; browner or black above and white below; dark feet; all-dark upperwing; usually paired.

Best Sites: coastal headlands; Pt. Partridge (Whidbey I.); Fort Casey bluffs; Discovery Park (Seattle); Cape Flattery; Ocean Shores and Westport jetties; Cape Disappointment (Columbia R. mouth).

MARBLED MURRELET
Brachyramphus marmoratus

Although Marbled Murrelets were first described as early as 1789, their nests were not found until 1961 in Asia and 1974 in North America. Most Marbled Murrelets nest high in old-growth rainforest trees. They visit their nests at night to avoid diurnal raptors and fly high, fast and directly to thwart nocturnal owls of the lower canopy. • Adults and young may stay together well past summer. Pair bonds are very strong, and pairs can be found well out to sea, even in winter. When one bird takes off from the water, it will call until it hears a reply from its partner. These stocky birds are sometimes seen in small flocks, especially when feeding close to nest sites.

nonbreeding

breeding

ID: appears flat-headed; small, dark bill. *Breeding:* mottled, dark brown throughout; paler on throat and undertail coverts. *Nonbreeding:* black "helmet," narrow nape line, back and wings; white "collar," underparts and shoulder stripe. *In flight:* all-dark wings; rocks from side to side.
Size: *L* 9–10 in; *W* 16 in.
Status: fairly common but declining year-round coastal resident; fairly common breeder; federal- and state-listed as threatened.
Habitat: *Breeding:* old-growth rainforests. *Foraging:* marine waters, usually within 3 mi of shore. *In migration* and *winter:* open ocean, usually close to shore; some birds may retain nest sites and territories over winter.

Nesting: in a tree crown or on a lower horizontal limb of a tall rainforest tree; nests in a depression in moss or lichens; pair incubates 1 dark-spotted, pale green egg for 28–30 days; both parents feed the chick until it jumps to the ground at 27–40 days.
Feeding: dives to 200 ft deep; eats mainly small schooling fish, adding small crustaceans in winter.
Voice: common location call in the water or in flight is a shrieking *keer;* gives various whistles and groans at the nest.
Similar Species: *Cassin's Auklet* (p. 195): sooty gray overall; rounder head; heavier bill; whitish crescent above yellowish eye; light stripe on underwing. *Rhinoceros Auklet* (p. 196): larger; generally grayish brown; heavier, yellow bill; white belly and undertail coverts; feeds farther offshore.
Best Sites: San Juans; west side of Whidbey I.; Salsbury Pt. (Kitsap Co.); Discovery Park (Seattle); Point No Point; Salt Creek CP (Clallam Co.); Pt. Brown and Westport jetties.

193

ANCIENT MURRELET
Synthliboramphus antiquus

During the breeding season, this proficient mariner's feathery white "eye-brows" and gray mantle give it a distinguished, aged look. Unfortunately, few Washington birders ever see the Ancient Murrelet in breeding plumage, because this small, relatively slender alcid is mainly an offshore migrant and winter resident along our coast. • The Ancient Murrelet's feet and wings are not as suited to diving as those of other small alcids, so it does not dive as deep. • At its island nesting colonies in Alaska and northern British Columbia, this murrelet typically raises two nestlings (most alcids raise one). Nestlings leave the nest burrow only one to three days after hatching and are reared entirely at sea. • The long and awkward genus name simply means "small bill."

breeding

ID: black "hood" with white upward extension at rear of neck; dark eyes; yellow bill; dark gray back; white-mottled, gray flanks; white lower neck and belly; pale blue legs and feet. *Breeding:* black throat; wispy white streaks on crown and nape. *Nonbreeding* and *immature:* upper head all or mostly black; white throat. *In flight:* all dark above; white underparts and wing linings; unique among alcids in commonly plunging directly underwater from the air to feed.
Size: *L* 9–10 in; *W* 17 in.
Status: uncommon resident from November to mid-March in marine waters,

particularly the eastern part of the Strait of Juan de Fuca and Puget Sound.
Habitat: from inshore tidal upwellings to the edge of the continental shelf; often seen from headlands, jetties and beaches; rarely occurs in harbors and protected bays.
Nesting: does not nest in Washington.
Feeding: swims and dives (often directly from flight) to 50 or 60 ft for krill, other crustaceans and very small fish.
Voice: generally silent; gives a clipped whistle at sea.
Similar Species: *Cassin's Auklet* (p. 195): generally sooty gray overall; white crescent over eye; dusky bill with light area on lower mandible base; white belly and undertail coverts; gray underwing with light stripe.
Best Sites: Point No Point; Fort Flagler; Fort Worden; Keystone ferry across Admiralty Inlet.

CASSIN'S AUKLET
Ptychoramphus aleuticus

The small size and the ground-nesting habits of the Cassin's Auklet make it extremely vulnerable to predators—including foxes, cats and rats—introduced where they can raid its island nesting colonies. Southern populations try to compensate for such losses by raising a second chick later in the breeding season. • Natural oils secreted by an alcid's uropygial gland help to waterproof the bird's feathers against cold water, but waterproofed feathers are useless against petrochemical spills. Matted, oil-contaminated feathers lose their insulative properties, and, in preening, the birds ingest much of the heavy oil, which then coats the digestive system, resulting in a slow and painful death by starvation and exposure.

ID: bold white crescent above pale yellow eye; stubby, dark bill with light area at base of lower mandible; sooty gray upperparts; paler gray underparts; white belly and undertail coverts. *In flight:* rounded wings; gray underwing with short lighter stripe near body; flies close to the water's surface.
Size: *L* 8–9 in; *W* 15 in.
Status: fairly common year-round resident of outer coastal marine waters; common but declining breeder on offshore islands; candidate for the state threatened list.
Habitat: *Breeding:* offshore islands, sea stacks, steep cliffs and slopes. *Foraging:* ocean waters, especially over upwellings along the continental shelf and deeper water near nest sites.

Nesting: colonial; pair digs an underground burrow or uses a natural rock crevice for the normally unlined nest; pair incubates 1 creamy white egg for 37–42 days; pair feeds the chick until fledging at 42 days; chick leaves the nest at 50 days and swims out to sea.
Feeding: swims underwater to a depth of 120 ft for small crustaceans, squid and small fish.
Voice: usually silent away from the nest site; foraging pair may utter short, sharp *krik* location notes.
Similar Species: *Rhinoceros Auklet* (p. 196): much larger; heavier, yellow bill; completely dark underwings. *Marbled Murrelet* (p. 193): brown, heavily mottled breeding plumage; slimmer, usually uptilted bill; completely dark underwings.
Best Sites: pelagic boat trips; occasionally seen from shore anywhere along the coast.

195

RHINOCEROS AUKLET

Cerorhinca monocerata

During winter storms, "Rhinos" ride out mountainous waves, seemingly unaffected by chill winds and ocean spray. These stocky, medium-sized alcids may be common along the coast in winter, but the better weather conditions of spring and summer allow more dependable viewing near their scattered breeding sites. • Feeding birds can remain submerged for up to two minutes. Unlike other alcids, Rhinoceros Auklets sometimes cooperatively herd sand lance and herring schools by blowing bubbles from the sides of their mouths, much as feeding humpback whales do, and they use their bills rather than throat pouches to carry food to their nests. • The striking "horn" that gives the Rhinoceros Auklet its name is present only during the breeding season from March to June.

breeding

ID: drab grayish brown overall; white belly and undertail coverts; pale, yellowish or bluish legs and feet. *Breeding:* yellow eyes; fleshy, ivory-colored, vertical "horn" at base of orangy yellow bill; 2 whitish plumes at side of head. *Nonbreeding:* paler eyes; dull yellow bill. *In flight:* all-dark wings.

Size: *L* 14–16 in; *W* 22 in.

Status: common spring and summer resident of coastal waters and uncommon in fall and winter; less common year-round in southern Puget Sound.

Habitat: *Breeding:* small islands, sea stacks and cliffs with enough soil for burrowing. *Foraging:* inshore coastal waters and offshore over the continental shelf; prefers deep water.

Nesting: colonial; in a burrow, up to 20 ft long, usually into a grassy slope at least 30 ft above sea level; nest is a cup of moss and twigs; pair incubates 1 lightly spotted, off-white egg for 42–49 days.

Feeding: dives up to 120 ft deep for small schooling fish and crustaceans; switches to pelagic fish and squid in winter.

Voice: usually silent; rasping squeak at sea; growling and braying at the nest site.

Similar Species: *Cassin's Auklet* (p. 195): much smaller; white crescent above eye; darker bill; light underwing stripe. *Common Murre* (p. 191): bulkier; long, dark, pointed bill; white sides and flanks; whitish wing linings. *Tufted Puffin* (p. 197): immature has wider bill and dark undertail coverts.

Best Sites: Protection Island NWR (no access—view from 200 yd offshore); San Juans; Admiralty Inlet; Point No Point; Cape Flattery; Pt. Brown jetty (Ocean Shores); Westport boat trips at mouth of Grays Harbor.

TUFTED PUFFIN

Fratercula cirrhata

Puffins, the clowns of the alcid world, are among the most photographed and painted of birds. • The Tufted Puffin, with its massive, brightly colored bill, may look awkward in the air and clumsy on land, but its stubby wings propel it with surprising speed and agility when it swims to pursue prey or avoid aerial predators. • During the breeding season, Tufted Puffins can be seen at the entrances to their burrows and on the water near colonies, but they forage well out to sea. In August, the adults abandon their chicks and move offshore. The chicks remain in the burrow for a week and then, still flightless, leap into the water and paddle out to sea, where they remain until they attain breeding maturity at four or five years.

breeding

ID: soot-black plumage; large head; yellow eyes; massive, laterally flattened bill; pinkish orange legs and feet. *Breeding:* white face; long, downcurved, yellow tuft behind eye; red eye ring; reddish orange and yellow bill. *Nonbreeding:* sooty face; short, golden gray tuft behind eye; dull orange bill with dark base.

Size: *L* 15–16 in; *W* 25 in.

Status: uncommon spring and summer resident on offshore islands and the outer coast; fairly common but dispersed at sea in winter; candidate for state threatened list.

Habitat: *Breeding:* offshore islands with enough soil to construct burrows; nearshore waters, especially with upwellings. *Winter:* open ocean offshore.

Nesting: colonial; burrow, usually 1–3 ft long (up to 20 ft), leads to a nest chamber, which may be lined with grass and feathers; pair incubates 1 dark-spotted, white egg for 41 days.

Feeding: dives to great depths, often for up to 2 minutes, to capture small schooling fish; also eats crustaceans, mollusks, sea urchins and, rarely, marine algae.

Voice: generally silent; softly growls and grunts at the nesting colony.

Similar Species: *Rhinoceros Auklet* (p. 196): smaller bill; white undertail coverts. *Surf Scoter* (p. 61): larger; male has white patches on forehead and nape, and his bill is orange, white and black. *Horned Puffin:* casual visitor only; white breast and underparts; paler face in nonbreeding plumage.

Best Sites: Diamond Pt. (Clallam Co.); Cape Flattery; La Push; Point Grenville; Protection Island NWR (no access; view from 200 yd offshore).

ROCK PIGEON
Columba livia

O ur Rock Pigeons (formerly called "Rock Doves") are the feral descendants of Eurasian birds first domesticated around 4500 BC. Introduced to North America in the 1600s, they have settled widely in cities, towns and agricultural areas. Some birds have reverted to nesting on tall cliffs—their original nesting habitat. • Rock Pigeons have been used as food, as message couriers (both Caesar and Napoleon used them) and as scientific subjects. Much of our understanding of bird migration, endocrinology, sensory perception, flight, behavior and other biological functions derives from experiments involving Rock Pigeons. • The Rock Pigeon's great variation in coloration is a result of extensive inbreeding over time.

ID: highly variable build and color; white rump, orangy pink feet and dark-tipped tail are typical; birds closest to their wild ancestors are gray overall, with bluish gray head, iridescent, green-and-purple neck and upper breast and 2 dark wing bars; other birds may be mostly white, tan or blackish brown. *In flight:* typically pale underwings; holds wings in deep "V" while gliding; clapping sound on takeoff; broad, fan-shaped tail; often in large flocks.
Size: *L* 12–14 in; *W* 28 in.
Status: common year-round resident statewide.
Habitat: urban and suburban areas, railroad yards, grain terminals, farms and ranches; cliffs and canyon walls; absent only from dense forests and alpine habitats.

Nesting: on ledges of structures and cliffs; flimsy nest of sticks and assorted vegetation is adorned with debris in urban sites; pair incubates 2 white eggs for about 18 days; parents feed the young with regurgitated food and crop "milk"; may raise up to 5 broods per year.
Feeding: gleans the ground for waste grain, seeds, fruits and scraps of human food; occasionally eats insects.
Voice: slow series of low hoots. *Male:* soft, *cooing coorrr-coorrr-coorrr* song. *Female:* occasional clucks.
Similar Species: *Band-tailed Pigeon* (p. 199): yellow bill; no wing bars; white half-"collar"; yellow feet; typically dark underwings; gray rump; dark band at base of paler tail. *Mourning Dove* (p. 200): much slimmer; grayish fawn overall, with less gray on head, breast and belly; shorter wings; dark wing spots; long, diamond-shaped tail.
Best Sites: cities; sites with waste grain; basalt cliffs along the Yakima R. canyon, above the Wanapum Dam (Kittitas Co.) and at Frenchman Coulee (Grant Co.).

BAND-TAILED PIGEON

Patagioenas fasciata

Clinging clumsily to twigs that may barely support their weight, Band-tailed Pigeons reach into adjacent foliage to pick nuts and fruit. Their presence overhead is often revealed by the occasional noisy slap of their broad wings as they shift position in the canopy. These large, heavy pigeons forage anywhere from sea-level forests to the upper limits of the coniferous forests, especially in mixed woodlands, such as fir and maple. They are also found in residential areas with large evergreens. Flocks can quickly empty a backyard bird feeder. • This bird's common and scientific names both refer to the broad, gray band on its tail—*fascia* means "a band" in Latin.

ID: gray overall; purple-tinged head and breast; dark eyes; black-tipped, yellow bill; white "half-collar" on iridescent, green nape; long, gray tail with broad darker band at base; yellow legs and feet. *In flight:* typically dark underwings; direct flight, often in small flocks.

Size: *L* 13–15 in; *W* 26 in.

Status: fairly common resident from spring through summer in coniferous and mixed forests from the coast to the western slopes of the Cascades and uncommon the rest of the year; very rare east of the Cascades.

Habitat: *Breeding:* mainly coniferous rainforests, especially riparian or moist bottomland ones. *In migration* and *winter:* agricultural lands, interior valleys and forested habitats throughout western Washington.

Nesting: in a tree; twig nest is lined with conifer needles, moss or breast feathers; female incubates at night, male by day, 1 all-white egg (rarely 2) for 16–22 days; young is fed regurgitated food and crop "milk"; pair raises 2–3 broods per year.

Feeding: seeds; grain; fruit; tree and shrub flower buds; attracted to salt licks.

Voice: call notes include a nasal *waaaaa*; male's song is a repetition of 2 owl-like *hwoo* notes.

Similar Species: *Rock Pigeon* (p. 198): variable build and color; usually has white rump and dark wing bars; no "half-collar"; typically light underwings. *Mourning Dove* (p. 200): much smaller; grayish fawn overall, less gray on head, breast and belly; dark wing spots; long, diamond-shaped tail.

Best Sites: coastal forests; Kitsap Peninsula; mixed woods on slopes of the Cascades; middle part of Skagit River Valley; Trout L.

MOURNING DOVE

Zenaida macroura

The soothing, rhythmic cooing of the Mourning Dove is an oft-heard sound in Washington's woodlands, farmlands and suburban parks and gardens. One of North America's most widespread and common land birds, it is ranked second to the Red-winged Blackbird in the number of breeding bird survey routes that it is found in and eleventh in relative abundance. • Like all members of its family, this dove feeds its young with a nutritious liquid ("milk") produced by glands in the bird's crop. • Mourning Doves are swift, direct fliers, and their wings make a distinctive whistling sound as the birds accelerate. • The Mourning Dove's common name reflects its sad-sounding song. The genus name *Zenaida* honors Zénaïde, Princess of Naples and wife of zoologist Charles-Lucien Bonaparte in the early 1800s.

ID: sleek profile; grayish fawn overall; slender, gray bill; pinkish tinges on neck and upper breast (especially on male); several blackish spots on upperparts; pinkish red feet. *In flight:* fast and direct flight on short, pointed wings; gray underwings; very long, diamond-shaped, black-and-white-trimmed tail.

Size: *L* 11–13 in; *W* 18 in.

Status: common resident east of the Cascades from spring through mid-October and fairly common the rest of the year; uncommon year-round resident in western lowlands.

Habitat: *Breeding:* open woodlands and forest edges next to grasslands and parks; rarely uses dense forests. *In migration* and *winter:* widespread in agricultural areas, waste areas, gravelly areas and suburbs.

Nesting: usually in a tree, but occasionally on the ground; flimsy twig platform is sometimes built on top of a songbird nest; pair incubates 2 white eggs for 14 days and feeds the young by regurgitation of digested seeds and crop "milk."

Feeding: picks seeds and waste grains from the ground; readily takes to city and suburban feeders, often arriving in small flocks.

Voice: mournful, soft, slow *oh-woe-woe-woe* is often misidentified as an owl hooting.

Similar Species: *Rock Pigeon* (p. 198): stockier; typically with iridescent neck, white rump and dark wing bars; broad, fan-shaped tail. *Band-tailed Pigeon* (p. 199): much larger; yellow bill; partial white "collar"; iridescent, green nape; yellow feet; broad, fan-shaped tail.

Best Sites: *Summer:* widespread east of the Cascades; agricultural areas of western Washington. *Winter:* agricultural areas.

BARN OWL
Tyto alba

This night hunter's haunting look and eerie screams have inspired superstitions. However, many people appreciate the Barn Owl's subtle beauty and the benefits it brings farmers by eating rodents. • Nest boxes have stabilized some populations, but intensive agriculture, particularly the loss of hedgerows and barns, have threatened others. Almost any open area serves as a foraging site, and Barn Owls are surprisingly tolerant of human activities as long as their nest sites are not threatened. Some birds have been known to roost even in large garages with people working below. With plentiful food, Barn Owls often raise a second brood in the same nest. • Birds in eastern Washington, at the northern edge of their range, often suffer during severe winters. • Even with their rather slow wingbeats, Barn Owls can achieve 50 miles per hour.

ID: heartlike reddish border around white face; dark brown or blackish eyes; ivory-colored bill; pinkish white cere; gray-patterned, tawny upperparts with lighter markings; white underparts; light gray feet and legs. *In flight:* mostly whitish below, with some gray underwing barring; feet extend beyond tail.

Size: *L* 13–15 in; *W* 34–35 in.

Status: common year-round statewide in agricultural lowlands; declining in the west because of habitat loss.

Habitat: almost any open habitat, including grasslands, deserts, marshes and farm fields.

Nesting: in a cavity in a tree, cliff, riverbank, building, haystack or nest box; female incubates 5–7 nest-stained, dull white eggs for 29–34 days; male delivers food while the female broods and tends the young.

Feeding: usually hunts in full darkness using superb hearing, flying close to the ground in quartering flights for small mammals; also eats some amphibians, reptiles, fish, invertebrates and roosting birds.

Voice: calls include harsh, raspy screeches and hisses; also makes metallic clicking sounds; often heard flying high over cities and residential areas late at night.

Similar Species: *Snowy Owl* (p. 205): winter only; larger; stockier; mostly white, often with dark barring and spots; yellow eyes. *Short-eared Owl* (p. 212): dark area accentuates yellow eye; vertical brown streaks on breast and belly; black "wrist" patches in flight; hunts by twilight.

Best Sites: agricultural lowlands; Samish Flats; Nisqually NWR; north of Ellensburg; Moxee Agricultural Station; Lower Crab Creek; Fishhook Park (Lower Snake R.).

FLAMMULATED OWL

Otus flammeolus

Just as the campfire settles into glowing embers, an odd, low-pitched sound comes from beyond the clearing edge. A Flammulated Owl has just shaken off its daytime lethargy and is preparing to begin its nocturnal hunt for large insects and anything else it can track down and overpower. • Once the summer supply of insects has dwindled and the season's youngsters have been safely fledged, the Flammulated Owl bids farewell to its mountain forests for another year and heads off for the warmth of Mexico or Guatemala. • Increased attention by birders and raptor researchers has revealed that this small, dark-eyed, nocturnal insectivore, once considered rare, is actually widespread and numerous in many areas.

gray morph

ID: variable gray or rufous overall; often shows small "ear" tufts; white "eyebrows" indent top of rusty or gray facial disc; dark eyes; grayish bill; dark-centered white spots on shoulders and wing coverts; dark-streaked, whitish breast. *In flight:* wings are generally brown and gray, with white barring.

Size: *L* 6–7 in; *W* 15 in.

Status: uncommon breeding eastern resident from late May through late July; candidate for state threatened list.

Habitat: forests of ponderosa pine alone or mixed with Douglas-fir, grand fir and western larch, often near clearings or in riparian areas with aspen and a brushy understory.

Nesting: uses a natural cavity or an old woodpecker hole, occasionally taking over an active nest of another species; female incubates 2–3 creamy white eggs for 21–24 days.

Feeding: strictly nocturnal; catches prey in flight, on the ground and from the foliage of both the canopy and understory; eats mostly arthropods, especially moths, beetles, crickets and grasshoppers.

Voice: utters low-frequency notes like those of a distant larger owl; very difficult to locate.

Similar Species: *Other small owls:* yellow eyes. *Western Screech-Owl* (p. 203): larger; generally brown or gray, with similar markings; face usually has less pronounced white markings and less rusty coloration. *Northern Saw-whet Owl* (p. 214) and *Northern Pygmy-Owl* (p. 206): heavier; no prominent "ear" tufts.

Best Sites: Old Blewett Pass; Liberty (Kittitas Co.); Loup Loup Creek and Rock Creek (Okanogan Co.); Bonaparte Lake Rd. (Okanogan Co.); Bethel Ridge (off US 12); Satus Pass (Klickitat Co.).

WESTERN SCREECH-OWL
Megascops kennicottii

L
ike many of the smaller owls, the Western Screech-Owl is a fierce and adaptable hunter, often adding birds larger than itself to its usual diet of insects, amphibians and small mammals. This chunky, open-woodland owl passes the daylight hours concealed in dense shrubs or roosting in a hollow tree, waiting until late evening to commence its hunting activities. The Western Screech-Owl requires little more than a secluded roosting site, a tree hollow for nesting and some semi-open ground that it can scout from low tree limbs. • Between March and June, the distinctive "bouncing-ball" courtship whistles indicate the presence of a pair of Western Screech-Owls. • Robert Kennicott, for whom this species is named, traveled across northern Canada and Alaska and collected owl specimens in the mid-1800s.

ID: usually streaky brown overall along the humid coastal plain and gray overall elsewhere; partially dark-bordered facial disc; often shows small "ear" tufts; gray bill; yellow eyes; narrow, dark, vertical breast stripes. *In flight:* pale-lined, barred, grayish or brownish wings; dark "wrist" patch; white spots on upperwing.
Size: *Male: L* 8–9 in; *W* 18–20 in. *Female: L* 10–11 in; *W* 22–24 in.
Status: uncommon to locally fairly common lowland resident.
Habitat: lowland forests of all types, including coniferous forests and riparian woodlands; also towns, orchards, farms, ranches and desert oases.
Nesting: in an abandoned woodpecker cavity or magpie nest, stump or nest box;

adds no nest material; female, fed by the male, incubates 2–5 white eggs for about 26 days; pair feeds the young through summer.
Feeding: nocturnal; swoops from a perch to capture invertebrates, mice, voles, amphibians and occasionally songbirds, often taking prey larger than itself.
Voice: courtship song is a distinctive series of soft, accelerating, even-pitched whistles and clear notes, with a rhythm like that of a bouncing ball coming to a stop; also gives a short trill followed by a longer trill; pairs often harmonize.
Similar Species: *Flammulated Owl* (p. 202): smaller; at least some rusty coloration on face and upperparts; whitish "eyebrows"; dark eyes; coarser breast markings.
Best Sites: lowland riparian areas, suburbs, towns and city parks.

GREAT HORNED OWL

Bubo virginianus

Unchallenged in any habitat from desert to dense forest, the large, powerfully built, aggressive Great Horned Owl normally lives a long life in almost any habitat except arctic-alpine areas. It is the most widely distributed avian predator in the Western Hemisphere and arguably the most formidable. Capable of severing the spinal columns of prey that outweigh it, this owl has talons that take 30 pounds of force to open. • The Great Horned Owl's acute hearing and sight allow it to hunt for a wide variety of nocturnal mammals, amphibians and other birds, including roosting waterfowl and hawks. With its poorly developed sense of smell, this owl happily hunts skunks, but even its molted feathers often retain the odor!

Habitat: almost any habitat below timberline, including agricultural areas and suburban parks. *Breeding:* usually trees or thick brush.

Nesting: typically uses a tree-platform nest of another species but sometimes uses a tree cavity, cliff, deserted building or artificial platform or nests on the ground; nest may be lined with bark shreds, leaves, downy breast feathers or fur; female, fed by the male, incubates 2–4 dull white eggs for 30–37 days.

Feeding: opportunistic; mainly nocturnal; usually from a perch but sometimes on the ground or from flight; eats large invertebrates and birds up to goose-sized, as well as rodents, amphibians and reptiles.

Voice: *Breeding male:* 4–6 deep hoots: *hoo-hoo-hoooo hoo-hoo* or *eat-my-food, I'll-eat you. Female:* in a pair duet, gives the higher-pitched hoots.

ID: interrupted brownish facial disc with partial dark border; prominent "ear" tufts; large, yellow eyes; heavily mottled, grayish brown upperparts; dark horizontal barring on white or buff underparts. *Immature:* paler; no "ear" tufts; whitish forehead. *In flight:* broad, barred wings, paler below; slow, measured wingbeats; short glides; will fly over open water.

Size: *Male: L* 18–22 in; *W* 3¼–3¾ ft. *Female: L* 21–25 in; *W* 3¾–4¼ ft.

Status: fairly common year-round resident statewide.

Similar Species: *Long-eared Owl* (p. 211): much smaller; very slim; startled-looking stare; narrower head and "ear" tufts; largely vertical breast markings; darker "wrist" patches in flight. *Barred Owl* (p. 209): smaller; no "ears"; bolder facial disc; coarse vertical belly streaks.

Best Sites: any wooded site.

SNOWY OWL
Bubo scandiacus

When the mercury dips and the landscape hardens in winter's icy grip, Snowy Owls move south from their arctic breeding sites in search of food. During particularly hard winters, when lemmings and voles are scarce in Canada and Alaska, these owls can be especially numerous in our area. Mostly immatures, plus a few adults, drift down into Washington, and they can be seen perching atop trees, power poles, coastal driftwood and anything else that affords a view over open country. At times, dozens of Snowy Owls may be scattered throughout the state, especially in the Samish Flats, in northeastern and north-central Washington and along the coast. They have even been observed in downtown Seattle.

ID: yellow eyes; black bill; white feet; black talons. *Male:* becomes almost entirely white with age; very little dark flecking. *Female:* white with dark barring on upperparts and breast. *Immature:* heavier, brownish gray barring. *In flight:* upperwings often have dark barring; underwings mostly or all white.

Size: *Male: L* 22–23 in; *W* 4¾ ft. *Female: L* 24–25 in; *W* 5¼–5½ ft.

Status: uncommon winter resident in north-central Washington from November to late March; irregular irruptive species in western Washington.

Habitat: open-country habitats, including farmlands, grasslands, marshes, wet meadows, salt marshes and sand dunes.

Nesting: does not nest in Washington.

Feeding: opportunistic; frequently hunts by day; usually uses a sit-and-wait technique; eats mostly rodents but is capable of catching large waterfowl and mammals as large as hares.

Voice: generally silent on wintering grounds but will utter low grunting sounds when flushed, as well as quite musical, soft warbles and soft barking sounds; may scream at territorial rivals during invasion years.

Similar Species: *Barn Owl* (p. 201): much smaller; slimmer; red-bordered, heartlike, white facial disc; dark eyes; gray-and-tawny upperparts; finely spotted, white underparts. *Short-eared Owl* (p. 212): much smaller; pronounced facial disc with dark areas around eyes; short, centrally placed "ear" tufts; mottled, tawny brown upperparts; bold brown streaks on breast; hunts by twilight. *Great Gray Owl* (p. 210): all-gray plumage; prominent facial disc; mainly nocturnal.

Best Sites: *Nonirruptive years:* Moses L.; Reardan; Davenport. *Irruptive years:* Samish Flats; Skagit Flats; Stillaguamish R. flats; Ocean Shores beaches.

NORTHERN PYGMY-OWL

Glaucidium gnoma

Ounce for ounce, the Northern Pygmy-Owl may be the fiercest predator in North America. Washington's smallest owl, it regularly catches prey that outweighs it. Prey may even be dragged some distance before the owl can finally subdue and dispatch its hard-won meal. • The Northern Pygmy-Owl is a daytime predator. With a poorly developed facial disc, it must depend more on vision than hearing to locate prey. • These owls are most likely to be seen outside of the breeding season, when individuals move into towns and farms to hunt birds and small mammals, and they often wreak havoc on wintering flocks at feeders. • The dark black "eyes" on the back of this owl's head trick predators into believing that the Northern Pygmy-Owl is watching them.

red morph

ID: 2 black "eyes" on back of large, rounded head; white-spotted crown, neck and back; indistinct facial disc; inconspicuous "ear" tufts; fierce, yellow eyes; gray to yellowish bill; brown upperparts; pale underparts with bold dark streaking; long, narrow, barred tail. *In flight:* rounded, white-and-dark-barred wings with brownish linings; usually short, woodpecker-like flights.

Size: *L* 7 in; *W* 15 in.

Status: uncommon year-round resident statewide.

Habitat: coniferous and mixed forests, including high-elevation conifers.

Nesting: in a tree cavity, sometimes lined with cedar strips or feathers; female incubates 3–7 glossy white eggs for about 28 days.

Feeding: mostly by day and early evening; eats large insects, birds up to woodpecker-sized, mammals as large as red squirrels, amphibians and reptiles.

Voice: often calls throughout the day for much of summer; main song is an easily imitated series of monotonous, low-pitched *toot* notes, sometimes preceded by a faster, quieter trill.

Similar Species: no other Washington owl has "eyes" on back of head. *Northern Saw-whet Owl* (p. 214) and *Boreal Owl* (p. 213): slightly larger; chunkier; prominent facial disc; white-spotted, dark brown upperparts; blurrier streaking on underparts; shorter, weakly barred or unbarred tail. *Western Screech-Owl* (p. 203): larger; unspotted head; prominent facial disc; often shows conspicuous "ear" tufts; gray bill; unbarred tail.

Best Sites: Mt. Rainier NP; Liberty (Kittitas Co.); Robinson Canyon (Kittitas Co.); Bethel Ridge (off US 12); North Fork, Entiat R.; Little Spokane River Natural Area (Spokane Co.); North Fork Coppei Creek Rd. (Walla Walla Co.).

BURROWING OWL
Athene cunicularia

Unlike most owls, the Burrowing Owl is strictly a ground dweller, choosing the shelter of an underground burrow for both nesting and roosting. The conversion of native grasslands to croplands and residential areas has greatly diminished foraging and nesting habitats for these inquisitive birds, and extermination campaigns against ground squirrels have reduced ready-made burrows. These birds have also been harmed by pesticide use. Burrowing Owls in Florida have been known to excavate their own 9-foot-long burrow in two days, but artificial nest burrows are now extensively used in Washington. • Some Burrowing Owls that breed in Washington spend their winters south of San Francisco. • *Athene* honors the Greek goddess of wisdom, and *cunicularia* is Latin for "burrower."

ID: generally slightly rufous brown with white spots; fine streaking on rounded head; white "eyebrow" and throat; yellow eyes; yellowish bill; horizontal belly barring; long, pale, feathered legs; upright stance. *Male:* plumage often sun-bleached lighter. *In flight:* short, white-barred wings, also spotted above, with pale linings; feet extend beyond tail.
Size: *L* 8–9 in; *W* 21–24 in.
Status: uncommon local breeding resident from April to early August in the Columbia Basin; populations declining; candidate for state threatened list.
Habitat: dry open grasslands and deserts; also agricultural lands.
Nesting: open terrain; in a 6–9 ft long burrow dug by a burrowing mammal or in a nest box or artificial nest burrow; female incubates 6–11 white eggs for 28–30 days; male guards the burrow and supplies food.

Feeding: opportunistic; active hunter mainly at dawn and dusk but often by day; eats mostly arthropods, small mammals and birds; takes some reptiles and amphibians.
Voice: utters a variety of clucks and rasping notes, screams or makes a snakelike rattle when threatened. *Male:* song is a loud, monotonous, dovelike *coo-cooo*.
Similar Species: *Short-eared Owl* (p. 212): larger; prominent facial disc; vertical breast streaking; short legs; longer wings. *Western Screech-Owl* (p. 203): stockier; stronger facial disc; often prominent "ear" tufts; vertical breast streaking; short legs; perches in trees.
Best Sites: Whitcomb Unit, Umatilla NWR; Rotha Rd. (Prosser); Dodson Rd. at Desert Wildlife Area; Frenchman Hill Rd.; Potholes Rookery; Othello area, east of SR 17 and north of SR 26; Hanford Reach (SR 24, milepost 63; Columbia R.).

SPOTTED OWL

Strix occidentalis

Late in the 20th century, the Spotted Owl became the focal point of discussions about timberland management across its range in the Pacific Northwest. The northern *caurina* subspecies needs large areas of old-growth rainforest to nest and forage—a pair may have a home range as large as 16 square miles. Unfortunately for the Spotted Owl, old-growth rainforest is favored for cutting by the forest industry. Another pressure on the Spotted Owl is the range expansion of its slightly larger relative, the Barred Owl, into Spotted Owl habitat. • The Spotted Owl hunts at night, usually by waiting patiently for a meal to scamper within range, usually an arboreal or terrestrial rodent.

and Douglas-fir to 6000 ft; forages in unlogged areas and tends to avoid crossing bushy areas and clear-cuts.

Nesting: in a stump or tree cavity or (rarely) on a tree platform; female incubates 2–3 white or pearly gray eggs for 28–32 days.

Feeding: strictly nocturnal; perches and waits to pounce on small mammals, especially ground squirrels, woodrats, voles and snowshoe hares; also eats insects, amphibians and birds (occasionally other owls).

Voice: often *whoo-whoo, hoo hoo,* similar to Barred Owl, but generally higher pitched and without pace changes; female makes loud barking and nasal cries.

Similar Species: *Barred Owl* (p. 209): slightly larger; often paler; horizontal breast bars; thick, vertical belly streaks; more likely in moist bottomlands. *Western Screech-Owl* (p. 203): much smaller; less white in plumage; often shows prominent "ear" tufts; yellow eyes; vertically streaked underparts.

Best Sites: La Push; Mt. Rainier NP; northeastern side of Mount St. Helens National Volcanic Monument; North Fork, Teanaway R. (Kittitas Co.); Swauk Creek basin; North Fork, Entiat R.; off Chinook Pass Highway (SR 410, east of Mt. Rainier).

ID: whitemottled brown overall; large, rounded head; large, dark eyes; pale yellowish bill; white-tipped, brown feathers give chest a spotted look; whitish throat. *In flight:* nearly rectangular, barred, brown wings, paler below and whitespotted above.

Size: *Male: L* 17–18 in; *W* 3¼ ft. *Female: L* 18–19 in; *W* 3½–3¾ ft.

Status: rare year-round resident in oldgrowth forests of the Cascades (most numerous on eastern slopes) and Olympics; federally listed as threatened and statelisted as endangered.

Habitat: old-growth rainforests, fir and mixed forests of ponderosa pine, white fir

BARRED OWL
Strix varia

Anyone who hears the excited *who-cooks-for-you, who-cooks-for-you-all* courtship call of this forest owl is tempted to mimic it. Imitating the call will almost certainly bring any Barred Owl that is within range, but it may also provoke an attack from this easily stressed, highly territorial bird. • Barred Owls are usually most active between midnight and 4 AM, when the forest floor rustles with the movements of mice, voles and shrews. These birds' eyesight in darkness is 100 times as keen as that of humans, but they can also locate prey using sound alone. • First discovered in Washington in Pend Oreille County in 1965, this owl may now be found in almost any forest in Washington. It is suspected to be replacing the Spotted Owl.

ID: large, round head; dark eyes; yellowish bill; white-spotted, brown upperparts; brown-barred, white breast; heavily streaked, white underparts. *In flight:* nearly rectangular, barred, brown wings; paler below and white-spotted above.
Size: *Male: L* 17–19 in; *W* 3¼–3¾ ft. *Female: L* 22–24 in; *W* 3¾–4¼ ft.
Status: fairly common year-round resident in Washington's moist forests.
Habitat: most mature and old-growth forests, including mixed, Douglas-fir and ponderosa pine; prefers riparian and low-elevation woodlands.
Nesting: in a cavity in a hardwood tree, especially a dead one; sometimes uses a nest box or platform nest of another species; nest is lined with lichens or fresh conifer twigs; female incubates 2–4 pure white eggs for 28–33 days; pair feeds the young.
Feeding: from a perch or, less often, from low, fairly direct flight; catches a wide range of invertebrates, reptiles, amphibians, smaller mammals and other birds.
Voice: gives the most characteristic call of all owls; loud, hooting, rhythmic, laughlike *who cooks for you? who cooks for you all?* is heard year-round, but mostly in spring.
Similar Species: *Spotted Owl* (p. 208): slightly smaller; paler bill; white-spotted, brown breast and underparts; limited to old-growth forests. *Great Gray Owl* (p. 210): larger; generally grayer; large, concentrically barred facial disc; small, deep-set, yellow eyes; partial white "collar" on throat has black center; diffusely patterned breast.
Best Sites: Hoh R.; Rockport SP; Discovery Park (Seattle); Swauk Creek basin; Stehekin Valley; Big Meadow L.; Kamiak Butte SP.

GREAT GRAY OWL

Strix nebulosa

This largely silent hunter is the only *Strix* owl to breed on both sides of the Atlantic. Although it is North America's largest owl, the Great Gray Owl owes its bulk largely to a mass of fluffy insulation, and the Snowy Owl and Great Horned Owl outweigh it by about 15 percent. • Often active by day, the Great Gray prefers areas near bogs, forest edges, montane meadows and other open areas offering an unobstructed view. Its small eyes are less important for hunting than its incredibly acute hearing, made possible by the large facial disc. • The Great Gray's habitat preferences restrict where it can breed, but Great Horned Owls or woodland hawks rarely disrupt its foraging and nesting activities.

resident in the Blue Mts.; rare, irregular winter visitor in the northern part of the greater Puget Trough.

Habitat: open pine forests or mixed conifers with nearby large meadows or open bogs for foraging; lower elevations in winter.

Nesting: in a broken-topped snag; may use an old raptor nest or an artificial platform; female incubates 3–5 dull white eggs for 28–31 days; male feeds the young for up to 3 months after fledging at 26–29 days.

Feeding: at dawn and dusk, from a perch or sometimes flight; eats mostly small rodents; can catch medium-sized or large birds.

Voice: hard-to-hear, very low, evenly spaced *hoo* note series; low, soft, doubled hoots.

Similar Species: *Barred Owl* (p. 209): smaller; less pronounced facial disc; dark eyes; horizontally barred breast; prefers moist, low-elevation woodlands. *Great Horned Owl* (p. 204): interrupted facial disc; conspicuous "ear" tufts; dark bill; dense horizontal underpart streaking.

Best Sites: meadow edges near Highlands Sno-Park (Okanogan Co.); Sitzmark Ski Area (from Havillah Rd., Okanogan Co.); Silver Creek Rd. (Ferry Co.); Sherman Pass area; Biscuit Ridge Rd. (Walla Walla Co.).

ID: white-marbled, grayish brown plumage; large, rounded head; prominent, concentrically barred facial disc; small, deep-set, yellow eyes; yellow bill; white partial "collar" with black center. *In flight:* large, nearly rectangular, mostly barred, brown wings; long, faintly banded tail.

Size: *Male: L* 25–28 in; *W* 4½–4¾ ft. *Female: L* 29–33 in; *W* 4¾–5 ft.

Status: rare, local year-round resident in mid-level forests in eastern Okanogan Co. and western Ferry Co.; rare year-round

LONG-EARED OWL

Asio otus

A master of disguise and illusion, the Long-eared Owl hides from intruders by assuming a thin, vertical form to blend into its wooded background. If that tactic fails, this medium-sized owl expands its air sacs, puffs up its feathers, spreads its wings to double its size and hisses defiantly in a threat display. • Most owl species are fiercely territorial, but nonbreeding Long-eared Owls often form communal roosts—typically fewer than two dozen birds but sometimes up to a hundred. • The "ear" tufts seen on many owls are purely ornamental feathers. The real ears are hidden under the facial disc feathers, and their asymmetrical size, shape and placement enhance the owl's judgment of distance and direction.

ID: slim body; pale rusty brown facial disc; long "ear" tufts; white "eyebrows" and "mustache"; large, yellow eyes; white-blotched, grayish brown upperparts; dark, roughly crisscross pattern on underparts. *In flight:* mostly gray upperwing with orangy patch near tip; dark-barred tips and trailing edges; prominent black "wrist" patch; pale buff underwing.

Size: *Male: L* 13–14 in; *W* 3–3¼ ft. *Female: L* 15–16 in; *W* 3¾–4 ft.

Status: uncommon year-round resident in the east; rare year-round visitor in the west, primarily in winter.

Habitat: *Breeding:* near open country in juniper forests, riparian woodlands and other coniferous and mixed forests. *In migration* and *winter:* open habitats; often groups in roosts.

Nesting: in an abandoned stick nest of another species; sometimes in a tree or cliff cavity or even on the ground; female incubates 5–7 slightly glossy white eggs for 26–28 days.

Feeding: actively searches for small rodents and birds, mostly by night; perches or flies along forest edges to flush prey.

Voice: gives a low, soft, ghostly *quoo-quoo* breeding call; utters *a weck-weck-weck* alarm call; also issues various shrieks, hisses, whistles, barks, hoots and dovelike coos.

Similar Species: *Short-eared Owl* (p. 212): buffier plumage; tiny "ear" tufts, usually hidden; light underpart streaking is denser at breast. *Great Horned Owl* (p. 204): larger; bulkier; wider-set "ear" tufts; darker around eyes; horizontally streaked underparts; plainer wings.

Best Sites: *Summer:* Ringer Loop Rd. (Ellensburg); Moxee Valley; Columbia Pt. (Tri-Cities). *Winter:* Lower Crab Creek; Lyons Ferry Hatchery; Lamoine; Bridgeport SP; Fishhook Park (Lower Snake R.).

SHORT-EARED OWL

Asio flammeus

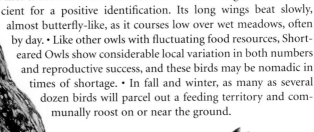

This open-country bird is the owl most likely to be seen hunting, and it is one of the easiest owls to identify. The Short-eared Owl flies so characteristically that after a first encounter even a distant view of one in flight can be sufficient for a positive identification. Its long wings beat slowly, almost butterfly-like, as it courses low over wet meadows, often by day. • Like other owls with fluctuating food resources, Short-eared Owls show considerable local variation in both numbers and reproductive success, and these birds may be nomadic in times of shortage. • In fall and winter, as many as several dozen birds will parcel out a feeding territory and communally roost on or near the ground.

ID: pale face; tiny, often hidden, close-set "ear" tufts; white "eyebrows" and "mustache"; black-socketed, yellow eyes; black bill; tawny golden dappling on brown upperparts; paler underparts; heavy vertical brown striping of upper breast thins on belly. *In flight:* barred, buff-and-brown upperwing; dark "wrist" patch and wing tip on buff underwing; bouncy, quartering flight.

Size: *L* 13–17 in; *W* 3–4 ft.

Status: fairly common local winter resident; uncommon from spring to fall in the east (declining because of habitat loss); uncommon to rare in the west in spring and fall and absent in summer.

Habitat: *Breeding:* wet meadows, marshes, grasslands, fields. *In migration* and *winter:* mountain meadows, deserts, coastal salt marshes, interior valleys; roosts communally in trees and brush.

Nesting: semicolonial in prime habitats; nests on the ground on matted-down vegetation; female incubates 4–10 nest-stained, creamy white eggs for 26–32 days.

Feeding: hunts by day or night, especially at twilight; eats small mammals and some small birds.

Voice: generally quiet; loud *keee-ow* in winter. *Breeding male:* soft *toot-toot-toot*.

Similar Species: *Long-eared Owl* (p. 211): grayer, more mottled plumage; pale rusty brown face; prominent "ear" tufts; criss-crossing underpart markings; infrequently perches in the open. *Burrowing Owl* (p. 207): smaller; white-spotted, slightly rufous brown plumage; yellowish bill; horizontal belly barring; long legs; stubbier wings; ground dweller.

Best Sites: *Winter:* Samish, Skagit and Stillaguamish flats; Nisqually NWR; north of Ellensburg; Black Rock Valley (near Moxee); Moses L. *Spring* and *summer:* Yakima Training Center (permission required); Swanson Lakes Wildlife Area (Lincoln Co.); Tucannon River Valley.

BOREAL OWL
Aegolius funereus

The Boreal Owl (known elsewhere as Tengmalm's Owl) lives primarily in the boreal forests of Canada and Alaska, as well as Eurasian boreal forests from Scandinavia to Siberia. It is also scattered across a number of the lower 48 states and was first discovered to be nesting in Washington in 1989. It is now known to be present in the Cascades, Kettle River Range, Selkirks, Blue Mountains and Mount Rainier, almost always above 4000 feet. This day-roosting owl may well be widespread and even fairly common in our high-elevation forests, but deep snow restricts observation from February to April, when it is most vocal, and, unlike other owls, it usually doesn't wander in winter.

ID: large, pale facial disc with partial dark border; white-speckled forehead; fluffy, white "eyebrows" and "mustache"; dark-ringed, yellow eyes; dusky ivory bill; white-spotted, dark brown upperparts; heavy, vertical brown streaks on white underparts. *Immature:* sooty brown upperparts; chocolate brown, unstreaked underparts; white forehead patch. *In flight:* coarsely brown-barred, whitish underwings; short, weakly barred tail.
Size: *Male: L* 9–10 in; *W* 22–24 in. *Female: L* 11–12 in; *W* 26–29 in.
Status: rare year-round resident at high elevations in the Cascades, Kettle River Range, Selkirk and Blue mts. and Mt. Rainier.
Habitat: subalpine pine, fir and spruce forests and transition forests just below.

Nesting: in a woodpecker cavity or a nest box; female incubates 2–5 dull white eggs for 26–32 days.
Feeding: mainly nocturnal hunter, from a low perch, for small mammals; also eats small birds and insects.
Voice: gives a loud, hoarse *hooo-aaak* and a grating, hissing threat call. *Male:* main spring song is a low, trilled *toot* series with increasing volume.
Similar Species: *Northern Saw-whet Owl* (p. 214): slightly smaller; warmer brown overall; dark bill; redder underpart streaks; paler underwings. *Western Screech-Owl* (p. 203): fiercer look; often shows "ear" tufts; streaky gray or brown upperparts; thinner dark vertical streaks on grayish or brownish belly.
Best Sites: Harts Pass (Okanogan Co.); Baldy Pass; Roger L.; Long Swamp; Sherman Pass; Salmo Pass (Pend Oreille Co.); upper Blue Mts.

213

NORTHERN SAW-WHET OWL

Aegolius acadicus

Northern Saw-whet Owls are opportunistic hunters that take whatever they can, whenever they can. When temperatures drop below freezing, these small owls catch and store extra food in tree caches, where it quickly freezes. When pickings are slim, a hungry owl can thaw out its frozen cache by "incubating" it as it would a clutch of eggs. • By day, Northern Saw-whets roost quietly in the cover of dense lower branches and brush to avoid attracting mobbing forest songbirds. • The immature Northern Saw-whet Owl differs more in color from the adult than any other North American owl except the Boreal Owl. • "Saw-whet" reflects the perceived likeness of the bird's call to the filing of a large saw, and *acadicus* refers to Acadia in Atlantic Canada, where the first specimen was collected.

ID: brown with fine white to buff streaking on facial disc, forehead and nape; thick, white "eyebrows"; dark-ringed, yellow eyes; dark bill; white-spotted, brown upperparts; rufous brown vertical streaks on white underparts. *Immature:* white forehead patch; buff-marked, brown upperparts; rich buff, unstreaked underparts. *In flight:* short tail; coarsely brown-barred, pale buff underwings.
Size: *Male:* L 7–8 in; W 16–17 in. *Female:* L 8–9 in; W 17–18 in.
Status: fairly common year-round resident statewide.
Habitat: favors low elevations. *Breeding:* moist woodlands, especially with conifers. *Winter:* dense riparian growth and hardwoods around farms and urban areas; coniferous forests; leaves snowy forests.

Nesting: in a woodpecker cavity or a nest box, usually lined with wood chips or other debris; male brings food while female incubates 5–6 white eggs for 27–29 days and broods the nestlings until the youngest is about 19 days old.
Feeding: mainly nocturnal; hunts from a perch; eats small rodents plus beetles, grasshoppers and small birds (especially in migration).
Voice: *Male:* easily imitated, evenly spaced, whistled song is repeated fairly rapidly, often for long periods.
Similar Species: *Boreal Owl* (p. 213): slightly larger; black-bordered, paler face; white-speckled forehead; pale bill; immature has browner underparts and indistinctly streaked belly.
Best Sites: Cougar Mountain Regional Park (Issaquah); Swauk Creek basin; Turnbull NWR; North Fork Coppei Creek Rd. (Walla Walla Co.). *Winter:* Bridgeport SP; Fishhook Park (Lower Snake R.). *Spring:* Kamiak Butte SP.

COMMON NIGHTHAWK
Chordeiles minor

During the day, the Common Nighthawk is mild-mannered and largely unnoticed, but it is a conspicuous, spectacular flier at dusk. The male's seemingly death-defying display dive terminates in a hard braking action of the wings, which produces a deep, hollow *vroom* sound. • Despite its name, the Common Nighthawk is often visible in the daytime as it roosts on a tree limb or on the ground, and it is most active at dusk and dawn. It sits along the length of a tree branch rather than across the branch the way most perching birds do. • The Common Nighthawk often migrates in loose flocks. • As with other members of the nightjar family, this bird's gaping mouth is surrounded by feather shafts that funnel airborne insects inside.

ID: large, dark eyes; cryptic, mottled upperparts of white, buff and brown; brown-barred underparts, whitish on male and buff on female; throat is white on male, pale buff on female; long tail extends to folded wing tips. *In flight:* narrow, pointed, dark wing with prominent white "wrist" patch; long, notched, barred tail, with white subterminal band on male; erratic, darting flight.
Size: *L* 8–10 in; *W* 23–26 in.
Status: common to uncommon from mid-May to mid-September in eastern Washington; uncommon (declining) from June to mid-August in western Washington.
Habitat: *Breeding:* coastal dunes; grassy hills; sagebrush and juniper deserts, mountain forest clearings; canyons; urban buildings. *In migration:* valleys and rivers; open woodlands; meadows and grasslands; sagebrush flats; urban areas.
Nesting: flat city roof or on the ground, in sand or gravel, without making a nest; female incubates 2 heavily speckled, white or pale gray eggs for 19–20 days.
Feeding: hunts by twilight, sometimes cooperatively with several birds; catches airborne insects, mainly queen ants, beetles and bugs.
Voice: *Male:* repeats a nasal *peent peent;* makes a deep, hollow *vroom* with wings during courtship flight.
Similar Species: *Common Poorwill* (p. 216): smaller; generally paler; bristles around mouth are more obvious; rounded wings without white patches; shorter, broader, rounded tail with white-tipped outer feathers; roosts on the ground.
Best Sites: *Summer:* low-elevation forest zones; open-country sage-steppe east of the Cascades; San Juans; prairies of Pierce Co.

215

COMMON POORWILL
Phalaenoptilus nuttallii

Back in 1946, the discovery of a Common Poorwill that appeared to be hibernating through winter in a rock crevice surprised the scientific community. Cold to the touch, it had no detectable breath or heartbeat. Apparently, poorwills that choose not to migrate to warmer climates enter a short-term torpor in which their temperature drops as low as 43° F and oxygen intake is reduced by over 90 percent, but it is not true mammal-style hibernation. This trait was known to the Hopi Indians, who named the bird *holchoko*, "the sleeping one," and to Meriwether Lewis of the Lewis and Clark expedition, who, in 1804, found a mysterious goatsucker "to be passing into the dormant state." • Another trait unusual among birds is the Common Poorwill's tendency to carry eggs and young to a safer location after disturbance. • This bird is most commonly seen on warm evenings on gravel roads.

ID: large head; dark eyes; prominent bristles around mouth; cryptic upperparts mottled with gray, white and black; finely barred underparts; pale throat band. *In flight:* short, rounded wings; brown-barred, cinnamon outer flight feathers; broad, rounded tail with white-tipped outer feathers (most prominent on male); flights usually short and low.
Size: *L* 7–8 in; *W* 16–17 in.
Status: fairly common breeding resident in the east from May to late June and uncommon from July to mid-September.
Habitat: dry open habitats, including sagebrush-covered hills and rocky country; oak and open ponderosa pine forests; isolated buttes.

Nesting: nests on bare ground, gravel, flat rock or bed of pine needles, usually partially shaded by a bush, log or rock; pair incubates 2 white, sometimes pink-tinged and dark-spotted eggs for 20–21 days; pair feeds the young regurgitated insects.
Feeding: sallies from a low perch or the ground, mostly at night, for large insects, such as moths and beetles.
Voice: mostly the male utters the familiar *poor-will* call, often adding an additional syllable.
Similar Species: *Common Nighthawk* (p. 215): larger; long, pointed wings with white "wrist" patches; dark underpart barring continues onto longer, narrower, notched tail (male has broad white subterminal band).
Best Sites: shrub-steppe and lower forest zones of the slopes of the eastern Cascades and Okanogan Highlands; Blue Mts.

BLACK SWIFT

Cypseloides niger

Few observers are lucky enough to see a nest of the Black Swift, North America's largest swift. This fast-flying bird has a limited distribution and prefers to nest on steep, vertical walls well concealed behind the sheets of cascading spray of inland waterfalls. Only four Washington nest sites have been confirmed, but several candidate sites exist. • Although Black Swifts forage high in the air when skies are clear, rain or low overcast conditions bring them closer to the ground and even out into the Puget Sound lowland. They hunt insects on the wing for much of the day, but, as the sun sets, the birds rocket back to their nests. • Swifts cast a characteristic boomerang silhouette in flight. They are shaped much like swallows—long, tapering wings, small bills, wide gape and long, sleek bodies—but they are only distantly related.

ID: slender, sleek body; black overall; feathers with whitish tips around fore-head; very small legs. *Immature:* fine, white barring on underparts. *In flight:* long, tapering wings angle backward; longish tail can appear slightly forked; often glides in broad circles.

Size: *L* 7 in; *W* 18 in.

Status: fairly common in the Cascades, Okanogan Mt. and Olympics from the end of May to mid-August and uncommon to mid-September.

Habitat: *Breeding:* steep, usually wet cliffs in interior canyons and along ocean coasts. *Foraging* and *in migration:* over forests, woodlands, canyons, valleys, grasslands and even cities.

Nesting: semicolonial; on a cliff, in a crevice, in a cavity or on a ledge, often near or behind a waterfall; nest is made of moss, mud and algae; pair incubates 1 white egg for 24–27 days; pair feeds the young.

Feeding: feeds in flight; eats flying insects, especially stoneflies, caddisflies and mayflies.

Voice: high-pitched *plik-plik-plik-plik* near the nest site.

Similar Species: *Vaux's Swift* (p. 218): much smaller; lighter color overall; pale throat and rump; short, stubby, comblike tail; flaps more and glides less. *White-throated Swift* (p. 219): white underneath from "chin" to vent; white flank patches; white tips on secondaries.

Best Sites: Big Four Ice Caves (Verlot); Skagit R. near Newhalem; Stehekin; Snoqualmie Falls; upper Cle Elum R.; Chinook Pass (SR 410, east of Mt. Rainier); Marymoor Park (Redmond; when Cascades are clouded over).

VAUX'S SWIFT
Chaetura vauxi

Soon after their arrival in April and May, and again in September, increasingly larger flocks of Vaux's Swifts circle above the state's towns and cities. They plunge collectively into chimneys to roost—a habit shared with the Chimney Swift *(C. pelagica)* of the eastern U.S. Roosting is very important for swifts year-round, so they favor habitats with suitable cavities. Rather than perching like most birds, they use their small, strong claws to grab onto vertical surfaces. • Even these most aerial of birds can be forced close to the ground by fog banks or low cloud. • The Vaux's Swift was named for William Sansom Vaux, an eminent mineralogist, member of Philadelphia's Academy of Natural Sciences and friend of John Kirk Townsend, who first described this bird in 1839 from specimens collected on the Columbia River.

ID: brownish gray overall; lighter at throat and rump. *In flight:* paler below than above; long, swept-back, scimitar-shaped wings; hard-to-see comblike points on short tail; shallow, rapid wingbeats and glides; rarely leaves the air.

Size: *L* 5 in; *W* 12 in.

Status: fairly common forest breeder from May to September; fairly common migrant in late April and September.

Habitat: *Breeding:* cities; open country; mixed and coniferous old-growth forests. *In migration:* cities, roosting in chimneys; forests and open areas with tree cavities, particularly in grand fir; mountain ridges.

Nesting: open half-circle of loosely woven twigs is glued together and to the inside of a hollow tree or chimney with sticky saliva; pair incubates 6–7 white or creamy white eggs for 18–19 days; a 3rd adult may help with feeding.

Feeding: hawks for flying ants, true bugs, flies, moths, spiders and aphids.

Voice: several high-pitched *chip* notes followed by an insectlike trill in flight; uses wings to produce a booming sound in midair and at the nest, perhaps to discourage predators.

Similar Species: *White-throated Swift* (p. 219): larger; black with white areas, mainly on underparts; long, forked tail. *Black Swift* (p. 217): much larger; black overall; tail often forked; variable wingbeats; more commonly soars. *Swallows* (pp. 264–70): relatively shorter, broader wings; notched or forked tails; usually whiter below; darting, fluid flight.

Best Sites: widespread in forested zones statewide.

WHITE-THROATED SWIFT

Aeronautes saxatalis

This avian marvel certainly earns its wings as a true *aeronaut* ("sky sailor"). During its lifetime, the average White-throated Swift will likely travel more than a million miles—enough to take it around the world more than 40 times! Only brief, cliff-clinging rest periods and annual nesting duties keep the White-throated Swift grounded, because it feeds, drinks, bathes and even mates while flying. This scimitar-winged aerial insectivore also lives up to its family common name, having been timed at up to 200 miles per hour, which is fast enough to avoid any Prairie Falcons wanting to devour it. • A familiar sight in mountainous areas and even some cities of the western U.S., the White-throated Swift is easily recognized by its loud, sharp, scraping notes, black-and-white coloring and rapid, rather erratic flight.

ID: dark upperparts; white on throat tapers to undertail coverts; black flanks with white hind patches. *In flight:* long, tapering, back-angled wings; long, slightly forked tail is often held in a point.
Size: *L* 6–7 in; *W* 15 in.
Status: uncommon to fairly common eastern resident from late March until late August.
Habitat: *Breeding:* high cliffs in open country; high desert fault blocks; river canyons; ranges widely in search of food. *In migration:* more likely at lower elevations.
Nesting: on a cliff or ridge; cup made from materials gathered on the wing, including feathers, grass, moss, cotton, straw and plant down, is stuck together with gluelike saliva; pair incubates 4–5 white or creamy eggs for 24 days; young are expert fliers on leaving the nest.

Feeding: snatches insects and other arthropods in midair; eats almost anything edible carried aloft by wind currents.
Voice: gives a loud, shrill, descending *skee-jee-ee-ee-ee-ee-ee*.
Similar Species: *Vaux's Swift* (p. 218): smaller; brown above, paler below; stubby, comb-pointed tail. *Black Swift* (p. 217): slightly larger; black overall; tail often appears notched; variable wingbeats; often soars. *Violet-green Swallow* (p. 266) and *Tree Swallow* (p. 265): smaller; blue, green or olive brown upperparts; all-white underparts.
Best Sites: Ginkgo Petrified Forest SP (Kittitas Co.); Frenchman Coulee (Grant Co.); Chopaka Rd.–Palmer L. (Okanogan Co.); Yakima R. canyon; Selah Creek Rest Area (I-82); Painted Rocks (Yakima); Palouse Falls SP.

BLACK-CHINNED HUMMINGBIRD

Archilochus alexandri

The Black-chinned Hummingbird is the western counterpart of the Ruby-throated Hummingbird *(A. colubris)* of eastern North America, and the females are virtually indistinguishable in the field. • The most noteworthy thing about the Black-chinned Hummingbird is that it is so average. This low-elevation species uses many different habitats, is in the middle size range of North American hummingbirds, has a fairly large breeding range and lacks defining colors. • The *alexandri* part of the name honors a doctor who collected specimens in Mexico. The genus name was chosen by naturalist and hummingbird taxonomist H.G.L. Reisenbach. Deeply influenced by Greek mythology, he named several hummingbird genera after famous Greeks, including the notable poet Archilochus.

ID: green crown and nape; small white spot behind eye; long, thin, black bill; green upperparts; gray-mottled, white underparts; green-washed flanks; white breast. *Male:* black throat with iridescent, bluish violet gorget (may appear dark). *Female* and *immature:* blackish eye line; gray-streaked, whitish throat. *In flight:* many-pointed, black tail (white-tipped on female).

Size: *L* 3¾ in; *W* 4½–5 in.

Status: fairly common summer resident in lowland forest east of the Cascades from May through August; absent from the Columbia Basin.

Habitat: *Breeding:* low mountain foothills and valleys; arid canyons; open and riparian woodlands. *In migration:* desert oases; city and town feeders.

Nesting: on a branch or outer twig; female molds a nesting cup using her belly and bill to smooth out plant down mixed with spiderwebs and insect cocoon fibers; female incubates 2 white eggs for 16 days; family stays together throughout summer.

Feeding: sips sugar water from feeders and nectar from flowers; catches flying insects by hovering in midair; gleans insects from vegetation, spiderwebs, soil and crevices.

Voice: buzzy and chipping alarm calls. *Male:* soft, high-pitched, warbling courtship song accompanied by wing-buzzing.

Similar Species: *Anna's Hummingbird* (p. 221): female has more gray and green on underparts, red-spotted throat and more rounded tail.

Best Sites: Nile Rd. (Yakima Co.); W.E. Johnson Park (Richland); Leavenworth; Sinlahekin Wildlife Area; Kettle River Valley (Ferry Co.); Cusick (Pend Oreille Co.).

ANNA'S HUMMINGBIRD

Calypte anna

Washington has six hummingbird species that could arrive at a well-stocked sugarwater feeder, but none can compare with the male Anna's Hummingbird for sartorial splendor. He may not have the rufous coat of a Rufous male, but a male Anna's impresses with the rose red "bib" that covers his head and neck. • Once restricted as a nesting species to the Pacific slope of northern Baja California and southern California, the Anna's Hummingbird expanded its range northward along the coast after the 1930s. Using cultivated exotic plants and year-round hummingbird feeders, it has also expanded eastward as far as Texas. • By nesting from December to May, Anna's Hummingbird can take advantage of the abundant late-spring blooms.

ID: partial white eye ring; long, black bill; iridescent, emerald green upperparts; grayish underparts. *Male:* rosy pink of gorget extends to crown; greenish wash across lower breast and belly. *Female* and *immature:* green crown; light green flanks; several rosy feathers on throat. *In flight:* many-pointed, black tail (white-tipped on female).

Size: L 3–4 in; W 5–5½ in.

Status: fairly common year-round resident of the Puget Trough and the lower Columbia R. and present in winter in surrounding areas; rare year-round resident of eastern Washington, but population may be expanding.

Habitat: riparian areas; coastal scrubland; farmlands; urban gardens with exotic flowers or sugarwater feeders.

Nesting: often on a tree or shrub branch; cup nest of plant down and spiderwebs is lined with downy material; female incubates 2 white eggs for 16–17 days.

Feeding: hovers, sometimes perches, to sip flower nectar and sugar water; gleans insects from flowers and shrubbery; territorial, but tolerates other hummingbirds if food is plentiful.

Voice: high, short call note; excited, chattering chase call. *Male:* complex songs include a varied series of high, scratchy, dry notes from a perch and sharp squeaks to end the diving display.

Similar Species: *Black-chinned Hummingbird* (p. 220): smaller female has whiter underparts and plainer throat.

Best Sites: Discovery Park (Seattle); Point Defiance Park (Tacoma); coastal settled places with gardens; Vancouver; Lyle.

CALLIOPE HUMMINGBIRD

Stellula calliope

listening in the slanting rays of sunlight announcing dawn, the iridescent, streaked gorget of the male Calliope Hummingbird suggests nectar dripping from the bird's needlelike bill. • The Calliope Hummingbird is North America's smallest breeding bird and smallest long-distance migrant—individuals routinely travel up to 5000 miles annually to and from wintering territory in Mexico. • Although they feed among clusters of wildflowers, male Calliopes often perch high atop shrubs or small trees to flash their unusual, pinkish red gorgets and make dazzling, high-speed dips and dives to entice the females to mate. • *Stellula* is Latin for "small star," and Calliopeia, "the fair voiced," was the muse responsible for epic poetry in ancient Greece.

ID: slender bill; iridescent, green upperparts. *Male:* light green flanks; whitish breast and belly; narrow, pinkish red gorget streaks extend down white throat from bill. *Female:* peach-washed flanks; white underparts; dark green throat spots. *In flight:* blackish tail (white-tipped on female).

Size: *L* 3 in; *W* 4–4½ in.

Status: fairly common eastern resident from mid-May to August and uncommon along the Columbia Gorge; rare western migrant.

Habitat: *Breeding:* mid-elevation open forests and riparian woodland edges,

occasionally higher. *In spring migration:* coastal mountains and valleys. *In fall migration:* higher elevations, valleys and desert oases east of the Cascades.

Nesting: usually on a conifer branch under foliage; tiny cup nest of plant down, moss, lichen and spiderwebs is often reused; female incubates 2 white eggs for up to 16 days.

Feeding: hovers and probes flowers for nectar; takes sugar water at feeders; also eats small insects, often in short sallies from a perch.

Voice: high-pitched *chip* calls. *Male:* sings high-pitched, chattering *tsew* notes in his relatively short courtship display.

Similar Species: *Anna's Hummingbird* (p. 221): slightly larger; longer, wider tail; male has red gorget; female has greenish flanks. *Costa's Hummingbird* (p. 364): male has bright violet crown and extended gorget; female has grayish green flanks.

Best Sites: lower Cle Elum R. (Kittitas Co.); Liberty (Kittitas Co.); Wenas Campground (Yakima Co.); Conconully SP; Sanpoil River Valley (Ferry Co.); Indian Canyon Park (Spokane).

RUFOUS HUMMINGBIRD

Selasphorus rufus

The tiny Rufous Hummingbird may spend part of its year in tropical regions, but its wings take it as far north as southern Alaska in summer. • Male hummingbirds are aggressively territorial and do not tolerate other males of their own, or other, species. The feistiness of male hummingbirds is clearly demonstrated at feeder stations, with males unwilling to concede space to any of their own kind yet perfectly content to let females of any species feed alongside them. • At the onset of nesting, Rufous males abandon the females and head inland or upslope to higher elevations to take advantage of early-blooming flowers, with the females and juveniles following later. They all head to Mexico and beyond for winter, with their return timed to coincide with the first salmonberry and currant flowers.

ID: long, thin bill; rufous flanks. *Male:* mainly rufous upperparts with green on wings and brownish crown (crown and back may be green); iridescent, orangy red gorget; white breast. *Female:* green back; white underparts; reddish throat spot. *In flight:* multi-pointed tail; male performs high-speed, whirring, oval courtship display flight.
Size: *L* 3–4 in; *W* 4¼–4½ in.
Status: fairly common to common western resident from early March to mid-September; uncommon to common eastern resident from late April to early September; most birds leave by mid-August.
Habitat: *Breeding:* open forests, especially secondary succession and glades; meadows;

brushy habitats. *In fall migration:* high-elevation montane meadows and disturbed areas for males; lower on mountains for females and immatures. *In spring migration:* through the lowlands, especially along the coast.
Nesting: in a tree or shrub; well-hidden cup is lined with soft, downy plant materials and decorated with lichen, moss or bark fragments; female incubates 2 white eggs for 15–17 days.
Feeding: darts and hovers to catch insects and sip flower nectar; outside the nesting season, also gleans for insects; visits sugar-water feeders.
Voice: gives a loud, emphatic *chip chip chip* warning call and a raspy *eeech* or rapid, repeated *eeeeeedidayer* notes.
Similar Species: *Black-chinned Hummingbird* (p. 220): green-and-white plumage with no rufous or peach.
Best Sites: forested areas statewide.

BELTED KINGFISHER

Ceryle alcyon

Never far from its beloved water, the stockily built Belted Kingfisher is generally found perched on a bare branch surveying the food prospects swimming below. With a precise headfirst dive, it can catch fish up to 2 feet beneath the water's surface. It can also launch itself from a hovering flight. • Easily identified by its outsized head and bill, shaggy, blue crest and distinctive rattling call, this bird is territorial year-round. • During the breeding season, a kingfisher male and female will excavate their nest burrow using their bills to chip away at the soil. They then kick the loose material out of the tunnel with their tiny feet. When digging in ideal soil, they may extend the burrow as far as 15 feet back into the bank.

ID: shaggy crest; small white area ahead of eye; long, straight bill; bluish upperparts; mostly white underparts; bluish gray breast band; white collar; short legs. *Female:* rusty flanks and "belt" (occasionally incomplete). *In flight:* white underwing with bluish trailing edge; white-marked outer flight feathers on bluish upperwing; dark and white bars on squarish tail; flies low over water; often hovers.
Size: *L* 11–14 in; *W* 20–21 in.
Status: fairly common year-round resident statewide; uncommon in winter in eastern Washington.
Habitat: *Breeding:* rivers, large streams, lakes, marshes and beaver ponds, especially near exposed soil banks, gravel pits or bluffs; brackish and saltwater estuaries; tidal creeks. *In migration* and *winter:* coastal swamps, brackish lagoons, oxbows, reservoirs and rivers.
Nesting: near water; in a cavity at the end of a burrow in earth or soft rock, often up to 6 ft deep or more, dug by pair; pair incubates 6–7 white eggs for 22–24 days.
Feeding: dives headfirst, either from a perch or from a hover above water; eats mostly small fish, aquatic invertebrates and tadpoles.
Voice: fast, repetitive, cackling rattle resembles a heavy teacup shaking on a saucer.
Similar Species: *Blue Jay* (p. 364) and *Steller's Jay* (p. 257): brighter blue plumage; smaller heads; backswept crests; smaller bills; longer legs; completely different behaviors.
Best Sites: almost any water body.

LEWIS'S WOODPECKER

Melanerpes lewis

This green-and-pink woodpecker has rejected the ordinary life of a woodpecker—the Lewis's does much of its foraging in the manner of a tyrant flycatcher, catching insects on the wing. It is also the only woodpecker that often perches on wires, but it is most likely to be seen in semi-open country high in oaks or pines or atop poles or snags. • Competition with European Starlings for nesting holes and the loss of favored snag habitats for feeding have greatly diminished this bird's numbers. • The Lewis's Woodpecker is named for Meriwether Lewis of the Lewis and Clark expedition of the early 1800s. Although not a formal naturalist, he recorded in his diary a great many concise and original natural history observations.

ID: dark red face; sharp, stout bill; glossy, dark green upperparts; dark undertail coverts; pinkish belly; light gray breast and "collar." *In flight:* appears mostly dark, especially from above; long wings and tail; crowlike flight with flapping and gliding.

Size: *L* 11 in; *W* 21 in.

Status: fairly common breeding resident from May through mid-September on eastern Cascade and Okanogan Mt. slopes; uncommon for the rest of the year; candidate for state threatened list.

Habitat: now confined to areas east of the Cascades; open woodlands; prefers Garry oak woodlands, riparian ponderosa pines and cottonwoods; favors snags by watercourses.

Nesting: male selects a dead stub of a live tree in which to excavate a cavity; pair incubates 6–7 white eggs for 13–14 days.

Feeding: sallies from a perch to catch flying insects; also eats acorns and other nuts, pine seeds and berries; caches acorns and nuts in natural crevices for use in the nonbreeding season and defends stores from other woodpeckers.

Voice: quiet away from the nest site; utters a wheezy contact call and harsh *churring* notes.

Similar Species: *Other woodpeckers* (pp. 226–36): none are dark green. *Pileated Woodpecker* (p. 236): flies in a similar fashion but is larger, with black-and-red plumage.

Best Sites: Fort Simcoe SP; Manastash Canyon (Kittitas Co.); Oak Creek Wildlife Area (Yakima Co.); Lyle; Swakane Canyon (Chelan Co.); Sinlahekin Valley.

ACORN WOODPECKER

Melanerpes formicivorus

The highly social Acorn Woodpecker is well known for its communal lifestyle, which is unusual in the generally territorial woodpecker family. During the breeding season, only one or two pairs in each group actually mate and produce eggs—nonbreeding members of the group help incubate the eggs and raise the young. • Communal groups place surplus acorns in one or two storage sites near the center of the group territory—dead trunks and limbs are studded with acorns jammed tightly into shallow holes. As many as 50,000 acorns have been stored in a single snag. All the woodpeckers in the group defend their acorns, which are often so tightly jammed that they cannot be removed without signaling that a robbery is in progress. • The Acorn Woodpecker is at its extreme northern limit in Washington, with only a few birds resident near Lyle.

♂

ID: clownlike face with white and pale yellow areas and black "cheek" and "chin"; pale eyes; glossy, black upperparts; pale underparts with heavily black-streaked breast; red nape. *Male:* red crown. *Female:* black crown. *In flight:* white upperwing patch; whitish underwing; white rump; black tail; flaps and glides.
Size: *L* 9 in; *W* 17½ in.
Status: casual year-round resident in very limited numbers near Lyle.
Habitat: hardwood woodlands that include oaks.

Nesting: colonial; cavity in a hardwood snag, especially oak, or a pole, is lined with wood chips; helped by the young of previous years, the pair incubates 3–7 white eggs for 11–12 days; larger clutches result from laying by several females.
Feeding: eats large numbers of acorns and some fruit, sap and corn; gleans ants or other insects or catches them on the wing; occasionally drills into wood for insects.
Voice: very vocal; gives a nasal *wheka wheka* series and a raucous *jay-cup, jay-cup, jay-cup,* with all group members joining in.
Similar Species: *White-headed Woodpecker* (p. 232): white head, except at back, and throat; black underparts and rump; solitary. *Williamson's Sapsucker* (p. 227): male has black face with white stripes, yellow belly, white shoulder patch and red throat.
Best Sites: Balch Rd. (Lyle).

WILLIAMSON'S SAPSUCKER
Sphyrapicus thyroideus

Male and female Williamson's Sapsuckers are so radically different in appearance that naturalists long believed them to be separate species. The male is boldly patterned in black and white, but the female, with her barred back and wings, brown head and dark breast, resembles the juveniles of other sapsuckers. The male and female also occupy separate winter territories. • A stiff tail helps brace woodpeckers against tree trunks when foraging or drumming. Because each foot has two toes facing forward, another at a 90 degree angle and, on most woodpecker species, a small, generally backward-pointing hind toe, these birds can move vertically up and down trunks. • Robert S. Williamson was a topographical engineer and U.S. Army lieutenant who led the Pacific Railroad Survey across Oregon during the mid-1800s.

ID: yellowish belly. *Male:* generally black; red "chin"; white "mustache" and "eye-brow"; broad white wing patch; white-streaked, blackish brown flanks. *Female:* brown head; dark brown and white bars on upperparts; blackish "bib" and upper breast; dark-barred flanks. *In flight:* white-barred, dark underwing; white rump.
Size: *L* 9 in; *W* 17 in.
Status: uncommon spring and summer breeding resident from May to early September on the eastern slopes of the Cascades and in the Okanogan Highlands and Blue Mts.
Habitat: coniferous forests, especially in Douglas-fir, grand fir, ponderosa pine or pine-aspen stands associated with western larch, usually at low to mid-elevation; sometimes uses hardwood riparian areas.
Nesting: in a tree, often used over several years and riddled with cavities; cavity is lined with wood chips; pair incubates 5–6 white eggs for 12–14 days.

Feeding: drills parallel lines of holes in hemlock, fir, pine and aspen for sap and insects; also gleans for ants; female eats more berries than the male.
Voice: loud, shrill *chur-cheeur-cheeur;* initially fast drumming slows, with lengthening pauses between the taps.
Similar Species: *Acorn Woodpecker* (p. 226): clownlike face; paler underparts; communal. *Other sapsuckers* (pp. 228–29): extensive red on head and throat; heavily white-marked back; narrower white upper-wing area.
Best Sites: Havillah (Okanogan Co.); Loup Loup Campground (Okanogan Co.); Swauk Pass (Kittitas Co.–Chelan Co.); Buck Meadows (Kittitas Co.); Bethel Ridge (off US 12); Blue Mts. above 5000 ft.

RED-NAPED SAPSUCKER

Sphyrapicus nuchalis

Not having reinforced skulls like other woodpeckers, sapsuckers have evolved a successful variation of the typical woodpecker foraging strategy: they drill parallel lines of sap wells in the bark of living trees and shrubs. The Red-naped Sapsucker, one of four North American species using this feeding method, is quick to make its rounds once the wells fill with sap, collecting trapped insects and oozing fluid as it makes its rounds. • A sapsucker does not "suck" sap—the bird laps it up with a long tongue that resembles a frayed toothbrush. Most healthy trees and shrubs can withstand a series of sapsucker wells, which also help sustain other woodpeckers, hummingbirds, waxwings, kinglets and warblers in times of need. • This species sometimes interbreeds with the Yellow-bellied Sapsucker or the Red-breasted Sapsucker.

Habitat: coniferous forests, aspen or cottonwood woodlands, riparian areas and residential woodlots; absent from oaks.

Nesting: excavates cavity in a live birch, cottonwood or aspen, often near water; pair incubates 4–5 white eggs for 12–13 days.

Feeding: drills a series of parallel lines to drink sap or pine pitch and eats attracted insects; eats cambium, fruit and berries; also catches insects in flight.

Voice: catlike *neeah* common call; also utters a loud *kweear* on its territory and a series of wavering *wika* notes; several fast drumming taps, then slower single and double taps.

Similar Species: *Red-breasted Sapsucker* (p. 229): redder head and breast; generally blacker back. *Williamson's Sapsucker* (p. 227): male has red only on "chin" and has all-dark back; female resembles immature Red-naped but has black upper chest and yellow belly.

Best Sites: Wenas Campground (Yakima Co.); Bethel Ridge (off US 12); Swakane Canyon (Chelan Co.); Methow Valley (Okanogan Co.); Little Spokane River Natural Area (Spokane Co.); North Fork, Coppei Creek (Walla Walla Co.).

ID: striped, black-and-white head; red forehead, nape spot, throat and "chin" (often white on female); white-marked, black back and wings; brown chevrons on pale underparts; yellow-washed upper breast; black "bib." *In flight:* white upperwing patch; short, rapid flight.

Size: *L* 8 in; *W* 16 in.

Status: fairly common breeding resident from May to mid-August east of the Cascade crest, in northeastern Washington and the Blue Mts.

RED-BREASTED SAPSUCKER

Sphyrapicus ruber

Bold in appearance, yet shy and reclusive by nature, the Red-breasted Sapsucker is one of three species that used to be considered subspecies of the Yellow-bellied Sapsucker. Especially in migration and winter, the Red-breasted Sapsucker is the most likely of the three species commonly found in Washington to occur in urban areas. It is also more likely to be seen in dense coniferous forests, especially coastal rainforests, where it is the only regular sapsucker present. In the few places in inland mountains and valleys where their ranges overlap, the Red-breasted is known to interbreed with the Red-naped Sapsucker. • The wells that Red-breasted Sapsuckers drill also benefit other birds, such as other woodpeckers and warblers, and even chipmunks and squirrels.

ID: red head, "chin," throat and breast; small white patch above bill; black-and-white back and wings; dark-streaked, yellow-washed, pale belly and sides. *In flight:* white upperwing patch.
Size: *L* 8 in; *W* 16 in.
Status: fairly common year-round resident west of the Cascade crest.
Habitat: moist rainforests, interior coniferous and broken, mixed woodlands, often close to riparian areas. *In migration* and *winter:* urban parklands, orchards and gardens.
Nesting: in a live alder, cottonwood, aspen, fir, riparian alder or willow (occasionally a snag); cavity is lined with wood

chips; pair incubates 4–5 white eggs for 12–13 days.
Feeding: drills and strips bark to produce sap wells; also eats insects, especially ants, and fruit; occasionally flycatches for insects.
Voice: loud, hoarse, descending *queeoh* spring call is often repeated several times; also utters a softer *cheer;* drumming starts with several fast taps, then becomes an irregular single- and double-tap series.
Similar Species: *Red-naped Sapsucker* (p. 228) and *Yellow-bellied Sapsucker* (p. 364): Red-naped is restricted mainly to eastern Washington, and Yellow-bellied is rare; pattern of black, red and white on head, throat and "bib"; usually more white on back.
Best Sites: coniferous and mixed forests west of the Cascade crest. *Winter:* lowland forests west of the Cascades.

DOWNY WOODPECKER

Picoides pubescens

A regular, welcome patron of backyard suet feeders, the Downy Woodpecker is often the first woodpecker a novice birder can confidently identify. Any small, black-and-white woodpecker seen in Washington is most likely a Downy, especially if it is feeding on the outer twigs of hardwood trees or low in shrubbery. Easily approachable, the Downy often travels with chickadees, kinglets and warblers in winter, gleaning the limbs of trees and uttering brisk, staccato contact calls as it goes. • The small bill is amazingly effective at poking into tiny crevices to extract dormant invertebrates and wood-boring grubs. Like many woodpeckers, this one has downy nostril feathering to filter out the sawdust produced in hammering, and it has a flexible, reinforced skull, strong neck and bill muscles, and a brain that is tightly packed in its protective cranium.

Habitat: hardwood and mixed woodlands; city woodlots and parks; prefers riparian willows, alders and cottonwoods.

Nesting: female selects a dead tree limb; pair excavates a hole, sometimes concealed, and lines it with wood chips; mostly the male incubates 4–5 white eggs for 12 days.

Feeding: male prefers smaller branches, the upper canopy and angled limbs; female favors trunks and upright limbs; eats mainly insects, especially wood-boring beetles and larvae, but also fruit, seeds and sap from sapsucker wells; takes suet in winter.

Voice: calls include a long, unbroken trill, sharp *pik* or *ki-ki-ki* and whiny *queek queek*; drums more than the Hairy, usually at a higher pitch on smaller trees and dead branches.

ID: white-striped, black head; stubby bill; black back with white patch; white (eastern) or pale buff (western) underparts; black tail with black-spotted, white outer feathers. *Male:* small, red hindcrown patch. *In flight:* white-barred, black wings with white linings; comparatively direct flight.

Size: *L* 6–7 in; *W* 12 in.

Status: fairly common year-round resident in low-elevation forests.

Similar Species: *Hairy Woodpecker* (p. 231): larger; larger bill; white, usually unspotted outer tail feathers; mostly feeds on tree trunks or large branches. *American Three-toed Woodpecker* (p. 233): larger; muted wing barring; white-barred, black back; finer white head stripes; 3-toed foot; male has yellowish crown.

Best Sites: lowland hardwood and mixed woods.

230

HAIRY WOODPECKER
Picoides villosus

Looking like an oversized Downy Woodpecker, the Hairy Woodpecker usually bullies its way to the forefront at a shared suet feeder. Too heavy to feed at a tree's outer extremities, the Hairy is often seen hammering away on the trunk or a large branch of a conifer or mature hardwood. It is proficient at opening up the shallow probings of a Black-backed Woodpecker or American Three-toed Woodpecker and digging deeper into the huge excavations of Pileated Woodpeckers. • The secret to any woodpecker's success is its long tongue—in some cases more than four times the bill length. Stored in twin structures that wrap around the skull's perimeter, it uncurls like the proboscis of a butterfly. Its finely barbed, saliva-sticky tip helps ease out the most stubborn wood-borers.

ID: black back with large white patch; white (eastern) or dusky buff (western) underparts; flanks may have dark streaks; black-and-white-patterned head; heavy, straight bill; black tail with white, usually unmarked outer feathers. *Male:* red hindcrown. *In flight:* barred, black-and-white wings with white linings.
Size: *L* 8–9 in; *W* 15 in.
Status: fairly common year-round resident.
Habitat: coniferous, mixed and, less often, hardwood forests, especially burns, wooded swamps and alder woodlands with many dead trees.
Nesting: male selects a soft tree; pair makes a cavity and lines it with wood chips; pair incubates 4 white eggs for 11–15 days.
Feeding: drills and enlarges holes in bark to reach wood-boring insects and larvae; also drinks sap in summer; winter diet consists of live and cached insects and nuts; male feeds higher on tree trunks than female, especially in winter; occasionally takes suet in winter.
Voice: calls include a loud, sharp *peek peek* and a long, unbroken *keek-ik-ik-ik-ik-ik* trill; drums less regularly than the Downy Woodpecker and at a lower pitch on tree trunks and large branches.
Similar Species: *Downy Woodpecker* (p. 230): smaller; daintier; shorter bill; prefers outer twigs or being close to the ground. *American Three-toed Woodpecker* (p. 233): black-and-white back; muted wing barring; black-barred, white flanks and sides; thinner "eyebrow" and "mustache" stripes; 3-toed feet; yellow crown patch on male and juvenile.
Best Sites: coniferous forests; burned areas. *Winter:* feeders.

WHITE-HEADED WOODPECKER
Picoides albolarvatus

Unique among woodpeckers with its largely white head and throat, the White-headed Woodpecker is a reclusive specialty of ponderosa pine forests. Pine seeds are an important part of its diet, so the White-headed Woodpecker forages chiefly among old and mature forests of three- and five-needle pines. Such a dry diet means that a reliable nearby source of drinking water is a necessity. • Throughout most of the year, their habit of quietly tapping flaking, loose bark high on trunks and out on the limbs makes these woodpeckers harder to detect than their relatives, but pairs of White-headed Woodpeckers can be heard engaging in territorial drilling in spring. At other times, these birds are most likely to be seen flapping overhead from one foraging area to another.

ID: mostly black; largely white head and throat; brown eyes. *Male:* red nape patch. *Immature:* red crown. *In flight:* dark wing with white patch above and below; slow, lazy but direct flight.

Size: *L* 9 in; *W* 16 in.

Status: uncommon year-round resident on the eastern slopes of the Cascades; possibly declining; candidate for state threatened list.

Habitat: ponderosa pine forests, frequently close to riparian areas with aspen.

Nesting: in a dying or dead pine, oak or aspen or a stump; pair excavates a cavity and lines it with wood chips; pair incubates 4–5 pitch-stained, white eggs for 14 days.

Feeding: female forages in ponderosa pine in winter, but male feeds at higher elevations; drills less than other woodpeckers; eats wood-boring insects and larvae plus pine seeds and other plant material; drinks more water than other woodpeckers.

Voice: usual call is a sharp, rattling, sometimes extended *tea-deek* or *tea-dee-deek;* long, unevenly paced drumming sessions.

Similar Species: *Acorn Woodpecker* (p. 226): red head patch on both genders; pale eyes surrounded by black; black "chin"; yellowish throat; white rump; communal. *Pileated Woodpecker* (p. 236): much larger; black-and-white head with red crest; longer, heavier bill; dark-tipped, white underwing feathers.

Best Sites: Wenas Campground (Yakima Co.); Bethel Ridge (off US 12); Leavenworth National Fish Hatchery (Chelan Co.); Entiat National Fish Hatchery (Chelan Co.); Lake Chelan SP; Silver Creek Rd. (Ferry Co.).

AMERICAN THREE-TOED WOODPECKER

Picoides dorsalis

Evidence of its foraging activities often betrays the American Three-toed Woodpecker long before it is seen. In seeking insects and their eggs, this resourceful bird flakes off bits of bark from old and dying conifers, exposing the red inner bark. Intent on extracting every last morsel from a tree, the American Three-toed Woodpecker returns again and again. After months or years, the tree is a distinctive conspicuous reddish color and is skirted with bark chips. Major insect infestations in Washington's high mountains have greatly expanded foraging opportunities for this woodpecker. • A feeding bird's tapping and flaking noises can often be heard at short range, and its contact calls are often quite musical. Every so often, it stops working to listen for the telltale sounds of grubs hidden beneath the bark or in the wood.

ID: white-striped and partly speckled, black head; black-and-white barring on back (mostly white patch on interior birds); white underparts; black-barred sides; 3-toed feet; black tail has mostly white outer feathers. *Male:* yellow crown patch. *In flight:* barred, black-and-white wings; typically short, fluttering flights.

Size: *L* 8–9 in; *W* 15 in.

Status: uncommon year-round resident on the eastern slopes of the Cascades and eastward mountains; very occasional in the west.

Habitat: variety of high-elevation subalpine forest types, especially Engelmann spruce–lodgepole pine forests, burns and areas of insect outbreaks.

Nesting: partly colonial when food is plentiful; usually in a fir, but possibly a hardwood snag, especially near burns, or in a pole; pair digs a cavity and lines it with wood chips; pair incubates 4 white eggs for 11–14 days.

Feeding: strips bark in search of wood-boring beetles; also eats other insects and drinks sap.

Voice: low *pik* or *teek* call; relatively noisy young; prolonged series of short drumming bursts.

Similar Species: *Black-backed Woodpecker* (p. 234): glossy, black back; stronger call and drumming. *Hairy Woodpecker* (p. 231): thicker white (or buff) head markings; large white (or buff) back patch; white or black-streaked, buff flanks.

Best Sites: FR 39 at Roger L. (Okanogan Co.); FR 37 at Baldy Pass; Harts Pass; Highland Sno-Park (Okanogan Co.); Sherman Pass; Salmo Pass (Pend Oreille Co.); Lewis Peak and Misery Springs Campground (Blue Mts.).

BLACK-BACKED WOODPECKER
Picoides arcticus

The Black-backed Woodpecker is most active in recently burned forest patches, where wood-boring beetles thrive under the charred bark. So focused is this bird on finding food that it can easily be approached and seldom flies far if disturbed. • With just three toes, Black-backed Woodpeckers and American Three-toed Woodpeckers cannot perch like other woodpeckers, but they can nevertheless climb and descend tree trunks. • In years when food is scarce, a few birds may descend from high-elevation coniferous forests to foothill parks or even urban woodlots. At such times, they tend to remain in a relatively small area and can be found by locating their foraging tree, which is worked until no wood-boring beetles or larvae remain.

ID: mainly black head with broad, white "mustache" stripe and tiny, white "eyebrow"; glossy, black back; white underparts with black-barred sides; black tail has unmarked, white outer feathers; 3-toed feet. *Male:* yellow crown. *In flight:* black-and-white-barred wings.
Size: *L* 9–10 in; *W* 16 in.
Status: rare year-round resident from the eastern slopes of the Cascades eastward; candidate for state threatened list.
Habitat: moderate- to high-elevation coniferous forests, especially recently burned Engelmann spruce–lodgepole pine and ponderosa pine areas.
Nesting: usually in a fir, with the nest entrance below a branch, or in a debarked snag; pair excavates a cavity and lines it with wood chips; pair incubates 4 white eggs for 12–14 days; family stays together until late fall.
Feeding: strips bark in search of wood-boring beetle larvae; also eats ants; prefers to forage in trees with easily stripped bark.
Voice: low *kik* call; prolonged drumming in a series of short bursts.
Similar Species: *American Three-toed Woodpecker* (p. 233): barred, black-and-white back; weaker call and drumming. *Williamson's Sapsucker* (p. 227): male has red throat, yellow belly, all-black tail and large white upperwing patch.
Best Sites: Surprise Lakes (Mt. Adams); Haney Meadow (Table Mt., Kittitas Co.); Taneum Ridge (Kittitas Co.); Entiat National Fish Hatchery (Chelan Co.); Thirty-mile Meadow (Okanogan Co.); Little Pend Oreille Lakes (Stevens Co.); Mt. Spokane SP.

NORTHERN FLICKER

Colaptes auratus

Want to watch a Northern Flicker foraging for food? Check the ground. Flickers are partial to ants, which form a substantial part of their diet and serve as unwilling participants in flicker hygiene. After bathing in a dusty depression to remove oils and bacteria, a flicker will pick up ants and preen rigorously. Ants contain formic acid, which is lethal to small parasites on the skin and feathers. Many other birds use this method, but the Northern Flicker is the only one to eat ants in quantity. • Although the "Red-shafted" race is the widespread breeding Northern Flicker in Washington, some "Yellow-shafts" appear as migrants and winter residents. Hybridizing in other parts of their shared summer range produces many intermediate forms that often show up in Washington.

"Red-shafted Flicker"

ID: long, straight bill; brown, neatly black-barred back and wings; heavily black-spotted, pale underparts; black "bib"; white rump; black-spotted, white tail coverts; black tail. *"Red-shafted":* brown crown and nape; mostly gray face. *"Yellow-shafted":* grayish crown; mostly brown face; red nape patch. *"Red-shafted" male:* red "mustache." *"Yellow-shafted" male:* black "mustache." *In flight:* undertail and wings, especially below, are pinkish red on "Red-shafted" and yellow on "Yellow-shafted."
Size: *L* 12–13 in; *W* 20 in.
Status: common year-round resident.
Habitat: wide variety of habitats but rarely dense forests; prefers woodland edges, open forests, grasslands and deserts; favors farmlands and towns in winter.
Nesting: usually in dead wood in a tree, snag or pole, but possibly in a post, house, natural bank, haystack, nest box or usurped burrow of a Belted Kingfisher or Bank Swallow; cavity is usually unlined; pair incubates 5–8 white eggs for 11–14 days.
Feeding: gleans the ground, tree trunks, stumps and mounds for ants; also eats seeds, nuts and grain; visits feeders in winter.
Voice: male gives a loud, rapid, laughlike *kick-kick-kick-kick-kick-kick;* issues a *wika-wika-wika* during courtship; drums less often and more variably than other woodpeckers.
Similar Species: *Williamson's Sapsucker* (p. 227): female is smaller, with all-brown head, yellow belly and fine, white barring on black upperparts.
Best Sites: any suitable habitat. *Winter:* often visits urban gardens.

235

PILEATED WOODPECKER

Dryocopus pileatus

With its flaming red crest, breathtaking flight and loud, maniacal call, this impressive deep-forest dweller is successful at stopping most hikers in their tracks. Considering its distinctive laugh, quirky looks and animated behavior, it is no surprise that the Pileated Woodpecker is reputed to have inspired a cartoon character. • Life is, however, a serious business for this crow-sized avian wood-carver. Using its powerful, dagger-shaped bill, the Pileated Woodpecker chisels out rectangular cavities in an unending search for grubs and ants. • A pair requires more than 100 acres of mature forest to survive and successfully raise its young. As a pair moves around its territory, it provides foraging sites for other woodpeckers, and the abandoned nesting cavities serve as bed-chambers for broods of tree-nesting ducks, falcons, owls and small mammals.

♂

♀

ID: mostly black plumage; flaming red crest; white "eyebrow" and "chin"; yellow eyes; white stripe from stout, dark bill to shoulder. *Male:* red forehead and "mustache." *Female:* black forehead and forecrown feathers have buff tips. *Immature:* pinkish crest; dark eyes. *In flight:* white wing lining and upperwing patch; distinctive crowlike flaps and glides. **Size:** *L* 16–19 in; *W* 28–30 in.
Status: fairly common year-round resident in the west; uncommon year-round resident in the east; candidate for state threatened list.

Habitat: mature forests, including those dominated by conifers, maples, oaks or cottonwoods, and some urban woodlands; rare in or absent from open country, juniper forests and isolated pine and aspen stands east of the Cascades.
Nesting: in a conifer, with the hole often facing east or south and often on a bark-free surface; cavity is lined with wood chips; pair incubates 4 white eggs for 15–18 days.
Feeding: drills and excavates large, rectangular holes in search of insects; also eats fruit and nuts, especially in fall and winter, and drinks sap.
Voice: loud, fast, rolling, laughlike *woika-woika-woika-woika;* long series of *kuk* notes; loud, resonant drumming.
Similar Species: *Other woodpeckers* (pp. 225–35): much smaller; no crest.
Best Sites: widespread.

Flycatchers

Shrikes & Vireos

Jays & Crows

Larks & Swallows

*Chickadees,
Nuthatches & Wrens*

*Kinglets, Bluebirds
& Thrushes*

*Mimics, Starlings
& Waxwings*

*Wood-warblers
& Tanagers*

*Sparrows, Grosbeaks
& Buntings*

*Blackbirds
& Orioles*

Finchlike Birds

Passerines are also commonly known as "songbirds" or "perching birds." Although these terms may be easier to comprehend, they are not as strictly accurate, because some passerines neither sing nor perch, and a number of nonpasserines do sing and perch. In a general sense, however, these terms represent passerines adequately: they are among the best singers, and they are typically seen perched on a branch or wire.

It is believed that passerines, which all belong to the order Passeriformes, make up the most recent evolutionary group of birds. Theirs is the most numerous of all orders, representing about 37 percent of the bird species in Washington and nearly three-fifths of all living birds worldwide.

Passerines are grouped together based on the sum total of many similarities in form, structure and molecular details, including such things as the number of tail and flight feathers and reproductive characteristics. All passerines share the same foot shape, with three toes facing forward and one facing backward, and none have webbed toes. Also, all passerines have a tendon that runs along the back side of the knee; tightening it gives the bird a firm grip when perching.

Some of our most common and easily identified birds, such as the Black-capped Chickadee, American Robin and House Sparrow, are passerines, but so are some of the most challenging and frustrating birds to identify—until their distinctive songs and calls are learned.

OLIVE-SIDED FLYCATCHER

Contopus cooperi

This flycatcher's enthusiastic courtship call makes it a favorite with many birders: *quick free beer!* (or, alternatively, *quick three beers!*) the male cries from the top of a spire. In late summer, he changes his call notes to a subdued but persistent *pip-pip, pip*. Without the distinctive calls, the Olive-sided Flycatcher would probably escape attention, because the drab plumage and preference for the upper canopy can make it difficult to see. • One of the largest flycatchers, the Olive-sided Flycatcher perches with a distinctive upright and attentive stance before launching out to capture insects that fly by. • Like other "tyrant flycatchers" of the family Tyrannidae, Olive-sided Flycatchers are fierce defenders of their nests that will harass and chase off squirrels and other predators.

ID: dark eyes; large bill with largely pale lower mandible; olive brown upperparts; olive gray "vest"; light throat and belly; white rump patches (often hard to see); barred undertail coverts; squared tail.

Size: *L* 7 in; *W* 13 in.

Status: fairly common but declining summer resident; uncommon in spring and fall; federal species of concern.

Habitat: *Breeding:* coniferous or mixed forests with snags or tall trees with dead branches. *In migration:* woodlands of all types, including juniper and oak, riparian areas and desert oases.

Nesting: usually high in a conifer, on a horizontal branch far from the trunk; compact cup nest of twigs, rootlets, lichen and pine needles is firmly attached with cobwebs and lined with lichen, grass and rootlets; female incubates 3–4 brown-marked, pale eggs for 14 days.

Feeding: sallies from a high perch to catch flying insects, especially honeybees (where available).

Voice: utters a descending *pip-pip-pip* when excited. *Male:* gives a flat *quick free beer!*

Similar Species: *Western Wood-Pewee* (p. 239): smaller; more uniform coloration below; 2 faint gray wing bars; different calls. *Cedar Waxwing* (p. 302): immature has obvious crest, black "mask," white facial lines, smaller bill and yellow-tipped tail.

Best Sites: Mt. Rainier NP; Dungeness River Audubon Center (Sequim); Blewett Pass (Chelan Co.); Loup Loup Campground (Okanogan Co.) Stevens Pass (Chelan Co.); Kamiak Butte SP.

WESTERN WOOD-PEWEE
Contopus sordidulus

Found mostly in forest clearings or edge habitats, this small, drab songster will sing persistently throughout the heat of a summer afternoon. Only by its nasal, down-slurred song can the Western Wood-Pewee be confidently distinguished from the nearly identical Eastern Wood-Pewee *(C. virens)* of eastern North America. • The Western Wood-Pewee will occasionally launch itself into aerobatic looping ventures in search of flying insects. It usually returns to the same perch. • The nest is a model of concealment—the completed structure resembles a bump on a horizontal limb. When cryptic conceal-ment fails to provide enough protection against predators, this unassuming fly-catcher will vigorously defend its nest, chasing away hawks, jays, squirrels and chipmunks. • The word *sordidu-lus* refers to this bird's dusky, "dirty" color.

ID: slightly peaked hind-crown; mainly dark bill; dark olive brown upperparts; 2 faint gray wing bars; pale underparts with blurry dark "vest"; pale throat; light undertail coverts; long, slightly notched tail.
Size: *L* 5–6 in; *W* 10½ in.
Status: common summer resident east of the Cascades and uncommon in spring and fall; fairly common summer resident west of the Cascades and uncommon in spring and from late summer to fall.
Habitat: *Breeding:* open hardwood and coniferous forests, orchards, riparian growth and residential woodlots. *In migra-tion:* almost any woodland habitat.

Nesting: on a horizontal limb of a tree far from the trunk; fairly large, deep cup of plant fibers and down is bound to a branch with spiderwebs and lined with fine mate-rials; female incubates 2–4 creamy white eggs, marked with brown and purple, for 12–13 days.
Feeding: sallies, hovers and gleans for insects and some berries.
Voice: whistles down-slurred, nasal *peeer;* also utters other short, whistled and sneezy notes.
Similar Species: *Olive-sided Flycatcher* (p. 238): larger; more distinct "vested" appearance; white rump patches may be visible. Empidonax *flycatchers* (pp. 240–45): smaller; rounded heads; white eye rings; paler, often gray or yellow-tinged under-parts; shorter wings; more contrast in underwing; some dip their tails.
Best Sites: woodland sites statewide; residential woodlots and farmsteads.

239

WILLOW FLYCATCHER

Empidonax traillii

Just as the spring movement of songbirds wanes, Willow Flycatchers begin appearing in low-growth areas near water. Most of them continue onward to more northern latitudes, but many remain to nest in Washington's lowland areas and locally in the mountains. • Similar plumages make the various *Empidonax* flycatchers the most difficult of any genera to distinguish. Subtle differences in habitat preferences, calls and such difficult-to-observe details as mandible color and the lengths of the outer flight feathers provide clues to identity. Only since the 1970s has the Willow Flycatcher been recognized as separate from the more widespread Alder Flycatcher *(E. alnorum)* of eastern North America, based mainly on song and call characteristics. • The *traillii* part of the name honors Scotsman Thomas Stewart Traill, who helped John James Audubon secure a British publisher for his book *Ornithological Biography* in the 1830s.

ID: indistinct white eye ring; pink lower mandible; olive brown upperparts; 2 whitish wing bars; pale olive breast; yellowish belly; white undertail coverts; whitish throat.

Size: *L* 5–6 in; *W* 8½ in.

Status: common, late-arriving western summer resident; fairly common, late-arriving eastern summer resident; uncommon migrant; does not breed in the Columbia Basin; federal species of concern.

Habitat: *Breeding:* willow thickets at stream outlets; woodland edges; young alders; tall brush at field margins. *In migration:* brushy habitat, usually near water.

Nesting: female selects an upright or slanting fork of a hardwood sapling or bush;

compact cup nest of bark, weed stems and grass is lined with grass, hair, plant down and feathers; pair incubates 3–4 brown-spotted, buff eggs for 12–13 days.

Feeding: flies from a perch to hover and catch flying insects; also eats berries and some seeds.

Voice: mellow *whit* call; mostly the male sings a quick, sneezy *fitz-bew*.

Similar Species: *Alder Flycatcher:* usually more olive green on back and rump; whiter wing bars; flatter *pip* call; song is usually *ree-bee-a*. *Other* Empidonax *flycatchers* (pp. 241–45): whiter eye rings and (generally) wing bars; less white throats; different calls and songs.

Best Sites: almost any wetland or shrubby habitat; Marymoor Park (Redmond); Nisqually NWR; Skagit Game Range; Nile Rd. (Yakima Co.); Sinlahekin Valley; Turnbull NWR; Rose Creek Preserve (Pullman).

LEAST FLYCATCHER

Empidonax minimus

This small bird might not look like a bully, but the Least Flycatcher is one of the boldest and most pugnacious songbirds where it occurs—it is a rare but probably increasing resident of a few localized aspen and cottonwood stands in Washington. During the nesting season, the Least Flycatcher is noisy and conspicuous, cheerily calling out its diagnostic simple, two-part call throughout much of the day. Even though it is not as glamorous as other aspen residents, the Least Flycatcher is conspicuous. • A fighting male Least Flycatcher is a pint-sized fluff of terror. In a territorial battle, the victor wins the right to select and chase a female for considerable distances in the hope of mating with her. The courtship might not be romantic, but afterward the male does his best to defend his mate. • Female Least Flycatchers are extremely persistent incubators—a toppled tree was once found with a female still on the nest.

ID: white eye ring; pale bill with upper mandible often half-dark; olive brown upperparts; 2 white wing bars; light throat; long, narrow, dark tail.

Size: *L* 5 in; *W* 7³/4 in.

Status: rare migrant and summer resident in Okanogan Co. and northeastern Washington.

Habitat: aspen and cottonwood forests; alder and willow thickets.

Nesting: on a horizontal branch in a small tree or shrub; female builds a small cup nest with plant fibers and bark and lines it with grass, plant down and feathers; female incubates 4 creamy white eggs for up to 15 days.

Feeding: flycatches insects and gleans the foliage of trees and shrubs for insects; also eats fruit and seeds.

Voice: constantly repeated, whistled *che-bec che-bec.*

Similar Species: *Other* Empidonax *flycatchers:* identification should be confirmed by voice. *Willow Flycatcher* (p. 240): no eye ring. *Hammond's Flycatcher* (p. 242): darker underparts and throat. *Dusky Flycatcher* (p. 244): outer tail feathers have whitish edges.

Best Sites: Wenas Valley (Yakima Co.); Champneys Slough (Okanogan Co.); Sanpoil River Valley (Ferry Co.); north Kettle River Valley (Ferry Co.); Turnbull NWR.

241

HAMMOND'S FLYCATCHER

Empidonax hammondii

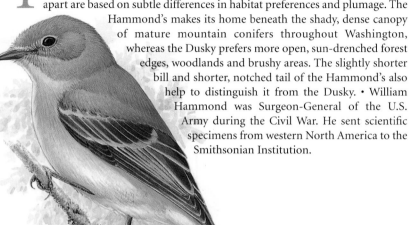

The retiring, diminutive Hammond's Flycatcher is easily confused with the very similar-looking Dusky Flycatcher. Strategies for telling the two species apart are based on subtle differences in habitat preferences and plumage. The Hammond's makes its home beneath the shady, dense canopy of mature mountain conifers throughout Washington, whereas the Dusky prefers more open, sun-drenched forest edges, woodlands and brushy areas. The slightly shorter bill and shorter, notched tail of the Hammond's also help to distinguish it from the Dusky. • William Hammond was Surgeon-General of the U.S. Army during the Civil War. He sent scientific specimens from western North America to the Smithsonian Institution.

ID: slightly peaked head; distinct white eye ring; very small, narrow, darkish bill with partly orangy lower mandible; olive gray upperparts; 2 white wing bars; pale gray "vest"; yellowish underparts and undertail coverts; long flight feathers make notched tail look comparatively short at rest.

Size: *L* 5 in; *W* 8½–9 in.

Status: fairly common migrant and summer resident in mountain areas; uncommon lowland migrant in late April and mid-September.

Habitat: *Breeding:* dense, humid, mid- to high-elevation coniferous forests; rarely in more open forests. *In migration:* lowlands; sometimes along the coast.

Nesting: on a horizontal limb of a tall tree, usually a conifer; cup of leaves, bark and grass is lined with feathers, grass and hair; female incubates 3–4 unmarked, creamy white eggs for 12–15 days.

Feeding: flycatches and hover-gleans for insects; usually in the mid-canopy; perches less in the open than similar flycatchers.

Voice: usual calls include a *pip* or a short *peek*. *Male:* song usually consists of a low, rapid 3-part *chi-pit*, a low-pitched *brrrk* and a rising *griip*, but part may be dropped.

Similar Species: *Dusky Flycatcher* (p. 244): longer bill; longer tail has pale-edged outer feathers; clearer whistles and *whit* call notes; usually 2-phrased song. *Gray Flycatcher* (p. 243): paler gray overall; longer, pale-based bill; dips tail persistently. *Other* Empidonax *flycatchers* (pp. 240–45): longer bills with conspicuously pale lower mandibles.

Best Sites: County Line Ponds (SR 20, Skagit Co.–Whatcom Co.); Tolt MacDonald Park (Carnation); Mt. Walker (Kitsap Co.); North Fork, Teanaway R. (Kittitas Co.); Buck Meadows (Kittitas Co.); Sinlahekin Rd. (Okanogan Co.).

GRAY FLYCATCHER

Empidonax wrightii

Distinctions between *Empidonax* flycatchers usually rely on subtle differences in plumage, vocalization and habitat, but the Gray Flycatcher can easily be identified by its habit of slowly dipping its pale-edged tail downward. Further clues are that it prefers low vegetation, tends to drop to the ground to pursue insects and makes its summer home in open ponderosa pine forests. All other small flycatchers flick their tails quickly upward, flycatch from higher perches (except in migration) and tend to prefer less open habitat. • For a flycatcher, the Gray has a relatively short migration range, with many birds overwintering in southern Arizona. • Spencer Fullerton Baird named this distinctly western species in honor of Charles Wright, who was a botanist with the North Pacific Exploring and Surveying Expedition of the mid-1800s.

ID: faint white eye ring; long, dark-tipped bill with pale lower mandible; drab, grayish upperparts; 2 pale wing bars; whitish underparts; long tail with thin white border.

Size: *L* 5–6 in; *W* 8½–9 in.

Status: uncommon late-spring and early-summer migrant and breeding resident on the lower slopes of the Cascades and in the northern Columbia Basin.

Habitat: *Breeding:* open ponderosa and lodgepole pine forests. *In migration:* low, brushy habitat, often well away from breeding habitats and mountains.

Nesting: in a crotch of a juniper or sage, or near the base of a thorny shrub; cup of bark, plant down, weed stems and grass is lined with feathers and hair; female incubates 3–4 unmarked, creamy white eggs for 14 days.

Feeding: sallies from a perch for flying insects; gleans foliage and the ground for insects and larvae.

Voice: dry *wit* or *pit. Male:* 2-syllable *chuwip* song is often followed by a *wit* or *pit.*

Similar Species: *Dusky Flycatcher* (p. 244): usually darker, with more contrast; darker lower mandible; does not dip tail. *Hammond's Flycatcher* (p. 242): darker; smaller bill with duskier lower mandible; darker "vest"; often flicks wings and short, thin tail. *Willow Flycatcher* (p. 240): browner upperparts; does not dip tail; prefers wetter habitats.

Best Sites: Wenas Creek (Yakima Co.–Kittitas Co.); Robinson Canyon (Kittitas Co.); Klickitat R. (Klickitat Co.); Washtucna (Adams Co.); Swanson Lakes Wildlife Area (Lincoln Co.); Riverside SP (Spokane).

DUSKY FLYCATCHER

Empidonax oberholseri

Many novice birdwatchers despair of trying to distinguish the very similar-looking Dusky, Hammond's and Gray flycatchers, so why not lump them together to make life a little easier? Prominent ornithologists did at one time consider the Dusky Flycatcher and the Gray Flycatcher to be one species, but closer inspection of collected specimens, DNA analysis and detailed studies of bird behavior and habitat requirements have confirmed separate species status. • In the breeding season, the Dusky Flycatcher favors mid- and high-elevation forests and other montane habitats that are more open than the Hammond's prefers, but less open, dry and shrubby than those of the Gray Flycatcher. • The *oberholseri* part of the name honors renowned 20th-century ornithologist Dr. Harry C. Oberholser, who worked for the U.S. Fish and Wildlife Service and the Cleveland Natural History Museum.

ID: rounded head; pale, elongated eye ring; small, dark bill with orangy lower mandible; olive brown upperparts; 2 faint white wing bars; whitish throat; pale gray "vest"; pale yellow belly and undertail coverts; long, dark tail with lighter edges.

Size: *L* 5–6 in; *W* 8–8½ in.

Status: fairly common resident of dry open slopes of the eastern Cascades, the Okanogan Mts. and the Blue Mts. from late spring to early fall; rare western migrant.

Habitat: *Breeding:* dry open conifers; high sagebrush-aspen areas. *In migration:* riparian, hardwood and coniferous woodlands at lower elevations.

Nesting: in a crotch of a juniper or sagebrush, or near the base of a thorny shrub; cup nest of weed stems and grass is lined with feathers, grass and hair; female incubates 3–4 unmarked, creamy white eggs for 12–15 days.

Feeding: flies from a perch to hover-catch flying insects; gleans for caterpillars and other larvae.

Voice: call is a flat *wit. Male:* song is a quick, whistled *chrip ggrrreep pweet,* rising at the end; breeding period song is sometimes a repeated *du...DU-hic.*

Similar Species: *Hammond's Flycatcher* (p. 242): smaller bill; shorter tail; prefers denser shade. *Gray Flycatcher* (p. 243): paler gray overall; dips tail persistently.

Best Sites: Wenas Campground (Yakima Co.); upper Cle Elum R.; Buck Meadows (Kittitas Co.); L. Wenatchee (Chelan Co.); Sinlahekin Valley; Silver Creek Rd. (Ferry Co.); Field Springs SP (Asotin Co.).

PACIFIC-SLOPE FLYCATCHER
Empidonax difficilis

ortunately for birders, the song of the Pacific-slope Flycatcher is much more distinctive than its plumage. When you enter any moist woodland during spring, this small flycatcher's upslurred *suweeet* call is often one of the first sounds you'll hear. Nonetheless, *difficilis* is an appropriate designation given the difficulties of flycatcher identification. Until late in the 20th century, this common songbird and the Cordilleran Flycatcher *(Empidonax occidentalis)* were collectively known as "Western Flycatcher."
• Like other members of the family, the Pacific-slope Flycatcher hunts primarily by "hawking": after launching from an exposed perch, it seizes a flying insect in midair and then loops back to alight on the same perch, ready for its next sally.

ID: white eye ring; small crest; dark bill with orange lower mandible; olive brown upperparts; 2 pale wing bars; brownish "vest"; yellowish throat; pale yellow underparts; brownish rump.
Size: *L* 5 in; *W* 8 in.
Status: common western summer resident and uncommon to fairly common spring and fall migrant; fairly common eastern summer resident.
Habitat: *Breeding:* moist hardwood or mixed forests in foothills and valleys. *In migration:* more varied habitats, but rarely away from treed areas.

Nesting: in a cavity in a stream bank, among the roots of an upturned tree, under building eaves or in a small tree; female constructs a nest of moss, lichen, rootlets, grass, leaves and bark that is lined with shredded bark, hair and feathers; female incubates 3–4 brown-spotted, creamy eggs for 14–15 days.
Feeding: sallies from a perch and hover-catches flying insects; also gleans for insects and eats some berries and seeds.
Voice: *Male:* call is a single, upslurred *suweeet* or *fe-oo-eeet!;* song is a series of high-pitched, repeated phrases *siLEEK...tup...P'SEET!* Female: call is a brief, high-pitched *tink.*
Similar Species: *Gray Flycatcher* (p. 243) and *Dusky Flycatcher* (p. 244): pale gray throats; use more open sites.
Best Sites: moist forests with well-developed understories in western Washington; riparian habitats east of the Cascades.

SAY'S PHOEBE

Sayornis saya

The Say's Phoebe, with its sandy brown and apricot plumage, is partial to dry environments. It thrives in sun-parched grassy valleys and hot, dry canyons, and it is particularly common where abandoned or little-used farm buildings provide safe, sheltered nest sites that can be reused every year and where livestock conveniently stir up insects. Waiting quietly on a fence post or other low perch, a Say's Phoebe can confidently sally forth to hawk an easy meal. • The Say's Phoebe is named for Thomas Say, a versatile naturalist known more for his expertise in the field of entomology. The name "phoebe" comes from an approximation of the call of a close relative, the Eastern Phoebe *(S. phoebe)*, in much the same way as "pewee" is derived from the call of the Eastern Wood-Pewee *(Contopus virens)*.

ID: pale gray head; stoutish, all-dark bill; dark eye line; pale gray throat, breast and upperparts; apricot buff belly and undertail coverts; dark legs; frequently bobs long, squared, black tail.

Size: *L* 7 in; *W* 13 in.

Status: fairly common spring migrant and summer resident in eastern open areas but uncommon as fall migrant; rare spring western migrant.

Habitat: *Breeding:* steep canyons, open country and foothills. *In migration:* streamsides, pond margins and other open and semi-open habitats, even at higher elevations.

Nesting: attached to a wall or under building eaves or a bridge; cup nest of soft plant materials is lined with fine materials, especially hair; female incubates 4–5 mostly unmarked, white eggs for 14 days.

Feeding: sallies and hovers from a perch, often just above the water, to catch flying insects; eats some berries.

Voice: calls are low, mellow whistles. *Male:* vireo-like song consists of 2 alternating 3-note phrases.

Similar Species: *Western Wood-Pewee* (p. 239): slightly smaller; pale yellow and brownish underparts; grayish wing bars; pale lower mandible; pointier wings; brown tail.

Best Sites: Ginkgo Petrified Forest SP Interpretive Center (Kittitas Co.); Frenchman Coulee (Grant Co.); Columbia NWR; Northrup Canyon SP; Turnbull NWR; Wawawai Canyon (Whitman Co.).

ASH-THROATED FLYCATCHER

Myiarchus cinerascens

The shrill, whistled calls of the Ash-throated Flycatcher are familiar summer sounds in the canyons and river valleys in the Garry oak zone of south-central Washington. These infrequent, burry notes from somewhere in the shadows of the heat-hazed oaks are to many people the voice of the dry woodlands. • The only Washington representative of a large group of subtropical and tropical crested *Myiarchus* flycatchers with rufous tails, the Ash-throat is a paler version of the Great Crested Flycatcher *(M. crinitus)* familiar to eastern North America. • Although it spends summer in arid terrain, the Ash-throated Flycatcher requires a shaded cavity in which to nest. If a suitable tree cavity cannot be found, this opportunistic secondary cavity nester uses a bluebird box, a crevice in junked machinery or an unused mailbox.

ID: fluffy crest; stout, dark bill; grayish brown upperparts; 2 indistinct pale wing bars; pale yellow underparts and undertail coverts; pale gray throat and breast; dark brown tail with rufous in central strip.

Size: *L* 8–9 in; *W* 12 in.

Status: fairly common breeding resident from mid-May to late July in the Garry oak zone of Klickitat Co.; rare summer breeder on lower eastern slopes of the Cascades.

Habitat: *Breeding:* juniper woodlands; cottonwoods, willows and other hardwood areas in canyons and river valleys; oak and oak–ponderosa pine woodlands. *In migration:* variety of tree and shrub habitats.

Nesting: in a natural cavity, nest box or other suitable cavity; soft nest consists of hair, fur, feathers and grass, and sometimes snakeskin; female incubates 4–5 creamy eggs, marked with brown and lavender, for 15 days.

Feeding: hawks from a perch and searches on the ground for insects; also eats some small fruit and sips flower nectar.

Voice: common migratory call is a *prrrt*. *Male:* song sounds like repeated toots of a referee's whistle with occasional more musical phrases.

Similar Species: *Western Kingbird* (p. 248): uncrested, pale gray head; bright yellow underparts and wing linings; darker, all-brown upperwing; thinly white-edged, black tail.

Best Sites: Rowland L. (SR 14, Klickitat Co.); Lyle CP (Klickitat Co.); Rock Creek Rd. (Klickitat Co.); Satus Pass (Klickitat Co.); Fort Simcoe SP; Wenas Rd. (Kittitas Co.).

247

WESTERN KINGBIRD

Tyrannus verticalis

The male Western Kingbird's tumbling aerial courtship display is sure to enliven a tranquil spring scene. Twisting and turning all the way, he flies about 60 feet into the air, stalls and then tumbles, flips and twists as he plummets to earth. • The Western Kingbird is often seen surveying for prey from fence posts, barbed wire and power lines. Once a kingbird spots a flying insect, especially a dragonfly, bee or butterfly, it will quickly give chase and pursue its prey for 40 feet or more if necessary. • Like any kingbird, the Western Kingbird will not hesitate to take on much larger birds that it considers a threat to its nest and young, and it is often seen harassing Red-tailed Hawks. • The word *verticalis* refers to the small, hidden red crown patch that this bird flares in courtship and territorial displays.

ID: pale gray head and breast; normally concealed orangy red crown patch; whitish "cheek" and throat; dark eye line; black bill; yellowish brown upperparts; yellow belly, sides and undertail coverts; long, black tail with narrow white edges.
Size: *L* 8–9 in; *W* 15–16 in.
Status: common spring and summer resident and fairly common migrant in eastern Washington; rare spring and summer resident in western Washington.
Habitat: *Breeding:* open country near ranch buildings, towns, isolated groves and cottonwood-lined stream courses. *In migration:* almost any open habitat, even in suburbs.
Nesting: usually on a horizontal tree branch, against or near the trunk, or on an artificial structure (often on telephone poles); cup nest of available materials is well lined with hair, cotton and plant down; female incubates 3–4 heavily mottled, white to pinkish eggs for 18–19 days.
Feeding: darts out from a perch to pounce on insects; also eats some berries.
Voice: feisty and argumentative; chatty, twittering *whit-ker-whit;* also *pkit-pkit-pkeetle-dot.*
Similar Species: *Tropical Kingbird* (p. 364): regular fall coastal visitor; much heavier bill; no white on outer tail feathers. *Ash-throated Flycatcher* (p. 247): browner upperparts and crested head; rufous in tail and wings; paler yellow underparts.
Best Sites: most any open habitat in eastern Washington, including ranches and farmsteads.

EASTERN KINGBIRD

Tyrannus tyrannus

When you think of a tyrant, an image of a ruthless despot might spring to mind. Most people wouldn't think of a small bird, except maybe those who are familiar with the exploits of the tyrant flycatchers, of which the Eastern Kingbird is North America's most widespread representative. This black-and-white kingbird is a bold brawler, a street fighter willing to attack crows, hawks and even humans audacious enough to invade its territory. These intruders are often vigorously pursued and pecked, and their feathers plucked for some distance, until the kingbird is satisfied that no further threat exists. • Fiercely argumentative on its breeding territory, the Eastern Kingbird can be quite gregarious in migration, when birds can be seen spaced out on power lines and fencelines.

ID: concealed, reddish crown patch; stout, black bill; dark gray to blackish upperparts; white underparts; grayish breast; white "bib"; dark tail with conspicuous white tip.
Size: *L* 8 in; *W* 15 in.
Status: fairly common summer resident in eastern Washington; rare local summer visitor and resident in western Washington.
Habitat: *Breeding:* irrigated valleys, open or riparian woodlands and woodland edges. *In migration* and *winter:* any fairly open habitat.
Nesting: halfway up a tree on a horizontal limb, or on a fence post or stump;

bulky cup of weed stems, grass and plant down is lined with fine grass, rootlets, hair and feathers; female incubates 3–4 darkly marked, white to pinkish eggs for 16–18 days.
Feeding: perches in the open and flycatches aerial insects; also swoops to the ground and hovers to catch other invertebrates; infrequently eats berries in migration.
Voice: utters quick, loud, chattering *kit-kit-kitter-kitter* and buzzy *dzee-dzee-dzee* calls in flight and when perched.
Similar Species: *Olive-sided Flycatcher* (p. 238): paler, grayish brown upperparts and flanks. *Black Phoebe:* casual visitor in Washington; smaller; all-blackish upperparts, neck, breast and tail.
Best Sites: most open riparian areas of eastern Washington.

LOGGERHEAD SHRIKE
Lanius ludovicianus

Patient and skilled hunters, Loggerhead Shrikes are commonly seen perched atop shrubs or small trees, using their keen vision to search for prey. Victims are quickly dispatched in a swift swoop and added to a storage cache of food impaled on thorns or barbs. Shrikes have been known to return to these caches up to eight months later. • Although the Loggerhead Shrike looks somewhat like the Northern Mockingbird, it differs greatly in its hunting techniques, dietary preferences and habitat requirements. • Pesticide use, from which the Loggerhead Shrike has been slow to recover, and habitat destruction have caused population declines across North America. • This masked songbird is named "Loggerhead" because of its large head.

ID: gray crown and back; black "mask" extends above short, dark, hooked bill; white-marked, black wings and tail; pale gray underparts; white throat; gray flanks. *In flight:* white "wrist" patch and outer tail feathers; quick wingbeats; short glide to perch.

Size: *L* 9 in; *W* 12 in.

Status: uncommon eastern migrant and breeding resident from mid-March to late August.

Habitat: open country with short vegetation (such as shrub-steppe), open juniper woodlands and rangelands.

Nesting: usually well hidden in a crotch or on a large branch of a tree, occasionally in a vine tangle; bulky, woven cup of twigs, plants and bark strips is lined with finer materials; female incubates 5–6 grayish buff eggs, marked with brown and gray, for 16–17 days.

Feeding: perches for long periods and then stoops down to the ground or actively pursues prey in flight; eats mostly large insects; also eats some small birds, rodents, frogs and lizards.

Voice: harsh screeches and harsh, scolding *jaaa* calls. *Male:* summer call is a bouncy hiccup: *hugh-ee hugh-ee;* infrequently uses a harsh *shack-shack* against aerial predators. *Female:* bill clicks.

Similar Species: *Northern Shrike* (p. 251): present in winter only; narrower "mask"; longer bill; lightly barred underparts. *Northern Mockingbird* (p. 365): narrow, black eye line; brownish yellow eyes; slimmer bill; longer legs; different behavior.

Best Sites: Old Vantage Highway (Kittitas Co.); Umtanum Rd. (Kittitas Co.); Toppenish NWR; Fort Simcoe SP; Potholes Wildlife Area (Grant Co.); Lower Crab Creek Rd. (Grant Co.); Cameron Lake Rd. (Okanogan Co.).

NORTHERN SHRIKE

Lanius excubitor

When the Loggerhead Shrikes retreat to warmer climates for winter, the small rodents, reptiles and amphibians of open country might expect a break. Unfortunately for them, and for small wintering songbirds, the respite is brief, because Northern Shrikes soon arrive from their subarctic breeding grounds. Each winter, a small number of these predatory songbirds migrate into Washington, where they perch, hawklike, to survey semi-open hunting grounds. • *Lanius* is Latin for "butcher," and *excubitor* is Latin for "watchman" or "sentinel." "Watchful butcher" does seem a good description of the Northern Shrike's tactics, and the macabre habit of impaling its prey on thorns and barbs has earned it the nickname of "Butcher Bird" throughout its range in the Northern Hemisphere.

ID: gray crown and forehead; black "mask" extends no higher than all-dark, hooked bill; gray back; white-marked, black wings and tail; pale, gray-barred underparts; white throat. *Immature:* initial overall brownish tinge; "scaly" underparts. *In flight:* white "wrist" patch and outer tail feathers; quick wingbeats; short glide to perch; often hovers.

Size: *L* 10 in; *W* 15 in.

Status: uncommon October migrant and fairly common winter resident until mid-March in eastern Washington and uncommon during this period in western Washington.

Habitat: semi-open country; scrub; low-elevation orchards, farmlands and ranches; migrants often appear among dunes or in coastal scrub.

Nesting: does not nest in Washington.

Feeding: perches on a small tree, bush or wire and swoops to the ground or pursues prey in flight; eats small mammals and birds and large insects; impales prey on plant spines or barbed wire for later consumption.

Voice: usually silent; calls are typically harsh and nasal; infrequent long, grating, laughlike *raa-raa-raa-raa*. *Male:* may utter a high-pitched, hiccupy *hee-toodle-toodle-toodle* song in spring.

Similar Species: *Loggerhead Shrike* (p. 250): present from March to late August, rarely until November; broader "mask"; shorter bill; grayer underparts; white throat; immature has barred crown and back and less heavily barred underparts. *Northern Mockingbird* (p. 365): narrow eye line; paler eyes; slimmer bill; longer legs; different behavior.

Best Sites: Marymoor Park (Redmond); Nisqually NWR; Skagit and Samish flats; Umtanum Ridge (Kittitas Co.); Lower Crab Creek Rd. (Grant Co.); Moses L.; Waterville Plateau (Douglas Co.).

CASSIN'S VIREO

Vireo cassinii

Distinct white "spectacles" set against a gray head mark the Cassin's Vireo, a compact and nimble forest songbird. This western breeder, the brighter colored Blue-headed Vireo *(V. solitarius)* of eastern and northern North America and the duller Plumbeous Vireo *(V. plumbeus)*, which breeds in the mountains and deserts of the Southwest and Mexico and rarely visits Washington, were all formerly considered subspecies of the Solitary Vireo *(V. solitarius)*. • Some birders report that the Cassin's Vireo is a fearless nester, often allowing brief close-range observations during incubation. It is one of the vireos most likely to be seen accompanying migrating warblers in fall. • The Cassin's Vireo is named for John Cassin, a Philadelphia ornithologist who published the descriptive accounts of many Pacific Coast birds.

ID: grayish head; bold white "spectacles"; fairly heavy, slightly hooked bill; olive gray back and rump; 2 white wing bars; white throat and underparts; yellowish sides and flanks.

Size: *L* 5–6 in; *W* 9–9½ in.

Status: fairly common breeding resident from May through September in eastern dry forests; uncommon breeding resident from late April through mid-September in western dry forests.

Habitat: open woodlands, especially mixed conifer-hardwood woodlands; prefers drier situations, especially pine-oak and oak woodlands and riparian growth.

Nesting: in an oak or conifer, suspended from a forked twig and attached by spiderwebs and cocoon silk; deep basket of soft plant materials is lined with fine grass and hair; pair incubates 4 dark-spotted, white eggs for 14–15 days.

Feeding: slowly and deliberately, with frequent pauses, gleans foliage and bark for insects, spiders and berries; sometimes hawks or hovers to catch insects.

Voice: harsh *ship* and *shep* call notes are often followed by a rising *zink* note. *Male:* song is a series of slowly spaced, high-pitched phrases: *See me...Detroit...Surreal.*

Similar Species: *Hutton's Vireo* (p. 253): more uniform yellowish olive brown overall; incomplete "spectacles"; smaller bill. *Warbling Vireo* (p. 254): more uniform overall coloration; creamy white "eyebrow" and lores; plain upperwings; warbling song.

Best Sites: Discovery Park (Seattle); Rasar SP (SR 20, Skagit Co.); Teanaway River Basin (Kittitas Co.); Taneum Creek (Kittitas Co.); Wenas Campground (Yakima Co.); Bethel Ridge Rd. (off US 12, Yakima Co.).

HUTTON'S VIREO

Vireo huttoni

During late winter and early spring, the male Hutton's Vireo may wage continuous vocal battles throughout the day to defend his nesting territory. • This early-nesting species is underrepresented in breeding bird surveys. With coloration and size so similar to those of the Ruby-crowned Kinglet, it is often overlooked, but the odds of seeing a Hutton's are good. It is far more numerous than many people believe. • A persistent "pishing" or a convincing rendition of a Northern Pygmy-Owl call (a series of low-pitched *toot* notes) will attract this year-round sprite of deep woodland shadows. Its lazier feeding style helps distinguish it from any small flycatchers and fall-plumaged warblers that resemble it. • John Cassin was persuaded by Spencer F. Baird to name this bird for his friend William Hutton, a field collector who first obtained this bird for scientific study in the 1840s.

ID: incomplete pale "spectacles"; short, slim, hook-tipped bill; olive brown upperparts; 2 white wing bars; olive tan underparts.

Size: *L* 4–5 in; *W* 8 in.

Status: fairly common year-round resident in western Washington.

Habitat: lowland mixed forests, especially coastal rainforests; valley foothills; Douglas-fir and western hemlock mixed with oak, maple or madrone.

Nesting: usually in a tree or bush, suspended in a twig fork; deep, round cup of tree lichen is bound with spiderwebs and lined with fine, dry grass; pair incubates 4 brown-spotted, white eggs for 14 days.

Feeding: hops from twig to twig; gleans foliage and twigs for insects, spiders and berries.

Voice: call is a rising, rather chickadee-like *reeee-dee-ree. Male:* monotonous song is a nasal, buzzy series of tirelessly repeated 2-syllable notes: *zuWEEM, zuWEEM, zuWEEM.*

Similar Species: *Cassin's Vireo* (p. 252): gray head; complete white "spectacles"; whiter throat and underparts. *Ruby-crowned Kinglet* (p. 288): slightly smaller; thinner bill; dark area between wing bars; shorter, notched tail; thinner, darker legs with yellowish feet; very active feeder.

Best Sites: Discovery Park (Seattle); Dungeness River Audubon Center (Sequim); Bayview SP; Tolt MacDonald Park (Carnation); Point Defiance Park (Tacoma); Nisqually NWR; Capitol State Forest (Thurston Co.).

WARBLING VIREO
Vireo gilvus

This vireo lives up to its name—its velvety voice has a warbling quality not present in the songs of other vireos. In eastern North America, the varied phrases end on an upbeat, as if asking a question, but songs heard in the West frequently have a dropping, fuzzy ending. • Common and widespread in Washington, the Warbling Vireo prefers the upper canopy of hardwood woodlands to dense, mature evergreen forest, so its range has probably been expanding over the years. It is the vireo most likely to be found in hardwood habitats and residential areas. Seeing one requires a lot of patience, however, because its rather drab plumage and slow, deliberate foraging make it difficult to spot among the dappled shadows of its wooded background.

breeding

ID: creamy white "eyebrow" and lores; dark eyes; shortish, hook-tipped bill; olive gray upperparts; unbarred wings; dull whitish or pale yellowish underparts; yellowish wash on flanks.

Size: *L* 5½ in; *W* 8½ in.

Status: common spring and summer resident and fairly common to uncommon fall migrant statewide.

Habitat: *Breeding:* riparian wooded areas; open bigleaf maple forests; mixed forests. *In migration:* almost any woodlands; prefers hardwood stands and residential areas.

Nesting: usually high in a hardwood tree or shrub, suspended from the prongs of a forked twig and secured by spiderwebs or cocoon silk; well-made, compact, deep cup nest consists of bark strips, leaves, plant fibers and grass; pair incubates 3–4 darkly spotted, white eggs for 13–14 days.

Feeding: feeds mostly in trees; gleans foliage, often from underneath, and makes hovering flights for insects; also eats spiders, berries and flower buds.

Voice: utters *eah* and *vit* calls. *Male:* song is a squeaky but appealing musical warble: *receiver receiver receiver receipt!*

Similar Species: *Red-eyed Vireo* (p. 255): slightly larger; greener upperparts; black-edged, bluish gray "cap"; white "eyebrow" contrasts with dark eye line; red eyes; larger bill. *Cassin's Vireo* (p. 252): 2 white wing bars; gray head; bold white "spectacles"; stouter bill.

Best Sites: Discovery Park (Seattle); Tolt MacDonald Park (Carnation); Sehome Hill Arboretum (Western Washington University, Bellingham); Bethel Ridge (off US 12); Columbia R. parks (Tri-Cities); Turnbull NWR.

RED-EYED VIREO

Vireo olivaceus

The male Red-eyed Vireo is North America's undisputed champion of vocal endurance. In early spring and summer he sings throughout the day and well into the night before taking a well-earned break until sunrise. One patient ornithologist estimated that a male Red-eye may sing his well-rehearsed phrases up to 21,000 times per day. This bird utters his robinlike song not from a perch but while hopping diagonally along branches and twigs. • Ornithologists do not yet agree about the reason for this vireo's eye color. Most other vireos, and young Red-eyed Vireos as well, have brown irises. Very uncharacteristic among songbirds, red eyes tend to be more prevalent in such nonpasserines as accipiters, grebes and herons.

ID: black-edged, bluish gray "cap"; bold white "eyebrow"; red eyes; olive green "cheek" and upperparts; white underparts; yellow-washed flanks and undertail coverts.
Size: *L* 6 in; *W* 10 in.
Status: fairly common summer resident in the west from mid-June to late July and in the east from early June to mid-August; uncommon migrant in the west in early June and August and in the east from mid-May to early June and from mid-August to mid-September.
Habitat: *Breeding:* favors riparian woodlands, especially with large cottonwoods. *In migration:* prefers hardwood woodlands.
Nesting: in a tree, suspended from a forked twig and secured by spiderwebs; dainty, deep cup of bark, grass, wasp-nest

paper and other materials is lined with finer materials; female incubates 2–4 chestnut-spotted, white eggs for 11–15 days.
Feeding: hops along branches, gleaning upper-canopy foliage, also hovers and fly-catches; eats insects, especially caterpillars, plus small fruits in late summer and fall.
Voice: short, scolding *neeah* call. *Male:* song is a continuous, variable run of quick, short phrases separated by short pauses: *Look-up, way-up, in-tree-top, see-me, here-I-am, there-you-are.*
Similar Species: *Warbling Vireo* (p. 254): paler overall; unbordered crown; dark eyes; shorter bill; warbling song. *Hutton's Vireo* (p. 253): whitish eye ring; shorter bill; 2 white wing bars; sings earlier in the year.
Best Sites: County Line Ponds (SR 20, Skagit Co.–Whatcom Co.); Marymoor Park (Redmond); Tolt MacDonald Park (Carnation); Sanpoil River Valley (Ferry Co.); Kettle River Valley (Stevens Co.); Sullivan L. (northern Pend Oreille Co.).

GRAY JAY

Perisoreus canadensis

Few birds in Washington rival Gray Jays for boldness. Outwardly unspectacular, they are inquisitive, endearing and gregarious by nature, always ready to seize any opportunity. Small family groups glide slowly and unexpectedly out of coastal and mountain coniferous forests, attracted by the slightest commotion or movement and willing to show themselves to any passersby, especially if food is available. • Gray Jays build their well-insulated nests, lay their eggs and begin incubation as early as late February, allowing them to supply their nestlings with the first foods of spring. • Gray Jays often store food for future use. By coating it with a sticky mucus from specialized salivary glands, they both preserve it and render it unappetizing to other birds and forest mammals.

ID: fluffy, light gray plumage, darker and browner above and paler below; dark "hood" (reduced on inland northeastern birds); pale forehead; white "cheek" and nape; short, black bill; long, rounded, white-tipped tail. *Immature:* darker gray overall. *In flight:* distinctive, bouncy flight with alternating fast flaps and short glides, usually close to the ground.
Size: *L* 11 in; *W* 18 in.
Status: fairly common year-round resident.
Habitat: montane coniferous forests; occasionally uses spruce habitat at sea level.
Nesting: usually on a horizontal conifer branch near the trunk or in a crotch; bulky cup of sticks, bark strips, moss and grass is fastened together with spider silk and insect cocoons and lined with soft materials;

female incubates 3–4 finely spotted, grayish white eggs for 16–18 days.
Feeding: gleans foliage and searches for food on the ground; eats mostly insects, fruit and carrion; caches partly digested food in conifers; steals or accepts food at campsites and picnic areas.
Voice: complex vocal repertoire includes soft, whistled *quee-oo,* chuckled *cla-cla-cla* and *churr;* also imitates other birds.
Similar Species: *Clark's Nutcracker* (p. 259): mostly pale gray; much longer bill; black-and-white wings and tail. *Shrikes* (pp. 250–51): black "masks"; larger, hooked bills; black-and-white wings and tails; favor open country.
Best Sites: Hoh River Campground and Hurricane Ridge Picnic Area (Olympic NP); Washington Pass Overlook (SR 20, Okanogan Co.); Paradise and Sunrise (Mt. Rainier NP); Meadows Campground–Harts Pass (Okanogan Co.); Mt. Spokane SP (Spokane Co.).

STELLER'S JAY

Cyanocitta stelleri

Normally noisy and pugnacious, the stunning Steller's Jay suddenly becomes silent, cautious and elusive at its nest, sitting tight on its eggs until action is required. It approaches the nest in a stealthy way to avoid being seen. • Most common in dense coniferous and evergreen hardwood forests, Steller's Jays regularly visit backyards in the foothills and lowlands, especially in winter, often descending upon feeders in search of peanuts and sunflower seeds. Inquisitive and bold like all jays, these crested opportunists are not averse to raiding the picnic sites and campgrounds of inattentive occupants for food scraps, but they rarely allow hand-feeding the way Gray Jays do. • When George Wilhelm Steller, the naturalist on Vitus Bering's ill-fated expedition to Alaska in 1740–42, saw his first Steller's Jay, the similarity to paintings of the Blue Jay convinced him he had arrived in North America.

ID: blackish brown head, nape and back; prominent, shaggy crest; dark eyes; stout, black bill; largely glossy, deep blue upperparts, finely brown-barred on wings and tail; medium blue underparts. *In flight:* grayish underwings with blue linings; round-tipped, blue tail; leisurely flight with short glides and little upward lift.
Size: *L* 11 in; *W* 19 in.
Status: fairly common year-round resident.
Habitat: *Breeding:* mixed woodlands; coastal and mountain conifers to timberline. *In migration* and *winter:* mostly coniferous woodlands.

Nesting: usually on a horizontal conifer branch or in a crotch, occasionally in a hardwood tree or shrub; bulky cup of twigs and dry leaves is cemented with mud and lined with rootlets, pine needles and grass; female incubates 4 brown-marked, pale greenish blue eggs for 16 days.
Feeding: gleans foliage and searches the ground for acorns, seeds, fruit, small invertebrates, bird eggs and nestlings.
Voice: varied; harsh, far-carrying *shack-shack-shack;* grating *kresh, kresh.*
Similar Species: *Western Scrub-Jay* (p. 258): no crest; blackish "cheek"; sky blue upperparts with grayish brown back; prefers open woodlands and brush. *Blue Jay* (p. 364): rare here; blue crest; grayish white face; sky blue upperparts with white wing and tail markings; thin, black "collar"; prefers oak and other hardwood woodlands.
Best Sites: virtually any low- to mid-elevation coniferous forest.

WESTERN SCRUB-JAY

Aphelocoma californica

The slender, uncrested Western Scrub-Jay is often seen foraging among leaf litter or surveying its tree-dotted habitat from a perch atop a tall shrub. • Each fall, these open-country jays gather fallen acorns and store them individually in holes they have dug in the ground with their strong bills. When it's time to eat the acorns, which form a staple of the winter diet, these intelligent birds often use a rock or concrete slab as an anvil to assist in cracking open the hard covering to get at the edible part inside. Because Western Scrub-Jays do not retrieve all of their hidden hoard, many acorns germinate, thus renewing the stand and keeping the resident scrub-jays supplied for life—a clear case of good forest management. • The Western Scrub-Jay is expanding its range northward, with breeding pairs seen as far north as Seattle.

ID: blackish "cheek"; white "eyebrow"; dark, pointed bill; sky blue upperparts with grayish brown back; pale grayish brown underparts; faintly streaked white throat bordered with blue "necklace"; long, unmarked, blue tail. *In flight:* tail and wings are bluish gray below.
Size: *L* 11 in; *W* 16 in.
Status: fairly common year-round resident in southwestern lowlands; expanding range.
Habitat: open hardwood habitats, including agricultural and residential areas, brushy hillsides, oak woodlands and juniper forests.

Nesting: in a shrub or small conifer; platform of twigs and some moss supports a grass cup lined with fine rootlets and hair; female incubates 3–6 dark-spotted, pale green eggs for 15–17 days.
Feeding: mostly a ground feeder; in summer, largely eats insects, plus other invertebrates and small vertebrates, including bird eggs, nestlings and fledglings; winter diet is mostly acorns, seeds and fruit.
Voice: perch call is a harsh, repetitive *wenk wenk wenk* series or a rough, frequently repeated *quesh quesh quesh*.
Similar Species: *Blue Jay* (p. 364): blue crest; all-blue back; thin, black "collar"; white-marked wings and tail.
Best Sites: Ridgefield NWR; Tenino (Thurston Co.); Olympia; Old Highway 8 (Lyle).

CLARK'S NUTCRACKER

Nucifraga columbiana

L ike other corvids, the Clark's Nutcracker stores food for winter. Its ground caches may be spread miles apart and hidden under deep snow along the high ridges of our mountain chains. A bird will often cache 30,000 or more seeds annually, and enough cached seeds remain unrecovered for the species to be a significant agent of whitebark pine dispersal. • This jay can apparently be either left-footed or right-footed when handling pine seeds. • The Clark's Nutcracker, like some of its cousins, has learned that a quick meal can be expected in campgrounds and day-use areas. • When explorer Captain William Clark of the Lewis and Clark expedition saw the large, straight bill, he thought this raucous and gregarious bird was a woodpecker, so he placed it in the new genus *Picicorvus*, meaning "woodpecker-crow." The species has since been reclassified.

ID: generally light gray head and body; long, straight, black bill. *In flight:* black wing with small white area near body; white tail with black center strip above; direct flight, usually to high location in pines.

Size: *L* 12 in; *W* 24 in.

Status: fairly common year-round resident high in the Olympics, Cascades, Selkirks, Kettle Range and Blue Mts.; may descend to lower elevations.

Habitat: high-elevation conifers; ponderosa pine and juniper forests at lower elevations.

Nesting: on a horizontal conifer limb; platform of twigs, secured with bark strips, supports an inner cup of fine material; pair incubates 2–4 dark-marked, pale green eggs for 16–18 days.

Feeding: searches the ground and gleans foliage for pine nuts and other seeds, fruit, insects, bird eggs and nestlings; carries pine seeds in throat pouch in summer and fall to ground caches that supply winter food.

Voice: quite varied; usual call is a grating *skraaaaaaa*, usually from high perch, plus higher pitched and yelping calls.

Similar Species: *Gray Jay* (p. 256): smaller; generally brownish gray, with dark "hood" and pale belly; stubby bill; forages more in lower canopy of dense coniferous forests.

Best Sites: Paradise and Sunrise (Mt. Rainier NP); White Pass (US 12); Chinook Pass (SR 410, east of Mt. Rainier); Washington Pass (SR 20, Okanogan Co.); Meadows Campground–Harts Pass (Okanogan Co.); Salmo Mt. (Pend Oreille Co.).

BLACK-BILLED MAGPIE

Pica hudsonia

Magpies are among the more strikingly plumaged of North America's birds, but their habits leave a little to be desired. Many magpies specialize in stealing the eggs of other birds, and some have taken to the widespread corvid habit of scavenging at roadkills—Black-billed Magpies will even eat the remains of their own kind. • Until recently, the Black-billed Magpie, which is largely confined to western North America, was considered to be the same species as the widespread Magpie *(P. pica)* of many parts of Europe, North Africa and Asia. • A magpie's nest is an elaborate dome of sticks held together with mud, offering excellent protection to the young. The magpie searches high and low for decorative touches—many a wedding ring or gemstone has ended up in a nest, and brightly colored material of any kind is highly prized by this interior decorator.

ID: black head; stout, black bill; black back; iridescent, blackish blue wings; white shoulders and belly; black breast, "leggings" and undertail coverts; long, dark-tipped, iridescent, green-and-blue tail; long, black legs. *In flight:* rounded wings with large white areas near tips.
Size: *L* 18–22 in; *W* 24–26 in.
Status: common year-round resident in eastern lowlands.
Habitat: sagebrush-juniper areas and agricultural areas with scattered trees; less often in dense juniper stands or treeless open country.

Nesting: in a tall shrub or conifer; large, conspicuous, domed platform of heavy, often thorny sticks contains a bowl of mud or cow dung lined with rootlets, fine plant stems and hair; female incubates 5–8 brown-marked, greenish gray eggs for 16–21 days.
Feeding: searches the ground, gleans foliage and hawks; eats carrion, invertebrates, small vertebrates, fruit and seeds; fall and winter diet is largely cached seeds and carrion.
Voice: many vocalizations, including a loud, nasal, frequently repeated *queg-queg-queg*.
Similar Species: none.
Best Sites: Ellensburg area; Yakima Valley; Moxee; Columbia NWR; Methow Valley; Okanogan Valley.

AMERICAN CROW

Corvus brachyrhynchos

Wary and intelligent, the American Crow has flourished despite consider-able efforts by humans to reduce its numbers. Much of its survival strength lies in its ability to adapt to a variety of habitats, food resources and environmental conditions. Because of this adaptability, this species remains year-round in lowland areas, preferring farmlands and urban areas; populations breeding at higher elevations usually flock together and migrate to warmer locations for winter. • Crows are highly gregarious birds with a complex social structure. Flocks can be composed of hundreds of birds, and these impressive, often noisy groups were once known as "murders." The purpose of flocking, however, is merely to prepare for evening roosts or migration. It is interesting to watch one of these late-afternoon gatherings with birds streaming in from all directions and "talking" together.

ID: all black; sleek head and throat; stout, black bill; typically has some iri-descent, green or purple back feathers; rounded tail.

Size: *L* 17–21 in; *W* 3–3½ ft.

Status: common year-round resident statewide.

Habitat: interior valleys, urban areas, agricultural lands and ranches, open coun-try forests, coastal mountains and along the coast.

Nesting: partly colonial; in a hardwood or coniferous tree or shrub, rarely on the ground; cup of branches, twigs and bark is lined with shredded bark, moss, grass, feathers, hair and leaves; pair incubates 4–6 bluish green or olive green eggs, with brown or gray markings, for 18 days.

Feeding: ground feeder; eats insects and other invertebrates, carrion, bird eggs and nestlings, seeds (especially corn), fruit and nuts; coastal birds break mollusk shells by dropping them onto rocks (probably learned by watching gulls).

Voice: utters a distinctive loud, repetitive *caw-caw-caw;* other calls are somewhat hoarse and hollow-sounding.

Similar Species: *Northwestern Crow* (p. 365): restricted to coastal northwestern Washington, and some experts doubt it is a true distinct species; slightly smaller; hoarser, lower-pitched calls. *Common Raven* (p. 262): larger and much heavier; heftier bill; throat looks shaggy; rough wedge shape to tail; glides with wings held flat; often soars and engages in spectacular courtship and bonding flights.

Best Sites: widespread.

COMMON RAVEN

Corvus corax

Whether stealing food from a flock of gulls or a Bald Eagle, harassing a Great Horned Owl or Golden Eagle, or scavenging from a carcass miles from its nest site, the Common Raven substantiates its reputation as a bold, clever bird. Glorified in many cultures, including those of many American Indians, as a magical being, the largest member of the crow family exhibits behavior that people often think of as exclusively human. It executes tumbling acrobatic feats that put the current crop of extreme sports practitioners to shame, and it performs everything with an individuality and practiced complexity that goes far beyond the instinctive behavior of most other birds. • Few birds boast the Common Raven's wide distribution, from the bitter winter cold and darkness of the arctic tundra to the hottest and most arid deserts, and few others demonstrate such an apparent enjoyment of life and such a loyalty to their mate.

ID: iridescent, purplish, all-black plumage; large head; heavy, black bill; shaggy-looking throat; powerful talons. *Immature:* grayish at neck; shorter bill. *In flight:* diamond-shaped tail; much soaring.
Size: *L* 24 in; *W* 4½ ft.
Status: common year-round resident statewide, except in Puget Sound urban corridor.
Habitat: mountains, open country, cattle ranches, large freshwater marshes, sage-juniper scrubland, coastal habitats. *Winter:* lowlands.
Nesting: on a cliff ledge or in a conifer; bulky cup of branches and twigs is lined with shreds of bark and hair; female

incubates 4–6 brown- or olive-marked, greenish eggs for 18–21 days.
Feeding: searches for food from the air; eats mainly carrion and also small vertebrates, bird eggs and nestlings (especially at seabird colonies), invertebrates, seeds and fruit; some birds scavenge in garbage.
Voice: gives a deep, loud, guttural, repetitive *craww-craww* or *quork quork* and many other vocalizations, including remarkably varied songs heard only at close range.
Similar Species: *American Crow* (p. 261): smaller and slimmer; smaller bill; rounded tail; smooth throat; higher-pitched calls; more often seen in urban locations.
Best Sites: Hurricane Ridge (Olympic NP); Paradise and Sunrise (Mt. Rainier NP); Yakima R. canyon; White Pass (US 12); Harts Pass (Okanogan Co.); FR 39 (Tiffany Mt., Okanogan Co.).

HORNED LARK

Eremophila alpestris

A small, uniquely patterned ground bird, the Horned Lark is a widespread migrant along the coast and freshwater shorelines. Nearly always encountered in open country, it nests in the mountains and on open grasslands. Its tinkling song and high, swooping breeding flight are a springtime treat. The three subspecies in Washington are the "Streaked" *(E. a. strigata)* along the coast, the "Pallid" *(E. a. alpina)* in the mountains and the "Dusky" *(E. a. merrilli)* in eastern Washington. Loss of habitat has reduced the "Streaked Horned Lark's" breeding range to coastal sand spits and dunes around Ocean Shores.

• To evade predators, Horned Larks rely on their disruptive coloring, mouselike foraging technique and a low profile among scattered grass tufts. Flushed flocks scatter and reassemble later. • Linnaeus, who encountered the species in Europe, named it *Alauda alpestris,* "lark of the mountains."

ID: yellow face and throat; bluish gray bill; mostly light brown above; white underparts; dark legs. *Male:* small, black "horns"; tapered black mark from bill to "cheek"; black breast band; rufous tints are common. *Female:* duller brown replaces rufous and black; paler yellow areas; no "horns."

Size: *L* 7 in; *W* 12 in.

Status: common year-round eastern lowland resident; fairly common alpine breeder in the Olympics and Cascades; uncommon year-round western resident.

Habitat: *Breeding:* bare alpine sites, shortgrass habitats, deserts and farmlands. *In migration* and *winter:* open grasslands, beaches, dunes and salt marshes; forages on roadsides, feedlots and fields.

Nesting: in a natural cavity in the ground; concealed nest of grass, small roots and shredded cornstalks is lined with soft materials; female incubates 3–4 cinnamon-spotted, gray eggs for 11–12 days.

Feeding: forages mainly on the ground for insects and seeds.

Voice: thin *seet* or *see-dirt* flight call; delicate song is a lilting, upward-spiraling tinkle of soft notes: *TEEP, tip, TOOP-pit-tip-pit-tip-pit-ittle-EEE.*

Similar Species: *American Pipit* (p. 300): muted facial colors; no "horns"; buffier, often streaked breast and underparts; wider white tail edges. *Lapland Longspur* (p. 336): stout, paler bill; no "horns"; streaked upperparts are brown, white and black; chestnut nape; breeding male has mostly black head and throat

Best Sites: Hurricane Ridge (Olympic NP); Damon Pt. (Ocean Shores); Paradise and Sunrise (Mt. Rainier NP); Columbia NWR. *Winter:* Waterville Plateau (Douglas Co.); SR 24 (Black Rock Valley, Yakima Co.); Davenport–Reardan.

PURPLE MARTIN

Progne subis

Attempting to hold its own at scattered locations across Washington, the Purple Martin, the largest of our swallows, struggles against pushy Eurasian immigrants—mostly European Starlings and House Sparrows that get a head start on nesting in spring. • In 1831, John James Audubon noted that pub owners were placing nest boxes above tavern signs to encourage Purple Martins to nest and bring good luck. Less than 70 years later, almost all birds in the eastern U.S. were using nest boxes, but, in the later-colonized West, most birds still used natural cavities and woodpecker holes. Because of competition with starlings, by the 1990s Purple Martin numbers had crashed in Washington, but they have since recovered remarkably through the use of nest boxes and hollowed-out gourds over water. • The genus name *Progne* refers to Procne, a daughter of Pandion; according to Greek mythology, she was transformed into a swallow.

In migration: various habitats, including urban parklands and ponds.

Nesting: colonial; usually in an old log piling or a nest box, but occasionally in a woodpecker hole in a snag; male helps female incubate 4–5 pure white eggs for 15–18 days.

ID: small bill. *Male:* glossy, dark bluish black overall. *Female:* brown-smudged, grayish white forecrown, forehead, "collar," throat and underparts; dusky blue back.

Size: *L* 7–8 in; *W* 18 in.

Status: fairly common local resident of Puget Sound, coastal Washington and the lower Columbia R. from late April through late August; uncommon migrant in early April and late August along Puget Sound and the Columbia R.; candidate for state threatened list.

Habitat: *Breeding:* clear-cuts, ridges and open woodlands near rivers and estuaries; forages over water and open country.

Feeding: hawks for flying insects; occasionally gleans from foliage, picks off the ground or skims from the water's surface.

Voice: rich, fluty, robinlike *pew-pew,* often uttered in flight; song is a vibrant, congested warble, often uttered high in the sky.

Similar Species: *European Starling* (p. 299): longer bill; green-and-purple gloss; pale spotting; wedge-shaped tail. *Barn Swallow* (p. 270): smaller; red forehead, throat and neck; glossy, blue upperparts; orangy to pale underparts; longer tail.

Best Sites: Seattle waterfront; Everett marina; English Boom (Camano I.); Ocean Shores; Ilwaco marina; Skamania marina.

TREE SWALLOW
Tachycineta bicolor

nyone with Tree Swallows nesting in the vicinity appreciates this bird's enormous appetite for flying insects, especially mosquitoes, which it brings back to its nestlings as often as 20 times per hour. Cavity nesters such as Tree Swallows benefit greatly when landowners and progressive foresters allow some dead trees to remain standing. In areas where natural tree cavities are scarce, the number of nest boxes available may well determine the size of the Tree Swallow (and mosquito) population.
• The back of a male Tree Swallow appears steely blue in bright spring sunshine but looks much greener in late summer and fall. Unlike our other swallows, a female Tree Swallow does not acquire full adult plumage until her second or third year.

ID: small bill; folded wings do not project beyond short, forked tail. *Male:* iridescent, bluish green upperparts and "cap" that extends below eyes; white throat and underparts; mostly dark rump. *Female:* slightly duller than male or drab brown above; darker "mask."

Size: *L* 5–6 in; *W* 14–15 in.

Status: common western resident from mid-March to late July and half a month later in eastern Washington; fairly common to uncommon migrant in March and from early August to mid-September.

Habitat: open areas, usually near water, including urban lawns. *Breeding:* places with suitable nesting cavities.

Nesting: primarily single, occasionally loosely colonial; in a natural cavity, old woodpecker hole or nest box; nest of weeds, grass, feathers, rootlets and other plant materials is lined with fine grass, feathers and sometimes pine needles; fed by male, female incubates 4–7 white eggs for 14–15 days.

Feeding: hawks for flying insects low over land or water; requires insects in spring but, unlike other swallows, can subsist for extended periods on seeds and berries.

Voice: gives a liquid *buli-dulu-dulit* contact call and a metallic, buzzy *klweet* alarm call. *Male:* song is a liquid, chattering repetition of 2- or 3-note phrases.

Similar Species: *Violet-green Swallow* (p. 266): wing tips extend past tail at rest; male has green "cap," nape and back, with white on face extending above eyes, plus purplish wings, rump (white sides) and tail; often duller female has smudgy head pattern.

Best Sites: throughout Washington.

VIOLET-GREEN SWALLOW

Tachycineta thalassina

Demonstrating a greater aptitude for taking advantage of Washington's diverse habitats than the Tree Swallow, the Violet-green Swallow is found around cliffs and treeless open areas far more than its cousin and is less reliant on riparian habitats. It often travels to higher altitudes, where it feeds with swifts, and clouds of birds can frequently be seen feeding on the wing. The Violet-green nests in cliff crevices, sandbanks, stream banks or old Cliff Swallow or Barn Swallow nests. • Swallows occasionally eat mineral-rich soil, eggshells and shellfish fragments, possibly to renew the minerals lost during egg formation. • *Tachycineta* is from Greek words that mean "I move fast," and *thalassina* is Latin for "sea green," the latter a reference to the male's upper plumage, which is reminiscent of shallow inshore waters.

Habitat: *Breeding:* open woodlands, wooded canyons, towns and open areas near water. *In migration:* any open area.

Nesting: loosely colonial; in a cavity in a tree, cliff or bank, or in a nest box or old swallow nest; cup of grass stems, small twigs, rootlets and straw is topped with feathers; female incubates 4–6 white eggs for 14–15 days.

ID: tiny bill; white underparts; white-sided rump; long, pointed wings extend well beyond short, notched tail at rest. *Male:* iridescent, green "cap," nape and back; white on face extends above and behind eyes; purplish wings, rump and tail; white underparts. *Female:* duller; can be more bronzy brown, with dark-barred "cheek."

Size: *L* 5 in; *W* 14 in.

Status: common spring and summer resident statewide from April through August; uncommon March and September migrant.

Feeding: hawks for flying insects, especially leafhoppers, leaf bugs, flies and ants.

Voice: exuberant, irregular chatter: *ch-ch-ch-ch-chairTEE, chairTEE-ch-ch.* *Male:* song is a squeaky series of single notes and rapid *tsip* repetitions.

Similar Species: *Tree Swallow* (p. 265): white on face stops abruptly below eyes; blue or bluish brown above; folded wings do not project beyond tail.

Best Sites: throughout Washington.

NORTHERN ROUGH-WINGED SWALLOW

Stelgidopteryx serripennis

The Northern Rough-winged Swallow is the cool-temperate representative of a group of swallows that wear almost the same colors as the earthen banks in which they live. These low-flying aerialists nest in burrows alongside streams and roadcuts; they don't make their own burrows but most often make use of the abandoned diggings of other birds and rodents. Usually seen in small numbers, they frequently join mixed flocks of swallows hawking insects over rivers or lakes. • In 1819, at a Bank Swallow colony in Louisiana, John James Audubon was the first to scientifically record Northern Rough-wings. Noticing the curved barbs along the outer edges of the outer flight feathers, he named them *Stelgidopteryx* (Greek for "scraper-wing") *serripennis* (Latin for "saw-feathered").

ID: plain, earthy brown upperparts, darkest on wings; pale underparts; light brown throat; wings extend just beyond tail at rest. *In flight:* broad wings; square tail, often spread when soaring; less erratic flight than other swallows.

Size: *L* 5–6 in; *W* 14 in.

Status: fairly common resident from mid-April to early August; uncommon migrant in mid-April and from mid-August to early September.

Habitat: *Breeding:* open areas with earthen banks, such as gorges, roadcuts, gravel pits, stream margins and coastal ridges. *In migration:* with other swallows over fairly open forest and grassland areas, freshwater lakes, marshes and lagoons.

Nesting: usually near water, in a cavity or crevice in a cliff or bank, such as an abandoned burrow, or a gutter, culvert, drainpipe or a hole in a wall; nest is a pile of various materials with a neat inner cup of softer materials, rarely feathers; female incubates 5–7 white eggs for 16 days.

Feeding: hawks at low levels over land, and especially water, for flying insects, particularly flies and beetles; occasionally picks floating insects off the water's surface.

Voice: generally quiet; gives an occasional quick, short, squeaky *brrrtt*.

Similar Species: *Bank Swallow* (p. 268): paler lower back and rump contrasts with darker wings; white at throat continues up behind dark ear patch; complete, distinct brown breast band. *Purple Martin* (p. 264): much larger female and immature have broader wings, whitish underparts indistinctly marked with gray and brown, and narrow, forked tails.

Best Sites: throughout Washington.

BANK SWALLOW

Riparia riparia

A Bank Swallow breeding colony seems to be in a constant flurry of activity as the adults fly back and forth delivering mouthfuls of insects to their insatiable young. All this activity tends to attract predators, yet few birds are caught, because the adults are swift and agile fliers, and the nest entrances are situated to make access from above or below very difficult. • In medieval Europe, it was believed that swallows overwintered in mud at the bottom of swamps, because the huge flocks seemed to disappear overnight after breeding. • *Riparia* is from the Latin word for "riverbank," which remains the preferred nest site for this bird, although in eastern Washington they are increasingly found near exposed sandbanks away from water.

ID: sandy brown head, upperparts and complete breast band; small, thin bill; white underparts, throat and foreneck; short, dark legs. *In flight:* dainty wings; long, narrow, forked tail; fluttering wingbeats; sudden direction changes; almost always in flocks.

Size: *L* 5 in; *W* 13 in.

Status: common resident from mid-April to mid-August in eastern Washington; fairly common to uncommon migrant in the east in early April and from late August to mid-September; rare local resident from mid-April to mid-September in the west.

Habitat: *Breeding:* stabilized banks, usually at low elevations; feeds mostly over wetlands, riparian woodlands, farmlands and shrublands. *In migration:* open areas near water.

Nesting: colonial; in a burrow up to 4 ft long, near the top of a cliff face or bank;

male helps the female incubate 3–5 white eggs for 13–15 days.

Feeding: captures airborne insects; feeds on the ground in insect infestations.

Voice: noisy at nesting colonies; *speed-zeet speed-zeet* twittering chatter. *Male:* sings a repeated series of short, clear notes.

Similar Species: *Violet-green Swallow* (p. 266) and *Tree Swallow* (p. 265): females and immatures have greenish, bluish or smudgy brown upper heads, partly white sides on rumps and broader tails. *Northern Rough-winged Swallow* (p. 267): darker head and back; brownish underparts, fading from breast to belly.

Best Sites: Wenas L. (Yakima Co.); lower Yakima Valley canals; White Bluffs, Hanford Reach (publicly accessible; Grant Co.); Conners L. (Sinlahekin Valley); Corkindale Creek (Skagit Co.); North Fork, Toutle R. (Coldwater Ridge Visitor Center, Mount St. Helens National Volcanic Monument).

CLIFF SWALLOW
Petrochelidon pyrrhonota

Silvestre Vélez de Escalante of Spain saw and described nesting colonies of Cliff Swallows in Utah in 1776. If named more recently, these birds would probably be called "Bridge Swallows," because many bridges seem to have their colonies underneath. Dramatic clouds of stocky, square-tailed swallows will suddenly swirl up along either side of the bridge, and a close inspection of the underside will reveal dozens to hundreds of gourd-shaped mud nests stuck to the pillars and structural beams. Some Cliff Swallows forego the tedium of raising young by dumping eggs in the nests of neighbors, who treat them as a gift and give them the same attention as their own eggs. When gathering mud for nests, both males and females usually hold their wings upright above their backs to prevent indiscriminate copulation attempts by other Cliff Swallows.

ID: bluish black "cap" and throat; white forehead; rusty "cheek"; bluish black back with 2 white stripes; dark brownish gray wings and tail; buff rump; white underparts; pale buff breast and nape joined by thin "necklace"; brown spots on undertail coverts. *In flight:* broad-based, triangular wings; dark, square-ended tail; fairly direct flight.

Size: *L* 5 in; *W* 13 in.

Status: common resident from mid-April to mid-July; fairly common to uncommon migrant from late March to mid-April and from mid-July to late August.

Habitat: *Breeding:* various upland and riparian habitats, especially canyons, and sites with suitable artificial structures. *Foraging:* stream edges, wetlands, grasslands and other open country and towns, though less often cities.

Nesting: colonial; attached to a rock face or rough wall of a building with mud gathered by the pair and applied together with saliva; gourd-shaped nest of mud and some grass is lined with dry grass stems, very rarely feathers; pair incubates 3–4 finely marked, whitish eggs for 11–16 days.

Feeding: catches flying insects on the wing; ingests gravel, probably to aid digestion.

Voice: *nyew* alarm call; thin, high notes; also makes twittering *churrr-churrr* chatter. *Male:* song sounds creaky and rattly.

Similar Species: *Barn Swallow* (p. 270): brighter, more extensively blue upperparts; orangy red to white underparts; longer, deeply forked tail.

Best Sites: throughout Washington's lowlands.

BARN SWALLOW
Hirundo rustica

The much-loved Barn Swallow is the world's most widespread and well-known swallow. In Europe, 2000 years of association with humans have resulted in a preference for nesting on buildings, and a swallow's nest is universally considered a good luck omen. • Pairs often raise two broods per year in heavy traffic areas without any problem. Not everyone appreciates the craftsmanship of the Barn Swallow's mud nest or the mess left behind, though, and many Barn Swallow lives are extinguished each summer before they have begun. Such a course of action is all the more regrettable given that this natural pest controller is more effective at keeping insect populations under control than any insecticide. • The scientific name means simply "rural swallow."

Status: common resident statewide from spring to early fall; uncommon to fairly common spring and fall migrant statewide; rare winter resident in western Washington.

Habitat: open country near water, including farmlands, freshwater wetlands and suburban areas. *Breeding:* needs cliffs or artificial structures for nesting.

Nesting: on a vertical wall, occasionally on a crossbeam or ledge, attached by a mixture of mud gathered by both birds and saliva; half-cup (if attached to a wall without support) or full cup (if supported) is lined with fine grass stems, horsehair and many large feathers; male helps female incubate 3–5 creamy white eggs, dotted and streaked with brown, for 13–15 days.

Feeding: opportunistic; hawks for various flying insects over land and water; sometimes collects dead and dying insects on the ground in cold or wet weather.

Voice: utters continuous *zip-zip-zip* twittering chatter and a *kvick-kvick* call. *Male:* gives a husky, squeaky but pleasant, lilting song with intermittent rattles.

Similar Species: *Cliff Swallow* (p. 269): browner upperparts; pale buff breast; white underparts; shorter, square-ended tail.

Best Sites: throughout Washington.

ID: rusty forehead and throat; short, dark bill; blue-glossed upperparts; blue "necklace"; long, deeply forked tail with white inner edges; short, blackish legs. *Male:* buff to orangy red underparts; longer tail streamers. *Female:* whitish to buff underparts. *In flight:* underwing has bluish flight feathers and orangy or pale lining; leisurely, measured flight, rarely to any significant height.

Size: *L* 6–7 in; *W* 15 in.

BLACK-CAPPED CHICKADEE
Poecile atricapillus

Throughout the Northern Hemisphere, titmice and chickadees are among the friendliest and most cheerful of woodland inhabitants. The well-known and widespread Black-capped Chickadee is a common sight throughout most of Washington. • Black-caps travel in family groups throughout summer and then band together in flocks that have both regular members and "floaters" that move between flocks. These flocks of fall and winter often attract other chickadees, woodpeckers, nuthatches, creepers, kinglets, vireos and warblers. • When foraging, chickadees often swing upside down on the tips of twigs, gleaning insects or plucking berries. • Eastern Washington birds show more contrast and less buff than western ones. • The closest relative of the Black-capped Chickadee may well be the Mountain Chickadee and not the Carolina Chickadee *(P. carolinensis)*, which it most resembles.

ID: black "cap" and "bib"; white "cheek" and foreneck; stubby, dark bill; grayish olive back and rump; gray wings with white-edged feathers; white underparts, becoming pale buff or light rufous on sides and flanks; dark, bluish gray legs.
Size: *L* 5 in; *W* 8 in.
Status: common year-round resident statewide, except for the San Juans and parts of the Columbia Basin.
Habitat: hardwood and riparian woods, orchards, parks, residential areas and urban woodlots, especially those with maple and alder.
Nesting: in a cavity, typically in a dead snag or rotten branch, or in a woodpecker hole or nest box; moss foundation is lined with rabbit fur or hair; female incubates 6–8 brown-dotted, white eggs for 12–13 days.

Feeding: gleans foliage in summer, mostly for caterpillars and small bugs; in winter, probes in bark and sometimes on the ground for insects, spiders, seeds and berries; takes seeds at urban feeders from fall until early spring.
Voice: clear *chip* contact call, usually extended into familiar *chick-a-dee-dee-dee;* song is a clear, whistled *fee-bee.*
Similar Species: *Mountain Chickadee* (p. 272): white "eyebrow"; pale gray below, with less buff; harsher calls; longer song. *Chestnut-backed Chickadee* (p. 273): dark brown "cap"; rufous brown back, flanks and sides; shorter tail; buzzier calls; song is a *chip* series.
Best Sites: almost any hardwood habitat statewide; easy to find at feeders in fall and winter.

MOUNTAIN CHICKADEE
Poecile gambeli

Breeding at higher elevations than other chickadees, the Mountain Chickadee routinely nests in subalpine conifers between 8000 and 10,000 feet and is often seen foraging up to treeline. This year-round resident spends much of its time feeding on seeds and insects high in the conifer canopy, perching on twigs, branches and trunks. Not easily foiled, it has even been seen using a splinter to assist in reaching into deep cracks. • Harsh winter weather can cause Mountain Chickadees to freeze or starve, and many move to lower elevations in search of more comfortable temperatures and abundant food sources. • The *gambeli* part of the name honors William Gambel, a 19th-century ornithologist who died of typhoid fever in the Sierra Nevada at the age of 28. "Chickadee" is an onomatopoeic description of the call most typical of the Black-Capped species.

ID: white "eyebrow" through black "cap"; white "cheek"; black "bib"; gray upperparts; light gray underparts; gray tail.

Size: *L* 5¼ in; *W* 8½ in.

Status: common year-round resident in eastern Washington; fairly common year-round resident in western Washington.

Habitat: montane coniferous forests and lower portions of subalpine forests from 2400–10,500 ft (occasionally up to 12,000 ft); irregular downslope flights to various woodland types in coastal and interior lowlands and foothills.

Nesting: in a natural cavity or an abandoned woodpecker nest; can excavate a cavity in soft, rotting wood; nest is lined with fur, feathers, moss and grass; female incubates 5–9 often chestnut-speckled, white eggs for up to 14 days.

Feeding: gleans vegetation, branches and the ground for small insects and spiders; visits backyard feeders for seeds; also eats conifer seeds and invertebrate eggs.

Voice: call is a drawling *chick a-day, day, day;* song is a sweet, clear, whistled *fee-bee-bay.*

Similar Species: *Black-capped Chickadee* (p. 271): no white "eyebrow"; buff sides. *Chestnut-backed Chickadee* (p. 273): dark brown "cap"; rusty back and flanks.

Best Sites: FR 39 (Okanogan Co.); Meadows Campground (Harts Pass); Teanaway River Basin (Kittitas Co.); Buck Meadows (Kittitas Co.); Bethel Ridge (off US 12); Mt. Rainier NP; Sanpoil River Valley (Ferry Co.); Mt. Spokane SP (Spokane Co.); Field Springs SP (Asotin Co.).

CHESTNUT-BACKED CHICKADEE

Poecile rufescens

The smallest of the North American chickadees, the colorful Chestnut-backed Chickadee inhabits the dense forests of the Pacific Northwest. Its habit of foraging widely within the forest canopy—from the lowermost boughs to the crown tips—allows it to survive in smaller ranges than most other forest birds. Like the Black-capped Chickadee, the Chestnut-back forms winter flocks that attract kinglets, vireos, nuthatches, creepers and lingering warblers. Preferring to stay in denser cover than its cousin, the Chestnut-back is less regular at feeders away from its evergreen nesting habitats, but, in severe winters, small parties may join other wintering songbirds in urban areas. • The tree cavities favored by chickadees in search of a nest site occasionally also attract insects. Bumblebees intent on establishing a new hive have been known to invade a chickadee cavity and chase the small birds from their nest.

ID: dark brown "cap" and darker "bib"; white "cheek"; stubby, dark bill; rufous brown back and sides; whitish underparts; dark brownish gray wings and tail; darkish legs.

Size: *L* 4½–5 in; *W* 7½ in.

Status: common year-round resident in western Washington; fairly common year-round resident of wet slopes of the eastern Cascades, the Selkirks and the Blue Mts.

Habitat: moist coniferous forests, especially Sitka spruce, western hemlock and Douglas-fir; some downslope movement and dispersal in winter.

Nesting: excavated cavity in a soft, rotting trunk or stub, natural cavity or abandoned woodpecker nest is lined with fur, feathers, moss and plant down; male helps female incubate 6–7 rufous-marked, white eggs for up to 15 days.

Feeding: gleans foliage, bark and twigs for insects, larvae, spiders, seeds and small fruits; visits seed and suet feeders near protective cover.

Voice: gives higher, buzzier call notes than other chickadees. *Male:* song is a *chip* series.

Similar Species: *Black-capped Chickadee* (p. 271): black "cap" and "bib"; grayish back; paler, buffier flanks; whistled song; prefers hardwoods.

Best Sites: along the coast; dense forests from the Cascades west; wet forests on the eastern slopes of the Cascades; San Juans.

273

BOREAL CHICKADEE

Poecile hudsonica

With four species and ample numbers, Washington is well blessed with chickadees. Birders generally love these energetic little "tits," and the Boreal Chickadee is especially sought out as the most northern representative of this endearing troupe to grace any of the lower 48 states. Softer-spoken and more introverted than the Black-cap, the Boreal slips into the great forest communities in the northern parts of our state and may go unnoticed. • Chickadees burn so much energy that they must replenish their stores daily to survive winter—they have insufficient fat reserves to survive a prolonged stretch of cold weather. Chickadees store food for winter in holes and bark crevices. • During cold winter nights, all chickadees enter into a state of torpor, in which the bird's metabolism slows so that it uses less energy. • The *hudsonica* part of the name refers to the northern (Hudsonian) region of Canada.

ID: grayish brown "cap"; black "bib"; gray brown flanks; light gray under-parts; light brownish back; white "cheek" patch. *In flight:* appears browner than other Washington chickadees.
Size: *L* 5¹/₂–6¹/₂ in; *W* 8 in.
Status: uncommon localized year-round resident in eastern Washington.
Habitat: mature and young Engelmann spruce and subalpine fir forests.
Nesting: excavates a cavity in soft, rotting wood or uses a natural cavity or abandoned woodpecker nest in a conifer tree;

female lines the nest with fur, feathers, moss and grass; female incubates 5–8 finely chestnut-dotted, white eggs for about 15 days.
Feeding: gleans vegetation, branches and infrequently the ground for small tree-infesting insects (adults, pupae and eggs) and spiders; also eats conifer seeds.
Voice: soft, nasal, whistled *scick-a day day day.*
Similar Species: *Black-capped Chickadee* (p. 271): black "cap"; buff flanks. *Mountain Chickadee* (p. 272): white "eyebrow"; black eye line.
Best Sites: Meadows Campground (Harts Pass, Okanogan Co.); Roger L. and Tiffany Spring Campground (FR 39, Okanogan Co.); Salmo Pass (Pend Oreille Co.).

BUSHTIT
Psaltriparus minimus

A fastidious perfectionist when it comes to nests, the Bushtit will test every fiber to ensure that the structure fulfills all tenets of Bushtit architecture, and it will desert both nest and mate if its sanctity is violated. • Hyperactive in everything they do, these tousled, fluffy, gregarious birds are constantly on the move, either as individual nesting pairs or in roaming postbreeding bands of up to 40 members. They bounce from one shrubby perch to another, examining everything of interest, filling the neighborhood with charming, bell-like, tinkling calls, and doing it all with panache. In cold weather, flocks will huddle together in a tight mass to reduce heat loss. • *Psaltriparus* is derived from Greek and Latin roots that mean "a harpist" and "titmouse."

ID: gray head (with brown "cap" in coastal birds); tiny, dark bill; dull gray back and wings; pale buff wash on grayish underparts; long, dull gray tail; black legs. *Male:* dark eyes. *Female:* pale yellow eyes.

Size: *L* 4–4½ in; *W* 6 in.

Status: common year-round resident in western Washington, except scarce along the outer coast; uncommon year-round resident in south-central Washington and along the lowland base of the eastern slopes of the Cascades.

Habitat: juniper, oak and mountain mahogany woodlands; riparian brushlands; residential plantings; brushy habitats in mixed forest in the west.

Nesting: in a shrub; pair builds a socklike hanging nest, intricately woven with moss, lichen, cocoons, spider silk, fur and feathers; pair incubates 5–7 white eggs for 12 days.

Feeding: gleans lower vegetation for insects, small fruits and seeds; birds in foraging flocks stay within visual and auditory distance of each other at all times.

Voice: flocks keep in contact with a series of short, high, buzzy notes that often resemble the calls of kinglets and titmice; a high, falling series of notes warns of an aerial predator.

Similar Species: *Chickadees* (pp. 271–74): slightly larger; dark "caps" and "bibs"; faces mostly white; heavier bills; different calls.

Best Sites: virtually anyplace from coastal Whatcom Co. through Puget Sound lowland, west to Hood Canal and into southwestern Washington; appropriate habitats along the Columbia R.; Rock Creek (Klickitat Co.); Satus Pass (Klickitat Co.); Umtanum Creek at Yakima R. (Kittitas Co.).

RED-BREASTED NUTHATCH

Sitta canadensis

Red-breasted Nuthatches often announce their presence with distinctive nasal calls. They are easily "pished" into view, where their bright colors, chubby bodies and headfirst movement down trunks set them apart from their traveling companions. Differing foraging techniques help to identify the three nuthatch species roaming Washington's woods in fall and winter. The result of this specialization is a thorough haul of what the forest has to offer without over-extending any particular resource.

• Nuthatches are unique among tree-climbing songbirds in that they use one foot to brace themselves while the other holds onto the bark—in contrast, woodpeckers and the Brown Creeper use their tails for stability.

ID: white "cheek" and "eyebrow"; black eye stripe; dark eyes; pointed, slightly upturned bill; bluish gray upperparts and flank feathers; blackish legs. *Male:* black "cap"; rusty underparts. *Female:* bluish "cap"; orangy buff belly.

Size: *L* 4½ in; *W* 8½ in.

Status: common year-round forest resident statewide.

Habitat: *Breeding:* almost any coniferous forest from sea level to timberline. *In migration* and *winter:* almost any woodland.

Nesting: in a natural cavity or old woodpecker nest in a tree; entrance is smeared with sap or pitch to catch insects; nest is lined with bark, grass and fur; female incubates 5–6 rufous-marked, white to pinkish eggs for 12 days.

Feeding: creeps along boughs or moves headfirst down a trunk while probing under loose bark for wood-boring beetles and larvae and other invertebrates; switches to pine and spruce seeds and visits feeders in winter.

Voice: gives a slow, continually repeated, nasal *yank-yank-yank* or *rah-rah-rah-rah* or short *tsip.*

Similar Species: *White-breasted Nuthatch* (p. 277): larger; plain white head with dark crown stripe; longer bill; grayish white underparts with rufous brown upper legs and undertail coverts; longer wings; prefers hardwoods. *Pygmy Nuthatch* (p. 278): stockier; brown "cap" descends to eye line; stouter bill; paler underparts; more gray on flanks; gray wing linings.

Best Sites: statewide, except for the arid Columbia Basin.

WHITE-BREASTED NUTHATCH

Sitta carolinensis

This acrobat of the bird world defies gravity by foraging upside down on tree trunks. So proficient is the White-breasted Nuthatch at maintaining its grip on a tree trunk that it will frequently pause in mid-descent, arch its head at a right angle to survey its surroundings and then announce to the world with its curious, noisy, nasal calls that all is well. • Pairs of White-breasted Nuthatches remain in permanent, year-round territories in open pine stands or mature oak and other hardwood woodlands and store their gathered food items in cache sites, each containing just one type of food. Stored foods are supplemented by regular visits to any feeders in the territory; each visit lasts just long enough to select a seed, pick it up and then flutter off.

ID: black nape and "cap"; white face; uptilted, dark bill; grayish blue back; white-edged, grayish blue wing feathers; black shoulders; gray flanks and sides; white throat and breast; rufous toward undertail coverts. *In flight:* broad wings; gray underwing with white arc; white flashes on short, rounded, gray tail.

Size: *L* 5½–6 in; *W* 11 in.

Status: fairly common year-round resident on the margins of the Columbia Basin; rare year-round western resident (largely Ridgefield NWR); federal species of concern, candidate for state threatened list.

Habitat: open woodlands, preferring oak woodlands in western Washington and ponderosa pine–Garry oak forests on the eastern slopes of the Cascades.

Nesting: in a natural cavity or old woodpecker hole in a hardwood or ponderosa pine; lined with soft materials; female incubates 5–9 chestnut-spotted, whitish eggs for 12 days.

Feeding: hops across trunks and main branches, exploring for various insects; also eats acorns and other nuts, grain and large seeds.

Voice: *tuck* location call; *quark* alarm call; song is a simple repetition of 6–10 persistent, high, whining notes.

Similar Species: *Red-breasted Nuthatch* (p. 276): smaller; black eye stripe; buff or orangy underparts and underwings; prefers conifers. *Pygmy Nuthatch* (p. 278): smaller; brown "cap"; warm buff breast and undertail coverts.

Best Sites: Ridgefield NWR; Washougal (Clark Co.); Sinlahekin Wildlife Area; Lake Chelan SP; Wenas Campground (Yakima Co.); Fort Simcoe SP; Satus Pass (Klickitat Co.); Turnbull NWR.

PYGMY NUTHATCH

Sitta pygmaea

When you're as small as the Pygmy Nuthatch and live high in the mountains year-round, a lot of your time is spent finding food. During daylight hours, this energetic Washington resident hops along the limbs and twigs of pines, probing and calling incessantly. With a body designed mainly for foraging among clumps of needles, the Pygmy Nuthatch seems barely capable of keeping itself airborne as it flutters awkwardly between adjacent trees. • Like the larger nuthatches, the Pygmy is gregarious by nature, usually forming flocks in fall and winter. At night, when the temperature drops, this resourceful bird seeks the shelter and warmth of communal roosts in tree cavities—as many as 100 birds have been recorded in one cavity.

ID: brown "cap"; black eye line; white "cheek" and throat; uptilted, stout, black-and-gray bill; grayish blue back; dark-and-white edges to wings; pale buff underparts; grayish blue flanks; dark legs.

Size: *L* 4 in; *W* 7½–8 in.

Status: fairly common year-round resident in eastern Washington.

Habitat: ponderosa pine forests and adjacent areas; rarely leaves breeding areas.

Nesting: uses an old woodpecker cavity or excavates its own hole; lining is soft plant material, wood chips, fur and feathers; female incubates 6–8 sparsely red-spotted, white eggs for 15–16 days; up to 3 unmated males may assist with nesting duties.

Feeding: forages in outer limbs for adult and larval insects and other invertebrates, including spiders; also eats pine seeds and suet at feeders.

Voice: varied, persistent, loud chipping and squeaking notes.

Similar Species: *Red-breasted Nuthatch* (p. 276): larger; black eye stripe; smaller bill; orangy buff or rusty underparts; nasal calls. *White-breasted Nuthatch* (p. 277): larger; white head with dark "cap"; grayish and white underparts with rufous confined to above legs and undertail coverts; nasal calls; usually in pairs.

Best Sites: Wenas Campground (Yakima Co.); Cle Elum; FR 1713 at Rocky Prairie (Yakima Co.); Antilon L. (Chelan Co.); Havillah Rd. (Okanogan Co.); Sanpoil River Valley (Ferry Co.); Riverside SP headquarters (Spokane); Turnbull NWR; Field Springs SP (Asotin Co.).

BROWN CREEPER

Certhia americana

Various nearly identical creeper species inhabit Europe and Asia, but the Brown Creeper is one of a kind in North America. Favoring sizable stands of large trees most of the year, this small, fragile-looking bird usually goes unnoticed until what looks like a flake of bark suddenly comes alive. The camouflage is so effective that even when a creeper is detected, it may once again blend into the background until it moves again. Completely at home among the flaking bark, the Brown Creeper even builds its nest there. • The Brown Creeper usually spirals methodically up a tree trunk until it reaches the upper branches and then darts down to the base of a neighboring tree to begin again—the opposite of what nuthatches do. The long, stiff, pointed tail feathers and long claws help to stabilize this bird against the trunk in a woodpecker-like manner. It is thought the white breast and throat act to startle insects on the tree trunk where the creeper is feeding.

ID: white "eyebrow"; pointed, downcurved bill; mottled, dark-streaked upperparts of gray, brown and white; white underparts and throat; buff undertail coverts; long, spiked tail.

Size: *L* 5 in; *W* 7½ in.

Status: fairly common year-round resident in western Washington; fairly common resident in eastern Washington from April through September, becoming uncommon from October to April.

Habitat: *Breeding:* coniferous (except juniper) and hardwood woodlands. *In migration* and *winter:* low-elevation woodlands, including small woodlots, parklands and coastal forests.

Nesting: suspended under loose bark; nest of grass and conifer needles is woven together with spider silk; female incubates 5–6 faintly marked, white eggs for 14–17 days.

Feeding: ascends trunk in a spiral or straight course and then drops down to another trunk; most prey is picked from beneath loose bark.

Voice: gives a high *tseee* call; also utters faint, very high *zip* notes in flight. *Male:* song is a faint, high-pitched *trees-trees these-trees, see the trees.*

Similar Species: *Wrens* (pp. 280–85): upraised, barred tails; forage on the ground, in woodpiles and foliage; harsh calls and powerful songs.

Best Sites: mature moist woodlands.

ROCK WREN

Salpinctes obsoletus

This endearing, mysterious bird with dull, cryptic markings can be hard to find in its rocky habitat. It doesn't help that the male Rock Wren expertly bounces his songs off surrounding rocks to maximize their effectiveness. One of western North America's best songsters, he might use up to 100 or more song types. He may perch out in plain sight, profiled against the sky, or frustrate us by singing from a hidden location. • Hidden in cracks and crevices, Rock Wren nests typically have their entrances "paved" with small pebbles, bones, shells and other flat items (up to 1500!). This "welcome mat" may be intended to protect the nest from moisture, make it easier to find in confusing terrain or reduce the risk of marauding ants. • *Salpinctes*, from the Greek word for "trumpeter," refers to this genus's loud calls.

ID: pale "eyebrow"; long, slightly downcurved bill; white-speckled, brownish gray upperparts; light buff belly and flanks; finely gray-streaked, white throat and breast; cinnamon rump; black-barred, white undertail coverts, pale buff tips to tail feathers.
Size: *L* 6 in; *W* 9 in.
Status: common eastern resident from May to mid-August; fairly common to uncommon eastern migrant; uncommon to rare in winter in the Columbia Basin; rare in spring and summer in western Washington.
Habitat: arid or semi-arid rocky areas, including rock outcroppings, rimrock,

canyons, talus slopes, gravel quarries and recent rock-strewn clear-cuts.
Nesting: in a cavity or crevice, with a "paved" entranceway; female incubates 5–6 brown-spotted, white eggs for 14–16 days.
Feeding: gleans from the surface, probes in cracks and crevices (often entering cavities) and flycatches for insects and other arthropods.
Voice: buzzy calls. *Male:* song consists of loud, buzzy, trilled phrases, each repeated 3–6 times: *tra-lee tra-lee tra-lee.*
Similar Species: *Canyon Wren* (p. 281): largely brown-barred, cinnamon rufous; longer bill; white throat; downward cascading song. *House Wren* (p. 283): smaller; shorter bill; plainer, browner upperparts; duskier underparts; bubblier song; prefers woodland edges.
Best Sites: Huntzinger Rd. (Kittitas Co.); Frenchman Coulee (Grant Co.); Yakima R. canyon; Cowiche Canyon (Yakima Co.); Bethel Ridge (off US 12); Sinlahekin Wildlife Area; Little Spokane River Natural Area (Spokane Co.).

CANYON WREN

Catherpes mexicanus

Visitors to western North America's broad, steep-sided, moist canyons have probably heard the song of the male Canyon Wren without catching sight of the bird itself. In fact, most people are surprised to discover that the songster is a small bird. The song, which echoes off the canyon walls, ripples and cascades downward in pitch as if it were recounting the action of tumbling boulders. • You might be lucky enough to spot a Canyon Wren busy squeezing its somewhat flattened body into a nook or crevice in its tireless search for prey. The bird may look like a small rodent until it quickly raises and lowers its tail and hindquarters, which it does every few seconds. • *Catherpes* is the latinized form of the Greek word *katherpein*, meaning "to creep."

ID: gray-streaked "cap"; very long, down-curved bill; brown-barred, cinnamon rufous back, wings, tail and underparts; clean white throat and upper breast.
Size: *L* 5–6 in; *W* 7½ in.
Status: uncommon year-round resident in eastern Washington.
Habitat: rocky canyons and boulder fields with access to moving water or large, year-round wetlands.
Nesting: in a crevice under rocks, on a ledge or on a cave shelf; cup nest of moss, twigs and spider silk is lined with fur and feathers; female incubates 5–6 chestnut-flecked, white eggs for up to 18 days.
Feeding: gleans rocks, exposed ground and vegetation for insects and spiders.

Voice: gives high-pitched, far-carrying calls. *Male:* song is a startling cascade of descending 1- and 2-note whistles: *dee-ah dee-ah dee-ah dah-dah-dah.*
Similar Species: *Rock Wren* (p. 280): shorter bill; brownish gray upperparts; unbarred underparts; lightly streaked throat and breast; buzzy, trilling song. *House Wren* (p. 283): much shorter bill; plainer, browner upperparts; more bubbly song; prefers woodland edges.
Best Sites: Frenchman Coulee (Grant Co.); Yakima R. canyon; Umtanum Creek (Yakima Co.); Cowiche Canyon (Yakima Co.); Moses Coulee (Douglas Co.); Lenore Caves (Grand Coulee, Grant Co.); Chelan Falls Overlook (Chelan Co.); Little Spokane River Natural Area (Spokane Co.).

BEWICK'S WREN
Thryomanes bewickii

The Bewick's Wren investigates all the nooks and crannies of its territory with endless curiosity and exuberant animation. As this charming resident briefly perches to scan its surroundings for food, its long, narrow tail flits and waves from side to side, occasionally flashing with added verve as the bird scolds an approaching intruder. • The songs of Bewick's males in the western U.S. are simpler than those of eastern ones, perhaps because a scattered distribution in the East (resulting from habitat loss) has made mating more competitive than among stabler western populations. Nevertheless, western Bewick's males can still produce a bewildering variety of songs and calls at different times of the year. • The first scientific specimen, collected in Louisiana in 1821, was identified by John James Audubon and named for his friend Thomas Bewick, a talented British wood engraver who wrote and illustrated *History of British Birds*.

ID: white "eyebrow"; downcurved, gray bill; brown or grayish brown upperparts; pale underparts; white throat; dark-barred undertail; long, banded tail.
Size: *L* 5 in; *W* 7 in.
Status: common year-round resident in western Washington; fairly common year-round resident of eastern Washington's river valleys (populations may die back in severe winters).
Habitat: woodland edges, urban woodlots, shrubbery and chaparral; dense riparian maple, cottonwood and ash understory; late-summer dispersal to timberline in the Cascades.

Nesting: in a cavity or structure, such as a brush pile, rock crevice or outbuilding; open cup of fine plant materials is lined with feathers and fine materials; female incubates 3–8 dark-marked, white eggs for 14–16 days.
Feeding: gleans invertebrate eggs, larvae and adults from trees and shrubs, mostly close to the ground.
Voice: extremely variable calls, such as a harsh *dzheer;* alarm call is a *dzeeeb* or *knee-deep. Male:* song is a bold, clear *chick-click, for me-eh, for you.*
Similar Species: *Marsh Wren* (p. 285): stockier; rufous-tinged plumage; white-streaked, black back. *Winter Wren* (p. 284): compact; darker brown; more mottling and barring; smaller bill; smaller tail.
Best Sites: almost any brushy understory area in western Washington; Yakima Area Arboretum; Paterson Unit, Umatilla NWR; W.E. Johnson Park (Richland); Little Spokane River Natural Area (Spokane Co.); Madame Dorion Park (Walla Walla Co.); Rose Creek Preserve (Pullman).

HOUSE WREN

Troglodytes aedon

With their bubbly singing and spirited disposition, House Wrens enhance any neighborhood. All it usually takes to attract these feathered charmers is some shrubby cover, plus a small cavity in a dead tree or a nest box. Sometimes even an empty flowerpot, vacant drainpipe, abandoned vehicle or forlorn shoe will serve as a nest site. • Male House Wrens, like several of their relatives, build a number of "dummy" nests for potential partners to inspect and complete. An offering rejected by one female may become another's "dream home." • In Greek mythology, Zeus transformed Aedon, the Queen of Thebes, into a nightingale. It says much for the appeal of the House Wren's song that an early ornithologist used such a heady comparison.

ID: faint buff "eyebrow" and eye ring; long, downcurved bill with yellow lower mandible; grayish brown upperparts, barred on wings and tail; grayish underparts; whitish throat; brown rump and undertail coverts; pale pink legs and feet.

Size: *L* 4½ in; *W* 6 in.

Status: common late-spring and summer resident in eastern Washington; fairly common local spring and summer resident in western Washington; uncommon spring and fall migrant statewide.

Habitat: semi-open habitats, including lodgepole pine forests, montane conifer parklands, cottonwood and aspen woodlands, oak and oak-fir forests, oak-juniper hillsides and riparian woods; restricted to dry prairies in oak woodlands in western Washington.

Nesting: in a tree cavity, often an old woodpecker hole, a nest box or one of various artificial objects; female completes nest started by male; female incubates 4–8 chestnut-marked, whitish eggs for 12–13 days.

Feeding: more arboreal than other wrens, gleaning small invertebrates from the lower tree canopy, shrubs, low vegetation and the ground.

Voice: call is a harsh, scolding rattle. *Male:* song is a rapid, chattering, unmusical 2–3-second series of notes: *tsi-tsi-tsi oodle-oodle-oodle-oodle.*

Similar Species: *Marsh Wren* (p. 285): strong "eyebrow"; rustier plumage; white-streaked, black back; shorter tail; prefers aquatic vegetation. *Winter Wren* (p. 284): stockier; shorter bill; more mottling and barring; prefers moist woodlands; long, tumbling, warbling song.

Best Sites: Wenas Campground (Yakima Co.); Klickitat Wildlife Area (Klickitat Co.); Manastash Canyon (Kittitas Co.); White River Canyon (Yakima Co.); Fort Casey SP (Whidbey I.); San Juans; Vancouver lowlands.

WINTER WREN

Troglodytes troglodytes

Wrens are tiny, combative bundles of energy, and the males have vocal abilities unmatched by most other songbirds. The loudest singer of his size, the male Winter Wren has one of the most vibrant songs of any species. Long and melodious, the bubbly song stands out both by its length (15–20 seconds) and its sheer exuberance, and none of the many phrases are repeated. His distinctive song makes his presence known, but heavy growth often hides the singer. • The male delivers food to his nesting mate but sleeps apart in an unfinished "dummy" nest built prior to egg laying. • Outside of the breeding season, several Winter Wrens may huddle together in a nest or sheltered crevice, but usually each bird lays claim to its own patch of moist coniferous forest, defending it against other wrens.

ID: pale "eyebrow"; barred, dark brown upperparts (migrants are paler); lighter brown underparts; barred flanks and undertail coverts; short, upraised, barred tail.

Size: *L* 4 in; *W* 5½ in.

Status: common year-round western resident; fairly common eastern resident from spring to early fall, becoming uncommon through late fall and winter.

Habitat: lowland forests, woodlands and thickets; prefers wet forests.

Nesting: in a natural cavity or old woodpecker hole, under bark or in an artificial item; bulky nest consists of twigs, moss, grass and fur; female incubates 5–8 chestnut-flecked, creamy to pinkish eggs for 12–14 days.

Feeding: forages on the ground, around tree trunks and in woodpiles and tangles for invertebrates; also picks aquatic insects and larvae from small pools.

Voice: calls include a sharp *chat-chat* and occasional churring. *Male:* song is an outpouring of rapid trills and twitters, lasting several seconds and repeating.

Similar Species: *House Wren* (p. 283): paler brown overall; longer tail; paler legs; shorter song; prefers drier and more open habitats. *Marsh Wren* (p. 285): more rufous; largely unstreaked; white-streaked, black back; longer tail; rattling song; inhabits aquatic vegetation.

Best Sites: most any western wet coniferous forest; Yellowjacket Creek (Wenas Campground, Yakima Co.); Bateman I. (Kennewick) in winter; L. Wenatchee (Chelan Co.); Silver Falls Campground (Chelan Co.); Sherman Pass Campground (Ferry Co.); Little Spokane Natural Area (Spokane Co.).

MARSH WREN

Cistothorus palustris

The energetic but often reclusive Marsh Wren keeps a low profile by staying hidden in the dense aquatic vegetation of its marsh home. However, the male is one of our most aggressive and noisy songbirds. John J. Audubon dismissed the song as sounding like "the grating of a rusty hinge," but many birders appreciate the reedy, gurgling outpouring of emotion. For other birders, the frustration of being able to hear this vociferous songster, but rarely able to see him, is almost more than they can bear. Although some notes are harsh, competing males may use as many as 200 riffs in their complex songfests to attract mates. • A male will build as many as a dozen nests, and a successful male may mate with several females. Additional nests are often used for a second brood or for roosting, but unsuccessful males—and even females—often destroy the nests of their neighbors.

ID: brown crown; white "eyebrow"; long, down-curved bill with yellow base; white "chin"; rusty brown nape, shoulders and rump; white-striped, black back; banded wings; buff-washed underparts; near-upright, banded tail.

Size: *L* 5 in; *W* 6 in.

Status: common western resident from spring to fall, becoming fairly common from fall to spring; common eastern resident from spring to fall, becoming uncommon by winter.

Habitat: freshwater and brackish marshes; aquatic vegetation bordering ponds, lakes and rivers.

Nesting: in cattails, reeds or sedges; dome-shaped nest of reeds, grass and aquatic plant stems has a side entrance and is lined with fine materials; female incubates 4–5 brown eggs for 14–15 days.

Feeding: forages near the water's surface, on aquatic vegetation, for insects, spiders and snails; hawks for flying insects.

Voice: harsh calls reminiscent of a blackbird's. *Male:* song is a rapid-fire series of *zig* notes and squeaking and rattling notes.

Similar Species: *Bewick's Wren* (p. 282): plain brown back; longer, banded tail; prefers drier habitats; simpler, trilled song. *House Wren* (p. 283): paler; faint "eyebrow"; brown overall; prefers drier habitats; bubbly, warbling song.

Best Sites: most any marshy area in western Washington; Potholes Wildlife Area (Grant Co.); Toppenish NWR; Turnbull NWR.

AMERICAN DIPPER

Cinclus mexicanus

The unusual, wrenlike American Dipper (also known as "Water Ouzel") is often seen standing on an exposed boulder in the middle of a raging torrent performing deep knee-bends before plunging into the frigid water. Below the surface, this songbird may use its wings to dive and maintain its position in the water and its long legs and claws to walk along the streambed of rocks and gravel in search of hidden aquatic insect larvae. Suddenly, it pops back into view, returns to the midstream boulders and emits a series of loud calls or flies to another watery perch. Fitted with scaly nose plugs, strong claws, dense plumage, "eyelids" to protect against water spray and an oil gland to protect its feathers, the American Dipper can survive a lifetime of ice-cold forays. No other songbird has a similar combination of plumage, foraging technique and song.

ID: slate gray overall; brownish head; straight, dark bill; short, wrenlike tail, often raised; long, pale legs.

Size: *L* 7½ in; *W* 11 in.

Status: uncommon year-round statewide resident.

Habitat: fast-flowing, rocky streams and rivers with cascades, riffles and waterfalls.

Nesting: usually on a cliff ledge, behind a waterfall or on a midstream boulder, but possibly in tree roots or a hollow tree stump close to water; domed or ball-like nest, with a side entrance, is made of moss, grass and leaves; female incubates 4–5 white eggs for 13–17 days.

Feeding: forages in streams by walking, swimming and diving for aquatic insects and other invertebrates and their larvae and fish fry and eggs; picks small prey from snow or flycatches for flying insects.

Voice: gives high-pitched, buzzy call notes; loud, clear, repetitive, high whistles most of the year.

Similar Species: *Gray Catbird* (p. 297): leaner; dark "cap"; rusty undertail coverts; long tail; inhabits thickets.

Best Sites: Dungeness River Audubon Center (Sequim); SR 10 at Teanaway R. crossing (Kittitas Co.); US 12 along Tieton R.; Mt. Rainier NP; Little White Salmon Fish Hatchery (Skamania Co.); Klickitat River Canyon (Klickitat Co.).

GOLDEN-CROWNED KINGLET

Regulus satrapa

With a voice beyond the hearing of many people, the tiny Golden-crowned Kinglet often goes unnoticed. What this little jewel of the coniferous forest canopy lacks in size—it is North America's smallest songbird—it more than makes up for in its friendliness and approachability. In winter's mixed foraging flocks, the first bird to be "pished" out of cover is often a kinglet. • The Golden-crowned Kinglet can withstand lower temperatures than the Ruby-crowned Kinglet—it ranges even to coastal Alaska in winter—and it is efficient at finding wintering insect eggs and other small items. Even if some individuals die over winter, the normally large clutches help maintain population sizes. • Quite frequently these diminutive wonders are seen hanging upside down, or hovering, and picking insect eggs from the undersides of leaves.

ID: black-bordered crown; white "eyebrow"; dark eye stripe; white below eye and on throat; tiny bill; grayish olive back; gray-and-yellow wings with blackish bar and white bar; gray-washed underparts. *Male:* orangy crown. *Female:* yellow crown.
Size: *L* 4 in; *W* 7 in.
Status: common year-round resident in the west, northeast and Blue Mts.; uncommon migrant and winter resident in eastern lowlands.
Habitat: *Breeding:* dense subalpine spruce, hemlock and fir forests and localized conifer stands; occasionally in Douglas-fir and riparian woodlands. *In migration* and *winter:* forests, particularly coastal ones, riparian areas and desert oases.

Nesting: in the upper tree canopy, usually well out on a twig; squarish nest of spider silk, cottongrass bristles and thin bark is lined with fine materials; female incubates 8–9 whitish eggs, speckled with brown and gray, for 15 days.
Feeding: gleans foliage and bark for insect adults and eggs, frequently hanging upside down; sometimes hovers; also eats spiders, berries and tree sap.
Voice: very high-pitched *tsee tsee tsee* call. *Male:* song is a faint, high-pitched, accelerating *I...am...not...a...CHEST-nut-backed CHICK-a-dee*.
Similar Species: *Ruby-crowned Kinglet* (p. 288): plain head with white eye ring (male has normally hidden red crest); buffier flanks; harsh calls and powerful song. *Hutton's Vireo* (p. 253): olive brown head and back; pale eye ring; 2 white wing bars.
Best Sites: most woodland habitats.

287

RUBY-CROWNED KINGLET
Regulus calendula

The male Ruby-crowned Kinglet, with a voice second in power-to-weight ratio only to the Winter Wren's, sings a loud, rollicking song that enlivens many a walk past lowland thickets in spring or upper-elevation conifers in summer. Normally quite drab, he adds to the effect by raising his red crest as he sings to impress a prospective mate or chase off a rival. As spring advances, his displays of his red crest become more frequent, and his sudden dashes at rivals become much more persistent. • The female Ruby-crown lays the largest egg clutches of any North American songbird her size. • This tiny, hyperactive woodland sprite continually flicks both tail and wings, a behavior that is enough to distinguish it from the similar Hutton's Vireo and small *Empidonax* flycatchers in roving bands of mixed passerines.

ID: white eye ring; pale lores; tiny bill; olive green upperparts; prominent white wing bar bordered behind by black wing bar; buff olive underparts; dark legs; yellow to orangy feet. *Male:* ruby red crest, usually hidden.
Size: *L* 4 in; *W* 7½ in.
Status: common western lowland resident from winter through spring; fairly common eastern summer resident; uncommon high-elevation summer resident in the western Cascades; uncommon to common migrant and rare winter resident in eastern Washington.
Habitat: *Breeding:* spruce-fir, mountain hemlock, Douglas-fir and lodgepole pine forests. *In migration* and *winter:* forests, streamside willows and suburban backyards.

Nesting: in a tree, protected by overhanging foliage; structure of materials such as moss, spiderwebs, bark pieces, twigs and conifer needles is lined with feathers, fine grass, plant down and fur; female incubates 5–9 lightly brown-speckled, white or buff eggs for 13–14 days.
Feeding: eats small arthropods and berries.
Voice: gives harsh *tit* calls. *Male:* song is a loud, spirited combination of clear notes and whistles, such as *see si seeseesee here-here-here ruby ruby ruby see.*
Similar Species: *Golden-crowned Kinglet* (p. 287): black-bordered, orangy or yellow crown; black-and-white face; grayer underparts. *Hutton's Vireo* (p. 253): plain olive brown face and back; thicker bill; 2 white wing bars. Empidonax *flycatchers* (pp. 240–45): larger; larger bills; longer tails; perch upright; dark toes; simple songs.
Best Sites: woodland habitats.

WESTERN BLUEBIRD
Sialia mexicana

E ach feather's microscopic structure, not pigmentation, creates the blue of the Western Bluebird and most other blue birds. Iridescence produces shiny blues, whereas dull blues result from the same scattering of light that makes the sky blue. • Along with the Mountain Bluebird, the Western Bluebird is a brilliant harbinger of spring. Formerly numerous on western Washington's prairies, the Western is now limited, by habitat modification and competition, mainly to the Fort Lewis prairies. • Pairs of Westerns in Washington usually manage to raise a second clutch of eggs after the first brood leaves the nest. Both parents may maintain another mate to help raise their young. Almost every brood has uncles, aunts, nieces, nephews and cousins on hand to lessen the load.

Habitat: open Douglas-fir and pine forests, wooded riparian areas, oak woodlands, areas with snags; forest edges and farmlands.

Nesting: in a tree cavity, beneath the bark of a pine or riparian hardwood or in a nest box; nest consists of available natural and artificial material; female incubates 5 pale blue eggs for 13–14 days.

Feeding: forages from a perch or from hovering; flycatches and gleans insects in summer; picks small fruits from trees and shrubs; takes seeds from beaches in winter.

Voice: calls are a low, chippy warble, a *chuk* and dry chatter. *Male:* harsh but upbeat *cheer cheerful charmer* song.

Similar Species: *Mountain Bluebird* (p. 290): male is blue overall; female is paler and grayer. *Lazuli Bunting* (p. 339): smaller; male has sturdy bill, white wing bars, whiter underparts and shorter wings.

Best Sites: Swauk Prairie (Kittitas Co.); Umtanum Rd. (Kittitas Co.); Wenas Campground (Yakima Co.); Goldendale–Bickleton (Klickitat Co.); Okanogan Valley; Fort Lewis (permit required).

ID: short, dark bill; dark legs. *Male:* deep blue head and upperparts; deep rusty breast, shoulder patches and flanks; blue-washed, white belly and undertail coverts. *Female:* paler than male; partial whitish eye ring; brownish gray upperparts, pale blue mostly on tail and wings. *Immature:* white spotting on dark gray back, breast and flanks.

Size: *L* 7 in; *W* 13½ in.

Status: fairly common eastern resident from spring through summer and uncommon in early spring and fall; year-round in parts of Yakima Co. and Klickitat Co.; uncommon local western resident from spring through fall; rare to casual winter resident statewide.

289

MOUNTAIN BLUEBIRD
Sialia currucoides

The Mountain Bluebird differs from most thrushes in that it prefers more open terrain, nests in cavities, frequently hovers and eats more insects. • The almost-fluorescent sky blue of the male Mountain Bluebird dazzles on sunny spring mornings. Few birds rival him for good looks, cheerful disposition and boldness—it is not surprising that bluebirds are viewed as the "birds of happiness." • Bluebirds have profited from the clearing of forests, raising of livestock and installation of nest boxes, but they have suffered from the practice of fire suppression and the introduction of European Starlings and other aggressive competitors. • During migration and winter, it is common for flocks of 100 or more Mountain Bluebirds to travel and forage together.

ID: short, dark bill; dark legs. *Male:* sky blue upperparts, slightly paler below; whitish undertail coverts. *Female:* bluish gray head and back; white eye ring; pale "chin"; gray underparts, sometimes pale rufous buff on breast. *Immature:* darker back; white-spotted flanks.

Size: *L* 7 in; *W* 14 in.

Status: fairly common from March through early September in open eastern habitats; fairly common but very localized from March through mid-August in western Washington; uncommon spring and fall migrant in eastern Washington.

Habitat: pine forests. *Breeding:* short-grass prairies with groves of trees, juniper woodlands, burns and clear-cuts, farms and meadow edges. *In migration* and *winter:* junipers, sagebrush and hedgerows.

Nesting: in a natural cavity, stump or artificial shelter, such as a nest box; female selects 1 of several sites where male displays; female incubates 5–6 pale blue eggs for 13 days.

Feeding: pounces from a perch on the ground or above; also flycatches, hovers and hawks; eats mainly insects, especially caterpillars, in summer; takes small fruits and seeds mostly in winter.

Voice: varied calls include a *chik*, a whistled *cheeeer* and a *turf*. *Male:* song is a series of low, churring whistles, less mellow than for other bluebirds.

Similar Species: *Western Bluebird* (p. 289): rusty breast; male is deeper blue; female's back is usually buffier; immature's spotting includes back.

Best Sites: Hidden Valley Rd. (Kittitas Co.); Umtanum Rd. (Kittitas Co.); Wenas Campground (Yakima Co.); Goldendale–Bickleton (Klickitat Co.); Okanogan Valley; Old Vantage Hwy. (Kittitas Co.); Sunrise (Mt. Rainier NP).

TOWNSEND'S SOLITAIRE

Myadestes townsendi

Few birds characterize our upper-elevation mountain forests better than Townsend's Solitaires. Slim and elegant but generally inconspicuous, these thrushes will drop to the ground to snatch food in the manner of bluebirds. They nest in open coniferous forests within the zone of winter snows, where undergrowth is sparse and the ground lies exposed. During the colder months, Townsend's Solitaires move southward and to lower elevations, defending feeding territories among junipers and mistletoe-bearing trees. They are often found with Mountain Bluebirds in open areas in eastern Washington. • Generally quiet, the male may suddenly burst into a bout of sustained song.
• The Townsend's Solitaire was named for John Kirk Townsend. He found the first specimen, in Oregon's Willamette Valley, in 1835.

ID: warm gray overall; bold white eye ring; peach-colored wing patches; shortish, dark bill; dark legs; broad, triangular, white-edged, dark gray tail. *In flight:* buff stripe on dark wing.

Size: *L* 8 in; *W* 14½ in.

Status: fairly common resident in eastern Washington from late spring to early fall and uncommon the rest of the year; uncommon from spring through summer in western Washington; uncommon in winter in the Dungeness area and the San Juans.

Habitat: *Breeding:* high-elevation conifers, clear-cuts, burns and open forests. *In migration* and *winter:* juniper forests; interior foothills and valleys; riparian woodlands; suburban areas.

Nesting: in a concealed hollow on the ground or in a cavity in dead wood; nest of twigs and pine needles is lined with plant materials; female incubates 3–4 gray-blotched, brown-dotted, pale eggs for 11–14 days; pair feeds young by regurgitation.

Feeding: forages at lower levels for insects and spiders—caught in midair or picked off trunks—or on the ground; eats berries and female juniper cones, mostly in winter.

Voice: whistled calls. *Male:* often long (10–30 seconds) and rambling song is a mixture of whistled and mumbled notes.

Similar Species: *Northern Mockingbird* (p. 365): rare in Washington; slightly larger; paler underparts; longer, often upraised tail; bold white wing patches in flight; inhabits lowlands.

Best Sites: Hurricane Ridge (Olympic NP); Rainy Pass (SR 20); Blewett Pass (Chelan Co.); Wenas Campground (Yakima Co.); Paradise and Sunrise (Mt. Rainier NP); Sinlahekin Valley. *Winter:* Lower Crab Creek Rd. (Grant Co.); Bassett Park (Washtucna, Adams Co.).

291

VEERY

Catharus fuscescens

Like a musical waterfall, the male Veery's voice descends through thick undergrowth in liquid ripples. Even more reclusive than other *Catharus* thrushes, the Veery is the one that spends the most time on the ground—it nests and forages among tangled vegetation and gets around in short, springy hops. Its reddish plumage distinguishes it from Washington's other thrushes, except some Swainson's Thrushes. • The Veery was first described by Alexander Wilson in 1831 as "Wilson's Thrush" or "Tawny Thrush"; its present name is an interpretation of the male's song. *Catharus* is a latinized version of the Greek *katharos*, which means "pure," referring to the songs of the thrush family, and *fuscescens* means "dusky."

ID: streaked "cheek"; thin, buff eye ring; straight, pale bill; reddish brown upperparts; white underparts; buff, lightly brown-spotted breast; gray flanks; pale throat.

Size: *L* 7 in; *W* 12 in.

Status: fairly common summer resident and uncommon late-summer migrant in eastern Washington; rare midsummer visitor to western Washington.

Habitat: moist woodlands with hardwood trees and shrubs next to watercourses.

Nesting: on or near the ground, in a bush or small tree; nest of dead leaves, bark, weed stems and moist leaf mold is lined with rootlets and fibers; female incubates 4–5 bluish green eggs for 10–14 days.

Feeding: insects and fruit eaten in summer are mostly taken on the ground, but insects are sometimes gleaned from foliage or taken in short flycatching sallies.

Voice: call is a high, whistled *feeyou*. *Male:* song is a fluty, descending series of whistled notes: *da-vee-ur, vee-ur, vee-ur, veer, veer, veer.*

Similar Species: *Swainson's Thrush* (p. 293): pale "spectacles"; red-tinged, olive brown upperparts and flanks; rising, flutelike song. *Hermit Thrush* (p. 294): rufous tints are limited to tail, back and wings; darker breast spotting; flutelike song has ascending and descending phrases.

Best Sites: Cle Elum R. (at Bullfrog Rd., Kittitas Co.); SR 10 at Teanaway R. (Kittitas Co.); Wenas Creek and Wenas Campground (Yakima Co.); Oak Creek Rd. (off US 12; Yakima Co.); Conners L. (Sinlahekin Valley); South Fork Coppei Creek Rd. (Walla Walla Co.).

SWAINSON'S THRUSH

Catharus ustulatus

The word "ethereal," often applied to thrush songs, is particularly appropriate for the Swainson's Thrush. Frequently seen in silhouette against the colorful sunset sky, perching atop the tallest tree in his territory, the male Swainson's is one of the last forest songsters to be silenced by nightfall. Continuing well into spring evenings, his phrases rise ever higher and then disappear, as if he has run out of air or inspiration. • Migrating Swainson's Thrushes, preferring the understory, skulk about the ground under low shrubs and tangles, occasionally visiting backyards and neighborhood parks. Ever alert to potential danger, they often vanish after giving a sharp warning call. • The "Olive-backed Thrush" *(C.u. swainsoni)* prefers eastern Washington, whereas the "Russet-backed Thrush" *(C.u. ustulatus)* favors the west. • The Swainson's Thrush was named for 19th-century English zoologist and illustrator William Swainson.

ID: pale "spectacles"; streaked "cheek"; straight bill; olive brown ("Olive-backed") to reddish brown ("Russet-backed") upperparts and flanks; pale gray underparts; brown-spotted breast; pale, brown-bordered throat; pale orangy pink legs.

Size: *L* 7 in; *W* 12 in.

Status: common summer lowland resident; fairly common to uncommon migrant, arriving in early May in the west and late May in the east; "fall" migration is from mid-August to late September.

Habitat: *Breeding:* coniferous and mixed forests with dense undergrowth, riparian thickets and aspen woodlands. *In migration:* low-elevation woodlands or thickets, including moist and riparian woodlands, canyon bottoms and city parks.

Nesting: in the understory, usually in a fork of a hardwood shrub or conifer sapling; outer layer of plant materials is lined with fine materials; female incubates 4 brown-speckled, greenish blue eggs for 10–14 days.

Feeding: gleans vegetation and forages on the ground for invertebrates, including spiders; eats berries and other small fruits.

Voice: gives a single, sharp *whit* but also issues generic harsh calls. *Male:* flutelike song, heard mostly at dusk or dawn, spirals upward and ends quickly.

Similar Species: *Veery* (p. 292): redder overall; indistinct eye ring; white belly; gray flanks; descending song. *Hermit Thrush* (p. 294): rufous tints only on tail, back and wings; ascending and descending song phrases.

Best Sites: *Summer:* widespread in mid-level conifers and mixed woods. *In migration:* residential areas and urban parks.

HERMIT THRUSH

Catharus guttatus

True to its name, the generally very quiet and unobtrusive Hermit Thrush spends much of its time hidden in the lower branches of the undergrowth or on the forest floor. If seen, it is most likely to be perched close to the ground, quickly raising and slowly lowering its tail, or flitting off to cover. This apparent shyness vanishes in spring and early summer, when the male Hermit Thrush takes up a prominent perch and sings his beautiful, flute-like song in the choruses of dawn and dusk (and on cloudy days). Many observers consider this song to be the most beautiful of any North American bird song. • Like many *Catharus* thrushes, the Hermit Thrush shows noticeable regional differences in plumage and size. Coastal birds are smaller and darker, whereas interior mountain birds are larger, paler, grayer and more heavily spotted.

ID: thin, white eye ring; streaked "cheek"; pale, dark-tipped bill; brown to grayish upperparts, reddish on wings and tail; heavily dark-spotted breast; faintly spotted, white underparts; grayish brown flanks; pale pink legs.

Size: *L* 6–7 in; *W* 11–12 in.

Status: common resident from spring through summer and fairly common migrant; uncommon western lowland resident in winter; rare winter resident in mild parts of eastern Washington.

Habitat: *Breeding:* mountain coniferous forests, bogs and watercourses. *In migration* and *winter:* coniferous and hardwood woodlands with dense undergrowth; forest edges; towns and ranches with berry-bearing trees and bushes.

Nesting: on a conifer branch or in a snag or tree roots; bulky nest consists of grass, leaves and hair; female incubates 3–4 light blue eggs for 11–13 days.

Feeding: forages on the ground or gleans vegetation; eats mostly insects, earthworms and spiders but also small salamanders; small fruits are important in winter.

Voice: gives a low *chup* or fluty *treeee*. *Male:* sings a series of ethereal, flutelike notes, some rising and others falling, in no set order.

Similar Species: *Swainson's Thrush* (p. 293): bold "spectacles"; buff-washed lower "cheek" and breast; tail colored like back; ascending song. *Veery* (p. 292): indistinct eye ring; generally reddish brown; white belly; gray flanks; descending song.

Best Sites: *Summer:* high-elevation forests. *Winter:* western lowland forests and dense urban parks.

AMERICAN ROBIN

Turdus migratorius

The well-loved American Robin, the most widespread and commonest North American thrush, is one of the easiest birds to recognize. It is well known for seeking worms in gardens and grassy areas, yet it occurs in more habitats and has a more varied diet than most Washington songbirds. • Many American Robins form flocks, move to lower elevations and seek berries over winter. Check these flocks, which attract waxwings, starlings and other thrushes, for any rare species caught up in the crowd. Winter also often brings flocks of darker, more colorful American Robins from farther north in Canada. • A hunting American Robin that appears to be listening for prey is actually looking for movements in the soil—with its eyes on the sides of its head, a robin must tilt its head sideways to look down.

ID: *Male:* blackish head and white-streaked throat; broken white eye ring; yellow bill; gray upperparts and tail; reddish orange underparts; white undertail coverts; dark legs. *Female:* generally paler than male; whiter throat; white-mottled, rusty underparts. *Immature:* buff-spotted upperparts; dark-spotted breast.
Size: *L* 10 in; *W* 17 in.
Status: common year-round statewide resident and migrant; numbers may be larger in fall and winter.
Habitat: *Breeding:* hardwood and coniferous forests, including juniper forests, farmlands, chaparral, riparian oases and residential areas. *In migration:* open grassy areas. *Winter:* sites with berries, especially juniper forests.

Nesting: in a tree or shrub, possibly in a building or on a ledge; twig-and-grass platform has an inner cup of mud and grass with moss and shredded bark; female incubates 4 pale blue eggs for 12–14 days.
Feeding: forages on the ground and among vegetation for insects, earthworms, snails and other small invertebrates; eats small fruits in fall and winter.
Voice: typical thrush calls and unique ones, such as a rapid, clucking *tut-tut-tut. Male:* sings a series of low whistles with long pauses and repeated or alternated phrases, such as *cheerily cheer-up cheer-up cheerio.*
Similar Species: *Varied Thrush* (p. 296): orangy eyebrow, breast, sides (gray "scales"), throat and wing stripes; black to gray breast band. Catharus *thrushes* (pp. 292–94): smaller; dark-spotted, pale breasts; buff underwing bars.
Best Sites: found in almost all habitats statewide. *Spring:* residential lawns. *Winter:* berry bushes.

VARIED THRUSH

Ixoreus naevius

Amidst migrant and wintering American Robins in urban parks and gardens, the Varied Thrush rarely gets a second glance, yet this bird is among the most attractive of North America's many thrushes. • The whistling tones of the male's long, drawn-out song easily penetrate the dense vegetation and drifting mist enshrouding his forest habitat, with each tone at a different pitch and seeming to come from a different location. When finally revealed, the songster shows a plumage pattern unmatched by any other North American bird. • Heavy snowstorms often drive the Varied Thrush into the lowlands in abundance. Although it does well in cold, humid conditions, severely cold spring storms can dampen its plumage and kill it just before summer's warm days and abundant food arrive.

ID: dark eyes; dark bill; white belly and undertail coverts; pinkish orange legs. *Male:* dark head; orange "eyebrow" and throat; dark gray upperparts; orange wing bars; orange belly and upper breast; black breast band; "scaly" gray flanks. *Female:* paler than male, especially on head and breast band. *Immature:* gray-blotched breast.

Size: *L* 9 in; *W* 16 in.

Status: common year-round western resident; fairly common summer resident in the east and otherwise uncommon.

Habitat: *Breeding:* dense mountain and foothill coniferous forests, especially old-growth; damp coastal hemlock, redcedar and spruce forests. *In migration* and *winter:* Douglas-fir forests, riparian woodlands, juniper forests, madrone stands, lowland suburbs and orchards.

Nesting: near the trunk or branch tip of a conifer; loose, open cup of twigs, bark, leaves and lichen is filled with rotten wood and lined with grass, leaves and moss; female incubates 3–4 light blue eggs for 12–13 days.

Feeding: forages on the ground and gleans vegetation for small invertebrates; eats fruits, seeds and acorns in winter.

Voice: *chup* call. *Male:* unique song is a series of whistles of different pitches, often about 10 seconds apart.

Similar Species: *American Robin* (p. 295): orangy-lined, plain gray wings; plain breast; immature is more heavily spotted, with no peach on wings or head.

Best Sites: Hoh River Valley (Olympic NP); Hurricane Ridge–Heart O' the Hills (Olympic NP); Rockport SP (Skagit Co.); Snoqualmie Pass (I-90); Mt. Rainier NP; Baldy Pass–FR 37 (Okanogan Co.); Mt. Spokane SP.

GRAY CATBIRD
Dumetella carolinensis

Sometimes revealed only by its mewing call, the Gray Catbird prefers to remain concealed in shrubbery. The male does come out in the open, however, to perform a most unusual "mooning" courtship display: he raises his long, slender tail to show off his bright rusty undertail coverts. • As with other members of the mimic thrush family, the male Gray Catbird can counter-sing by using each side of his syrinx separately. • The Gray Catbird vigorously defends its nesting territory, often to the benefit of neighboring warblers, towhees and sparrows. Although this species is one of the few that can distinguish cowbird eggs from its own, confused individuals have been seen expelling their own eggs in error. • *Dumetella*, Latin for "small thicket," reflects the Gray Catbird's favorite habitat.

ID: medium gray overall, with darker "cap" and tail; dark eyes; thin, straight bill; extensively rusty undertail coverts; dark legs.

Size: *L* 8 in; *W* 11 in.

Status: fairly common summer resident in eastern Washington, becoming an uncommon migrant in late May and from late August to early September.

Habitat: *Breeding:* hardwood growth along watercourses, forest edges and clearings, roadsides, dense shrubbery and vine tangles; rarely found in suburban areas. *In migration:* tangles and thickets, even in residential areas.

Nesting: in a shrub, sapling, small tree or vine; bulky open cup, usually in 3 layers, with a lining of rootlets and tendrils; female incubates 3–4 turquoise green eggs for 12–14 days.

Feeding: forages on the ground and in vegetation, largely for insects and spiders; also eats berries; sometimes visits feeders.

Voice: usual call is catlike. *Male:* song, sung at a slow, uneven pace, is an unstructured babble of whistles, chattering notes, squeaks and limited mimicry.

Similar Species: *Townsend's Solitaire* (p. 291): large eyes; white eye ring; shorter bill; buff wing bars; gray undertail coverts; prefers mountain areas in summer.

Best Sites: major river valleys of north-central and northeastern Washington, including the Okanogan, Sanpoil, Kettle, and Pend Oreille; SR 10 at Teanaway R., Robinson Canyon and Manastash Canyon (all Kittitas Co.); South Fork, Coppei Creek (Walla Walla Co.).

SAGE THRASHER

Oreoscoptes montanus

The Sage Thrasher, which depends heavily on the open sagebrush flats east of the Cascades, is the smallest and plainest of the thrashers. However, the male redeems himself by performing both a melodious song that can last several minutes and an exaggerated, undulating courtship flight. Because of these two attributes, this species is considered a closer relative to mockingbirds than to other thrashers—it was even originally named "Mountain Mockingbird." Other mockingbird-like mannerisms include slowly raising and lowering its tail while perched and holding its tail high while running along the ground. • *Oreoscoptes* is Greek for "mimic of the mountains," a misnomer for this bird that is usually not found in mountainous habitat.

ID: yellowish eyes; short, slim, straight bill; pale grayish brown upperparts; 2 thin white wing bars; brown-streaked, buffyish underparts; dark legs; plumage fades by late summer.

Size: *L* 8 in; *W* 12 in.

Status: fairly common eastern resident from spring through early summer and uncommon migrant in early spring and late summer.

Habitat: *Breeding:* sagebrush, low greasewood flats and dry areas with scattered junipers. *In migration* and *winter:* dry open-country areas, especially with scrub or sagebrush; grassland with scattered bushes; open pine-juniper woodlands.

Nesting: in sagebrush, occasionally in a juniper or on the ground; bulky structure of coarse twigs is lined with grass, rootlets and fur; pair incubates 3–5 boldly spotted, rich blue eggs for 11–13 days.

Feeding: gleans sagebrush for insects and spiders; also eats berries and other fruits, especially in winter.

Voice: low *tup* call. *Male:* song, often nocturnal, is a sustained, complex, mellow warble with repeated phrases and little change in pace or pitch.

Similar Species: *Northern Mockingbird* (p. 365): plainer underparts; blackish eye line; large white wing patches in flight; longer, darker, white-edged tail. *Swainson's Thrush* (p. 293) and *Hermit Thrush* (p. 294): stockier; dark eyes; browner upperparts; spotted breasts; unmarked bellies; pinkish legs; prefer forest habitats.

Best Sites: Quilomene Wildlife Area (Kittitas Co.); Ryegrass Summit (I-90); Umtanum Rd. above Ellensburg (Kittitas Co.); Rattlesnake Mt. (Benton Co.); Columbia NWR; County Rd. H SE (Grant Co.); Beezley Hills Preserve (north of Quincy); Swanson Lakes Wildlife Area (Lincoln Co.).

EUROPEAN STARLING

Sturnus vulgaris

European Starlings were released into New York's Central Park in 1890 and 1891 as part of the local Shakespeare society's misguided plan to introduce all the birds mentioned in the author's works. Starlings quickly spread across North America. In spite of their attractive, iridescent plumage, their ability to mimic almost any other bird and their appetite for insects and other pests, many ornithologists dislike European Starlings because they have outcompeted many native birds for cavity nest sites. Their success is largely a result of their association with urban areas (buildings and other structures provide them with plenty of nesting and roosting habitats), their flocking tendency (which reduces the chance of predation) and a unique bill-muscle structure (which helps detect and expose hidden prey).

breeding

ID: generally shiny black; dark eyes; straight, pointed bill; orangy edges to wing feathers; blunt tail; orangy pink legs. *Breeding:* glossy purple head, neck and breast; bright yellow bill; greenish back; pinkish buff spots on upperparts and undertail coverts. *Nonbreeding:* finely white-streaked head; black bill; white-spotted back and underparts. *Immature:* drab gray-brown all over; buff edges to wing feathers.

Size: *L* 8 in; *W* 16 in.

Status: common year-round resident statewide.

Habitat: favors urban areas, farmlands and open forests up to 7000 ft.

Nesting: in a cavity or crevice; messy nest of grass, twigs and straw; female incubates 4–6 brown-marked, bluish or greenish white eggs for 12–14 days; raises 2–3 broods per year.

Feeding: omnivorous and opportunistic; searches the ground and gleans foliage for insects, berries, seeds and human scraps; flycatches for flying termites and ants; picks off small invertebrates behind farm machinery; scavenges from garbage.

Voice: common call is harsh chatter; flight call is typically buzzy. *Male:* sings a mixture of mellow whistles, squeaks and mimicked sounds of other birds.

Similar Species: *Brewer's Blackbird* (p. 345): male has purplish iridescence on head and breast, yellow eyes, stouter, black bill, unmarked, shiny greenish black plumage, rounded wings, longer tail and black legs; usually in looser flocks. *Brown-headed Cowbird* (p. 346): smaller; often-greenish, shiny black male has brown head, sturdier bill and more rounded wings.

Best Sites: almost anywhere except dense forests and mountaintops.

AMERICAN PIPIT

Anthus rubescens

Here in Washington, American Pipits breed only in open, treeless, alpine environments. Many birds are already paired when they reach the breeding territories, having gone through the preliminaries of courtship and pair formation at lower elevations. • In fall migration, flocks of American Pipits carpet open areas, especially short grasslands, barren fields, park lawns and lowland shorelines. Pipits can often be seen with flocks of shorebirds on salt marshes and grasslands. Their plain wardrobe and habit of continuously bobbing their white-sided tails make American Pipits instantly recognizable. They forage by walking with an upright posture, rather than hopping or bent over. Tail-wagging, a common feature of the Northern Hemisphere pipits and wagtails, may help to stir up hidden prey.

ID: pale "eyebrow"; large, dark eyes; white eye ring; grayish "ear" patch; weakly streaked grayish brown upperparts. *Dark morph:* pale buff lower face and underparts, strongly dark-streaked, particularly on breast, with breeding bird showing white areas and darker streaking. *Light morph:* buff parts are cinnamon-tinged, unmarked (with smaller "ear" patch) in breeding plumage and lightly streaked otherwise.

Size: *L* 6–7 in; *W* 10½ in.

Status: common lowland migrant from April to May and from September to October; fairly common high-elevation summer resident in the Cascades and Olympics; uncommon in winter in the western lowlands.

Habitat: *Breeding:* open, windswept alpine meadows and slopes. *In migration* and *winter:* shorelines and other areas with low or no vegetation.

Nesting: concealed in grass, a bank or a burrow; base of dried grass and sedges is lined with finer grass and hair; female incubates 3–7 brown-spotted, pale eggs for 14–15 days.

Feeding: forages on the ground and pecks or gleans land and aquatic invertebrates in summer; eats plant seeds in fall and winter.

Voice: high, thin calls, often repeated. *Male:* high, repeated *tiwee* courtship song.

Similar Species: *Sparrows* (pp. 320–34, 365–66): stouter bills; shorter legs; plainer tail coloration. *Lapland Longspur* (p. 336): female and nonbreeding male have pinkish, conical bills, rusty necks, back and wing bars, darkish breast bands and shorter legs. *Sage Thrasher* (p. 298): larger; yellowish eyes; tail often upraised; prefers sagebrush.

Best Sites: *Summer:* Hurricane Ridge (Olympic NP); Paradise and Sunrise (Mt. Rainier NP); Harts Pass (Okanogan Co.). *In migration* and *winter:* Damon Pt. (Ocean Shores); Othello area.

BOHEMIAN WAXWING
Bombycilla garrulus

A flock of waxwings swarming over a suburban neighborhood is guaranteed to dispel even the most severe winter blues. Faint, quavering whistles announce an approaching flock, which may swoop down to perch and then take turns stripping berries from mountain-ashes, junipers and other trees and bushes. • Bohemian Waxwings normally breed in Canada and Alaska. In winter, they appear in eastern Washington suburbs, orchards and other places where fruit remains on trees. Somewhat larger than any Cedar Waxwings among them, these birds usually arrive just in time to be tallied in reasonable numbers on Christmas bird counts and depart for their boreal homes before most songbirds arrive back in Washington. • Waxwings get their name from the "waxy" red spots on their secondary feathers. Actually enlargements of the feather shafts, these spots get their color from the berries the birds eat. • This nomadic avian wanderer is named for Bohemia, once considered the ancestral home of the Gypsies.

ID: prominent rear-pointing, brown crest; reddish forehead and "cheek"; black "mask" with white line below; short, gray bill; grayish brown upperparts and breast; darker wing tip with yellow stripe, "waxy" red spot and 2 white areas; black throat; rufous undertail coverts; grayish rump; grayish tail with black band and yellow tip.
Size: *L* 8 in; *W* 14½ in.
Status: fairly common visitor to eastern Washington from winter to very early spring and uncommon as a late-November migrant; often irruptive.

Habitat: open or juniper woodlands; townsites, cities and suburbs with berry-bearing trees and shrubs.
Nesting: not known to nest in Washington.
Feeding: forages in flocks; eats mostly berries, other fruits and some tree seeds in winter; gleans vegetation or catches flying insects on the wing.
Voice: usual call is a series of high notes.
Similar Species: *Cedar Waxwing* (p. 302): smaller; tawnier; only a red spot on wing tip; yellowish belly; white undertail coverts; slightly higher call notes.
Best Sites: Cle Elum; Ellensburg; Wanapum SP (Kittitas Co.); Bridgeport; Grand Coulee–Electric City–Coulee Dam; Methow Valley (Okanogan Co.); Okanogan River Valley.

301

CEDAR WAXWING

Bombycilla cedrorum

Cedar Waxwings, unlike the larger, winter-only Bohemian Waxwings, inhabit Washington year-round. In cold winters, most breeding birds migrate southward, but, if food is plentiful in warm winters, they will remain to join flocks of other Cedar Waxwings and Bohemian Waxwings from boreal breeding locations. Flocks show little site loyalty. • Waxwings gorge themselves on fruit left hanging on tree and shrub branches in fall and winter, occasionally eating themselves to flightless intoxication on fermented fruit. In summer, Cedar Waxwings add insects to their diet, capturing them by gleaning or by flycatching near streams and ponds. • Cedar Waxwings nest later than most songbirds, timing their arrival for when the first fruits appear.

ID: prominent rear-pointing, brown crest; black "mask" with white border; short, gray bill; tawny brown upperparts and breast; wing is grayer and darker toward tip and has "waxy" red spot; black throat; white undertail coverts; grayish rump; grayish tail with black band and yellow tip.

Size: *L* 7 in; *W* 12 in.

Status: common western resident in late spring and summer; fairly common migrant in the west and uncommon in winter; common in eastern Washington from late spring to late summer and uncommon the rest of the year at lower elevations.

Habitat: *Breeding:* hardwood and mixed forests, woodland edges, fruit orchards, young pine plantations and riparian hardwoods among conifers. *In migration* and *winter:* open woodlands and brush, often near water; desert watercourses and oases; residential areas; any habitat with nearby berries.

Nesting: in a fork of a branch or trunk, in a vine or on a branch; bulky, open cup nest is lined with fine plant materials, spider silk and hair; female incubates 3–5 sparsely dark-spotted, very pale blue eggs for 11–13 days.

Feeding: forages in branches of fruit trees and shrubs for fruits, flowers and insects; sallies from high, exposed branches near fresh water; gleans bark for insects.

Voice: high-pitched purrs and trills that intensify in large flocks; simple song is similar.

Similar Species: *Bohemian Waxwing* (p. 301): larger; grayer overall; reddish face; gray belly; rufous undertail coverts; white areas and yellow stripe on wing.

Best Sites: woodlands, trees with berries and blackberry brambles.

ORANGE-CROWNED WARBLER

Vermivora celata

Unlike many birds, the Orange-crowned Warbler is best identified by its lack of field marks—no wing bars, no flashing rump, no visible color patch, not even a memorable song. Its plain appearance is all the more surprising considering that most of the 109 New World wood-warblers, of which 56 species occur north of Mexico, boast at least one of those features, even in their confusing fall plumages. • Some fall migrants of the boreal-nesting "Taiga" race—with grayish olive on the back, gray on the head and yellow confined to the undertail coverts—can easily be confused with Nashville Warblers or casual Tennessee Warblers. • *Vermivora* is Latin for "worm-eating," and *celata*, derived from the Latin word for "hidden," refers to the male's crown patch.

ID: olive green to dull yellow overall; faint yellow "eyebrow"; broken yellow eye ring; faint dark eye line; faintly greenish-streaked underparts; yellow undertail coverts; dusky legs. *Male:* orange crown patch (usually hidden).
Size: *L* 5 in; *W* 7½ in.
Status: common western summer resident and fairly common migrant; fairly common eastern resident from late spring through September and uncommon migrant in late April and early October.
Habitat: *Breeding:* brush, understories of dense forests, chaparral, oak woodlands and aspen, willow and mountain mahogany stands. *In migration* and *winter:* hardwood and brushy habitats, especially berry-bearing thickets.

Nesting: on the ground or low in a shrub; well-hidden nest of coarse grass and bark strips is lined with finer materials; female incubates 4–5 russet-marked, white eggs for 12–14 days.
Feeding: gleans foliage for invertebrates and berries; feeds on flower nectar; visits sapsucker "wells" and hummingbird feeders.
Voice: high-pitched, chippy calls. *Male:* faint trill song rises slightly, then breaks downward at midpoint.
Similar Species: *Nashville Warbler* (p. 304): grayer head; prominent white eye ring; greener back and wings; yellower below. *Yellow Warbler* (p. 305): female has brighter yellow head and underparts, larger eyes and complete eye ring.
Best Sites: Hoh Rain Forest (Olympic NP); Cape Disappointment (Columbia R. mouth); Dungeness River Audubon Center (Sequim); Discovery Park (Seattle); Marymoor Park (Redmond); Fort Ebey SP (Whidbey I.); Sherman Pass (Ferry Co.); Field Springs SP (Asotin Co.).

NASHVILLE WARBLER

Vermivora ruficapilla

The male Nashville Warbler has plenty to sing about: his plumage is a bright mixture of green, yellow and bluish gray, with splashes of rufous and white thrown in for good measure. Fortunately for beginning birdwatchers, this species retains the same plumage from juvenile to adult, although only the breeding male has the crown patch reminiscent of a kinglet's. • Compared to most other warblers, Nashville Warblers are partial to drier, more open woodlands and brush. Quite conspicuous in summer, in migration they are much more retiring and can easily slip by unnoticed. • The Nashville Warbler—like the Tennessee, Cape May and Connecticut warblers—bears a name that reflects where it was first collected in migration and not its breeding or wintering range. • *Ruficapilla* refers to the hidden red crown patch of the male.

August to September; uncommon western resident from spring through summer.

Habitat: *Breeding:* dry, brushy areas and foothills; high-elevation brushy wetlands. *In migration:* lowland habitats.

Nesting: on the ground; well-hidden nest of coarse materials and moss is lined with fur and fine materials; female incubates 4–5 white eggs wreathed in reddish brown for 11–12 days.

Feeding: gleans foliage for insects, such as caterpillars, flies and aphids; occasionally hover-gleans or feeds on the ground.

Voice: usual call is a rather sharp *twit*. *Male:* song is a 2-part descending trill.

Similar Species: *MacGillivray's Warbler* (p. 313): larger; gray "hood" extends to upper breast; broken white eye ring; pink bill; pink legs; longer tail. *Wilson's Warbler* (p. 315): yellow head; black or olive "cap."

Best Sites: eastern slopes of Mt. Adams (Yakima Co.); Swauk Campground (FR 7320 Kittitas Co.); Reecer Creek Rd. (near Ellensburg); Wenas Campground (Yakima Co.); Harts Pass (Okanogan Co.).

ID: thin, dark bill; dusky legs. *Male:* bluish gray head; rufous crown patch (often hidden); prominent white eye ring; plain, olive green back; brownish green wings and tail; yellowish green rump; yellow throat and underparts. *Female:* paler head; gray crown; whitish throat and lower belly.

Size: *L* 4 in; *W* 7½ in.

Status: fairly common breeding resident on the eastern slopes of the Cascades and in the northeast in late spring and summer; uncommon eastern migrant in mid-April and from

YELLOW WARBLER

Dendroica petechia

Active and inquisitive, flitting from branch to branch in search of plant-eating insects, this small warbler is the home gardener's perfect houseguest. With golden plumage and a cheerful song, it is easy to see why the Yellow Warbler is a welcome addition to any neighborhood. • The Yellow Warbler is also popular with the Brown-headed Cowbird, which deposits an egg or two of its own into this warbler's nest. Unlike most forest songbirds, the Yellow Warbler recognizes the foreign eggs and either abandons the nest or builds over the clutch. Some persistent pairs build over and over, creating bizarre, multilayered high-rise nests. Despite this vigilance, the Yellow Warbler is in decline, with the trend toward exotic ornamental plants and undergrowth removal in residential areas also being responsible.

ID: large, black eyes; small, black bill. *Male:* yellowish green crown, "cheek," nape, back and rump; bright yellow underparts; reddish streaks on breast and sides. *Female:* drabber; smudgy olive streaks on breast and flanks; white-edged inner flight feathers.

Size: *L* 5 in; *W* 7½ in.

Status: common breeding resident in late spring and summer; fairly common western migrant in May and from August to mid-September; fairly common eastern migrant in late May and from early to mid-August.

Habitat: *Breeding:* riparian willows, cottonwoods and hardwood thickets; aspen groves; shade trees in residential areas. *In migration:* second-growth or shrubby habitats, including urban ones.

Nesting: in a fork of a hardwood tree or small shrub; female builds a neat, compact nest of weed stalks, shredded bark and lichen and lines it with plant down, spider silk and other fine materials; female incubates 4–5 variably marked, off-white eggs for 11–12 days.

Feeding: gleans foliage, bark and vegetation for invertebrates, especially caterpillars and cankerworms, beetles and aphids; also hawks and hover-gleans for insects.

Voice: lackluster chipping call, sometimes repeated. *Male:* song is a fast, repeated *sweet-sweet-sweet summer sweet.*

Similar Species: *Wilson's Warbler* (p. 315): dark crown; smaller bill; greener upperparts; plain yellow underparts; chipping, trilled song. *Orange-crowned Warbler* (p. 303): olive green to dull yellow overall; faintly streaked underparts; dry, dull, trilling song.

Best Sites: widespread in riparian and other wetland edge habitats with willows and hardwood trees.

YELLOW-RUMPED WARBLER

Dendroica coronata

The Yellow-rumped Warbler is North America's most abundant and widespread warbler. Even though it is a common sight for most birdwatchers, its energetic behavior and the male's attractive breeding plumage make it welcome at all times, especially during the cold, sometimes misty days of fall and early winter. • Other warblers also seem to appreciate the Yellow-rump's company and its alertness, and they tag along with it in fast-moving foraging flocks. • Although all breeding Yellow-rumps in Washington are of the western "Audubon's Warbler" race, migrants and wintering birds are equally likely to be of the more widespread "Myrtle Warbler" race, which commonly migrates down the Pacific Coast from breeding sites in northwestern Canada and Alaska.

breeding

"Audubon's Warbler"

ID: 2 white wing bars, merging in "Audubon's"; yellow rump and side patch. *Breeding male:* yellow crown patch; blackish "mask" and white "eyebrow" (boldest on "Myrtle"); heavily streaked, gray back; black breast; white underparts; black-streaked flanks; yellow ("Audubon's") or white ("Myrtle") throat; gray tail. *Breeding female:* like male but drabber, with more streaking below; all-gray crown.
Size: *L* 5½ in; *W* 9–9½ in.
Status: *"Audubon's":* common statewide resident from spring to fall. *"Myrtle":* uncommon statewide migrant and winter resident, albeit less numerous in the east.
Habitat: *Breeding:* any coniferous or mixed forests. *In migration* and *winter:* hardwood and mixed thickets and woodlands along the coast and in interior valleys.
Nesting: in a conifer; female constructs a compact nest of shredded bark, weed stalks, twigs and rootlets and lines it with fine materials; female incubates 4–5 brown-marked, creamy white eggs for 12–13 days; may raise 2 broods per year.
Feeding: hawks, hover-gleans or gleans vegetation and branches for insects; also feeds on the ground; eats mostly berries in fall and winter.
Voice: *"Audubon's":* utters a more liquid, rising *swip*. *"Myrtle":* gives a sharp, dry *kep* call. *Male:* song varies from a tinkling trill to a more varied warble.
Similar Species: *Townsend's Warbler* (p. 308) and *Hermit Warbler* (p. 309): mostly yellow face, often with darker markings and black on throat; greenish rump; buzzy songs.
Best Sites: widespread in woodlands, especially in migration, but also present in winter.

BLACK-THROATED GRAY WARBLER

Dendroica nigrescens

Once seen, the Black-throated Gray Warbler is instantly recognizable—it looks like a yellow-challenged Townsend's Warbler. It is a close relative of the Townsend's Warbler and the Hermit Warbler, but these two species both have a moderate amount of yellow in their plumages, whereas the Black-throated Gray has just one small yellow facial spot. Another distinction is that the Black-throated Gray Warbler frequents the transition zone between low-elevation mixed woodlands and higher conifer forests, whereas the other two warblers prefer the higher conifers. The male's shrill, buzzy song, however, is typical for a warbler. • The Black-throated Gray Warbler is one of the very few western warblers that rarely crosses the Continental Divide.

breeding

ID: yellow spot ahead of eye; blackish legs. *Male:* black head and throat; white "eyebrow" and "mustache"; black-marked, gray nape and upperparts; 2 white wing bars; white underparts; black-streaked breast and sides. *Female:* black markings less pronounced than male's; white or black throat; paler back.
Size: *L* 5 in; *W* 7¾ in.
Status: fairly common spring-to-summer resident on the slopes of the Cascades and uncommon late-April migrant; uncommon migrant on the western slopes of the Cascades in mid- to late September and rare on the eastern ones from mid-August to September.
Habitat: hardwood and mixed forests, second-growth clear-cuts and juniper woodlands. *In migration:* towns and riparian areas.

Nesting: far out on a horizontal conifer branch; small cup nest consists of weed stalks, grass and plant fibers; female incubates 3–5 brown-marked, white eggs for about 12 days.
Feeding: hawks, hover-gleans and gleans for insects.
Voice: usual call is a low *tep. Male:* song is a series of wiry musical notes with a loud final flourish.
Similar Species: *Black-and-white Warbler:* rare here; white-streaked back; white crown stripe; yellowish feet. *"Myrtle" Yellow-rumped Warbler* (p. 306): white throat; yellow rump and side patch; less white in tail. *Townsend's Warbler* (p. 308): yellow on head and breast; olive green back.
Best Sites: Cape Disappointment (Columbia R. mouth); Dungeness River Audubon Center (Sequim); Discovery Park (Seattle); County Line Ponds (Skagit Co.–Whatcom Co.); west of Roslyn (Kittitas Co.); Lyle CP (SR 142, Klickitat Co.).

307

TOWNSEND'S WARBLER

Dendroica townsendi

Hardier than many of its close relatives, the stripe-headed Townsend's Warbler is found nesting throughout most of Washington. As the male utters his wheezy song from the tip of a conifer branch in the upper canopy, he is difficult to locate amidst the dense, dark foliage. In winter, however, when the Townsend's joins other cold-hardy warblers in dense cover along the coast and in sheltered valleys in western Washington, it sometimes offers a much better look at its attractive plumage as it forages at suet feeders. • Some Townsend's Warblers bear evidence of hybridization with the yellow-headed Hermit Warbler, which occurs in some of the same mountainous areas, but usually at slightly higher elevations. The latest evidence indicates that this hybridization is more extensive than formerly believed.

♂

♀

breeding

ID: small, black bill; blackish legs. *Male:* yellow face with black "cheek" patches, crown and throat; dark olive green back and rump; bluish gray wing with 2 bold white bars; heavily black-streaked, yellow breast; white belly, flanks and undertail coverts. *Female:* black largely replaced by dark olive; white throat.

Size: *L* 5 in; *W* 8 in.

Status: common summer resident; fairly common eastern migrant in mid-May and late September; uncommon western migrant and resident from fall to spring.

Habitat: *Breeding:* mountain fir forests and other coniferous forests. *In migration and winter:* coniferous and mixed woods, urban parks and coastal thickets.

Nesting: far out on a horizontal branch of a fir; shallow nest of grass, moss, cedar bark, fir twigs and plant fibers is lined with moss, feathers and hair; male helps female incubate 4–5 brown-marked, white eggs for 12 days.

Feeding: gleans vegetation and hawks for invertebrates; eats seeds and plant galls in winter; often forages high in trees; occasionally visits suet feeders.

Voice: chippy call. *Male:* unevenly patterned song consists of wiry *zee* and *zoo* notes and ends with a flourish.

Similar Species: *Hermit Warbler* (p. 309): all-yellow (male) or gray-smudged (female) face; more streaked, grayish back; unmarked, white underparts.

Best Sites: *Summer:* Olympics; Fort Ebey SP (Whidbey I.); Rockport SP (Skagit Co.); Blue Mts. *Fall:* lowland areas in western Washington. *Winter:* coastal forests; Discovery Park (Seattle); Marymoor Park (Redmond).

HERMIT WARBLER

Dendroica occidentalis

Upon arriving on his nesting territory, the male Hermit Warbler begins patrolling the crowns of the tall conifers marking its boundaries. Each tree-top offers a superb singing perch and a vantage point from which to welcome potential mates or thwart the intrusions of other males. • The south side of Mount St. Helens and the Capitol State Forest are good locations to see "pure" Hermit Warblers—but Townsend's Warbler × Hermit Warbler hybrids are regularly reported. Some of these hybrids resemble the Black-throated Green Warbler (*D. virens*), which has been sighted once in Washington. The similarity of the songs of the Hermit Warbler and the Townsend's Warbler males can also lead to misidentification. • During migration, Hermit Warblers travel in mixed-species flocks.

breeding

ID: dark eyes; small, black bill; blackish legs. *Male:* bright yellow crown and face; heavy black streaking on gray nape, back and rump; bluish black wing with 2 bold white bars; unmarked, white underparts; cleanly defined black throat and upper breast. *Female:* smudgy crown, ear patch, lores and throat patch.

Size: *L* 5 in; *W* 8 in.

Status: uncommon resident from spring to midsummer in the west and possibly in the higher reaches of eastern slopes of the southern Cascades.

Habitat: coniferous forests.

Nesting: on a horizontal conifer branch, far from the trunk; deep, compact cup of weed stems, pine needles, fine twigs, moss, spiderwebs and lichen; male helps female incubate 4–5 brown-flecked, creamy white eggs for about 12 days.

Feeding: forages on branches, gleaning and hawking for insects and larvae; male usually feeds higher in the canopy than the female.

Voice: call is a sharp *tsik* or *te*. *Male:* song is a series of buzzes at the same pitch, often with a final flourish of higher or lower notes.

Similar Species: *Townsend's Warbler* (p. 308): dark crown and ear patch; yellow breast with heavy, dark streaks continuing onto white flanks; plainer, greener back.

Best Sites: eastern slopes of the Olympics; Capitol State Forest (Thurston Co.); southern slopes of Mt. St. Helens.

309

PALM WARBLER

Dendroica palmarum

One of the habitual "tail-waggers," the Palm Warbler can easily be picked out in mixed-species foraging flocks, even when its plumage details are hard to observe. The tail-wagging occurs whether the bird is at rest on a perch or hopping on the ground in search of food. • The Palm Warbler was found overwintering in the vicinity of palms when first collected, hence its name, but it breeds in tamarack and spruce bogs in boreal Canada, the Great Lakes states and the northern part of the eastern seaboard. Along the Washington coast, it is a regular migrant, with the number of birds varying considerably from year to year. The great majority of Palm Warblers seen in Washington are of the western race, and there are a few records of individuals of the eastern race as well.

nonbreeding

ID: dark eye line; dark-streaked, grayish brown upperparts; yellow undertail coverts; white corners to tail; constantly pumps tail at rest and when feeding. *Breeding:* rufous crown; dark-streaked, whitish belly; yellow throat. *Nonbreeding:* grayish brown crown; paler, smudgy underpart streaking.
Size: *L* 5 in; *W* 8 in.
Status: rare late-fall migrant and winter resident in the western lowlands, particularly along the coast.

Habitat: shrubby growth, especially on wet woodland edges, and coastal scrub.
Nesting: does not nest in Washington.
Feeding: forages mostly on the ground for insects and seeds; gleans foliage and hawks for insects; eats some berries in fall.
Voice: call is a clipped *chik. Male:* song is a monotonous, insectlike trill that is less even than a Swamp Sparrow's or a Dark-eyed Junco's.
Similar Species: *Yellow-rumped Warbler* (p. 306): chunkier; grayer; localized yellow patches; 2 white wing bars; brighter yellow rump; white undertail coverts. *Blackpoll Warbler:* rare in Washington; female has 2 white wing bars, olive green rump and white undertail coverts.
Best Sites: Ocean Shores Marina; Raymond Airport.

AMERICAN REDSTART

Setophaga ruticilla

Many species exhibit sexual dimorphism, but male and female American Redstarts are so different that it seems impossible that they are the same species. • American Redstarts are always in motion. It is as if they are eager to show off their contrasting plumage, which is continually displayed in an enthusiastic series of flutters, twists, turns and feather-spreading. This constant motion extends to darting out into midair and hawking after insects, much in the manner of flycatchers. They behave the same way on their Central American wintering grounds, where they are called *candelitas*—"little candles." • The song of the American Redstart is so variable that even experienced birders who are faced with an unknown warbler song will exclaim, "It must be a redstart!"

ID: dark eyes; small, dark bill; blackish legs. *Male:* black head, throat and upperparts; orangy red (yellow on immature) sides of breast, wing bar and tail patch; white belly and undertail. *Female:* gray head; pale "spectacles"; olive gray upperparts; yellow sides of breast, wing bar and tail patch; light gray underparts.
Size: *L* 5 in; *W* 7½ in.
Status: fairly common summer resident and uncommon migrant in northeastern and north-central Washington; rare, very localized summer resident in western Washington.
Habitat: *Breeding:* riparian and lake-edge hardwood woodlands, particularly in dense alder and willow wetlands. *In migration:* coastal thickets, woodlots, second-growth along streams and desert oases.

Nesting: in the fork of a low tree or shrub, occasionally on the ground; compact cup of plant fibers, grass and rootlets is lined with fine materials; female incubates 4 brown-wreathed, white eggs for 12 days.
Feeding: actively gleans foliage and hawks for insects and spiders; occasionally consumes flower nectar, seeds and berries.
Voice: call is a sharp, sweet *chip*. *Male:* song is a highly variable series of *tseet* or *zee* notes, often at different pitches.
Similar Species: male is distinctive. *Palm Warbler* (p. 310): nonbreeding female is browner, has streaked flanks and breast, yellow undertail coverts and pale "eyebrow."
Best Sites: willow wetlands from Pend Oreille Co. to Okanogan Co.; the only recorded western Washington breeding location is County Line Ponds (Skagit Co.–Whatcom Co.).

311

NORTHERN WATERTHRUSH

Seiurus noveboracensis

Although the Northern Waterthrush resembles a thrush, it is not one. With a stronger affinity for wet habitats than most ground-feeding warblers, this bird favors wet streamsides. Like many waterside foragers, it teeters along like a slightly out-of-practice Spotted Sandpiper. As it works along downed logs and branches and on the ground, its preferred gait is a tail-bobbing walk. • The earlier name "New York Warbler" is almost justified by the male's loud and raucous song. • The Northern Waterthrush is one of several "eastern" birds that breed in northeastern Washington. In spite of the effort involved in getting there for many Washington residents, the area is attractive to birders looking for specialties, including this attractive large warbler.

ID: brown crown and eye line; narrow, white or pale yellow "eyebrow"; pink bill; plain, dark brown upperparts and tail; heavily black-streaked, white or yellow-washed underparts; white or yellow undertail coverts; pink legs; pumps and "bobs" tail while walking.
Size: *L* 6 in; *W* 9½ in.
Status: fairly common northeastern summer resident and uncommon fall migrant; rare fall migrant in western lowlands.
Habitat: wooded swamps; riparian thickets in coniferous and hardwood forests; flooded scrubby growth.
Nesting: on the ground, among a fallen tree's roots, under an overhanging bank or on a broken stump or branch; small, concealed cup of moss, leaves, twigs and inner bark is lined with fine materials; female incubates 4–5 variably marked, white eggs for 12–13 days.
Feeding: feeds mostly on the ground, frequently tossing aside leaves with its bill in seeking invertebrates; also gleans foliage and dips into shallow water for invertebrates and small fish.
Voice: brisk *chip* or *chuck* call. *Male:* distinctive loud, 3-part song, *sweet sweet sweet, swee wee wee, chew chew chew chew,* usually down the scale and speeding up, with an ending flourish.
Similar Species: *Ovenbird:* rare here; black-bordered, rusty crown; bold white eye ring; warm brown above; distinctive song.
Best Sites: Myers Creek (near Chesaw, Okanogan Co.); West Fork Sanpoil Campground (Okanogan Co.–Ferry Co.); Little Pend Oreille NWR (Stevens Co.); Big Meadow L. (west of Ione, Pend Oreille Co.); West Sullivan Lake Campground (northern Pend Oreille Co.); Tacoma Creek Rd. (north of Cusick).

MACGILLIVRAY'S WARBLER

Oporornis tolmiei

The MacGillivray's Warbler is a difficult bird to get to know. Birders often have difficulty viewing this understory skulker, even when its loud, rich call note appears to be less than a binocular-view away. • Multiple wood-warbler species can coexist in one habitat by using different foraging niches and nest sites. Some species inhabit the upper canopy, with a few feeding and nesting along the outer branches and others restricting themselves to inner branches and trunks. The MacGillivray's Warbler claims the dense understory shrubbery and bushy tangles in conifer glades, hardwood woodlands or even residential parks. • Spring is the best time of year to look for this shy species, when the males ascend tall shrubs to impress the females with their courtship songs.

breeding

ID: dark eyes; broken white eye ring; slightly down-curved, pink-ish bill; plain, olive green upperparts; unmarked, lemon yellow underparts; brownish flanks; pink legs. *Male:* grayish blue "hood," darkest on breast, forehead and eye line. *Female:* paler, more uniform "hood"; whitish throat; longer tail.
Size: *L* 5 in; *W* 7½ in.
Status: fairly common statewide resident from late spring through midsummer; uncommon statewide migrant; absent from Columbia Basin and dense wet forests.
Habitat: *Breeding:* hardwood brush along streams and lakes; forest understory; early clear-cut and burn regeneration. *In migration:* any dense vegetation.
Nesting: usually close to the ground in thick shrubbery; small cup nest of weed stems and grass is lined with fine materials; female incubates 4 brown-marked, creamy white eggs for 11 days.

Feeding: gleans bark, low vegetation and the ground for beetles, bees, leafhoppers, insect larvae and other invertebrates; rarely moves higher than the understory.
Voice: call is a typical *chik. Male:* song is a somewhat buzzy *churr churr churr swee swee* with less clear final notes.
Similar Species: *Nashville Warbler* (p. 304): smaller; yellow throat and breast; complete white eye ring; may have white belly. *Wilson's Warbler* (p. 315): smaller; yellow head; dark "cap"; finer bill.
Best Sites: Sauk Mt. Rd. (Rockport SP); Newhalem; Tolt MacDonald Park (Carnation); Teanaway Rd. (west of SR 970, Kittitas Co.); Wenas Campground (Yakima Co.); Little Rattlesnake Creek (off Nile Rd., Yakima Co.); Chopaka Rd. (Loomis); Mt. Spokane SP.

COMMON YELLOWTHROAT

Geothlypis trichas

Other warblers avoid getting wet feet by frequenting dry areas or the forest canopy, but the Common Yellowthroat muddles around in the mud and muck of marsh and lakeshore vegetation. At home in the world of cattails and tules, the male fires off his salvo of loud, repetitive songs as his mate gets down to the job of raising a family—often including some "donated" Brown-headed Cowbird eggs. • Common Yellowthroats do not spend all their time hidden away in dense, wet vegetation. When nesting is over, they can be found in almost any damp, scrubby habitat. Here they fuel up for a short winter trip south, often no farther than California. • A Common Yellowthroat will often respond to "pishing," but look quickly, because these birds don't stay around long before dropping back into cover.

ID: dark eyes; dark bill; greenish brown nape and upperparts; bright yellow throat, breast and undertail coverts; dusky flanks; pink or orangy legs. *Male:* black "mask" from forehead to shoulder, white-bordered above. *Female:* greenish brown face; indistinct pale eye ring.

Size: *L* 5 in; *W* 6½ in.

Status: common western resident from mid-April to the end of August and fairly common to uncommon migrant; fairly common eastern resident from mid-May to late August and uncommon migrant.

Habitat: *Breeding:* marshes; damp, lush vegetation, especially wet areas with willows or brush; overgrown fields and hedgerows. *In migration* and *winter:* wet thickets, dense brush and weedy fields.

Nesting: in low, scrubby growth or shrubs; bulky, loosely made nest of weed stems, grass, bark, dead leaves and ferns is lined with fine material; female incubates 3–5 darkly marked, creamy white eggs for 12 days.

Feeding: gleans vegetation and bark, hover-gleans and flycatches for invertebrates; also eats some seeds, usually picked from the ground.

Voice: sharp *tcheck* or *tchet* call. *Male:* song is a clear, oscillating *witchety witchety witchety-witch* or other repetitions of 3 (rarely 2) syllables.

Similar Species: *MacGillivray's Warbler* (p. 313): gray "hood"; prominent broken white eye ring; deeper olive green upperparts; yellower underparts.

Best Sites: almost any wet, marshy patch of cattails or reeds, particularly ones bordered by willows or thick brush.

WILSON'S WARBLER

Wilsonia pusilla

E ven a casual glance into a streamside thicket is sure to reveal an energetic Wilson's Warbler as it flickers through tangles of leaves and branches in pursuit of its food as if every moment is precious. With more energy than many a larger bird, the Wilson's Warbler is also quick to jump to the defense of its hidden brood should an intruder come too close. • Often intensely golden over much of its plumage, this tiny warbler could be confused with the Yellow Warbler, but a closer look will usually reveal that error, especially if the male Wilson's flashes his black crown. • The Wilson's Warbler bears the name of birding pioneer Alexander Wilson—his energetic devotion to ornithology in the early 1800s inspired many careful studies of North American birds.

ID: large, black eyes; small, pink-and-dark bill; yellowish green upperparts; yellow underparts; pink legs. *Male:* black crown; bright golden yellow face; broad, yellow "eyebrow." *Female:* olive (or light-spotted black) forehead and crown.
Size: *L* 4 in; *W* 7 in.
Status: common western resident from May to late August and uncommon to fairly common migrant in late April and from late August through September; fairly common eastern migrant from mid-May to early June and in early to mid-September and uncommon resident from early June to late August.
Habitat: *Breeding:* dense hardwood understory and brush, usually near fresh water. *In migration:* conifers, hardwood brush and residential parks and gardens.

Nesting: on the ground or low in a coastal shrub or vine tangle; bulky nest of dead leaves, grass and moss is lined with fine grass and hair; female incubates 4–6 brown-marked, creamy white eggs for 10–13 days.
Feeding: gleans vegetation and bark, hover-gleans and hawks for adult and larval insects.
Voice: flat, low *chet* or *chuck* call. *Male:* rapid 2-part chattering song becomes louder and faster toward the end.
Similar Species: *Yellow Warbler* (p. 305): plainer face; heavier bill; male is bright yellow overall, with yellow crown and reddish orange breast streaks. *MacGillivray's Warbler* (p. 313): larger; gray "hood"; prominent broken white eye ring.
Best Sites: Fort Casey SP (Whidbey I.); Tolt MacDonald Park (Carnation); Mt. Rainier NP; Buck Meadows (Kittitas Co.); Long Swamp (Okanogan Co.). *Fall:* Indian Canyon Park (Spokane).

YELLOW-BREASTED CHAT

Icteria virens

With its bright yellow breast and intense curiosity, the Yellow-breasted Chat is a typical wood-warbler. Yet it seems too large and a trifle too clumsy, and it has a most unwarbler-like song. Although its inclusion in the wood-warbler family has been questioned, molecular studies seem to support this grouping. • The Yellow-breasted Chat is sorely taxed when it tries to find a summer home. The riparian buffer zones of scrubby and brushy habitat that it likes are being degraded by livestock grazing and are becoming scarce as a result of urban sprawl, but some suitable protected areas remain where you can still enjoy this unique songbird. • The two parts of the scientific name refer to the yellow underparts and olive green upperparts, respectively.

ID: white "spectacles" and "mustache"; heavy, dusky bill; unmarked, olive green upperparts; rich yellow (sometimes orange) breast and throat; buff flanks; white belly and undertail coverts; long tail, often held upraised.

Size: *L* 7 in; *W* 10 in.

Status: fairly common local eastern resident from mid-May to late July; uncommon eastern migrant in early May and early August.

Habitat: *Breeding:* dense streamside and bottomland willows and brush; open-country thickets; understory in open hardwood and mixed woodlands. *In migration:* almost any brushy habitat, including urban parks and overgrown gardens.

Nesting: low in a shrub or small tree; well-concealed, bulky nest of leaves, straw, weed stems and vine bark is thinly lined with fine weed stems and grass; female incubates 3–4 large, brown-marked, creamy white eggs for 11 days.

Feeding: gleans vegetation for insects and berries; usually feeds low in thicket growth.

Voice: calls include *whoit, chack* and *kook. Male:* song, which can be long, is an assorted series of whistles, squeaks, grunts, rattles and mews; often sings after dusk and before dawn.

Similar Species: *Common Yellowthroat* (p. 314) and *MacGillivray's Warbler* (p. 313): much smaller; no white "spectacles" or "mustaches"; finer bills; shorter tails.

Best Sites: Wenas Creek–Hardy Canyon, Umtanum Creek at Yakima R. and Cowiche Canyon (all Yakima Co.); Rock Creek Rd. (Klickitat Co.); W.E. Johnson Park (Richland); Champneys Slough (Okanogan Co.); South Fork Coppei Creek Rd. (Walla Walla Co.).

WESTERN TANAGER

Piranga ludoviciana

ew birds can match the tropical splendor of the tanagers. Four species of this Central and South American family have expanded northward into the U.S. The Western Tanager, the most northerly breeding species, is the only one regularly seen in Washington. • The male Western Tanager brings a splash of color to Washington's foothills and lower mountain slopes. His difficult-to-learn song closely parallels the phrases of an American Robin's song, but the notes are somewhat hoarser, as if the bird has a sore throat, and it ends with a distinctive, hiccuplike *pit-a-tik*. • Female tanagers are more cryptically colored than males, and the female Western Tanager is no exception. The spectacular male Western Tanager, however, is responsible for converting many people to birdwatching.

ID: stout, dull orangy bill; dark eyes; bluish gray legs. *Breeding male:* generally deep yellow; orangy red face and throat; black back, wings and tail; 1 yellow wing bar and 1 white one. *Nonbreeding male:* duller yellow; dusky wash on head and flanks; orangy only on forehead, lores and "chin"; duller back. *Female:* similar to nonbreeding male, but with less orange on face, dusky back, paler upper wing bar and white belly.
Size: *L* 7 in; *W* 11½ in.
Status: common resident in coniferous forests from mid-May through summer; uncommon to fairly common migrant from late April to early May and in September.
Habitat: *Breeding:* coniferous and mixed forests, locally in ponderosa pines.

In migration: hardwood and riparian woodlands.
Nesting: usually in a fork of a horizontal conifer branch, well out from the trunk; loose cup nest of twigs, rootlets and moss is lined with hair and rootlets; female incubates 3–5 brown-marked, blue eggs for 13 days.
Feeding: gleans vegetation and catches flying insects on the wing; eats wasps, beetles and other insects, flower buds and small fruits.
Voice: soft, whistled calls; fast, rattling notes when agitated. *Male:* song is a robin-like series of somewhat hoarse, slurred whistles often delivered very rapidly.
Similar Species: *Bullock's Oriole* (p. 347): larger; female has bright yellow head and breast, bluish bill, gray wings and whitish belly. *Summer Tanager:* unusual here; much heavier bill; wing bars absent or vague.
Best Sites: most any coniferous forest except for coastal rainforests.

GREEN-TAILED TOWHEE

Pipilo chlorurus

The cryptically colored Green-tailed Towhee often goes unrecognized as a close relative of the Spotted Towhee, which sports a striking plumage of red, white and black. Yet, a few moments of observation reveal the Green-tailed Towhee's classic towhee foraging style: leaping back and forth in the dappled shade of a brushy thicket floor, it scratches away loose leaf litter and debris with both feet in its search for insects and hidden seeds. • Green-tailed Towhees rarely venture far from the dense, low understory of brushy thicket openings. When startled, they prefer to run for cover or flutter off, often "mewing" their annoyance, and nesting females scurry away in a mouselike manner if approached. • In spring, male towhees gradually emerge from cover to produce a series of clear, whistled notes and raspy trills from exposed woody perches.

ID: orangy rufous crown; gray face; conical, gray bill; dull yellowish green back, wings and tail; bright yellowish to greenish edge on wings and tail; sooty gray neck and underparts; gray stripe on white throat; whitish belly; greenish undertail coverts.
Size: *L* 7 in; *W* 9½ in.
Status: rare local resident of the Blue Mts. from June to mid-August.
Habitat: *Breeding:* dry foothills and canyons; open and brushy slopes; ponderosa pine–juniper forests with dense brush cover; mountain mahogany; riparian areas in dry open country. *In migration:* brushy areas, including residential ones.

Nesting: on the ground or low in a bush; large, thick-walled nest of grass, bark, twigs and weed stems is lined with fine material; female incubates 3–4 heavily brown-spotted, white eggs for 11 days.
Feeding: scratches the ground for insects, seeds and berries; drinks morning dew from leaves; occasional, flighty visits to feeders.
Voice: calls are thin and wheezy, sometimes mewing. *Male:* song consists of several clipped notes, then a variable trill, such as *swee-too weet chur cheee-churr*.
Similar Species: none.
Best Sites: all in the Blue Mts.: Wenatchee Guard Station (Asotin Co.); Lewis Peak (Walla Walla Co.); Biscuit Ridge (Walla Walla Co.).

SPOTTED TOWHEE

Pipilo maculatus

Scratching for food on the forest floor, a Spotted Towhee puts both feet to use at the same time doing the "Towhee Dance," its long claws revealing anything hidden in the leaf litter. The resulting ruckus leads many people to expect a squirrel—what a surprise to see a bird not much larger than a sparrow! • Towhees like tangled thickets and overgrown gardens, especially if they offer blackberries or other small fruits. Many pairs nest in urban neighborhoods, where they take turns scolding the family cat or checking out any suspicious sounds. • The male Spotted Towhee often selects a prominent perch to spit out his curious, trilled song, puffing out his chest and exposing his striking rufous flanks, but at other times he can be curiously shy. • Eastern Washington birds have much whiter, more contrasting belly and wing spots than western ones.

ID: red eyes; dark bill; bright rufous sides and flanks; white belly; buff pink undertail coverts; light brownish legs; long claws. *Male:* all-black head; white-spotted, black back and wings; black tail. *Female:* paler, with brown replacing black in plumage.

Size: *L* 7–8 in; *W* 10½ in.

Status: common year-round resident in western Washington; common resident in eastern Washington from late April through August and fairly common the rest of the year.

Habitat: brushy habitats and scrub situations, including those in residential areas. *Breeding:* especially in valleys and coastal lowlands.

Nesting: low in a shrub or in a scratched depression on the ground; neat cup of leaves, grass, bark, twigs and rootlets is lined with fine grass and hair; male helps female incubate 3–4 brown-wreathed, white eggs for 12–13 days.

Feeding: scratches the ground vigorously to uncover seeds and insects; also eats berries and acorns, especially in winter; occasionally visits feeding stations.

Voice: catlike *meeew* call note. *Male:* song starts with a few simple notes and then accelerates into a fast, raspy trill.

Similar Species: *Black-headed Grosbeak* (p. 338): male has heavy, conical, bluish gray bill, bright orange nape, breast, belly, flanks and rump, and more white in wings.

Best Sites: widespread; Discovery Park (Seattle); Marymoor Park (Redmond); Riverside SP (Spokane).

AMERICAN TREE SPARROW

Spizella arborea

You know winter is near when you start to find more than the occasional American Tree Sparrow among the local sparrow flocks. Quietly arriving from the north, this bird is easily identified by its two-tone bill and the central breast spot on its otherwise clear underparts. The American Tree Sparrow finds its place in brushy and shrubby areas alongside summering species and remains after many other species have moved on. By March, the lengthening days encourage most birds to leave, and by mid-April every American Tree Sparrow has headed to its summer home in the arctic vegetation of Canada and Alaska. • Although its common and scientific names (*arborea* means "tree") imply that it is a forest-dwelling bird, this sparrow prefers semi-open areas where trees are at a premium.

Nesting: does not nest in Washington.
Feeding: forages on the ground and in low shrubs; eats insects, spiders, seeds, buds, catkins and berries.

ID: gray face; chestnut or rufous crown and eye line; white eye ring; gray-and-yellow bill; mottled, brown-and-chestnut upperparts; 2 prominent white wing bars; chestnut shoulder line; buff sides; gray underparts; dark central breast spot; whitish throat; creamy undertail coverts; long, gray tail.

Size: *L* 6 in; *W* 9–9½ in.

Status: uncommon resident in eastern Washington and rare in western Washington from mid-October to late March.

Habitat: riparian growth and low-elevation meadow brush.

Voice: *tseet* call. *Male:* song of late winter and spring migration is a high, whistled *tseet-tseet,* then a short, sweet, musical series of slurred whistles.

Similar Species: *Chipping Sparrow* (p. 321): smaller; nonbreeding bird has streaked brown crown, long, pale buff "eyebrow," thin, blackish eye line, yellowish pink bill and all-gray breast and underwings. *White-crowned Sparrow* (p. 333): immature has head striped with rusty brown and buff, all-pinkish or all-yellow bill, unmarked breast and brownish rump.

Best Sites: West Foster Creek Unit, Wells Wildlife Area (south of Bridgeport); Molson (Okanogan Co.); Lower Crab Creek west of SR 26 (Grant Co.–Adams Co.); rare in Skagit Game Range (Skagit Co.).

CHIPPING SPARROW

Spizella passerina

The Chipping Sparrow and the Dark-eyed Junco obviously do not share a tailor, but they must have attended the same voice lessons. Only subtle differences distinguish the two songs: the rapid trill of the Chipping Sparrow is just slightly faster, drier and more mechanical. • Habitat preferences are often the best means of distinguishing unseen singers. The Chipping Sparrow is more likely to be found in open or semi-open woodlands, whereas the junco prefers darker, denser forests once it has left its wintering flocks. • Commonly nesting at eye level, the Chipping Sparrow offers the opportunity to study its courtship and nest-building rituals at close range. • The common name refers to this bird's call, and *passerina* is Latin for "little sparrow."

breeding

ID: dark eyes; dark eye line; pink legs; long tail. *Breeding:* chestnut "cap"; gray "cheek"; white "eyebrow"; thin, grayish "mustache"; dusky yellow bill; dark-mottled, brown back and wings; 2 white wing bars; gray nape, rump and underparts; white throat. *Nonbreeding:* brown "cap"; buff "eyebrow"; pinkish orange bill. **Size:** *L* 5½ in; *W* 8½ in.

Status: common eastern resident from May to mid-August and uncommon to fairly common migrant in late April and from mid-August to mid-September; fairly common resident of western dry forests from spring to mid-August and migrant to mid-September.

Habitat: *Breeding:* grassy clearings in dry forests; open or semi-open grassy woodlands. *In migration* and *winter:* open grasslands with brushy cover, sagebrush scrub and residential woodlots.

Nesting: low to mid-level in a conifer or oak, occasionally in a vine tangle; compact cup of grass and other plant materials is lined with fur or hair; female incubates 2–5 blackish-marked, bluish green eggs for 11–14 days.

Feeding: forages on the ground or gleans in low foliage and trees for insects and seeds, especially those of grasses, dandelions and clovers.

Voice: usual call is a short, clipped *chip*. *Male:* song is a simple, long, dull trill.

Similar Species: *Clay-colored Sparrow* (p. 365): streaked, brown crown with white, central stripe; pinkish or orangy bill; brownish rump; nonbreeding and 1st-winter birds have buff breast bands and flanks. *American Tree Sparrow* (p. 320): winter resident only; usually redder crown and eye line; gray-and-yellow bill; dark central breast spot.

Best Sites: open, dry forests, particularly in eastern Washington.

BREWER'S SPARROW

Spizella breweri

The Brewer's Sparrow is the ultimate in sparrow design—its plumage is so non-descript and its song so insectlike that it would go completely unnoticed in a brushy woodland filled with bird songs. Fortunately for birders, the Brewer's Sparrow favors treeless sagebrush plains and brushy habitats instead. The male's song, often exceeding 10 seconds, is a remarkable outburst of rapid, buzzy trills that constantly change in speed, pitch and quality. • Ranging east of the Cascades, this sparrow starts to form migrant flocks in mid-August, and it is one of the commonest species in open-country flocks until its departure in late August. • This bird's name honors Dr. Thomas Brewer, who made significant contributions to understanding the breeding behavior of North American birds in the 19th century.

breeding

ID: unbroken white eye ring; small, pink bill; pink legs; long tail. *Breeding:* "cheek" patch with dark brown border; streaked, brown upperparts; light brown to whitish underparts; light throat. *Nonbreeding:* faint head and throat stripes; paler upperparts.
Size: *L* 5½ in; *W* 7½ in.
Status: common eastern resident from April to early August and uncommon to fairly common migrant in mid- to late April and mid- to late August.
Habitat: sagebrush; rocky, brushy breaks in lodgepole pine forests; grassland shrubbery.
Nesting: in a low, dense shrub, usually sagebrush, or a small tree; small, compact cup of soft plant materials is lined with finer materials; pair incubates 3–4 brown-marked, bluish green eggs for 11–13 days.

Feeding: forages on the ground and in low vegetation for insects, spiders and seeds; can eat seeds without water for up to 3 weeks.
Voice: high-pitched *psst* call. *Male:* long song of interspersed buzzes and trills changes in speed and pitch.
Similar Species: *Clay-colored Sparrow* (p. 365): white "eyebrow"; unstreaked, gray nape; unstreaked rump; grayer and more heavily patterned in breeding plumage; buffier, especially on underparts, in nonbreeding plumage. *Chipping Sparrow* (p. 321): chestnut on crown and upperparts; black eye line; plainer "cheek"; grayer rump.
Best Sites: Quilomene Wildlife Area (Kittitas Co.); Umtanum Ridge (Kittitas Co.); Ryegrass Summit (I-90); Beezley Hills Preserve (north of Quincy); Moses Coulee–Sagebrush Flat (Douglas Co.); Cameron Lake Rd. (near town of Okanogan).

VESPER SPARROW

Pooecetes gramineus

For birders who live on flat grasslands and shrublands that teem with confusing little brown sparrows, the Vesper Sparrow offers welcome relief—its white-edged tail and deeply undulating flight are reliable identification features. The Vesper is also known for the male's bold and easily distinguished song, which is often heard in the evening (*vesper* is Latin for "evening"), usually from an elevated perch or in a brief song flight. • The Vesper Sparrow's nest is usually in a grassy hollow at the base of a low shrub, thus providing camouflage, a windbreak and an umbrella. • Changing agricultural practices are reducing the preferred habitat of the Vesper Sparrow. It is still common east of the Cascades, but it is becoming rare in much of its former Washington breeding range west of the Cascades.

ID: white eye ring; pink bill; streaked, brown upperparts; whitish underparts and undertail; white-edged tail; pink legs. *Breeding:* pale "cheek" patch with brown border; dark "mustache"; chestnut shoulder patch; dark-streaked breast; faintly streaked flanks. *Nonbreeding:* paler; buff sides.
Size: *L* 6 in; *W* 10 in.
Status: common resident of eastern Washington from mid-April to mid-August; uncommon to fairly common migrant in eastern Washington from mid-March to mid-April and from mid-August to mid-September; rare, declining localized resident in western Washington from mid-April to mid-September.
Habitat: grasslands and farmlands. *Breeding:* sagebrush; dry, grassy hillsides.

In migration: low desert brush areas, open grassy areas and fields.
Nesting: in an excavated depression; well-concealed, bulky, loose nest of grass, other plants and rootlets; pair incubates 3–4 brown-marked, creamy or greenish white eggs for 11–13 days.
Feeding: walks or runs to catch grasshoppers, beetles and cutworms; picks up seeds; not known to drink or bathe in water.
Voice: short, hard *chip* call. *Male:* song begins with 4 low notes, with the 2nd higher in pitch, then a bubbly trill of *here-here there-there, everybody-down-the-hill.*
Similar Species: *Savannah Sparrow* (p. 326): pale "eyebrow"; stronger flank streaking; dark undertail; weak, buzzy song. *Lark Sparrow* (p. 324): chestnut head pattern; heavier bill; white-tipped tail feathers; slow-paced, uneven song.
Best Sites: widespread in eastern grassland habitats.

323

LARK SPARROW

Chondestes grammacus

Singing atop small bushes or low rock outcrops in their rural haunts, male Lark Sparrows reminded early naturalists of the famed Sky Lark *(Alauda arvensis)* of Eurasia and North Africa. Lark Sparrow males do occasionally indulge themselves in short display flights, but they do not fly as high or as skillfully as the Sky Lark. • Typically seen in dry scrubland, open shrub-steppe and edge habitats, Lark Sparrows occasionally venture into grassy forest openings, other woodland areas and meadows. • Lark Sparrows sometimes associate with Vesper Sparrows and Savannah Sparrows, but the pattern of white on the tail easily distinguishes the three species. • A summer-only bird in Washington, the Lark Sparrow is found year-round in much of western California.

ID: white-striped, chestnut crown; chestnut "cheek"; black eye line and "mustache"; heavy, grayish bill; brown-streaked back and wings; dark spot on pale breast; buff gray sides and flanks; grayish brown rump; uppertail has grayish brown center and darker outer feathers with white tips.
Size: *L* 6½ in; *W* 11 in.
Status: uncommon to fairly common eastern resident from May through mid-August.
Habitat: grasslands with scattered bushes and open woodlands. *Breeding:* farmlands, open pine and juniper forests and sagebrush.
Nesting: in a depression in the ground, in a shrub or in a rock crevice; bulky, twig-based shrub nest is covered with a cup of grass and other plants and lined with fine materials; female incubates 4–5 dusky-marked, creamy or grayish white eggs for 11–12 days.
Feeding: walks or hops on the ground to find seeds; also eats grasshoppers and other invertebrates.
Voice: utters a finchlike *pik* flight call and a loud, high alarm call. *Male:* song, occasionally given on the wing, has a variable pace and rhythm with rattling trills.
Similar Species: *Vesper Sparrow* (p. 323) and *Savannah Sparrow* (p. 326): plainer faces; thinner bills; heavily streaked breasts and sides; less white on uppertail.
Best Sites: Huntzinger Rd. (south of Vantage); Toppenish NWR; Klickitat Wildlife Area (west of Goldendale); Potholes Rookery (I-90, exit 174); Bridgeport SP.

SAGE SPARROW

Amphispiza belli

Washington's Sage Sparrows are almost entirely of the pale *nevadensis* subspecies, which forages and nests in areas dominated by sagebrush. Each year, the males return to the same breeding site, which they defend by singing from exposed perches. Breeding pairs often raise two broods of three or four young per year. The production of so many young may be in response to high predation. • The Sage Sparrow can often be distinguished from other sparrows by its habits of wagging and twitching its tail when perched and holding it upward in wrenlike fashion during short runs. • When assigning the scientific name for this bird, John Cassin of the Philadelphia Academy of Natural Sciences chose to honor John Graham Bell, the taxidermist who collected the first scientific specimen in the mid-1800s.

ID: grayish blue head; short, white "eyebrow"; unbroken white eye ring; white "mustache"; stubby, bluish bill; streaked, pale brown upperparts and wings; white underparts; dark "V" patch on breast; dark-bordered, white throat; buff gray flanks; long, dusky legs.

Size: *L* 5–6 in; *W* 8–8½ in.

Status: fairly common eastern resident from March to July and uncommon migrant in mid-February and early July.

Habitat: arid sagebrush and greasewood, occasionally in grasslands with scattered shrubs.

Nesting: low in sagebrush, occasionally on the ground; bulky nest of twigs, grass, other plants and bark is lined with grass, plant down and sometimes hair; female incubates 2–4 darkly spotted, bluish white eggs for 13–16 days; female will run from the nest rather than fly.

Feeding: forages on the ground and gleans foliage for insects, spiders and seeds.

Voice: most calls are a series of high, tinkling notes. *Male:* song is a mechanical, uninspired mixture of notes: *slip, slip freeee slip-slip freee you.*

Similar Species: *Black-throated Sparrow* (p. 365): very limited distribution; stronger black-and-white facial pattern; unstreaked back and underparts; large black throat area; shorter legs; buff undertail coverts; more white in undertail; runs with tail held flat.

Best Sites: Quilomene Wildlife Area (Kittitas Co.); Schnebly Coulee (Kittitas Co.); Rattlesnake Mt. (Benton Co.); Silica Rd. (I-90, exit 143); Beezley Hills Preserve (north of Quincy).

SAVANNAH SPARROW

Passerculus sandwichensis

Anyone wanting to study songbird plumage variations might well consider choosing the Savannah Sparrow as a model. At least four subspecies visit Washington at various times of the year, thereby helping to keep beginning birders on their toes as they try to make positive identifications. • Savannah Sparrows are common in open, grassy country, where their plumage conceals them perfectly among tall grasses. They like to remain hidden, often scurrying like feathered voles low in cover or making short, low flights to clumps of concealing grass. • Savannah Sparrows roost on the ground in short grass in small, compact groups. Disturbed migrating or wintering flocks will scatter, flushing from the ground one by one like miniature quails, and rejoin later.

ID: grayish brown head and dark-streaked back; dark eye line and "mustache"; pale "eyebrow"; pink bill; medium to reddish brown wings; dark-streaked, white breast and white or buff flanks; dark "V" spot on breast; pale throat; white belly and undertail coverts.

Size: *L* 5–6 in; *W* 6–7 in.

Status: common statewide resident from April through September; uncommon to fairly common statewide migrant in March and October; uncommon to rare winter resident in western Washington and very rare in the east.

Habitat: *Breeding:* most grassy habitats, including open forest glades. *In migration* and *winter:* grasslands and farmlands; lakeshores, coastal dunes and salt marshes; grassy suburban parks.

Nesting: on the ground, usually in a natural or excavated depression; small, well-concealed cup of coarse grass is lined with finer materials; pair incubates 3–5 brown-marked, pale greenish blue eggs for 12–13 days.

Feeding: forages on the ground for insects, spiders and grass seeds; also eats small snails.

Voice: gives a high, thin *tsit* call. *Male:* song is a high-pitched, clear, buzzy *tzip-tzip-tzip ztreeeeeee-ip*.

Similar Species: *Vesper Sparrow* (p. 323): chestnut shoulder patch; tail is white below and prominently white-edged above; undulating flight to a high perch. *Lincoln's Sparrow* (p. 330): buffier overall, particularly on breast; gray or olive face; all-brown tail; prefers scrubby cover.

Best Sites: widespread statewide in grassy habitats and coastal dunes. *In migration:* especially along the coast.

GRASSHOPPER SPARROW

Ammodramus savannarum

The Grasshopper Sparrow is one of Washington's most enigmatic summer songbirds. Its loose colonies are forever shifting from one place to the next in search of the optimal grassland nesting and foraging sites. • This species is named not for its diet, which consists largely of insects much smaller than grasshoppers, but for its buzzy, insectlike song. The male will pick the highest grass stalk on which to perch and sing. However, his flight song, which he uses in pursuit of females, is so high pitched as to be inaudible to humans. • The Grasshopper Sparrow prefers to run from danger rather than fly or hide, so the genus name *Ammodramus*—Greek for "sand runner"—is appropriate, and so is *savannarum*, in reference to the bird's grassland habitat.

ID: brown "cap" with whitish middle stripe; sloping forehead; buff face; large, dark eyes; thick, pale bill; chestnut-streaked nape and back; dark-centered wing feathers with rusty and white tips; plain buff underparts; pale pink legs.
Size: *L* 4–5 in; *W* 7–7½ in.
Status: uncommon and local resident of eastern Washington from May to mid-July.
Habitat: open grasslands, particularly dry, ungrazed ones in foothills, but also on prairies and old fields with scattered bushes.
Nesting: semi-colonial; in a low depression well concealed by overhanging grass and other plants; nest of dried grass, arched or domed at the back, is lined with fine materials; female incubates 4–5 russet-marked, white eggs for 11–12 days.
Feeding: forages on the ground and in low vegetation for insects, other invertebrates and the seeds of grasses and other plants.
Voice: calls are high-pitched and thin. *Male: tea-tea-tea zeeeeeeeeee* song is 1–3 high, thin, whistled notes followed by a high, faint, buzzy trill.
Similar Species: *Brewer's Sparrow* (p. 322): grayer overall; rounder head; streaked crown; dark "mustache"; smaller bill; less patterned back; prefers sagebrush.
Best Sites: Soap Lake Rd. (Okanogan Co.); Dodson Rd. (Grant Co.); Swanson Lakes Wildlife Area (Lincoln Co.); Crosby Rd. on Rattlesnake Mt. (Benton Co.); Fishtrap L. (east of Sprague); Turnbull NWR.

FOX SPARROW

Passerella iliaca

Scratching away leaf litter and duff to expose seeds and insects, the Fox Sparrow forages much like a towhee. • Several races of the Fox Sparrow, which is one of North America's largest sparrows, occur in Washington. Washington's two breeding populations are the medium brown "Sooty," on the outer Olympic Peninsula, and the gray-and-rusty "Slate-colored," which inhabits the Cascades, Okanogans, Selkirks, Kettle Range and Blue Mountains. There are also a few records of the widespread, more easterly "Red" race that has a coloration like that of a red fox. Each race has a different version of a beautiful, warbled song. • It is likely that ornithologists will soon split the Fox Sparrow into two or more species.

"Sooty"

ID: dark eyes; thick, gray or yellowish bill; rufous-and-gray or brown upperparts; mostly white underparts with lines of strongly contrasting black, gray, brown or rufous spots or chevrons; pinkish legs.

Size: *L* 7 in; *W* 10½ in.

Status: *"Sooty":* uncommon outer Olympic coast resident from May to late September; common western lowland resident from October through March. *"Slate-colored":* fairly common resident on mid-elevation slopes of the Cascades from April through September; fairly common in the Blue Mts., Selkirks, Kettle Hills and Okanogan Mts. from May through mid-October; rare eastern resident from mid-October through April.

Habitat: *Breeding:* dense brush and riparian thickets. *In migration* and *winter:* dense brush in open and forested habitats, including residential areas and coastal thickets.

Nesting: on the ground, low in a shrub, rarely in a tree; bulky nest of grass, moss, lichen, rootlets, shredded bark, leaves and twigs; female incubates 2–5 russet-marked, pale green eggs for 12–14 days.

Feeding: scratches the ground to uncover seeds, berries and invertebrates; feeds largely on small fruits, especially blackberries, in fall and early winter; visits feeders in winter and in migration.

Voice: explosive *tak* call. *Male:* burry, whistled songs of coastal birds sound patchy and uninspired; interior birds have a purer, ringing song with noticeable trills.

Similar Species: *Song Sparrow* (p. 329): streaked upperparts; breast and sides more streaked than spotted; brown-striped, grayish face; slimmer bill.

Best Sites: widespread in brushy habitats and low second-growth, best seen in winter.

SONG SPARROW

Melospiza melodia

When amateur birder Margaret Morse Nice began studying plumage variations in the widespread Song Sparrow in the 1920s, she had no idea how much interest she would eventually trigger among professional ornithologists. We now know that the dowdy Song Sparrow probably has the greatest variation in plumage of any North American songbird, which suggests that it has readily adapted to differences in factors such as climate, soil coloration and food selection. Given time and some separation, these subspecies could become so different that they are reproductively incompatible and thus distinct species.
• Other sparrows may have more beautiful songs, but the complexity, rhythm and sweetness of the male Song Sparrow's springtime rhapsodies justify the name.

ID: brown or rufous crown (with pale center stripe) and eye line; grayish face; thick, gray bill; streaked, rufous-and-brown upperparts; thickly brown-streaked, gray or brown flanks and breast with smudgy spot; whitish belly; pinkish legs.
Size: *L* 5–6 in; *W* 8–8½ in.
Status: common year-round resident statewide but absent from extremely arid or barren areas and dense wet forest.
Habitat: *Breeding:* hardwood brush in forests and open country; near water or in lush vegetation in chaparral, riparian willows, marshy habitats and residential areas.
Nesting: usually beneath a grass tuft or in a shrub or brush pile; bulky nest of twigs, bark strips, grass, other plants and leaves;

female incubates 3–4 russet-marked, pale blue or green eggs for 12–14 days; frequently has 2 broods.
Feeding: gleans the ground and foliage for insects and seeds; coastal birds eat crustaceans and mollusks; eats berries in winter; may visit feeders for seeds.
Voice: calls include a short *tsip* and nasal *tchep*. *Male:* song is 1–4 bright introductory notes, such as *sweet, sweet, sweet,* followed by a buzzy *towee* and a short, descending trill.
Similar Species: *Fox Sparrow* (p. 328): plainer head and upperparts; lines of spots or chevrons rather than streaks. *Lincoln's Sparrow* (p. 330): daintier; gray or olive face and back; buff "mustache," finer bill; brown-streaked, buff breast and flanks; more white on belly.
Best Sites: widespread in suitable low- to mid-elevation habitats, including residential ones.

LINCOLN'S SPARROW
Melospiza lincolnii

The subtle beauty of a Lincoln's Sparrow's plumage is greater than the sum of its feathers. The colors are not spectacular, yet they match and give the bird a distinctive, well-groomed look lacking in most other sparrows. • The Lincoln's Sparrow usually skulks among tall grasses and dense, brushy growth, but when the male sings, he sheds his shy nature and issues territorial challenges from a prominent perch. • Lincoln's Sparrows prefer wetter conditions than most sparrows, and most Washington breeders occupy mid-elevation territories in the Cascades and eastern mountains, often freshly emerged from melting snow and swollen streams. In fall, these birds generally move downslope or leave the state; meanwhile, others travel south from Alaska and Canada to join wintering sparrow flocks in our area.

ID: peaked, dark brown "cap" with gray median stripe; gray or olive nape and "eye-brow"; brown facial lines; buff "mustache" stripe; dark streaking on gray upperparts, often with rufous on wings and tail; lightly brown-streaked, buff-washed breast and flanks; white belly.

Size: *L* 5 in; *W* 7½ in.

Status: fairly common summer resident in the Cascades and northeastern mountains; fairly common winter resident in western Washington; statewide migrant.

Habitat: *Breeding:* wet meadows with willow patches; streamside marshes; deciduous brush. *In migration* and *winter:* tall grass and dense brush in wet areas; coastal brush; salt-marsh margins.

Nesting: in a grass tussock or a shallow depression in moss; well-hidden nest of grass or sedges is lined with fine grass and hair; female incubates 4–5 russet-marked, pale green eggs for 12–14 days.

Feeding: scratches on the ground for insects, spiders, millipedes and seeds; occasionally visits feeders.

Voice: calls include a buzzy *zeee* and a *tsup. Male:* sings a musical mixture of buzzes, trills and warbled notes, often at night.

Similar Species: *Song Sparrow* (p. 329): stockier; heavier bill; less tidy and coarser streaking; central breast spot; less bubbly song; prefers more open, shrubby areas by wetlands; less secretive.

Best Sites: *Summer:* Snoqualmie Pass (King Co.–Kittitas Co.); Tucquala L. (FR 4330, Kittitas Co.); Buck Meadows (Kittitas Co.); Roger L. (FR 39, Okanogan Co.). *Winter:* Skagit Game Range (Skagit Co.); Discovery Park (Seattle); Marymoor Park (Redmond); Yakima Area Arboretum (Yakima).

SWAMP SPARROW

Melospiza georgiana

Sharing its habitat with blackbirds, wrens and yellowthroats, the Swamp Sparrow is one of the most common wetland inhabitants in eastern and northern parts of North America. It is perfectly suited to life around water. Because it eats mostly insects and fewer hard seeds than other sparrows, its bill and associated muscles are comparatively small. • The male Swamp Sparrow's song would not win any awards, but, in this bird's open habitat, a simple, dry, rattling trill is all that is required to gain the necessary attention from females. • The first state record of this eastern species dates from 1955, but few representatives were seen until the early 1970s. Since then, the Swamp Sparrow has been recorded annually in small numbers, especially at coastal locations. It is eagerly looked for during Christmas bird counts.

nonbreeding

ID: dark stripe behind eye; small, grayish bill with yellow base; black and buff stripes on back; rusty brown wings and tail; buff chestnut flanks; grayish breast; dark-bordered, whitish throat; pink legs. *Breeding male:* chestnut crown with pale median stripe; mostly gray face and nape. *Breeding female:* like breeding male, but with dark brown crown. *Nonbreeding:* weaker brown crown; olive tinge on face; buffier gray on breast.
Size: *L* 5–6 in; *W* 7–7½ in.
Status: rare western migrant and winter resident from late October to late February.
Habitat: marshy river mouths; wet grass-sedge meadows; cattail marsh edges; brushy habitats.

Nesting: does not nest in Washington.
Feeding: forages on the ground, on mud and in low marshland vegetation for insects and seeds; rarely visits feeders.
Voice: emphatic *tchip* call. *Male:* simple trill song has separated notes.
Similar Species: *White-throated Sparrow* (p. 332): larger; black or dark brown crown; more clearly defined white throat; yellow lores; white or light buff "eyebrow"; indistinct white wing bars. *White-crowned Sparrow* (p. 333): larger; black and white crown stripes; yellowish to pinkish bill; unmarked, buff gray underparts.
Best Sites: Skagit Game Range (Skagit Co.); Stillwater Wildlife Area (King Co.); Crescent Lake Wildlife Area (Monroe area); Spencer I. (Snohomish Co.); Union Bay Natural Area (Montlake Fill, Seattle); Nisqually NWR. *Fall:* Crow Butte SP (Benton Co.); Burbank Slough (McNary NWR).

WHITE-THROATED SPARROW

Zonotrichia albicollis

Listen to almost any film soundtrack that features a woodland setting, and you are almost sure to hear the unmistakable whistled song of the White-throated Sparrow, even though this forest songbird's breeding range is limited to Canada, the Great Lakes area and the northern eastern seaboard. • In Washington, a few White-throated Sparrows join winter flocks of White-crowned Sparrows and Golden-crowned Sparrows in the lowlands. Most of these White-throats stay in the brushy fields and hedgerows, but a few venture away from these open habitats to visit bird feeders, where they are often the first "rare birds" to be identified by novice birders. • The especially handsome "White-striped" White-throated Sparrows are about as common as the "Tan-striped" ones, and the two morphs often mate with each other.

"*Tan-striped" morph*

ID: dark eye line; pale gray bill; patterned, 2-tone brown back; rufous-marked, brown wing with 2 indistinct white bars; finely streaked, grayish brown breast and flanks; whitish belly; pale brown rump and tail; pink legs. *"White-striped" morph:* black crown with bold white median stripe and "eyebrow"; bright yellow lores; sharply defined white throat patch. *"Tan-striped" morph:* light tan median crown stripe and "eyebrow"; smudgier facial markings; fainter yellow lores; brown-tinged neck and flanks; divided white throat patch.
Size: *L* 6–7 in; *W* 9 in.

Status: uncommon western visitor from mid-October through April; rare in the east from mid-September through March.
Habitat: woodlands with brush; brushy patches in open country and residential areas; often associates with Golden-crowned Sparrow.
Nesting: does not nest in Washington.
Feeding: scratches the ground for insects, spiders, millipedes, snails and seeds; also eats small fruits; occasionally visits feeders.
Voice: distinctive, sharp *chink* call; foraging flocks use low, chuckling calls.
Similar Species: *White-crowned Sparrow* (p. 333): more peaked head; grayer face, throat and breast; yellowish to pinkish bill; duller rufous on wings; buzzy, trilled song. *Golden-crowned Sparrow* (p. 334): partly yellow crown; dull gray face and underparts; broad, black "eyebrow."
Best Sites: Skagit Game Range (Skagit Co.); L. Terrell (west of Ferndale, Whatcom Co.); Marymoor Park (Redmond); Nisqually NWR; Horan Natural Area (Wenatchee); Yakima Area Arboretum (Yakima); Burbank Slough (McNary NWR).

WHITE-CROWNED SPARROW

Zonotrichia leucophrys

Highly visible and audible at its breeding grounds, the ubiquitous White-crowned Sparrow is also a common member of winter lowland sparrow flocks. One of the most common of wintering sparrows, the White-crown enlivens dull situations in brushy expanses and suburban parks and gardens with its perky attitude and bright song. • The White-crown is one of North America's most studied sparrows. It has given scientists an intriguing, and somewhat confusing, insight into avian speciation and the geographic variation in song dialects. • Most breeders east of the Cascades are of the black-lored "Interior" race *(Z.l. oriantha)*, whereas those nesting in western Washington are of the pale-lored coastal "Pacific" race *(Z.l. pugetensis)*. In fall and winter, they are largely replaced by the grayer, pale-lored, more northerly breeding "Taiga" race *(Z.l. gambelli).*

ID: black-bordered, white crown stripe; broad, white "eyebrow"; black eye line; white or gray lores ("Pacific" and "Taiga") or black ones ("Interior"); pinkish to yellow bill; black-striped, brown back; lightly rufous-marked, brown wing with 2 white bars; buff or brown flanks; brownish rump; gray underparts; pale undertail coverts; pinkish to yellow legs.

Size: *L* 7 in; *W* 9½ in.

Status: *"Pacific":* common western resident in spring and summer. *"Taiga":* common western resident in fall and winter; common to fairly common year-round in eastern Washington. *"Interior":* fairly common in the northeast from mid-May to mid-September.

Habitat: *Breeding:* prefers coastal and mountain shrubby areas. *In migration* and *winter:* brushy areas, sometimes residential ones.

Nesting: on the ground or in a shrub or small conifer tree; neat nest is lined with fine materials; female incubates 3–5 russet-marked, pale greenish blue eggs for 11–14 days.

Feeding: forages on the ground for seeds and insects; gleans foliage and hawks for insects; also eats plant buds and similar items; visits feeders.

Voice: high *seet* and crisp *pink* calls. *Male:* song is a repeated *O see me pretty pretty me;* coastal birds sing a cleaner, more rapid, 4-part song.

Similar Species: *Golden-crowned Sparrow* (p. 334): yellow crown stripe; no white "eyebrow"; all- or partly gray bill. *White-throated Sparrow* (p. 332): yellow lores; gray bill; more rufous in wings; white throat.

Best Sites: widespread.

GOLDEN-CROWNED SPARROW
Zonotrichia atricapilla

Shortly before Golden-crowned Sparrows leave their winter quarters in Washington's roadside hedgerows, residential parks and neighborhoods to head north, they acquire the bold black "eyebrow" and bright golden crown of their breeding plumage and fine-tune their songs. Unlike many wintering birds, male Golden-crowns regularly sing throughout the colder months. • While foraging for seeds and invertebrates, these sociable sparrows team up with other ground-feeding birds, especially White-crowned Sparrows and Dark-eyed Juncos, as they scour shrubby open ground, dense brush and backyards. • This large sparrow nests in the weather-beaten subalpine meadow edges and tundra of the western Canadian mountains and Alaska, where its dreamy, whistled song is often both the last sound snowline campers hear at night and their morning wake-up call.

nonbreeding

ID: gray face; buff and black streaks on back; rufous-tinged, brownish wing with 2 white bars; light brown rump; gray underparts; pale rufous or tan streaking on sides and flanks. *Breeding:* broad, black "cap" with median stripe of yellow and white; yellowish lower mandible. *Nonbreeding:* less black in crown patch.
Size: *L* 7 in; *W* 9½ in.
Status: common western resident from October to mid-May; uncommon in eastern Washington from late September to late May.

Habitat: brush patches; brushy woodland edges at lower elevations; willows and forest edges at higher elevations.
Nesting: does not nest in Washington.
Feeding: scratches the ground for insects and seeds; also eats berries and other small fruits, moss capsules, buds, blossoms and fresh leaves; visits bird feeders, often with White-crowned Sparrows.
Voice: gives a sharp, loud *seek* call. *Male:* usual song is a 3-note whistle, but birds from the Canadian Rockies add a slow trill.
Similar Species: *White-crowned Sparrow* (p. 333): black and white stripes on head; pinkish to yellow bill. *White-throated Sparrow* (p. 332): black and white (or tan) head stripes; yellow lores; clearly defined white throat.
Best Sites: widespread in western Washington.

DARK-EYED JUNCO
Junco hyemalis

The Dark-eyed Junco is a widespread sparrow with easily recognizable subspecies, several of which are found in Washington. The brownish-sided, black-headed "Oregon Junco" is the common nesting and year-round resident in Washington, and the mostly gray "Slate-colored Junco," sporting its black "mask," is an uncommon migrant and winter resident. Other subspecies can be expected in Washington as well. • Juncos are nervous and flighty. The scissorlike flash of their white outer tail feathers is a familiar sight along rural roadsides and mountain trails. When they aren't nesting, they are gregarious, flocking in shrubby openings that offer open ground on which to search for seeds. These birds are routine visitors to backyard feeders, where they typically form the center of large, mixed-species sparrow flocks.

"Oregon Junco"

ID: large, dark eyes; pink bill; white belly and undertail coverts; gray or brownish rump and tail with prominent white outer feathers; pinkish legs. *"Oregon" male:* reddish brown back with paler sides and flanks; gray-and-brown wings; black "hood" and breast. *"Oregon" female:* gray instead of black.

Size: *L* 6 in; *W* 9–9½ in.

Status: common year-round resident statewide.

Habitat: *Breeding:* coniferous and hardwood forests; riparian areas within forests and in open country; residential parks and woodlots. *In migration* and *winter:* brushy, open country, towns and forest edges at lower elevations.

Nesting: usually on the ground, in a depression, or low in a shrub or tree; deep cup consists of coarse grass, moss, rootlets, bark and twigs; female incubates 3–5 chestnut-marked, pale blue eggs for 12–13 days.

Feeding: gleans the ground and low vegetation for seeds, insects and spiders; also hawks for flying insects; eats berries and visits feeders in fall and winter.

Voice: call is a high, often-repeated, clicking *stip;* wintering flocks keep up a constant ticking chorus. *Male:* song is a brief trill.

Similar Species: *Spotted Towhee* (p. 319): much larger; red eyes; white-dotted, black (male) or brown (female) back and wings; brilliant rufous sides and flanks; buff undertail coverts.

Best Sites: widespread in most woodland habitats, common in backyards in winter.

LAPLAND LONGSPUR
Calcarius lapponicus

Longspurs are small songbirds of mostly treeless country that breed on extensive plains or tundra. Of the four North American species, only the Lapland Longspur occurs in any numbers in Washington. It is best found by inspecting roaming flocks of Horned Larks, Snow Buntings and American Pipits. • A Lapland Longspur's extremely long claws aid it in finding food, but they are not suited to gripping branches, so this bird prefers perches such as flat-topped boulders, logs or posts on which it can spread its toes. • Males arriving here in fall have long since molted out of their spectacular breeding plumage, and most birds leave again by March, but a few later males may already be sporting their unmistakable black-and-rufous breeding colors.

nonbreeding

ID: back and wings are mottled with black, white and brown; rufous patch and 2 thin, white bars on wing; streaked, gray rump; white underparts; blackish legs; long claws. *Breeding male:* black crown, face, throat and mid-breast; white (often partly yellow) "L" stripe from eye to upper breast; yellow bill; boldly dark-streaked flanks; chestnut nape. *Female and nonbreeding male:* nape and black areas on head and breast look "washed out," and white areas on head and flanks may be buff; pinkish bill.
Size: *L* 6 in; *W* 11½ in.
Status: uncommon, mostly coastal migrant from mid-September to late November; uncommon migrant in the east in March and from November to mid-December and rare winter visitor from mid-December to

March; rare visitor in the west from December to May.
Habitat: dunes, estuary edges and plowed and fallow farmlands.
Nesting: does not nest in Washington.
Feeding: forages in flocks on the ground for seeds, such as waste grain, and invertebrates, including spiders.
Voice: mellow, whistled contact calls; rattled *tri-di-dit* and descending *teew* flight calls. *Male:* flight song is a rapid, slurred warble.
Similar Species: *Chestnut-collared Longspur:* very rare here; smaller; breeding male has black belly and pale buff throat; other plumages show little color.
Best Sites: Ocean Shores Game Range and Damon Pt. (Ocean Shores); Dungeness Spit (Sequim); Black Rock Valley (SR 24 east of Moxee); Rattlesnake Mt. (Benton Co.); Waterville Plateau (Douglas Co.); plateau above Grand Coulee (Grant Co.).

SNOW BUNTING

Plectrophenax nivalis

When early fall frosts settle on Washington's north-central plateaus and grasslands, Snow Buntings are surely close behind. They arrive in fall and endure winter in tight, wandering flocks, often with a few Lapland Longspurs mixed in, using their long hind claws to scratch away the snow in a search for seeds and waste grains scattered beneath. Searching these plateaus in winter can be rewarding, but it can be a challenge when they are covered in snow and fog. • As spring approaches, the warm rufous tones of the winter plumage fade to leave the male with a decidedly formal black-and-white look. • One bird took the trek to its breeding grounds in the Arctic a little too far. It was reported close to the North Pole, thus setting a record not known to have been beaten or matched by any other songbird.

♀

♂

nonbreeding

ID: dark eyes; stubby bill; black legs. *Breeding male:* brilliant white with black bill, back, wing tips and "wrist" patch. *Breeding female:* faint dark streaking on crown, "cheek" and nape; dark gray bill; dark areas browner than on male; white mottling on back, and more extensive on wing. *Nonbreeding:* warm, golden rufous crown, "cheek" and partial breast band; yellow bill; dark-streaked, rufous back and rump.
Size: *L* 6–7 in; *W* 14 in.
Status: uncommon in eastern Washington from October through December and fairly common from late December to mid-March; rare through winter in western Washington.

Habitat: open country, especially farmlands and grasslands; coastal sand dunes and beaches.
Nesting: does not nest in Washington.
Feeding: forages on the ground in large flocks; diet includes insects, spiders, seeds and buds; spring migrants eat fresh leaves.
Voice: call is a whistled *tew;* flocks keep up a constant twittering on the ground and especially in flight.
Similar Species: *McKay's Bunting:* very rare here; more white on head, back and wings in each plumage.
Best Sites: Black Rock Valley (SR 24 east of Moxee); Rattlesnake Mt. (Benton Co.); Waterville Plateau (Douglas Co.); plateau southeast of Grand Coulee (Grant Co.); Davenport–Reardan; Timentwa Flat (above Brewster, Okanogan Co.); Okanogan Highlands (Okanogan Co.).

BLACK-HEADED GROSBEAK
Pheucticus melanocephalus

Almost any spring or summer visit to hardwood woodlands will reveal Black-headed Grosbeaks. They arrive in mid-May, and the first sign they are present is often the robinlike songs of the males as they advertise their territories with extended bouts of complex, accented caroling. Meanwhile, the females forage and conduct the household chores within dense foliage cover, frequently betraying their presence with sharp, woodpecker-like calls that reassure the males. • Both genders share incubation, and the male will often sing from the nest. • Characteristic of hardwood habitats, even ones within broken conifer forests, Black-headed Grosbeaks are sometimes found alongside Steller's Jays in campgrounds and picnic sites. During migration, they also visit feeders.

ID: heavy, conical, bluish gray bill; bluish legs. *Breeding male:* generally orangy chestnut; blackish head; white-streaked, dark brown back; dark brown wing with 2 white bars; yellowish belly. *Breeding female:* white "eyebrow" and "mustache"; paler upperparts than male; buff to whitish neck and underparts.

Size: *L* 7–8 in; *W* 12–13 in.

Status: fairly common in lowland forests from mid-May to mid-August; uncommon migrant in early May and from mid-August to mid-September.

Habitat: hardwood and mixed forests, including bottomland willows and cottonwoods, riparian and lakeshore woodlands, maple forests and high-elevation aspen groves.

Nesting: in a tall shrub or hardwood tree, often near water; loose, bulky nest is lined with fine stems and rootlets; pair incubates 3–4 bluish green eggs, with brown and purple marks, for 12–13 days.

Feeding: gleans upper canopy for invertebrates, seeds, buds and fruit; occasionally visits feeders for seeds and small fruits.

Voice: high, woodpecker-like *pik* contact call. *Male:* leisurely, whistled, warbling song with a robinlike cadence is huskier and less measured.

Similar Species: *Bullock's Oriole* (p. 347): male has orange face with dark eye line, slimmer bill, larger white patch on upperwing and brighter underparts. *Hooded Oriole:* rare here; smaller; male has orangy "hood," slim bill and all-black tail.

Best Sites: Dungeness River Audubon Center (Sequim); Discovery Park (Seattle); Marymoor Park (Redmond); Skagit R. (Skagit Co.); Nisqually NWR; SR 10 at Teanaway R. (Kittitas Co.); White R. (Yakima Co.); Champneys Slough (Okanogan Co.); Lewis and Clark Trail SP (Columbia Co.).

LAZULI BUNTING

Passerina amoena

S mall flocks of Lazuli Buntings work their way northward into Washington in spring, bringing a splash of color to feeders and desert oases. They do not demand much of their environment, making use of dry brushlands and woodland edges and often sharing their quarters with Black-headed Grosbeaks in the upper canopy. • From May to late July, the brightly colored male's crisp and varied songs punctuate the hot "siesta hours" during which only a handful of other species regularly vocalize. Singing intensity diminishes as broods are fledged. • By late August, most Lazuli Buntings have deserted their summer homes. They undergo a partial molt before they leave, completing their change of plumage at their wintering grounds.

ID: pale, stubby, conical bill; whitish belly and undertail coverts; bluish tail; dark legs. *Breeding male:* bright blue head, back and rump; gray-and-blue wing with 2 white bars; orangy chestnut breast; pinkish buff sides. *Nonbreeding male:* tan-mottled, blue upperparts; duller breast. *Female:* buff eye ring; dull grayish brown upperparts; 2 pale wing bars; off-white underparts; buff breast.
Size: *L* 5½ in; *W* 9 in.
Status: fairly common resident of eastern mid-elevations from early May to late July; uncommon eastern migrant from mid-April to early May and early to mid-August; uncommon in western lowlands from mid-May to mid-July.
Habitat: bottomland open woods; weedy fields with brushy margins; streamside or high-elevation willows; brushy slopes and chaparral. *In migration:* sagebrush, desert oases.
Nesting: in a crotch in a shrubby tangle; coarsely woven nest of dried grass and other plants is lined with fine grass and hair; female incubates 3–5 pale bluish white eggs for 12 days.
Feeding: feeds on the ground; gleans low shrubs; eats invertebrates and seeds; visits feeders.
Voice: buzzy, trilling flight calls and woodpecker-like *pik* notes. *Male:* song is a brief, varied warbling note series.
Similar Species: *Indigo Bunting:* rare here; breeding male is blue overall; breeding female has faintly streaked underparts and vaguer wing markings; hybrids are regularly seen.
Best Sites: Reecer Creek Rd. (Ellensburg); Taneum Creek (Kittitas Co.); Ellensburg Pass (Yakima Co.); Hardy Canyon (Yakima Co.); Lower Crab Creek Rd. (Grant Co.); Rock Creek Rd. (Klickitat Co.); Sinlahekin Valley; Field Springs SP (Asotin Co.).

BOBOLINK

Dolichonyx oryzivorus

The plumage and breeding strategies of the male Bobolink are unlike those of any other North American bird. Roger Tory Peterson described him as "wearing a backward tuxedo," but his courting tactics are very forward as he flashes his yellowish buff nape and white wing patches at any female within view. If that doesn't work, he launches into a bubbly, zestful song in a trembling song-flight or atop a low bush. • Once his early-summer duties have been performed, the male Bobolink acquires the same cryptic coloring as his mate and gets ready for fall migration. • "Bobolink" may be an abbreviation of "Robert O. Lincoln," the subject and title of a poem by William Cullen Bryant that used the phrase in its interpretation of the bird's song, but the name could have originated earlier.

Habitat: *Breeding:* grassy meadows interspersed with sedges and shrubs; alfalfa meadows and tall grass. *In migration:* mainly habitats close to breeding colonies.

Nesting: colonial; in a ground depression in dense plant cover; coarse nest is lined with fine materials; female incubates 5–6 purple-marked, gray to pale rufous eggs for 10–13 days.

Feeding: gleans the ground and low vegetation for adult and larval invertebrates, including spiders, and seeds.

Voice: *pink* flight call. *Male:* song, often issued in flight, is a series of bubbly notes and banjolike twangs: *bobolink bobolink spink spank spink.*

Similar Species: *Lark Bunting:* recorded in Oregon and British Columbia; breeding male has black nape and rump; female and nonbreeding male are browner, with dark breast spot and unevenly streaked underparts.

Best Sites: Chopaka Rd. (north of Loomis); Havillah Rd. (northeast of Tonasket); Aeneas Valley Rd. at SR 20 (Okanogan Co.); Chewelah (Stevens Co.); Cusick (Pend Oreille Co.).

ID: sharp-tipped tail feathers; pink legs. *Breeding male:* mostly black plumage; black bill; yellowish buff nape; white shoulder patch and rump. *Breeding female:* pale buff head and underparts; black crown and line behind eye; pink bill; sparrowlike, brown-striped back and wings; sandy brown rump. *Nonbreeding:* similar to breeding female, except yellower overall.

Size: *L* 6–8 in; *W* 11–12 in.

Status: fairly common local resident from late May to early July in Okanogan Co. and the northeast and very localized in Yakima Co. during this period.

RED-WINGED BLACKBIRD

Agelaius phoeniceus

Bright red shoulder patches and a raspy song are the male Red-winged Blackbird's most important tools in the often intricate strategy he uses to defend his territory. A richly voiced male who has established a high-quality territory can attract several mates to his cattail kingdom. His main role during summer is to defend his hard-won territory against encroaching males, usurping Yellow-headed Blackbirds and marauding Marsh Wrens (which may destroy the eggs and young, although not often for food). • With his breeding-season duties completed, the male Red-winged Blackbird becomes just another member of a large flock of foraging blackbirds roaming agricultural fields, grasslands and marshes. These flocks, augmented by other species and by northern immigrants, can number in the hundreds, and sometimes thousands, and are a regular feature of Washington winters.

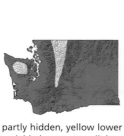

ID: *Male:* all-black, non-glossy plumage; orangy red shoulder patch with partly hidden, yellow lower border. *Female:* variable brown overall; heavily streaked, especially on belly and flanks; usually some rufous on upperparts.

Size: *L* 7–9 in; *W* 12–13 in.

Status: common year-round resident statewide.

Habitat: *Breeding:* freshwater bodies with standing aquatic vegetation, including ditches and flooded fields. *In migration and winter:* dry agricultural fields and marshes.

Nesting: usually in cattails, reeds or other vegetation; woven nest of sedges, dried cattails and grass; female incubates 3–4 dark-marked, pale bluish green eggs for 10–12 days.

Feeding: gleans the ground and vegetation for seeds, including waste grain, and invertebrates; catches insects in flight; eats fruit in fall and winter; sometimes visits feeders.

Voice: calls include a harsh *check* and high *tseert. Male:* song is a loud, raspy *konk-a-ree* or *ogle-reeeee. Female:* may give a *che-che-che chee chee chee.*

Similar Species: *Tricolored Blackbird* (p. 342): male has glossier plumage, white lower border to shoulder patch and different song; female's plumage is darker, with less contrast and no rufous.

Best Sites: *Summer:* wetland areas statewide. *Winter:* fields, feedlots.

341

TRICOLORED BLACKBIRD

Agelaius tricolor

Found solely along the Pacific coast of the U.S. and northern Mexico, the Tricolored Blackbird is not much of a migrator, although it does move from place to place within this range. • Birders should study any dense colony of nesting blackbirds for Tricolors, which are strictly colonial and nonterritorial. In Washington, the only known colony is small compared to the colonies composed of hundreds, sometimes thousands, of birds per acre found in California. • After the breeding season, males and females go their separate ways in nomadic, gender-specific flocks that include cowbirds, starlings and other blackbirds. • The draining of productive marshlands has accelerated the decline of this species, which lacks the nesting versatility of the Red-winged Blackbird.

ID: *Male:* glossy, all-black plumage; small, dark red shoulder patch has white (buff when fresh) lower border. *Female:* dark brownish gray overall; streaked and mottled, especially on belly; pale "eyebrow" and throat.
Size: *L* 7–9 in; *W* 13–14 in.
Status: rare but regular, localized breeding resident in eastern Washington; somewhat more widespread in migration and winter; casual in winter in the Columbia Basin and around the Vancouver lowlands.
Habitat: *Breeding:* cattail and tule marshes. *In migration* and *winter:* in farmlands with other blackbirds.

Nesting: colonial; in reeds, cattails or willows, near or over water, rarely in crop fields; bulky, woven nest of marsh vegetation and grass; female incubates 3–4 brown-marked, pale green eggs for 11–13 days; young fledge at 11–14 days.
Feeding: forages in flocks on the ground; gleans the foliage of trees and shrubs; eats insects, snails, seeds and waste grain.
Voice: gives calls similar to the Red-winged Blackbird's, but less accomplished. *Male:* harsh-sounding song is a poorly refined, less bubbly, short, falling *awnk-krr-awnngk.*
Similar Species: *Red-winged Blackbird* (p. 341): flat black plumage; shoulder patch has yellowish lower border; female is paler and crisper looking, often with rufous in plumage.
Best Sites: *Summer:* marsh on Crab Creek east of town of Wilson Creek (Grant Co.). *Winter:* Othello.

WESTERN MEADOWLARK
Sturnella neglecta

The Western Meadowlark displays a combination of cryptic coloration on the upperparts and bright courtship elegance on the underparts. To show off his plumage and vocal abilities to potential mates, the male finds a prominent perch or indulges in a brash display flight. If he notices human observers, the male will often turn away, hiding his brightly colored underparts. • When the female needs to draw predators away from her nest, she flashes her yellow, black and white plumage in a fast-moving blur. As soon as the nest is safe, she folds away her white tail flags, and her well-camouflaged back allows her to return to the nest undetected. • Western Meadowlarks have benefited from the conversion of sagebrush to grassland, and their numbers have declined wherever large expanses of grassland habitat have been degraded by overgrazing or replaced by monoculture crops or asphalt.

breeding

ID: long, sharp, pale bill; short, banded tail with whitish outer feathers. *Breeding:* dark-mottled, pale sandy brown overall; yellow throat, lower breast and belly; black "V" breast band; boldly black-streaked, whitish flanks and undertail coverts. *Nonbreeding:* paler, with indistinct breast band.
Size: *L* 8–10 in; *W* 14–15 in.
Status: common resident of eastern Washington from March to October, fairly common migrant and uncommon in winter; locally common to uncommon year-round in western Washington.

Habitat: grasslands, rough pastures and deserts. *Winter:* sandspits and airports.
Nesting: in a natural or scraped depression on the ground; domed canopy, with a side entrance, consists of grass, bark and plant stems interconnected with surrounding vegetation; female incubates 3–7 white eggs, marked with purple and brown, for 13–15 days.
Feeding: walks and runs on the ground, gleaning grasshoppers, crickets, sowbugs, snails and spiders; also eats seeds and probes the soil for grubs, worms and insects.
Voice: issues a *bluk* and a rattling call. *Male:* song is a rich series of flutelike warbles.
Similar Species: none.
Best Sites: Brady Loop Rd. (Grays Harbor Co.); Marymoor Park (Redmond); West Snoqualmie River Rd. (south of Carnation); Hidden Valley Rd. (Kittitas Co.); Umtanum Rd. (Kittitas Co.); open areas throughout eastern Washington.

YELLOW-HEADED BLACKBIRD
Xanthocephalus xanthocephalus

One of the first signs of spring in many freshwater marshes is the arrival of the male Yellow-headed Blackbird and his raw, rasping song. Standing head and shoulders above his Red-winged Blackbird neighbors, the later-arriving male Yellow-headed Blackbird bullies his way to the choicest areas, forcing the Red-wings to the outskirts, where predation is highest. • Once the males have staked out their territories, the females arrive. From their nest sites, pairs forage a mile or more into croplands and pastures. The bright yellow heads of the males make large colonies resemble fields of mustard. After the colony completes its breeding season, flocks gather to feed with other blackbirds. Most birds depart before winter's chill, but a few occasionally remain with wintering flocks of other blackbird species.

ID: *Male:* black body; orangy yellow head and breast; black lores; white wing patches. *Female:* dark brown overall; dull yellow face and breast.
Size: *L* 8–11 in; *W* 13–15 in.
Status: fairly common to common in eastern Washington from mid-April to late August and uncommon migrant in early spring and from September to November; rare winter resident in the Moses L.–Potholes area; uncommon, very local summer resident in western Washington.
Habitat: *Breeding:* large freshwater marshes. *In migration:* agricultural areas.
Nesting: colonial but territorial; over water in cattails or shoreline shrubs; bulky nest is firmly woven with wet vegetation and lined with dried grass; female incubates 4 greenish or grayish white eggs, with gray and brown markings, for 11–13 days.
Feeding: gleans vegetation and probes the ground for seeds and invertebrates; also opens cattail heads for larval invertebrates.
Voice: calls are harsher than those of the Red-winged Blackbird, except for a whistled trill and soft *kruk* or *kruttuk* flight call. *Male:* song is a strained, metallic grating similar to the sound of an old chainsaw.
Similar Species: none.
Best Sites: Rattlesnake Mt. (Benton Co.); Frenchman Coulee (Grant Co.); Dodson Rd. (Grant Co.); Para Ponds (Othello); Wilson Creek (with Tricolored Blackbirds; Grant Co.); Cassimer Bar (US 97 just east of Brewster); Conners L. (Sinlahekin Valley); Turnbull NWR.

BREWER'S BLACKBIRD

Euphagus cyanocephalus

Even in some residential areas, male Brewer's Blackbirds in their glossy plumage can easily be seen strutting their stuff to impress the dowdy females. Rather than gathering in large colonies, Brewer's Blackbirds nest in small groups or as widely dispersed pairs. For this reason, they are more widespread in summer than colony-nesting blackbirds. Following nesting, adults and juveniles form small flocks, which then team up with roving mobs of other blackbirds, Brown-headed Cowbirds and European Starlings to form large flocks that spread out over lowland fields and wetlands throughout winter. • Our network of highways provides a bounty of vehicle-struck insects for Brewer's Blackbirds, which exploit this roadkill resource better than any other songbird. They also use this resource in moving into urban areas around the state.

ID: walks with a head-up strut, with head nodding at each step. *Male:* all-black plumage, glossed purple on head and breast and green on back, wings and tail; pale yellow eyes. *Female:* dull grayish brown overall; eyes usually dark.
Size: *L* 8–9 in; *W* 15–15½ in.
Status: common year-round resident of low to mid-elevations west and east of the Cascades.
Habitat: *Breeding:* open areas near wetlands and farmlands; grasslands; sagebrush-greasewood deserts. *Winter:* agricultural areas, roadsides and suburbs.
Nesting: loosely colonial; in a tree, on the ground, in a shrub or in marsh vegetation; sturdy basket of twigs and grass is cemented with mud or cow dung and lined with grass, rootlets and hair or fur; female incubates 4–6 brown-marked, grayish eggs for 12–14 days.
Feeding: picks, gleans or chases food items; eats a wide variety of invertebrates, seeds and fruit; often wades in shallow water to feed.
Voice: unusually quiet for a blackbird; gives a plain *chek* call. *Male:* song is a creaking, 2-note *k-sheee*.
Similar Species: *Brown-headed Cowbird* (p. 346): smaller; stouter bill; dark eyes; male has brown head; sandy brown female has some streaking on underparts.
Best Sites: open fields and farmlands; sage shrub-steppe areas; along highways; increasingly in open areas in urban and suburban areas, particularly in winter.

BROWN-HEADED COWBIRD
Molothrus ater

The Brown-headed Cowbird once followed the great bison herds across the Great Plains and Prairies of central North America. With its nomadic lifestyle making building and tending nests impractical, it learned to lay its eggs in the nests of other birds, thus passing on the parental responsibilities. In spring, female Brown-headed Cowbirds are frequently seen exploring for potential host nests. • Some warblers and vireos recognize the odd eggs, but many birds simply incubate cowbird eggs along with their own. Often hatching earlier than the host's young, nestling cowbirds get most of the food provided by the often smaller foster parents. Because ranching expansion, forest fragmentation, urbanization and an increase in transportation corridors have allowed the cowbird's range to dramatically increase, more species, unable to discern the stranger in their midst, have become unwilling hosts.

ID: dark eyes; stout bill; dark legs. *Male:* brown head, green gloss on black body. *Female:* grayish brown overall, typically with fine-streaked underparts.

Size: *L* 6–8 in; *W* 12 in.

Status: common statewide resident from mid-April to late July; fairly common migrant west of the Cascades in early to mid-April and from August through October and uncommon from November to mid-April; fairly common migrant east of the Cascades in late April and August and uncommon from September to late April.

Habitat: *Breeding:* arid sagebrush and juniper country, farmlands, marshes, grasslands, conifers and hardwood woodlands.

Nesting: female lays up to 40 eggs singly in other birds' nests; brown-marked, grayish eggs hatch in 10–13 days.

Feeding: gleans the ground for seeds, waste grain and invertebrates, especially grasshoppers and beetles, often those flushed by livestock; gleans tree foliage for caterpillars and other items in summer.

Voice: issues squeaky, high-pitched *seep, psee* and *wee-tse-tse* calls, often given in flight; also gives a fast chipping note series. *Male:* song is a high, liquidy, gurgling *glug-ahl-whee* or *bubbloozeee.*

Similar Species: *Brewer's Blackbird* (p. 345): larger; longer bill and tail; male has purple-glossed head and yellow eyes; unstreaked female is darker brown.

Best Sites: *Summer:* woodlands. *Winter:* farmlands and suburban areas in western Washington; livestock pens in eastern Washington.

BULLOCK'S ORIOLE

Icterus bullockii

Although the Bullock's Oriole is common and widespread in much of Washington, most residents are unaware of its existence. The plumage of the male blends remarkably well with the sunlit and shadowed upper-canopy summer foliage where he spends much of his time. When clearly seen in bright sunlight, however, he never fails to elicit a "Wow!" from observers, particularly new birders. Drab plumage camouflages the female, and very elaborate hanging nests provide protection and shelter for the offspring. • The Bullock's Oriole is a good example of how bird names can change. Considered a separate species for more than a century, this oriole was then for a time lumped with the Baltimore Oriole *(I. galbula)* as the "Northern Oriole."

ID: dark eyes; bluish gray bill and legs. *Male:* black crown, upperparts and throat patch; bright orange face, underparts and rump; black eye line; large white wing patch; black-tipped, orange tail. *Female:* yellow head and breast; gray back and wings; 2 white wing bars; whitish underparts; yellowish orange rump and tail.

Size: *L* 7–9 in; *W* 11–12 in.

Status: common eastern resident from mid-May through most of July; uncommon western riparian resident from May through July; fairly common eastern migrant in early May and late July and uncommon in early August; rare western migrant in late April and early August.

Habitat: riparian cottonwoods and willows; semi-open oak and madrone woodlands; ranches and towns with shade trees; rarely in juniper forests.

Nesting: attached to a high, drooping hardwood branch; woven nest of plant fibers is lined with fine materials; female incubates 4–5 dark-marked, grayish or bluish white eggs for 12–14 days.

Feeding: gleans upper-canopy foliage and shrubs for caterpillars, wasps and other invertebrates; also eats small fruits and plant nectar; sometimes visits feeders.

Voice: 2-note whistles; dry chatters. *Male:* song is a rich, sharply punctuated series of 6–8 whistled and guttural notes.

Similar Species: *Black-headed Grosbeak* (p. 338): all-black head; short, heavy bill; orangy chestnut breast; smaller wing patches; all-dark tail.

Best Sites: Marymoor Park (Redmond); Tolt MacDonald Park (Carnation); Nisqually NWR; SR 10 at Teanaway R. (Kittitas Co.); Umtanum Creek upstream of Yakima R.; Oak Creek Rd. (off US 12; Yakima Co.); Rock Creek Rd. (Klickitat Co.); Okanogan R. valley; Lewis and Clark Trail SP (Columbia Co.).

347

GRAY-CROWNED ROSY-FINCH
Leucosticte tephrocotis

The remarkable rosy-finches spend summer around the summits and higher slopes of mountains with permanent snowfields and glaciers. During the nesting season, they conserve energy by taking slow, measured steps across patches of snow as they inspect crevices for chilled or weakened insects and other small invertebrates. At the end of summer, family groups assemble into larger flocks that remain in the alpine zone until driven into the lowlands by the first major winter storms. • Two fairly distinct races of Gray-crowned Rosy-Finch appear in Washington. Most of our winter Gray-crowns are the gray-cheeked "Hepburn's Rosy-Finch" *(L. t. littoralis)*, which also breeds here. The brown-cheeked "Interior" race *(L. t. tephrocotis)*, for which the species is named, also occurs here in winter, most often in the southeast.

"Interior"
breeding

"Hepburn's"
breeding

ID: dark eyes; conical bill; blackish legs. *Breeding male:* gray "cap" or "hood" with dark forehead and throat; black bill; brown back, wings and underparts; rosy wing coverts, flanks and rump; dark tail. *Female and nonbreeding male:* generally paler, with less pink in plumage; yellow bill.
Size: *L* 6 in; *W* 13 in.
Status: uncommon high-elevation summer breeder and lowland winter resident east of the Cascades; uncommon breeder at high elevations on the western slopes of the Cascades, with a small population in the Olympics, from mid-May to late September.
Habitat: *Breeding:* near summer snowfields, alpine glaciers and barren rocky areas above timberline. *Winter:* snowfields above timberline; open fields and exposed hillsides at lower elevations; often in rocky coulees.
Nesting: typically among rocks; bulky nest consists of moss, grass and lichen; female incubates 4–5 white eggs for 12–14 days.
Feeding: walks and hops on the ground or snow (and on the edge of water, ice or snow) gleaning small seeds and insects.
Voice: flight call is a soft chirp. *Male:* song is a long warble.
Similar Species: none.
Best Sites: *Summer* (all reached by hiking trails): Paradise and Sunrise (Mt. Rainier NP); Skyline Divide Trail and Ptarmigan Ridge Trail (Mt. Baker area); West Fork Pasayten River Trail (Harts Pass, Okanogan Co.). *Winter:* Huntzinger Rd. (south of Vantage); Frenchman Coulee (Grant Co.); Lower Grand Coulee and L. Lenore (Douglas Co.); south of Mansfield (Douglas Co.); Lower Granite Dam (Garfield Co.).

PINE GROSBEAK
Pinicola enucleator

Pine Grosbeaks favor the solitude of mountain forests and timberline scrub. Here they feed at leisure and occasionally introduce themselves with a distinctive loud, whistling call uttered from the highest point they can find. Every now and again, an early summer hiker might be surprised by what seems to be the song of a robin high atop a mountain, only to find that the songster is a particularly beautiful finch. Sometimes you can walk right past one as it sits still on a perch in the forest. Anyone fortunate enough to have Pine Grosbeaks visiting their feeder in winter may also get to hear this quiet, warbled song from a bird that has adorned many a Christmas card. • The Latin term *enucleator* refers to the bird's method of obtaining seeds hidden in protective cones.

ID: dark eyes; dark, conical bill with downcurved tip; dark wing with 2 white bars; dark tail; dark legs. *Male:* rosy red head, back, rump and underparts; grayish sides, belly and undertail coverts. *Female:* generally gray; yellowish olive or russet crown, face and rump.

Size: *L* 8–9 in; *W* 14–15 in.

Status: uncommon year-round resident of the Olympics, Cascades, northeastern mountains and Blue Mts.; uncommon winter visitor to adjacent lower slopes.

Habitat: *Breeding:* coniferous forests above the ponderosa pine zone. *In migration and winter:* coniferous and mixed forests; rarely in lowland wooded areas and towns.

Nesting: in a conifer or tall shrub; loose, bulky nest consists of moss, twigs, grass and lichen; female incubates 4 heavily marked, bluish green eggs for 13–15 days.

Feeding: forages on the ground for seeds; gleans foliage for insects; enjoys crab apples, mountain-ash berries, pine seeds and maple buds; visits gardens and feeders in winter and spring.

Voice: call is a 3-note *tew* whistle with a higher middle note; short, muffled trill in flight. *Male:* song is a short, sweet musical warble.

Similar Species: *Red Crossbill* (p. 353) and *White-winged Crossbill* (p. 366): much smaller; longer, crossed bills; White-winged has bolder wing patches.

Best Sites: *Summer:* high in the Olympics, Cascades and Selkirk Mts.; Harts Pass (Okanogan Co.); Rainy Pass (SR 20); Washington Pass (Okanogan Co.). *Winter:* places with lingering fruit; northern Okanogan Valley and Methow River Valley.

PURPLE FINCH

Carpodacus purpureus

Take a walk along forested lower mountain slopes or in riparian or mixed-oak woodlands, and you are almost certain to hear, emanating from the highest branch, the continuous, bubbly warble of a male Purple Finch. • Roger Tory Peterson described this finch best when he said the male looks like a "sparrow dipped in raspberry juice." Not all singing birds will appear this color—first-year males practice their songs before they get their adult coats, and some males are an aberrant yellow or orange, much like the more widespread House Finch. Females occasionally also sing softly during nest-building. • Unlike Purple Finches in the east and House Finches in the west, western Purple Finches show no affinity for highly developed urban and residential areas.

Habitat: coniferous and mixed forests. *In migration* and *winter:* hardwood forests, shrubby open areas and feeders with nearby tree cover.

Nesting: on a conifer branch, far from the trunk; female builds a cup nest of twigs, grass and rootlets lined with moss and hair; female incubates 4–5 dark-marked, pale greenish blue eggs for about 13 days.

Feeding: gleans the ground and vegetation for seeds (often from ash trees), buds, berries and insects; readily visits table-style feeders.

Voice: single, metallic *cheep* or *weet* call; song is a bubbly, continuous warble.

Similar Species: *Cassin's Finch* (p. 351): male has bright red forecrown; female's streaks are darker and clearer. *House Finch* (p. 352): squared tail; male has orangy crown and brown flanks; female has plainer face. *Red Crossbill* (p. 353): larger, crossed bill.

Best Sites: widespread but declining in western lowland mixed forests; Cle Elum; Wenas Campground area (Yakima Co.); Nile Rd. (Yakima Co.); Wolf Creek Rd. (Winthrop).

ID: black eyes; gray, sometimes pink-tinged bill; dull orangy legs. *Male:* raspberry red (occasionally yellow to salmon pink) head, throat, breast and nape; brownish "cheek"; streaked, brown-and-red back and flanks; red rump; pale, unstreaked belly and undertail coverts; notched tail. *Female:* dark brown "cheek" and jaw line; white "eyebrow" and lower "cheek" stripe; heavily streaked underparts; unstreaked undertail coverts.

Size: *L* 5–6 in; *W* 10 in.

Status: fairly common year-round resident of western lowlands to mid-elevation; uncommon resident of moist, low slopes of the eastern Cascades from April to early November and otherwise rare.

CASSIN'S FINCH

Carpodacus cassinii

The Cassin's, Purple and House finches are all present in Washington. Having three *Carpodacus* finches to contend with makes Christmas bird counts even more interesting, but these birds generally go their separate ways in summer. Cassin's Finches claim the eastern mountain ranges, Purple Finches nest mostly at lower elevations west of the Cascades, and House Finches are the common open-country and lowland species. The variability in the plumage of immature males, which may be orange or yellow in all three species, and their tendency to intermix in winter, add up to inevitable confusion. • Traveling in small flocks, the Cassin's Finch would probably go unnoticed except for its characteristic calls.

ID: pale, conical bill; pale-ringed, dark eyes; heavily dark-streaked, grayish brown upperparts. *Male:* pinkish wash on wings and back; whitish sides, flanks and belly; pinkish red on rump, breast and head; bright red crown. *Female:* distinctly dark-streaked, white underparts.

Size: *L* 6–6½ in; *W* 11–12 in.

Status: common resident of eastern dry forests from May to August; uncommon in eastern Washington from September to April; uncommon on open subalpine slopes of the western Cascades from mid-May to mid-September.

Habitat: *Breeding:* mid- to high-elevation forests, especially ponderosa and lodgepole pines but also firs and cottonwoods; aspen groves close to conifers. *In migration and winter:* moves to lower foothills and valleys.

Nesting: near the end of a large conifer limb, rarely in a shrub; nest consists of grass, moss, bark shreds, rootlets and lichen; female incubates 4–5 dark-spotted, bluish green eggs for 12–14 days.

Feeding: gleans foliage and the ground for conifer seeds, buds, berries and insects; often visits winter feeders.

Voice: flight call is a warbling *kiddileep*. *Male:* rich, warbling song.

Similar Species: *Purple Finch* (p. 350): no pale eye ring; shorter, slightly curved bill; more widespread pink on male; female has prominent white "eyebrow," less clear, browner streaks and unstreaked undertail coverts; song is lower and less lively. *House Finch* (p. 352): squared tail; male has orangy crown and brown flanks; female has plainer face.

Best Sites: Sinlahekin Valley; Loup Loup Campground (Okanogan Co.); Methow Valley (Okanogan Co.); Roslyn; Hidden Valley Rd. (Kittitas Co.); Wenas Campground (Yakima Co.); Bethel Ridge Rd. (off US 12); Northrup Canyon SP (Grant Co.).

HOUSE FINCH
Carpodacus mexicanus

Formerly restricted to the arid Southwest and Mexico, the House Finch has, with the help of humans, spread across all the lower 48 states and into southern Canada. Introductions to the eastern U.S. and the urbanization of much of California have both helped to establish this bird. • In 1918, the House Finch was a common permanent resident in Washington just from Walla Walla to the Okanogan. Since then, it has colonized all the valleys and coastal lowlands west of the Cascades and is now found throughout the state. • Depending on how well each individual male House Finch processes the carotenoids in his diet, he can be the usual reddish color or more of a yellowish orange. • The male's cheerful song may be heard year-round, and no berry bush, grassy patch or weedy shrub is beyond the interest of family parties in late summer and fall.

ID: gray, conical bill; dark eyes; dark legs. *Male:* reddish orange (sometimes yellow) crown, throat, breast and "cheek"; weakly streaked back; blurry brown streaking on whitish sides, flanks and belly. *Female:* pale eye ring; drab brown overall, with blurry streaking.
Size: *L* 5–6 in; *W* 9–10 in.
Status: common year-round lowland resident statewide.
Habitat: disturbed areas, including farms, ranches, towns, residential areas, open fields and woodlands; often visits feeders in winter.

Nesting: in a cavity, building, dense shrub or abandoned nest; nest consists of twigs, grass, leaves, rootlets and hair; female incubates 4–5 bluish eggs for 12–14 days.
Feeding: forages on the ground and in shrubbery for small insects, seeds and juniper berries; fond of maple sap and hardwood buds; eats dirt and gravel for minerals and salts.
Voice: gives a sweet *cheer* flight call singly or in a series. *Male:* song is a bright, disjointed warble lasting about 3 seconds, often ending with a harsh *jeeer* or *wheer.*
Similar Species: *Cassin's Finch* (p. 351): pale "spectacles"; male has bright red crown, and streaks on underparts are limited to flanks and undertail coverts; female's streaks are darker and clearer.
Best Sites: widespread, especially around urban and suburban areas and farms.

RED CROSSBILL

Loxia curvirostra

With crossed bill tips and nimble tongues, crossbills are uniquely adapted for extracting seeds from conifer cones. • Irregular cone distribution forces Red Crossbills into a nomadic existence. They can often be located by listening for their loud calls wherever the boughs of conifers are laden with ripe or ripening cones. If they discover a bumper crop, they might stay to breed regardless of the season (late winter or early spring is typical), and it is not unusual to hear Red Crossbills singing in midwinter or to find newly fledged juveniles begging for food in November or February. • Ongoing research, based on different vocalizations, bill sizes and seed preferences, suggests that the Red Crossbill may consist of up to eight (or more) "sibling species," of which six occur in Washington.

ID: heavy, obviously crossed bill; dark eyes; dark brown wings; dusky legs. *Male:* generally brick red; grayish bars on lower flanks; possibly 2 narrow, buff wing bars. *Female:* generally yellowish to olive green.
Size: *L* 5–6 in; *W* 10–11 in.
Status: fairly common year-round; may visit lowlands in winter.
Habitat: coniferous forests; occasionally in hardwood habitats as a nonbreeder; rarely at feeders.
Nesting: loosely colonial; on an outer conifer branch, usually high in the canopy; loose, bulky nest consists of twigs, grass, moss, rootlets and bark strips; female incubates 3–4 darkly spotted, pale blue or green eggs for 12–18 days.
Feeding: perches in conifers to extract seeds; sometimes feeds on the ground; eats insects, spruce buds, berries and seeds; licks

salt, ash or minerals from the ground or rocks.
Voice: distinctive *jip-jip* call note, often in flight. *Male:* typical finch song is a varied series of warbles, trills and *chip* notes.
Similar Species: *White-winged Crossbill* (p. 366): 2 prominent white wing bars; male is usually pinker; female has blurry underpart streaking. *Pine Grosbeak* (p. 349): larger; shorter, uncrossed bill; 2 prominent white wing bars; more gray in plumage.
Best Sites: Dungeness Audubon Center (Sequim); Cape Disappointment (Columbia R. mouth); Snoqualmie Pass (I-90); Mt. Rainier NP; Bethel Ridge Rd. (off US 12); Meadows Campground (Okanogan Co.); Loup Loup Campground (Okanogan Co.); Sherman Pass Campground (Ferry Co.); Mt. Spokane SP.

353

PINE SISKIN
Carduelis pinus

The abundance of Pine Siskins fluctuates seasonally and with the availability of favored food sources, so you can wait months or even years to see one. Your best strategy is to frequent conifer forests in summer and to be alert for rapidly moving flocks of small, finchlike birds in winter. • When plentiful, Pine Siskins consume seed in great quantities, and even a small lingering flock can necessitate daily feeder restocking. Keep the seed dry and disinfect the feeder regularly to prevent salmonellosis outbreaks that may weaken or kill siskins and other feeder users. • Pine Siskins are often heard before they are seen, their distinctive calls confirming their presence high in the canopy. Restless winter flocks are often observed flashing their yellow wing and tail patches as they move around their territories.

ID: small, sharp, dusky bill; dark-streaked, brown upperparts; whitish belly; brown legs. *Male:* large yellow wing bar and small white one; brown-streaked, white underparts; may have overall yellow wash. *Female:* brown lower border on "cheek"; white wing bars; brown-washed sides and breast.
Size: *L* 4–5 in; *W* 8–9 in.
Status: common year-round western resident and erratic migrant; common in eastern Washington from mid-March to late August and otherwise uncommon.
Habitat: *Breeding:* coniferous forests, especially firs, spruces and hemlocks; rarely in pines. *In migration* and *winter:* low-elevation woodlands, shrubbery and residential areas.
Nesting: loosely colonial; usually on an outer conifer branch; nest of twigs, rootlets and grass is lined with fine rootlets, moss, fur and feathers; female incubates 3–4 darkly spotted, pale greenish blue eggs for 13 days.
Feeding: gleans the ground, shrubby vegetation and tree foliage for seeds, buds and insects; attracted to road salt, mineral licks and ashes; regularly visits feeders for niger seeds and sunflower seeds.
Voice: utters a distinctive, buzzy, ascending *zzzreeeee* call. *Male:* song is a variable, bubbly mix of squeaky, metallic and raspy notes, sometimes resembling a jerky laugh.
Similar Species: *Carpodacus finches* (pp. 350–52): larger; longer tails; stouter bills; females have no yellow in wings or tail. *Sparrows* (pp. 320–34, 365–66): generally have thicker, stubbier bills; no yellow in wings or tail; pinkish or reddish legs.
Best Sites: *Summer:* widespread in conifers, except pines. *Winter:* often irrupts abundantly in residential areas.

LESSER GOLDFINCH

Carduelis psaltria

Lesser Goldfinches are often overlooked by people unfamiliar with their calls, but they enliven the margins of watercourses flowing through dry, weedy expanses—as well as various brushy or semi-open habitats. As uncommon, localized residents in our state, these cousins of the American Goldfinch just make it over the Columbia River from Oregon, where they are more numerous. • Despite their resemblance to American Goldfinches, Lessers breed early in the year and have young in their nests well before their late-nesting cousins produce their clutches. Family groups join up in fall and winter, congregating in weedy thickets, untilled gardens and meadows and at hillside seeps, sometimes flocking with American Goldfinches and Pine Siskins.

ID: dark eyes; thick, grayish bill, possibly with yellow; greenish back and rump; black wing with prominent white bar and "wrist" patch; bright yellow underparts. *Male:* black "cap." *Female:* olive-and-yellow head; often drabber or paler than male.
Size: *L* 4½ in; *W* 8 in.
Status: uncommon year-round resident in southern Klickitat Co.
Habitat: oak foothills; riparian woods and brushy valley floors; occasionally in high-elevation juniper forests. *In migration* and *winter:* residential areas.
Nesting: on an outer portion of a small tree or shrub; compact, woven nest of

plant fibers, grass stems, bark and moss is lined with plant down; female incubates 4–5 pale blue eggs for 12 days.
Feeding: gleans foliage and fruit of hard-wood trees, plants and grass; eats seeds and insects; attracted to salt-rich soil, seeps and mineral licks; visits birdbaths and sprinklers for water and feeders for niger seeds.
Voice: calls include high, thin notes and a coarse *shik shik shik* flight call. *Male:* sings a long, varied and unstructured series of trills, twitters and warbles.
Similar Species: *American Goldfinch* (p. 356): larger; breeding bird has chestnut pink bill and whitish undertail coverts; yellow on male's upperparts is more extensive; female's back and head are browner.
Best Sites: Lyle; Lyle–Balch Cemetery (Balch Rd., Klickitat Co.); Maryhill SP (Klickitat Co.); Locke L. (Klickitat Co.).

355

AMERICAN GOLDFINCH
Carduelis tristis

Uttering its familiar *po-ta-to-chip* call as it swings over suburban parks and gardens in bounding, deeply undulating flight, the highly social American Goldfinch, Washington's state bird, is hard to miss. • Seen along rural roads, at streamsides and in weedy fields and residential plantings most of the year, American Goldfinches concentrate in willow and cottonwood thickets to nest and raise their young. Afterward, family parties form larger flocks and roam the lowlands and foothills in search of weed seeds and other food. They particularly favor thistle seeds, which they gather one by one, twisting and turning to extract the tiny morsels from the seedhead. Birds can be closely approached at such times, but, if someone comes too near, they will move a short distance or rise as one in a flock.

breeding

ID: stout, chestnut pink (breeding) or dusky (non-breeding) bill; whitish undertail coverts. *Breeding male:* bright yellow overall; black "cap"; white rump; mostly black wing with narrow white bar; white-edged, brown tail feathers. *Breeding female:* brownish head and back; dark wing with broad yellowish wing bar and smaller white one; yellow underparts and throat. *Nonbreeding:* generally brownish to grayish; male retains some yellow.
Size: *L* 5–5½ in; *W* 9–9½ in.
Status: common western resident from mid-May to mid-November, fairly common migrant from April to mid-May and uncommon in late fall and winter; common to fairly common year-round in eastern Washington.
Habitat: *Breeding:* open country with weedy fields; other low-vegetation areas. *In migration* and *winter:* wanders from breeding areas, often visiting residential areas, ranches and farms.
Nesting: in the fork of a shrub or small tree; tightly woven nest of plant fibers, grass, cocoon silk and spider silk is lined with fur or plant down; female incubates 4–6 pale blue eggs for 10–12 days.
Feeding: gleans vegetation for thistle seeds, insects, flower buds and berries; visits feeders for sunflower and niger seeds.
Voice: calls include *po-ta-to-chip* or *per-chic-or-ee* (often in flight) and whistled *dear-me, see-me. Male:* song is a long, varied series of trills, twitters and warbles.
Similar Species: *Lesser Goldfinch* (p. 355): limited to southern Klickitat Co.; smaller; greenish back and rump; male has black "cap"; female's head is mostly olive green.
Best Sites: widespread.

EVENING GROSBEAK

Coccothraustes vespertinus

Anyone with a bird feeder knows the appetite of Evening Grosbeaks—it doesn't take long for a flock to finish a tray of sunflower seeds. Scattering husks and unopened seeds, they often create an unplanned sunflower garden. If they don't like what's offered, these picky eaters are quick to look elsewhere. • Dispersing in pairs to nest in coniferous forests in summer, Evening Grosbeaks appear scarce until after their young fledge. By late summer, flocks are assembling in the lowlands, ready to devour tender hardwood buds before launching an aerial assault on neighborhood feeders. • With their habit of appearing in large numbers in backyards and in flowering streetside trees, Evening Grosbeaks are almost unrivaled at sparking an interest in birds.

ID: large, conical, pale yellowish bill; pink legs. *Male:* dark olive brown head and throat; yellow "eyebrow"; brownish back and breast; black wing with white inner flight feathers; yellow "shoulder," belly and undertail coverts; all-black tail. *Female:* dull gray overall; black lores and vertical "chin" line; black wing with gray area; olive nape and flanks; black tail with white tip and spots.
Size: *L* 7–8 in; *W* 13–14 in.
Status: common breeding resident in May; fairly common wanderer and migrant in April and from June to mid-October; somewhat irregular in winter.
Habitat: *Breeding:* mid- to high-elevation coniferous and mixed forests. *In migration and winter:* lowland habitats, especially interior towns with bigleaf maples; sometimes desert oases.

Nesting: normally well out on a conifer limb; nest of twigs, sticks, roots, plant fibers and grass is lined with fine materials; female incubates 3–4 darkly marked, blue or bluish green eggs for 11–14 days.
Feeding: gleans the ground and foliage for seeds, insects and berries; fond of maple sap and hardwood buds; dirt and gravel provide minerals and salts; takes sunflower and safflower seeds at feeders.
Voice: high, clear, whistled *teew* call; flocks utter a low, dry, rattling *buzz*. *Male:* repeated call constitutes the song.
Similar Species: *Lesser Goldfinch* (p. 355) and *American Goldfinch* (p. 356): smaller; small bills; breeding males have yellow faces and black "caps."
Best Sites: Newhalem (SR 20, Whatcom Co.); Rattlesnake L. (King Co.); Roslyn (Kittitas Co.); South Cle Elum; Wenas Campground (Yakima Co.); Milk Pond (FR 1708, Kittitas Co.); Mt. Rainier NP; Bassett Park (Washtucna, Adams Co.); Conconully SP (Okanogan Co.); Indian Canyon Park (Spokane).

HOUSE SPARROW

Passer domesticus

Probably the most familiar songbird in the world—and one of the least prized—the House Sparrow is not a true sparrow but a weaver-finch from Eurasia and northern Africa. • Introduced to the U.S. in the 1850s to control insect pests, the House Sparrow immediately began to exploit human-modified habitats. Nonmigratory by nature, this bird nevertheless has a knack for colonizing far-flung settled areas and usurping territory from native species. The House Sparrow will nest in any nest box within practical flight distance of foraging sites. With its year-round breeding habits, it occupies nest boxes before most native cavity-nesting birds, such as bluebirds and swallows, have arrived. In a predator-scarce urban environment, the brazen and seemingly fearless House Sparrow is a survivor. Many people have seen this bird cleaning up discarded scraps around fast-food restaurants.

ID: conical bill is yellowish, pinkish or black (breeding male). *Breeding male:* gray crown, rump and tail; pale gray "cheek" and underparts; buff-streaked, chestnut brown upperparts; bright chestnut nape; black "bib." *Nonbreeding male:* duller plumage; mostly white breast. *Female:* grayish head; pale buff "eyebrow"; buff-striped, brown upperparts; 2 indistinct wing bars; drab grayish brown underparts.
Size: *L* 6 in; *W* 9–10 in.
Status: common year-round resident.
Habitat: never far from human settlements, especially where grain is stored or where other human-originated food can be found.

Nesting: communal but territorial; typically in a nest box, natural cavity or artificial cavity; nest is a sprawling, untidy mass of loosely woven grass and other materials; female incubates 4–6 pale eggs, marked with gray and brown, for 10–13 days; has 2–3 broods per year.
Feeding: gleans the ground, low foliage, livestock manure, grain stores and human environments for seeds, blossoms, insects, fruit and food scraps; visits feeders.
Voice: call is a hoarse *chirrup;* flocks chatter and squeak constantly. *Male:* song is a series of similar chirps.
Similar Species: *Black-throated Sparrow* (p. 365): rare in Washington; dark face with white stripes; unstreaked, grayish brown upperparts; found only in arid environments.
Best Sites: widespread, although absent from dense woodlands.

OCCASIONAL BIRD SPECIES

The following is a selection of 33 of the accidental and casual species known to occur in Washington. For a full listing of these species, see the checklist (pp. 370–74).

EMPEROR GOOSE
Chen canagica

The small, stocky, beautifully marked Emperor Goose of the Bering Sea is equally at home in saltwater or freshwater habitats, feeding either on eelgrass, sea lettuce and barnacles or on sedges and grasses. From November to late February, single birds can sometimes be seen, usually in sheltered coastal areas.

ID: "scaly" gray plumage; white head and nape; dark "chin" and foreneck; small, pink bill; orange legs. *In flight:* white tail band.
Size: *L* 25–27 in; *W* 3¹/₂–4 ft.

ROSS'S GOOSE
Chen rossii

Ross's Geese are diminutive "Snow Goose look-alikes" that nest in the Canadian Arctic and migrate to central California. Because they do not breed near our population of Snow Geese (which nest on Wrangell Island north of Siberia), our Ross's Geese are more often seen with flocks of ducks than with Snow Geese.

ID: white overall, occasionally rust-stained by iron in the water; no "grinning patch"; small, bluish or greenish "warts" on base of dark pink bill; black wing tips; dark pink feet. *Blue morph:* very rare; bluish gray body plumage; white head. *Immature:* gray plumage; dark bill and feet.
Size: *L* 21–26 in; *W* 3³/₄ ft.

AMERICAN BLACK DUCK
Anas rubripes

The American Black Duck is not native to Washington, but vagrants from eastern North America may appear at any time of year. Hybridization with Mallards has resulted in an overall decline of these dark dabbling ducks throughout their North American range.

ID: dark, brownish black body; light brown head and neck; bright orange feet. *Male:* yellowish olive bill. *Female:* dull green bill mottled with gray or black. *In flight:* violet speculum; whitish underwings;.
Size: *L* 20–24 in; *W* 35 in.

ARCTIC LOON
Gavia arctica

We see the Arctic Loon as an occasional migrant and winter visitor, most often in the Strait of Juan de Fuca, Admiralty Inlet and Puget Sound. It breeds in western Alaska and is also found across Eurasia. Until 1985, this bird was classified with the Pacific Loon as a single species.

ID: *Breeding:* silvery gray head and nape; dark back with large, bold white spots; white flank patch; black and white streaks on neck; purplish black throat patch. *Nonbreeding:* dark crown extends down around eye; dark grayish brown upperparts; white flanks and underparts.
Size: *L* 27–28 in; *W* 3¹/₂–4 ft.

YELLOW-BILLED LOON
Gavia adamsii

The largest of our five loon species, the Yellow-billed Loon overwinters largely to our north, but it is a very rare winter visitor to Washington. Although it mainly visits coastal estuaries, it occasionally uses large inland lakes and reservoirs. Most records are from late September to mid-May, but individuals have been seen every month of the year.

nonbreeding

ID: *Breeding:* dark green "hood"; pale yellow bill appears upturned; white "collar" and breast; large, white spots on back. *Nonbreeding:* yellowish bill; pale brown neck and "cheek."
Size: *L* 34 in; *W* 4 ft.

LAYSAN ALBATROSS
Phoebastria immutabilis

Occasionally encountered off the coast of Washington in migration, the Laysan Albatross breeds on warm islands in the Pacific Ocean, primarily on Midway Atoll and the Hawaiian Islands. In our state, this large seabird is best seen on pelagic boat trips between November and April.

ID: white head; large, pale pinkish bill; grayish brown upperparts; white underparts; white rump; dark tail. *In flight:* long, slender wings; dark markings on white underwings.
Size: *L* 30–32 in; *W* 6–6½ ft.

FLESH-FOOTED SHEARWATER
Puffinus carneipes

The Flesh-footed Shearwater breeds in the Southern Hemisphere and makes its way to the Northern Hemisphere in its nonbreeding season, generally from May through October. Best seen on boat trips, this pelagic species is often found scavenging near fishing vessels.

ID: pinkish bill; uniformly dark brownish black; pinkish feet. *In flight:* silvery bases of flight feathers visible in bright, direct light.
Size: *L* 18–19 in; *W* 3–3½ ft.

MANX SHEARWATER
Puffinus puffinus

Primarily an Atlantic species, the Manx Shearwater was first recorded in Washington in 1990 in Grays Harbor County. Reports are increasing. Most sightings occur offshore between March and October, although birds are occasionally seen from land during heavy storms with high onshore winds.

ID: white on throat extends to white crescent behind eye; long, slender bill with hooked tip; dark upperparts; white underparts. *In flight:* white underwing with dark wing border; white undertail coverts; stiff-winged flight.
Size: *L* 12–14 in; *W* 30–34 in.

SNOWY EGRET
Egretta thula

The Snowy Egret is distinguished by its size, spotless white plumage and bright yellow feet. More common from Oregon southward, this rare visitor is seen almost annually in Washington, usually in spring.

ID: white plumage; black bill and legs; bright yellow feet. *Breeding:* crown feathers can be raised; reddish orange lores; long plumes on throat and rump. *Immature:* more yellow on legs. *In flight:* yellow feet.
Size: *L* 22–26 in; *W* 3½ ft.

CATTLE EGRET
Bubulcus ibis

Often associated with livestock, the Cattle Egret is at the northern edge of its range in Washington. It occurs here with some regularity, but no breeding records exist. This African bird arrived in Florida in the late 1940s and has since expanded its range to include most of the U.S.

ID: mostly white overall; yellowish orange legs. *Breeding:* buff orange crown, throat and rump; purple lores; orangy red bill; long plumes on throat and rump; orangy red legs. *Nonbreeding:* yellower bill; black feet. *Immature:* dark bill.
Size: *L* 19–21 in; *W* 35–37 in.

nonbreeding

WHITE-FACED IBIS
Plegadis chihi

Western North America's large wetlands attract the White-faced Ibis, which has a preference for flooded croplands and the expansive reedbeds and muddy shallows of federal wildlife refuges. It is a rare summer visitor to Washington.

ID: *Breeding:* dark chestnut and dull green overall with glossy highlights; dark red eyes; white feathers border naked red facial patch; long, downcurved bill; long, rich red legs. *In flight:* outstretched neck.
Size: *L* 22–26 in; *W* 3 ft.

breeding

AMERICAN GOLDEN-PLOVER
Pluvialis dominica

Hunted nearly to extinction in the late 1800s, the American Golden-Plover has recovered somewhat, but it will likely never return to its historic numbers. It migrates across most of North America to breed in Alaska and northern Canada. Small numbers are found in western Washington in spring and fall, and a few sometimes overwinter. It is often seen with the Pacific Golden-Plover.

ID: straight, black bill; long, black legs. *Breeding:* black face; white S-shaped stripe from fore-head down to shoulders; dark upperparts speckled with gold and white; black underparts, including undertail coverts. *Nonbreeding:* broad, pale "eyebrow"; dark streaking on pale neck and underparts; much less gold on upperparts. *In flight:* gray underwings.
Size: *L* 10–11 in; *W* 26 in.

HUDSONIAN GODWIT
Limosa haemastica

Each fall, Hudsonian Godwits embark on a migratory journey from Alaska and northern Canada to southern South America. A few of these fall migrants, mostly immatures, occasionally appear in Washington.

ID: long, pinkish bill with dark, slightly upturned tip; white rump; black tail; long, bluish black legs. *Breeding:* heavily barred, chestnut red underparts; dark grayish upperparts; male is more brightly colored. *Nonbreeding:* white "eyebrow"; grayish upperparts; whitish underparts. *Immature:* less pink on bill; dark grayish brown upperparts; pale underparts. *In flight:* black "wing pits" and wing linings.
Size: *L* 14–15½ in; *W* 29 in.

nonbreeding

BAR-TAILED GODWIT
Limosa lapponica

Making one of the longest migratory journeys of any shorebird, the Bar-tailed Godwit flies from its western Alaska breeding grounds to New Zealand. The rare fall migrants that occur in Washington are usually immatures, and one or two birds may overwinter in Tokeland.

ID: long, pinkish bill with dark, upturned tip; dark legs. *Breeding:* mottled, brown back; rufous underparts; barred undertail coverts. *Nonbreeding:* white "eyebrow"; dark eye line; gray back with dark streaks; streaked, gray breast; white belly. *Immature:* buff wash on breast; buff-notched back feathers.
Size: *L* 16 in; *W* 30 in.

SHARP-TAILED SANDPIPER
Calidris acuminata

Sharp-tailed Sandpipers nest in Siberia and migrate to New Zealand and Australia. They occur as rare fall migrants in our state, almost always as immatures. Favoring salt marshes and mudflats, they are often seen in the company of Pectoral Sandpipers.

immature

ID: *Immature:* rufous crown; bright white "eyebrow"; dusky yellow bill; dark upperpart feathers with reddish tinges and white edges; unstreaked or very finely streaked, warm buff breast contrasts with pale belly and undertail coverts; long, yellow legs; sharply pointed tail.
Size: *L* 8 in; *W* 17 in.

BUFF-BREASTED SANDPIPER
Tryngites subruficollis

Argentina-bound Buff-breasted Sandpipers leaving the Arctic occur here rarely, mostly from mid-August to mid-September. Most sightings are along the coast on open coastal beaches, at the dry edges of estuaries and on fields, flats behind coastal dunes and airports. Almost all birds seen here have been immatures.

ID: small, dark spots on crown, nape, breast, sides and flanks; buff, unpatterned face and foreneck; large, dark eyes; very thin, straight, black bill; buff underparts; yellow legs. *Immature:* darker than adult; "scaly" back and upperwings. *In flight:* white underwing with dark trailing edge and dark crescent; no wing stripe.
Size: *L* 7 1/2–8 in; *W* 18 in.

RUFF
Philomachus pugnax

The Ruff is the most regular and widespread of the Eurasian vagrants that sometimes stray into North America. It tends to turn up in Washington in fall. Most birds seen here are immatures. Without their flamboyant breeding-season "ruffs," any adult males will resemble the smaller females (known as Reeves).

nonbreeding

ID: plump body; small head. *Nonbreeding:* mottled, gray-to-whitish head, neck and breast; white around base of black or dark-tipped, yellow bill; light-edged, brownish gray upperpart feathers; orangy yellow to pinkish legs. *Immature:* buff head, neck and breast; dark back feathers with buff edges. *In flight:* thin, white upperwing stripe; white rump divided by a dark central triangle.
Size: *L* 9–12 in; *W* 21 in.

SOUTH POLAR SKUA

Stercorarius maccormicki

After breeding in the Antarctic, the South Polar Skua "overwinters" in our region from May to November. A pelagic boat trip is the best way to see this far-offshore migrant.

ID: dark, hooked bill. *Dark morph:* dark grayish brown overall; pale nape. *Light morph:* pale body; dark wings with pale streaking. *In flight:* white crescent across outer flight feathers.
Size: *L* 21 in; *W* 4–4½ ft.

dark morph

LITTLE GULL

Larus minutus

This small, largely Eurasian gull was first identified in North America in 1820, as a specimen collected on the first expedition of explorer John Franklin. The Little Gull's dark underwing differentiates it from the white-underwinged Bonaparte's Gull, with which it usually mingles. Most sightings occur in fall in coastal areas.

ID: black bill; gray mantle; white neck, underparts, rump and tail; orangy red legs and feet. *Breeding:* black head. *Nonbreeding:* white head; dark "cap" and ear spot. *In flight:* white tip and trailing edge on wing; dark underwing (gray on immature).
Size: *L* 10–11 in; *W* 24 in.

nonbreeding

SLATY-BACKED GULL

Larus schistisagus

A breeder on the coasts of northeastern Russia, China and Japan, as well as on the coast of western Alaska, the Slaty-backed Gull is an accidental winter visitor to Washington.

ID: yellow bill with red spot; dark, slate gray mantle; white underparts and tail; pink legs. *Breeding:* white head and neck. *Nonbreeding:* brown-streaked head and neck. *In flight:* wide white trailing edge on wing, transitioning to white "string of pearls" against black on wing tips.
Size: *L* 24–26 in; *W* 4½–5 ft.

ELEGANT TERN

Sterna elegans

The Elegant Tern has a breeding range restricted to coastal Mexico and southern California, but it is occasionally seen along the southwestern Washington coast in summer. It winters as far south as Peru and Chile.

ID: black crown and conspicuous crest; white face; long, slender, orange bill; pale gray upperparts; white underparts; deeply forked tail; black legs. *Breeding:* black forecrown; subtle pinkish blush on underparts. *Nonbreeding:* white forecrown. *Immature:* yellow bill and legs. *In flight:* jabbing downstroke to each wingbeat.
Size: *L* 16–17 in; *W* 34 in.

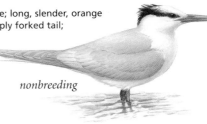

nonbreeding

COSTA'S HUMMINGBIRD
Calypte costae

After breeding, Costa's Hummingbirds (the "dry desert hummingbirds") leave the Sonoran Desert to visit other habitats
for nectar and flying insects. Several individuals have appeared at
scattered Washington locations. Although not as regular as other
hummingbirds, these birds grace feeders with brief visits and may
return for several seasons.

ID: green upperparts; pale underparts. *Male:* amethyst purple
of crown and throat extends down shoulders. *Female:* unmarked,
white throat; green-and-gray tail with white-tipped outer feathers.
Size: *L* 3–3¹/₂ in; *W* 5 in.

YELLOW-BELLIED SAPSUCKER
Sphyrapicus varius

Lines of parallel "wells" freshly drilled in tree bark are a sure sign that a sapsucker is in the neighborhood. Closely resembling the Red-naped Sapsucker but with a white nape, the Yellow-bellied
Sapsucker is an accidental winter visitor to Washington. It is much more common east of the Rockies
and in the boreal forest.

ID: black overall, with white barring on back, wings and tail; red forecrown; black and white
facial stripes; broad, black "bib"; large white shoulder patch; yellow wash on lower breast and
belly. *Male:* red "chin." *Female:* white "chin." *Immature:* generally brownish; distinctive white
shoulder patch.
Size: *L* 8–9 in; *W* 15¹/₂ in.

TROPICAL KINGBIRD
Tyrannus melancholicus

Like many herons and egrets, but quite uncharacteristi-
cally among songbirds, the Tropical Kingbird migrates north
after breeding before retreating south again for winter. This
unusual behavior results in sightings of this Central and South
American species, which breeds as far north as Arizona, along our
coastline almost every fall. Unlike the smaller-billed Western
Kingbird, it has no white on the outer tail feathers.

ID: gray head with dark ear patch; white "cheek" and
throat; robust black bill rivals length of head; grayish
olive back; dark wings and tail; bright yellow underparts.
Size: *L* 8–9¹/₂ in; *W* 14 in.

BLUE JAY
Cyanocitta cristata

Partly because of its ability to exploit human resources,
the Blue Jay has expanded its range westward, taking
advantage of forest clearing to establish new territories.
Winter invasions have brought several parties and individuals to our state. The Blue Jay remains, however, a very rare
visitor, primarily to eastern Washington.

ID: blue crest; black eye line; black bill; black "necklace";
blue upperparts; white bar and marks on folded wings; white underparts; dark bars and white corners on blue tail.
Size: *L* 11–12¹/₂ in; *W* 16 in.

NORTHWESTERN CROW
Corvus caurinus

Considered by some ornithologists to be a subspecies of the American Crow, the slightly smaller Northwestern Crow is best distinguished by its hoarser, lower-pitched calls. It can be found year-round on the northern Washington coast, especially on the northwestern Olympic Peninsula, around the Strait of Juan de Fuca and in the San Juans.

ID: iridescent, purplish gloss on black plumage; black bill; slightly rounded tail; black legs.
Size: *L* 16 in; *W* 34 in.

NORTHERN MOCKINGBIRD
Mimus polyglottos

Able to imitate almost anything, the Northern Mockingbird replicates sounds so accurately that even computerized auditory analysis may fail to differentiate between the original source and the imitation. This singer's amazing vocal repertoire reputedly includes over 400 different song types. Widespread in the U.S., this bird is a rare resident, most commonly seen in winter, both east and west of Washington's Cascades.

ID: narrow, black eye line; brownish yellow eyes; gray upperparts; dark wings; light gray underparts; 2 thin, white wing bars; long, dark tail with white outer feathers. *In flight:* large white patch at base of outer flight feathers.
Size: *L* 10 in; *W* 14 in.

CLAY-COLORED SPARROW
Spizella pallida

The dainty Clay-colored Sparrow generally lives east of the Rockies, but this easily overlooked species of special concern is a rare winter visitor in Washington, mostly in the west, and a rare and local breeder in the Spokane area. Bolder markings, particularly in the head area, distinguish it from the Brewer's Sparrow in spring. A buff-washed breast and a bolder-bordered jaw stripe differentiate it from the Chipping Sparrow in fall and winter.

ID: dark-streaked, brown crown with pale central stripe; white "eyebrow"; light brown "cheek" edged with darker brown; white jaw stripe bordered with brown; mostly pale bill; gray nape; white throat; buff breast wash; unstreaked, white underparts.
Size: *L* 5–6 in; *W* 7¹/₂ in.

BLACK-THROATED SPARROW
Amphispiza bilineata

Look for the Black-throated Sparrow as a rare and local breeder in sagebrush-dominated areas in south-central Washington and along the Columbia River near Vantage. Adapted to the arid, thorny shrub habitat of the Southwest and Mexico, it can survive for long periods without water, obtaining the moisture it needs from the seeds and insects it eats.

ID: gray "cap" and "cheek"; prominent, white "eyebrow"; dark bill; broad, white jaw line; black "chin," throat and "bib"; unstreaked, light underparts; black tail with white-edged outer feathers.
Size: *L* 4¹/₂–5¹/₂ in; *W* 7¹/₂–8 in.

HARRIS'S SPARROW
Zonotrichia querula

Most Harris's Sparrows overwinter in the central and southern Great Plains, but some birds arrive here in late October, mostly in eastern Washington. They enliven winter feeders or appear with other sparrows, often only one per flock, in brush patches in open country. As the birds prepare to head north to breed in April or May, more black facial feathers appear, and the brown head color gradually gives way to gray.

ID: pinkish orange bill; mottled, brown-and-black upperparts; white underparts. *Breeding:* black crown, ear patch, throat and "bib"; gray face; black streaks on sides and flanks; white wing bars. *Nonbreeding:* white flecks on crown; brown face; brownish sides and flanks.
Size: L 7–7½ in; W 10½ in.

RUSTY BLACKBIRD
Euphagus carolinus

Named for its fall plumage color, the Rusty Blackbird could just as easily have been named for its grating, squeaky song, which sounds very much like a neglected hinge. This rare winter visitor to Washington, which normally overwinters in the eastern U.S., prefers wet lowland areas and generally avoids human-altered environments, but it is often found in flocks with other blackbirds in grain-rich fields.

nonbreeding

ID: yellow eyes; long, sharp bill; dark legs. *Breeding male:* dark overall with subtle green gloss (may be bluish on head). *Breeding female:* paler than male, without gloss. *Nonbreeding male:* rusty crown, back and wings. *Nonbreeding female:* paler than male; rusty "cheek"; buff underparts.
Size: *L* 9 in; *W* 14 in.

WHITE-WINGED CROSSBILL
Loxia leucoptera

When news of an irregular winter White-winged Crossbill invasion reaches the rare-bird alerts, many birders willingly brave the cold to see this small, nomadic northern finch. It typically occurs in the North Cascades, Okanogan Mountains and northeastern areas of the state. The White-winged Crossbill's unusual bill is adapted for prying open conifer cones; in Washington, it favors those of Engelmann spruce.

ID: bill tips cross; 2 bold white wing bars. *Male:* pinkish red overall; black wings and tail. *Female:* streaked, brown upperparts; weakly brown-streaked, dusky yellow underparts; dark wings and tail.
Size: *L* 6–7 in; *W* 10½ in.

COMMON REDPOLL
Carduelis flammea

A predictably unpredictable winter visitor from the north or east, the Common Redpoll can appear in flocks of hundreds or a dozen or less, depending on the year. It occurs most frequently in northern and especially eastern parts of the state, often with Pine Siskins and American Goldfinches.

ID: red forecrown; small, yellowish bill; black "chin"; streaked upperparts, including rump; lightly streaked sides, flanks and undertail coverts; notched tail. *Male:* pinkish red breast (brightest in breeding plumage). *Female:* whitish to pale gray breast.
Size: *L* 5 in; *W* 9 in.

SELECT REFERENCES

American Ornithologists' Union. 1998. *Check-list of North American Birds.* 7th ed. (and its supplements). American Ornithologists' Union, Washington, DC.

Choate, E.A. 1985. *The Dictionary of American Bird Names.* Rev. ed. Harvard Common Press, Cambridge, MA.

Cox, Randall T. 1996. *Birder's Dictionary.* Falcon Publishing, Helena, MT.

Cullinan, Tim, compiler. 2001. *Important Bird Areas of Washington.* Audubon Washington, Olympia. (Lists the initial set of 53 sites selected in the Important Bird Area program.)

Jewett, Stanley G., W.P. Taylor, W.T. Shaw & J.W. Aldrich. 1953. *Birds of Washington State.* University of Washington Press, Seattle. (The classic discussion of the occurrence of birds in the State of Washington.)

Kaufman, K. 1996. *Lives of North American Birds.* Houghton Mifflin, Boston.

Kaufman, K. 2000. *Birds of North America.* Houghton Mifflin, New York.

Link, R. 1999. *Landscaping for Wildlife in the Pacific Northwest.* University of Washington Press, Seattle.

National Geographic Society. 2002. *Field Guide to the Birds of North America.* 4th ed. National Geographic Society, Washington, DC.

Opperman, Hal N. 2003. *A Birder's Guide to Washington.* American Birding Association, Inc., Colorado Springs. (Gives specific directions to many excellent Washington birding locations.)

Paulson, Dennis R. 1993. *Shorebirds of the Pacific Northwest.* University of Washington Press, Seattle. (The definitive book on the identification, distribution and occurrence of shorebirds in the Pacific Northwest.)

Sibley, D.A. 2000. *National Audubon Society: The Sibley Guide to Birds.* Alfred A. Knopf, New York.

Sibley, D.A. 2001. *National Audubon Society: The Sibley Guide to Bird Life and Behavior.* Alfred A. Knopf, New York.

Sibley, D.A. 2002. *Sibley's Birding Basics.* Alfred A. Knopf, New York.

Stepniewski, Andrew. 1999. *The Birds of Yakima County, Washington.* Yakima Valley Audubon Society, Yakima. (Detailed discussion of the birds of Yakima County and their distribution.)

Wahl, T.R., B. Tweit & S.G. Mlodinow, eds. 2005. *Birds of Washington: Status and Distribution.* Oregon State University Press, Corvallis.

Wahl, Terence R. 1995. *Birds of Whatcom County: Status and Distribution.* T.R. Wahl, Bellingham. (Occurrence and distribution of birds in Whatcom County.)

GLOSSARY

accipiter: a forest hawk (from the genus *Accipiter*), characterized by short, rounded wings and a long tail; feeds mostly on birds.

alcid: a seabird (from the family Alcidae), such as a murre, auklet or puffin, characterized by wings well suited to diving and swimming and that beat rapidly in flight; feeds largely on crustaceans and small fish.

brood: *n.* a family of young from one hatching; *v.* to incubate the eggs.

buteo: a high-soaring hawk (from the genus *Buteo*), characterized by broad wings and a short, wide tail; feeds mostly on small mammals and other land animals.

cere: the fleshy area above the base of the bill on some birds.

clutch: the number of eggs laid by the female at one time.

corvid: a member of the crow family (*Corvidae*); includes crows, jays, magpies and ravens.

covey: a flock of partridges, quail or grouse.

crop: an enlargement of the esophagus; serves as a storage structure and also (in pigeons) has glands that produce secretions to feed the young.

cryptic: a coloration pattern that helps to conceal the bird.

dabbling: a foraging technique used by ducks in which the head and neck are submerged but the body and tail remain on the water's surface; dabbling ducks can usually walk easily on land, can take off without running and have brightly colored speculums.

diurnal: most active during the day.

drake: a male duck.

eclipse plumage: a cryptic plumage, similar to that of females, worn by some male ducks in fall when they molt their flight feathers and consequently are unable to fly.

egg dumping: the laying of eggs in another bird's nest, leaving the "foster parent" to raise the young.

endangered: facing imminent extirpation or extinction.

extinct: no longer existing anywhere.

extirpated: no longer existing in the wild in a particular region but occurring elsewhere.

fledge: to grow the first full set of feathers.

hawking: attempting to capture insects through aerial pursuit.

irruption: a sporadic mass migration of birds outside their usual range.

lek: a place where males gather to display for females in spring.

mantle: the area covering a bird's back and wings.

morph: one of several alternate color phases displayed by a species.

peep: a sandpiper of the genus *Calidris.*

pelagic: open ocean habitat very far from land.

polyandrous: having a mating strategy in which one female breeds with several males.

riparian: along rivers and streams.

sensitive: likely to become threatened or endangered in all or part of its range (state listing).

sexual dimorphism: a difference in plumage, size or other characteristics between males and females of the same species.

species of concern: likely to become threatened or endangered in all or part of its range (federal listing).

stage: to gather in one place during migration, usually when birds are flightless or partly flightless during molting.

stoop: a steep dive through the air, usually performed by birds of prey while foraging or during courtship displays.

threatened: likely to become endangered in the near future in all or part of its range.

torpor: a temporary reduction in body temperature and metabolism in order to conserve energy, usually in response to low temperatures or a lack of food.

tubenose: an albatross, shearwater, petrel or storm-petrel.

vagrant: a transient bird found outside its normal range.

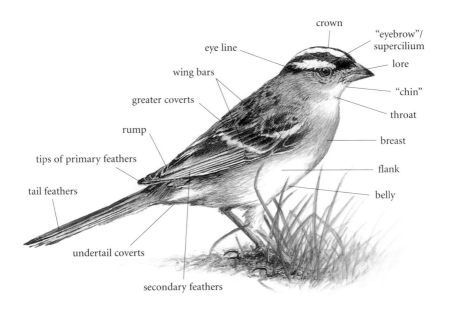

crown

"eyebrow"/ supercilium

eye line

lore

wing bars

"chin"

greater coverts

throat

rump

breast

tips of primary feathers

flank

tail feathers

belly

undertail coverts

secondary feathers

CHECKLIST

The following checklist contains 477 species of birds that have been officially recorded in Washington. Species are grouped by family and listed in taxonomic order in accordance with the A.O.U. *Check-list of North American Birds* (7th ed.) and its supplements.

Regularly appearing species are in plain text. Accidental species are in *italics*. Species in italics with an asterisk (*) are accidental species that have been identified by sight records only with no additional verification. A plus (+) indicates introduced species. In addition, the following Washington state risk categories are noted: extirpated (ex), endangered (en), threatened (th) and sensitive (se).

We wish to express our appreciation to the Washington Ornithological Society and the Washington Bird Records Committee for their permission to use this checklist.

Waterfowl (Anatidae)
- ❏ *Bean Goose*
- ❏ *Fulvous Whistling-Duck* (ex)
- ❏ Greater White-fronted Goose
- ❏ *Emperor Goose*
- ❏ Snow Goose
- ❏ Ross's Goose
- ❏ Cackling Goose
- ❏ Canada Goose
- ❏ Brant
- ❏ Mute Swan +
- ❏ Trumpeter Swan
- ❏ Tundra Swan
- ❏ Wood Duck
- ❏ Gadwall
- ❏ *Falcated Duck*
- ❏ Eurasian Wigeon
- ❏ American Wigeon
- ❏ American Black Duck +
- ❏ Mallard
- ❏ Blue-winged Teal
- ❏ Cinnamon Teal
- ❏ Northern Shoveler
- ❏ Northern Pintail
- ❏ *Garganey*
- ❏ Green-winged Teal
- ❏ Canvasback
- ❏ Redhead
- ❏ Ring-necked Duck
- ❏ *Tufted Duck*
- ❏ Greater Scaup
- ❏ Lesser Scaup
- ❏ *Steller's Eider*
- ❏ *King Eider*
- ❏ *Common Eider*
- ❏ Harlequin Duck
- ❏ Surf Scoter
- ❏ White-winged Scoter
- ❏ Black Scoter
- ❏ Long-tailed Duck
- ❏ Bufflehead
- ❏ Common Goldeneye
- ❏ Barrow's Goldeneye
- ❏ *Smew*
- ❏ Hooded Merganser
- ❏ Common Merganser
- ❏ Red-breasted Merganser
- ❏ Ruddy Duck

Grouse & Allies (Phasianidae)
- ❏ Chukar +
- ❏ Gray Partridge +
- ❏ Ring-necked Pheasant +
- ❏ Ruffed Grouse
- ❏ Greater Sage-Grouse (th)
- ❏ Spruce Grouse
- ❏ White-tailed Ptarmigan
- ❏ Blue Grouse
- ❏ Sharp-tailed Grouse (th)
- ❏ Wild Turkey +

New World Quails (Odontophoridae)
- ❏ Mountain Quail
- ❏ California Quail +
- ❏ Northern Bobwhite +

Loons (Gaviidae)
- ❏ Red-throated Loon
- ❏ *Arctic Loon*
- ❏ Pacific Loon
- ❏ Common Loon (se)
- ❏ Yellow-billed Loon

Grebes (Podicipedidae)
- ❏ Pied-billed Grebe
- ❏ Horned Grebe
- ❏ Red-necked Grebe
- ❏ Eared Grebe
- ❏ Western Grebe
- ❏ Clark's Grebe

Albatrosses (Diomedeidae)
- ❏ *Shy Albatross*
- ❏ Laysan Albatross
- ❏ Black-footed Albatross
- ❏ *Short-tailed Albatross*

Petrels & Shearwaters (Procellariidae)
- ❏ Northern Fulmar
- ❏ *Murphy's Petrel*
- ❏ *Mottled Petrel*
- ❏ *Cook's Petrel*

- ❏ Pink-footed Shearwater
- ❏ Flesh-footed Shearwater
- ❏ *Wedge-tailed Shearwater*
- ❏ Buller's Shearwater
- ❏ Sooty Shearwater
- ❏ Short-tailed Shearwater
- ❏ *Manx Shearwater*

Storm-Petrels (Hydrobatidae)
- ❏ *Wilson's Storm-Petrel*
- ❏ Fork-tailed Storm-Petrel
- ❏ Leach's Storm-Petrel

Tropicbirds (Phaethontidae)
- ❏ *Red-billed Tropicbird*

Boobies (Sulidae)
- ❏ *Blue-footed Booby* (ex)
- ❏ *Brown Booby*

Pelicans (Pelecanidae)
- ❏ American White Pelican (en)
- ❏ Brown Pelican (en)

Cormorants (Phalacrocoracidae)
- ❏ Brandt's Cormorant
- ❏ Double-crested Cormorant
- ❏ *Red-faced Cormorant*
- ❏ Pelagic Cormorant

Frigatebirds (Fregatidae)
- ❏ *Magnificent Frigatebird*

Herons (Ardeidae)
- ❏ American Bittern
- ❏ Great Blue Heron
- ❏ Great Egret
- ❏ *Snowy Egret*
- ❏ *Little Blue Heron*
- ❏ Cattle Egret
- ❏ Green Heron
- ❏ Black-crowned Night-Heron
- ❏ *Yellow-crowned Night-Heron*

Ibises (Threskiornithidae)
- ❏ *White Ibis*
- ❏ *White-faced Ibis*

Vultures (Cathartidae)
- ❏ Turkey Vulture
- ❏ *California Condor* (ex)

Hawks & Eagles (Accipitridae)
- ❏ Osprey
- ❏ White-tailed Kite
- ❏ Bald Eagle (th)
- ❏ Northern Harrier
- ❏ Sharp-shinned Hawk
- ❏ Cooper's Hawk
- ❏ Northern Goshawk
- ❏ *Red-shouldered Hawk*
- ❏ *Broad-winged Hawk*
- ❏ Swainson's Hawk
- ❏ Red-tailed Hawk
- ❏ Ferruginous Hawk (th)
- ❏ Rough-legged Hawk
- ❏ Golden Eagle

Falcons (Falconidae)
- ❏ *Eurasian Kestrel*
- ❏ American Kestrel
- ❏ Merlin
- ❏ *Eurasian Hobby*
- ❏ Gyrfalcon
- ❏ Peregrine Falcon (se)
- ❏ Prairie Falcon

Rails & Coots (Rallidae)
- ❏ *Yellow Rail*
- ❏ Virginia Rail
- ❏ Sora
- ❏ American Coot

Cranes (Gruidae)
- ❏ Sandhill Crane (en)

Plovers (Charadriidae)
- ❏ Black-bellied Plover
- ❏ American Golden-Plover
- ❏ Pacific Golden-Plover
- ❏ Snowy Plover (en)
- ❏ Semipalmated Plover

- ❏ *Piping Plover*
- ❏ Killdeer
- ❏ *Mountain Plover*
- ❏ *Eurasian Dotterel*

Oystercatchers (Haematopodidae)
- ❏ Black Oystercatcher

Stilts & Avocets (Recurvirostridae)
- ❏ Black-necked Stilt
- ❏ American Avocet

Sandpipers & Allies (Scolopacidae)
- ❏ Greater Yellowlegs
- ❏ Lesser Yellowlegs
- ❏ Solitary Sandpiper
- ❏ Willet
- ❏ Wandering Tattler
- ❏ *Gray-tailed Tattler*
- ❏ Spotted Sandpiper
- ❏ *Upland Sandpiper* (en)
- ❏ *Little Curlew*
- ❏ Whimbrel
- ❏ *Bristle-thighed Curlew*
- ❏ Long-billed Curlew
- ❏ *Hudsonian Godwit*
- ❏ *Bar-tailed Godwit*
- ❏ Marbled Godwit
- ❏ Ruddy Turnstone
- ❏ Black Turnstone
- ❏ Surfbird
- ❏ *Great Knot**
- ❏ Red Knot
- ❏ Sanderling
- ❏ Semipalmated Sandpiper
- ❏ Western Sandpiper
- ❏ Least Sandpiper
- ❏ *White-rumped Sandpiper*
- ❏ Baird's Sandpiper
- ❏ Pectoral Sandpiper
- ❏ Sharp-tailed Sandpiper
- ❏ Rock Sandpiper
- ❏ Dunlin

371

- ❏ *Curlew Sandpiper*
- ❏ Stilt Sandpiper
- ❏ *Buff-breasted Sandpiper*
- ❏ *Ruff*
- ❏ Short-billed Dowitcher
- ❏ Long-billed Dowitcher
- ❏ *Jack Snipe**
- ❏ Wilson's Snipe
- ❏ Wilson's Phalarope
- ❏ Red-necked Phalarope
- ❏ Red Phalarope

Gulls & Allies (Laridae)
- ❏ South Polar Skua
- ❏ Pomarine Jaeger
- ❏ Parasitic Jaeger
- ❏ Long-tailed Jaeger
- ❏ *Laughing Gull*
- ❏ Franklin's Gull
- ❏ Little Gull
- ❏ *Black-headed Gull*
- ❏ Bonaparte's Gull
- ❏ Heermann's Gull
- ❏ *Black-tailed Gull*
- ❏ Mew Gull
- ❏ Ring-billed Gull
- ❏ California Gull
- ❏ Herring Gull
- ❏ Thayer's Gull
- ❏ *Iceland Gull*
- ❏ *Lesser Black-backed Gull*
- ❏ *Slaty-backed Gull*
- ❏ Western Gull
- ❏ Glaucous-winged Gull
- ❏ Glaucous Gull
- ❏ *Great Black-backed Gull*
- ❏ Sabine's Gull
- ❏ Black-legged Kittiwake
- ❏ *Red-legged Kittiwake*
- ❏ *Ross's Gull*
- ❏ *Ivory Gull**
- ❏ Caspian Tern
- ❏ Elegant Tern
- ❏ Common Tern
- ❏ Arctic Tern
- ❏ Forster's Tern
- ❏ *Least Tern*
- ❏ Black Tern

Alcids (Alcidae)
- ❏ Common Murre
- ❏ *Thick-billed Murre*
- ❏ Pigeon Guillemot
- ❏ *Long-billed Murrelet*
- ❏ Marbled Murrelet (th)
- ❏ *Kittlitz's Murrelet*
- ❏ *Xantus's Murrelet*
- ❏ Ancient Murrelet
- ❏ Cassin's Auklet
- ❏ *Parakeet Auklet*
- ❏ *Whiskered Auklet*
- ❏ Rhinoceros Auklet
- ❏ *Horned Puffin*
- ❏ Tufted Puffin

Pigeons & Doves (Columbidae)
- ❏ Rock Pigeon +
- ❏ Band-tailed Pigeon
- ❏ *Eurasian Collared-Dove* +
- ❏ *White-winged Dove*
- ❏ Mourning Dove

Cuckoos (Cuculidae)
- ❏ *Black-billed Cuckoo*
- ❏ *Yellow-billed Cuckoo*

Barn Owls (Tytonidae)
- ❏ Barn Owl

Owls (Strigidae)
- ❏ Flammulated Owl
- ❏ Western Screech-Owl
- ❏ Great Horned Owl
- ❏ Snowy Owl
- ❏ *Northern Hawk Owl*
- ❏ Northern Pygmy-Owl
- ❏ Burrowing Owl
- ❏ Spotted Owl (en)
- ❏ Barred Owl
- ❏ Great Gray Owl
- ❏ Long-eared Owl
- ❏ Short-eared Owl
- ❏ Boreal Owl
- ❏ Northern Saw-whet Owl

Nightjars (Caprimulgidae)
- ❏ Common Nighthawk
- ❏ Common Poorwill

Swifts (Apodidae)
- ❏ Black Swift
- ❏ Vaux's Swift
- ❏ White-throated Swift

Hummingbirds (Trochilidae)
- ❏ *Ruby-throated Hummingbird**
- ❏ Black-chinned Hummingbird
- ❏ Anna's Hummingbird
- ❏ *Costa's Hummingbird*
- ❏ Calliope Hummingbird
- ❏ *Broad-tailed Hummingbird*
- ❏ Rufous Hummingbird
- ❏ *Allen's Hummingbird* (ex)

Kingfishers (Alcedinidae)
- ❏ Belted Kingfisher

Woodpeckers (Picidae)
- ❏ Lewis's Woodpecker
- ❏ Acorn Woodpecker
- ❏ Williamson's Sapsucker
- ❏ *Yellow-bellied Sapsucker*
- ❏ Red-naped Sapsucker
- ❏ Red-breasted Sapsucker
- ❏ Downy Woodpecker
- ❏ Hairy Woodpecker
- ❏ White-headed Woodpecker
- ❏ American Three-toed Woodpecker
- ❏ Black-backed Woodpecker
- ❏ Northern Flicker
- ❏ Pileated Woodpecker

Flycatchers (Tyrannidae)
- ❏ Olive-sided Flycatcher
- ❏ Western Wood-Pewee
- ❏ *Alder Flycatcher*
- ❏ Willow Flycatcher

❏ Least Flycatcher
❏ Hammond's Flycatcher
❏ Gray Flycatcher
❏ Dusky Flycatcher
❏ Pacific-slope Flycatcher
❏ *Black Phoebe*
❏ *Eastern Phoebe*
❏ Say's Phoebe
❏ *Vermilion Flycatcher*
❏ Ash-throated Flycatcher
❏ *Tropical Kingbird*
❏ Western Kingbird
❏ Eastern Kingbird
❏ *Scissor-tailed Flycatcher*
❏ *Fork-tailed Flycatcher*

Shrikes (Laniidae)
❏ Loggerhead Shrike
❏ Northern Shrike

Vireos (Vireonidae)
❏ *White-eyed Vireo**
❏ *Yellow-throated Vireo*
❏ Cassin's Vireo
❏ *Blue-headed Vireo**
❏ Hutton's Vireo
❏ Warbling Vireo
❏ *Philadelphia Vireo*
❏ Red-eyed Vireo

Crows & Jays (Corvidae)
❏ Gray Jay
❏ Steller's Jay
❏ Blue Jay
❏ Western Scrub-Jay
❏ *Pinyon Jay*
❏ Clark's Nutcracker
❏ Black-billed Magpie
❏ American Crow
❏ Northwestern Crow
❏ Common Raven

Larks (Alaudidae)
❏ Sky Lark +
❏ Horned Lark

Swallows (Hirundinidae)
❏ Purple Martin
❏ Tree Swallow

❏ Violet-green Swallow
❏ Northern Rough-winged Swallow
❏ Bank Swallow
❏ Cliff Swallow
❏ Barn Swallow

Chickadees (Paridae)
❏ Black-capped Chickadee
❏ Mountain Chickadee
❏ Chestnut-backed Chickadee
❏ Boreal Chickadee

Bushtits (Aegithalidae)
❏ Bushtit

Nuthatches (Sittidae)
❏ Red-breasted Nuthatch
❏ White-breasted Nuthatch
❏ Pygmy Nuthatch

Creepers (Certhiidae)
❏ Brown Creeper

Wrens (Troglodytidae)
❏ Rock Wren
❏ Canyon Wren
❏ Bewick's Wren
❏ House Wren
❏ Winter Wren
❏ Marsh Wren

Dippers (Cinclidae)
❏ American Dipper

Kinglets (Regulidae)
❏ Golden-crowned Kinglet
❏ Ruby-crowned Kinglet

Gnatcatchers (Sylviidae)
❏ *Blue-gray Gnatcatcher*

Thrushes (Turdidae)
❏ Western Bluebird
❏ Mountain Bluebird
❏ Townsend's Solitaire
❏ Veery

❏ *Gray-cheeked Thrush*
❏ Swainson's Thrush
❏ Hermit Thrush
❏ American Robin
❏ Varied Thrush

Mockingbirds & Thrashers (Mimidae)
❏ Gray Catbird
❏ Northern Mockingbird
❏ Sage Thrasher
❏ *Brown Thrasher*

Starlings (Sturnidae)
❏ European Starling +

Accentors (Prunellidae)
❏ *Siberian Accentor*

Wagtails & Pipits (Motacillidae)
❏ *Yellow Wagtail*
❏ *White Wagtail*
❏ *Black-backed Wagtail*
❏ *Red-throated Pipit*
❏ American Pipit

Waxwings (Bombycillidae)
❏ Bohemian Waxwing
❏ Cedar Waxwing

Silky-flycatchers (Ptilogonatidae)
❏ *Phainopepla**

Wood-Warblers (Parulidae)
❏ *Blue-winged Warbler*
❏ *Golden-winged Warbler*
❏ *Tennessee Warbler*
❏ Orange-crowned Warbler
❏ Nashville Warbler
❏ *Northern Parula*
❏ Yellow Warbler
❏ *Chestnut-sided Warbler*
❏ *Magnolia Warbler*
❏ *Cape May Warbler*
❏ *Black-throated Blue*

Warbler

- ❏ Yellow-rumped Warbler
- ❏ Black-throated Gray Warbler
- ❏ *Black-throated Green Warbler*
- ❏ Townsend's Warbler
- ❏ Hermit Warbler
- ❏ *Blackburnian Warbler*
- ❏ *Yellow-throated Warbler*
- ❏ *Prairie Warbler**
- ❏ Palm Warbler
- ❏ *Blackpoll Warbler*
- ❏ *Black-and-white Warbler*
- ❏ American Redstart
- ❏ *Prothonotary Warbler*
- ❏ *Ovenbird*
- ❏ Northern Waterthrush
- ❏ *Kentucky Warbler**
- ❏ *Mourning Warbler*
- ❏ MacGillivray's Warbler
- ❏ Common Yellowthroat
- ❏ *Hooded Warbler*
- ❏ Wilson's Warbler
- ❏ Yellow-breasted Chat

Tanagers (Thraupidae)
- ❏ *Summer Tanager*
- ❏ Western Tanager

Sparrows & Allies (Emberizidae)
- ❏ Green-tailed Towhee
- ❏ Spotted Towhee
- ❏ American Tree Sparrow
- ❏ Chipping Sparrow
- ❏ Clay-colored Sparrow
- ❏ Brewer's Sparrow
- ❏ Vesper Sparrow
- ❏ Lark Sparrow
- ❏ Black-throated Sparrow
- ❏ Sage Sparrow
- ❏ *Lark Bunting*
- ❏ Savannah Sparrow
- ❏ Grasshopper Sparrow

- ❏ *Le Conte's Sparrow*
- ❏ *Nelson's Sharp-tailed Sparrow*
- ❏ Fox Sparrow
- ❏ Song Sparrow
- ❏ Lincoln's Sparrow
- ❏ Swamp Sparrow
- ❏ White-throated Sparrow
- ❏ Harris's Sparrow
- ❏ White-crowned Sparrow
- ❏ Golden-crowned Sparrow
- ❏ Dark-eyed Junco
- ❏ Lapland Longspur
- ❏ *Chestnut-collared Longspur*
- ❏ *Rustic Bunting*
- ❏ Snow Bunting
- ❏ *McKay's Bunting*

Grosbeaks & Buntings (Cardinalidae)
- ❏ *Rose-breasted Grosbeak*
- ❏ Black-headed Grosbeak
- ❏ Lazuli Bunting
- ❏ *Indigo Bunting*
- ❏ *Dickcissel*

Blackbirds & Allies (Icteridae)
- ❏ Bobolink
- ❏ Red-winged Blackbird
- ❏ *Tricolored Blackbird*
- ❏ Western Meadowlark
- ❏ Yellow-headed Blackbird
- ❏ Rusty Blackbird
- ❏ Brewer's Blackbird
- ❏ *Common Grackle*
- ❏ *Great-tailed Grackle*
- ❏ Brown-headed Cowbird
- ❏ *Orchard Oriole*
- ❏ *Hooded Oriole*
- ❏ Bullock's Oriole
- ❏ *Baltimore Oriole*
- ❏ *Scott's Oriole*

Finches (Fringillidae)
- ❏ *Brambling*
- ❏ Gray-crowned Rosy-Finch
- ❏ Pine Grosbeak
- ❏ Purple Finch
- ❏ Cassin's Finch
- ❏ House Finch
- ❏ Red Crossbill
- ❏ White-winged Crossbill
- ❏ Common Redpoll
- ❏ *Hoary Redpoll*
- ❏ Pine Siskin
- ❏ Lesser Goldfinch
- ❏ American Goldfinch
- ❏ Evening Grosbeak

Old World Sparrows (Passeridae)
- ❏ House Sparrow +

INDEX OF SCIENTIFIC NAMES
This index references only the primary species accounts.

INDEX OF COMMON NAMES

Page numbers in **boldface** type refer to the primary, illustrated species accounts.